Feeding Victory

Feeding Victory

INNOVATIVE MILITARY LOGISTICS

FROM LAKE GEORGE TO KHE SANH

Jobie Turner

University Press of Kansas

Published by the University Press of Kansas (Lawrence, Kansas 66045), which was
organized by the Kansas Board of Regents and is operated and funded by Emporia
State University, Fort Hays State University, Kansas State University, Pittsburg State
University, the University of Kansas, and Wichita State University

Library of Congress Cataloging-in-Publication Data

Names: Turner, Jobie, author.
Title: Feeding victory : innovative military logistics from Lake George to Khe Sanh /
Jobie Turner.
Description: Lawrence, Kansas : University Press of Kansas, [2020] I Series: Modern war
studies I Includes bibliographical references and index.
Identifiers: LCCN 2019034848
  ISBN 9780700629147 (cloth)
  ISBN 9780700629152 (epub)
Subjects: LCSH: Logistics—History. I Logistics—Technological innovations—United
States—Case studies. I United States—Armed Forces—Transportation—History—20th
century. I United States—History, Military—Case studies.
Classification: LCC U168 .T87 2020 I DDC 355.4/11—dc23
LC record available at https://lccn.loc.gov/2019034848.

British Library Cataloguing-in-Publication Data is available.

Printed in the United States of America
10 9 8 7 6 5 4 3 2 1

The paper used in this publication is recycled and contains 30 percent postconsumer
waste. It is acid free and meets the minimum requirements of the American National
Standard for Permanence of Paper for Printed Library Materials Z39.48-1992.

CONTENTS

ACKNOWLEDGMENTS

My wife, Kara, my daughter, Avery, and my son, Gavin, have been my biggest fans and supporters. They are motivators, makers of fun, and a merry team indeed. Thank you. This work is yours.

My mom Trudy and step-dad Lonney have been a rock of support and provided love and good humor over the course of this work. They have also put up with us moving the grandkids to hither and yon with nary a complaint. My in-laws, Kemp and Nancy Smith, have welcomed me as part of the family and their connection to the Adirondacks is the sole reason that Lake George was a case study. Thanks to them for introducing me to such a special place and for their support.

Dr. Stephen Chiabotti is a steadfast friend and has been a mentor for over twenty-five years. He helped hatch the idea of this book inside of a thirty-minute conversation, and somehow it all worked to plan. As always, he encouraged me to be creative and treat this more of a labor of love and less like a project. Only he could be so certain that writing about three hundred years of history across five disparate campaigns would make sense. Along with Gen. (ret.) Stephen Lorenz, Dr. Chiabotti created the Lorenz fellowship, a dedicated program to allow Air Force officers to work on their PhD in military strategy. Thanks to them both for the vision to see the program through. In addition, Dr. Chiabotti, introduced me to Dr. Lina Svedin, who gave me much-needed direction and a due date to submit this idea as a book project. She is a tour de force of scholarship and a champion for military officers within academia.

In the field of history, there are none better than Dr. John Morrow. He took several days to read this work and make comments, when he had a full schedule himself. In doing so, Dr. Morrow gave a corrective to loose thinking and writing. Dr. (and Colonel) Timothy "Astro" Cullen provided comprehensive reading lists early during the research process on various topics of technology and warfare. In addition, he made vast improvements to the format and the structure of this work (especially regarding the overuse of parentheses).

During my time researching and writing for this program many people at the humble but intellectually mighty School of Advanced Air and Space Studies assisted, to include Shelia Mckitt, Dr. Richard Muller, Dr. Hal Winton, Dr. Stephen Wright, and Dr. Mel Korsmo. Most importantly, Dr. Tom Hughes reviewed the third chapter and pushed this work to a larger audience and his simple note of encouragement during a tough time saw the project through.

Mr. Matthew Keagle and the staff at the Fort Ticonderoga/Thompson-Pell Research Center meticulously scoured their entire archive for every snippet on the French and Indian War. At Air University, Barbara Jiles, Donna Billingsley, and Miranda Gilmore offered top-notch support. Chet Baker, Bruce Geiger, Dr. (and Colonel) Meg Martin, Dr. (and Colonel) Randy Oakland, Dr. Richard Weyhring, and Patrick Walsh all helped with research and ideas. VADM (ret.) Mark Harnitchek provided much needed edits to chapter 3 and lent his unparalleled expertise in logistics to this work. Leyton Barney and Avery Turner provided many of the maps and were patient with my requests.

Joyce Harrison at the University Press of Kansas took a chance on a work from a first-time author. Her counsel, guidance, and help were much appreciated. The staff at Kansas was incredible: Colin Tripp, Jeffrey Rubin, Derek Helms, Suzanne Galle, Michael Kehoe, and Andrea Laws all worked hard to improve and promote this work. Dr. William Allison and another anonymous reader provided invaluable source material and helped to point chapter 5 in the right direction.

Finally a small mention to my C-130 teammates from Herk Nation. You have been at the pointy-end of logistics since 1954 and getting the mission done without much fanfare. Many of the ideas in the book germinated from doing the business of tactical airlift. Thank you.

Feeding Victory

Introduction

A horse, a horse! My kingdom for a horse!
—Richard III, Act V, Scene IV

On 11 May 1745, a French force led by Marshal de Saxe bested an allied army led by the Duke of Cumberland of Great Britain at the Battle of Fontenoy in Flanders. In the daylong melee, the fifty-thousand-man armies clashed in one of the great set-piece battles of the Age of Enlightenment. The Duke of Cumberland quit the field, his army suffering ten thousand casualties.

Further crippling the British-led army was the lack of supplies and reinforcements flowing from the homeland. Cumberland's line of communication started in Great Britain, sailed across the English Channel, and journeyed sixty-five miles overland to Fontenoy. Transportation on land, in an age of wood, wind, and sail, was cumbersome, with rough-hewn wagons carrying cargo on rutted, muddy roads. Thus, in the weeks after the battle, the defeated army suffered from supply and food shortages. To maintain discipline, Cumberland resorted to draconian, if standard, practices of the day. He sentenced a man to death for "clipping" money—shaving precious metal from coins—and mandated five hundred lashes to another for robbing from a fellow soldier.[1] With Cumberland's army licking its wounds and starving, and the Jacobite rebellion threatening London, the Crown had no choice but to recall Cumberland.

Meanwhile, Marshal De Saxe, his army fresh from victory and

with his line of communication just six miles from French territory at the battle of Fontenoy, took the key ports of Nieuport and Ostend—sixty-five miles away. Thus, logistics—the combination of transportation and supply for a fighting force—undergirded de Saxe's success and failed the Duke of Cumberland. While the British Navy was a dominant force on the high seas, able to transport soldiers and supplies to any harbor on the globe, its ability to project power stopped at the port. Command of the sea could do little to help drag ammunition and food to Cumberland's beleaguered force. His army's extended line of communication, so close to French territory, pushed the advantage to de Saxe.

De Saxe's victory at Fontenoy and the following capture of the two ports cut the British ability to establish a line of communication through Flanders to France. French success forced the British to make peace with Frederick the Great and, according to Napoleon, "made the French monarchy live forty years longer than it would otherwise have done."[2] At Fontenoy the interplay between the modes of transportation across sea and land and the technology of the age—wood, water, and sail—had much to say about logistics, the outcome of battle, and, certainly for that age, geopolitics.

At Fontenoy, the muskets needed ammunition, the animals needed fodder, and the soldiers needed food. The side able to source, deliver, and sustain those needs won. For these unquenchable desires, Lewis Mumford declared that "an army is a body of pure consumers."[3] War as the "great consumer" is an apt customer for logistics, as the method to feed war's insatiable appetite for men and materiel.

In the three centuries since this long-forgotten battle, has the relationship among technology, logistics, and warfare (i.e., feeding the "great consumer") changed? Did technological innovations from the industrial age to the information age—the railroad, the machine gun, artillery, the airplane, the nuclear weapon, the computer, and many more—alter the equation? And if so, what was the impact on geopolitical dynamics through the aegis of combat power?

To answer these questions a framework is required, comprising two parts: a typology to describe the vast technological changes since the Age of Enlightenment, and a method to analyze the change within historical context. To define the technological changes of the past three hundred years in logistics and battle, Lewis Mumford provides a path tread by the "great

Table I.1. Typology of Time and Technology

Era	Timeline	Motive Power	Material	Technology
Preindustrial	Through 1755	Wind	Wood	Ship-of-the-line
Industrial	1756–1918	Coal	Iron	Railroad
Late Industrial	1918–1945	Electricity/Oil	Alloys	Airplane
Modern	1945–Present	Atom	Information	Nuclear weapon

Source: Based on the typology of technological eras set forth by Lewis Mumford in *Technics and Civilization*, New York: Harcourt, 1934.

consumer." Using Mumford's method from his classic work, *Technics and Civilization*, in Table I.1 the broad markers of technological eras are classified into general time periods, source of motive power, and dominant material, with representative technologies from 1755 to the present.[4]

To analyze technological changes in warfare, and more precisely logistics, five case studies will stand as representatives of these eras: (1) The campaign for Lake George from 1755 to 1759 during the Seven Years' War in North America; (2) the Western Front in 1917, during the First World War; (3) the Battle of Guadalcanal in 1942 during the Second World War; (4) the Battle of Stalingrad from 1942 to 1943 during the Second World War; and (5) the Battle of Khe Sanh in 1968, during the Vietnam War. Why these operational campaigns? In each of these, the logistics of the belligerents were at their limit because of geography or the vast material needs of war. An example of the former, Guadalcanal, was thousands of miles from Japan and the United States. The Western Front in 1917, the archetype of the latter, required the severe privation of its population during the campaign. With such limits of logistics, the case studies give a good accounting of the logistics for each era and the inflection points between success and failure.

The campaign for Lake George occurred at the apogee of the Preindustrial Era. Many participants on the French and British sides had fought at Fontenoy, taking with them the ideas of European war to the wilderness of the New World. The conflict at Lake George serves as a baseline for comparison for the changes wrought by technological revolutions over the next two centuries. Mumford's penance for the sin of industrial revolution was the Western Front in 1917, and the campaigns that year are the archetype of the Industrial Era.[5] Guadalcanal and Stalingrad took place in the fall of 1942 and are products of the late Industrial Era.

The Modern Era began with the atom as the power source, while information took the place of dominance over physical materials of the previous eras. Beyond its promise as a source of power, the atom also held the ambitions of the world's great powers at bay, epitomized in the Cold War struggle for supremacy between the United States and the Soviet Union. With the life of the state hostage to another's nation-ending nuclear arsenal, the capability to process large amounts of data was necessary to ensure survival. According to Antione Bousquet in *The Scientific Way of Warfare*, "Within this discourse, computers acted as powerful tools and metaphors promising 'total oversight, exacting standards of control, and technical-rational solutions to a myriad of complex problems.'"[6] The computer, like the internal combustion engine and the steam engine before it, was the invention of the age. Thus, in the Modern Era, information and ideas hold sway over physical objects. Khe Sanh, where the North Vietnamese Army laid siege to US Marines in 1968, represents the Modern Era—nuclear weapons, computers, and information all being components of the conflict.

The key variable of analysis in each case is the mode of transportation. Transportation is one-half of the equation of logistics, and materiel is the other.[7] Moving soldiers, armaments, and supplies forward is the critical link of war—connecting biology and industry with battle. As Winston Churchill said, "Victory is the beautiful, bright-colored flower. Transport is the stem without which it could never have blossomed."[8] At Fontenoy, and for the next 170 years, battle pitted transportation by water against transportation by land. Upon initial review, the American Civil War seems be missing in these cases; however, as we shall see, land transportation was not equal to water transportation until much further into the nineteenth century. With the Union blockade and limited rail capacity, the South lacked transportation and the industrial economy to compete with its foe. The conflict was less a contest of operational logistics and battle than of overmatch. As Theodore Ropp states in *War in the Modern World*, the Civil War "was the last great of the great wars for North America, one in which the power which commanded the sea defeated a people who were too dependent on water transportation."[9]

For the case studies presented here, the interplay between modes breaks down as follows in Table I.2:

Finally, there are critical questions to ask of each campaign: (1) What was

Table I.2. Case Studies and Modes of Transportation

Case	Modes
Lake George	Water and land
Western Front, 1917	Water and land
Guadalcanal	Major—Water
	Minor—Land and air
Stalingrad	Major—Land
	Minor—Air and Water
Khe Sanh	Land and Air

Source: Based on the typology of technological eras set forth by Lewis Mumford in *Technics and Civilization,* New York: Harcourt, 1934.

the dominant mode of transportation and why? (2) What are the continuities between eras in terms of logistics? (3) What does the campaign tell us about the relationship of technology to logistics and logistics to geopolitics? Said France Bacon in the age of Elizabeth, "He who commands the sea, is at great liberty, and can take as much or as little of the war as he will."[10] Could the same be true of the air and the electromagnetic spectrum?

Conestoga versus Canoes
Lake George, 1755–1759

*New York was . . . [as] Belgium or Flanders or the old Netherlands had
and has been for centuries in Europe, the battle-field between France and
England.*
—James Kent, 1877

In 1759, Thomas Davies was a colonial soldier in the British Army
stationed at Lake George, commanded by Major General Jeffrey
Amherst. After his experience, he painted the first known portrait
of the lake (Figure 1.1). In this painting, the waters of Lake George
and its steep terrain dominate the scenery. In the foreground, a wide
modern road with deep wagon ruts gives way to a clearing containing the eleven thousand men of the British Army, which recedes to
a thick wilderness on the edges of the frame leaving Lake George at
the center. The water stretches out like a smooth sheet of glass, while
the environs of the lake—from the shores to the mountaintops—
lack trails, roads, or natural clearings.

The geographical constraints of the steep terrain of the Adirondack Mountains of upstate New York, populated with heavy
forest of pine, birch, and oak, limited land travel in mid-eighteenth-
century North America. In an age of water, wind, and wood, boats
and ships bested horses and wagons in speed and capacity. As if to
underscore the limits of land transportation in the 1750s, Davies
painted the wagons as miniature vehicles moving toward the larger
boats to unload cargo, while in the foreground a Native American

Figure 1.1. Captain Thomas Davies, *View of the Lines at Lake George.* (Reprinted with permission from the Curator, Fort Ticonderoga/Thompson-Pell Research Center, New York.)

warrior and a Colonial Ranger, of Rogers' Rangers fame, sit aside the big wagon road. The road, a key line of communication, was the most frequent object of attack for Native and Ranger raiding parties. In a Preindustrial moment, Thomas Davies captured the bucolic yet harsh reality of travel on Lake George during the Seven Years' War in North America—transportation by water dominating movement by land.

While Davies' painting illustrated the temperate and sunny summer of a July day in the Adirondacks, it missed the harshness of winter. The first hard-freeze at Lake George happened around October, with the lake frozen by mid-December. The ice remained thick enough to drive heavy sleds over until the end of March. While the ice allowed easy transportation by snowshoe or sled, the weather that accompanied the freeze cut the food supply, transforming the lake into a "shining desert" in winter.[1] At the Ticonderoga point, just out of the far view of the painting and overlooking Lake Champlain and Lake George, the water kept ice until April.

Into this pastoral and brutal environment, the French, British, and their native allies fought for control of Lake George from 1755 to 1759. The line of troops, weapons, supplies, food, and strategic communication flowed from Europe west over the Atlantic Ocean, augmented with colonial support, and then followed two converging paths. For the French, the water passage flowed past Fort Havre Louisbourg into the St. Lawrence River; east of Montreal the route turned south and followed Lake Champlain to Fort Saint-Frédéric, which stood ten miles north of the peninsula the Native Americans called Ticonderoga. From Ticonderoga, a short and steep portage of a mile led to the north end of Lake George.[2]

The British path sailed from London west to New York City, then turned north on the Hudson River past Albany to the "Great Carrying Place." From there, a long portage of seventeen miles ended at the southern bank of Lake George (see Figure 1.2). The distance from the southern bank of the lake to the northern shore at Ticonderoga measured thirty-three miles Thus, in this age, when the dominant form of war transportation was water, Lake George separated London and Paris geopolitically by thirty nautical miles.

Lake George also stood astride two Native American empires: the Iroquois to the south and the Algonquian to the north. Because it stood abreast of these two enemies and was thus a waterway for war parties seeking scalps, prisoners, and territorial control, Lake George had few native residents. Lake George, with Lake Champlain, the Hudson River, the Mohawk River, and the Great Lakes made Colonial New York a road to war for Native American tribes, earning the moniker of "The Great Warpath."[3]

Because of the ease of water travel and its geographic position bifurcating European and Native empires, Lake George played a crucial role in deciding the outcome of the Seven Years' War on the North American continent. From 1755 to 1759, control of the lake seesawed between the French and British, and their native allies. Over fifty thousand soldiers and warriors took part in four major battles, dozens of minor skirmishes, and hundreds of small raids and individual acts of violence. Added to the men needed to fight the war were the impressive logistics needed to sustain battle at the edge of

Quebec

Louisburg

St. Lawrence

Montreal

Lake Champlain

Fort Ticonderoga/
Carillon

Lake George

Fort Edward

Lake Ontario

Atlantic Ocean

Albany ·

Hudson River

Lake Erie

New York City

N

Figure 1.2. Lake George Region Major Rivers and Lakes. (Map by Avery Turner.)

civilization—food, cannon, muskets, boats, wagons, timber for forts, and countless other supplies.

The English colonies dwarfed French Canada in weight of economic and human might available to buttress the material forces of war from 1755 to 1759. In 1755, the British plantations general reported 1,062,000 whites in the colonies, with 152,000 attached to a militia or available for military service.[4] The French, by comparison, had a meager population of 60,000, with a trained provincial force of 11,000 at the start of the conflict.[5] The British allied themselves with the Iroquois tribes of New York and Pennsylvania, while the French allied with over 25,000 constituents in tribes stretching from Lake Champlain to the western reaches of the Great Lakes.[6] Thus, in a simple math equation totaling the men and material available for war—it appears the British should have won in a rout.

Why then, with such material advantage, did it require five years for the British to gain control of Lake George? From the perspective of logistics, the key lies in the modes of transportation, dictated by geography, that both

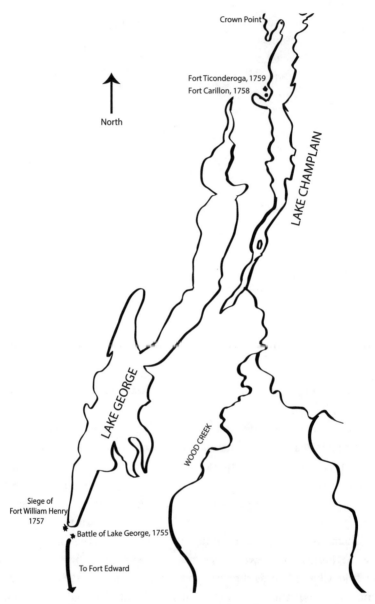

Figure 1.3. Lake George Campaign, 1755–1759. (Map by Avery Turner.)

sides used. The French and their larger contingent of native allies had internal lines of communication built on well-fortified waterways flowing from New France to Lake George, whereas the British had to move overland from the Hudson River to the lake.[7] Juxtaposed against this internal movement on the continent was the battle for control of the sea lanes from Europe to the New World, of which the British began the war with a dominant position. Thus, the campaign at Lake George forms an ideal test case to examine the interplay of supply; land and water modes of transportation; the Preindustrial technologies involved; and their impact on the geopolitics of war.

PRELUDE TO 1755

The campaign for Lake George campaign was at the heart of the global competition between the Duke of Newcastle's British government and Louis XV, the king of France. Although the battle for the lake began in 1755, its origins were much earlier. From the mid-seventeenth century onward, the English colonies spread westward from the seaboard to the Appalachians and toward the Ohio River Valley, encroaching on the territories of French Canada and those tribes aligned with them. As these contested areas became associated with the race for global empire, French and British colonists fought wars associated with European conflicts.

From 1689 to the 1740s, the British and French fought King William's War, Queen Anne's War, and King George's War in North America. These paralleled the Nine Years' War, the War of Spanish Succession, and the War of Austrian Succession on the continent.[8] All the wars in the New World centered on waterways—especially the control of Lake Champlain and the Hudson River—with Lake George astride them (see Figure 1.3).

None of these conflicts settled the geopolitical rivalry, and with the population of the British colonies exploding from 1700 to 1750, the push westward for land ran into 150 years of French dominance to the west of the Appalachians. In 1754, Lieutenant George Washington's mission to stake out British claims to the Ohio River Valley near Fort Duquesne and his defeat by the French set off the greater Seven Wars War and the French and Indian War in North America, two years before a declaration of war by England or France.[9]

Into the intensifying conflict, the British, led by the Duke of Newcastle, sent a proper European campaign to the Ohio comprising two regiments of British regulars led by Major General Edward Braddock during the summer of 1755. The prime minister wanted to place enough troops in the New World to gain the Ohio and then move to control the strategic Great Lakes waterways, forcing French capitulation before war began. Braddock was to take the French-controlled Fort Duquesne on the Ohio River, turn his forces to the north to take Fort Niagara, and move east to meet the other British operations converging on Crown Point. To meet Braddock, colonial leader William Johnson would take a force of colonial troops and move from Albany, New York, alight upon Lake George, row north, and take Crown Point, which the French called Fort St.-Frédéric. Once the British controlled Crown Point, they could control Lake Champlain (see Figures 1.2 and 1.3). At the same time, the British Navy was to drive the French from Nova Scotia, secure Louisbourg and the entrance to the St. Lawrence, and then intercept French troop transports bound for the New World.[10] With this three-pronged attack, the British planned to hem the French in via internal and external waterways and win the continent. Whereas previous conflicts between the French and British in North America involved only colonial forces, the British efforts in 1755 were the first time regular European armies led the fight. Although Braddock never saw Lake George, his campaign to take Fort Duquesne began the contest between the French and British for control of the water.

While Braddock led British efforts in the colonies, Pierre de Rigaud de Vaudreuil de Cavagnial, Canadian-born son of a past governor, led the French in North America. Braddock's chain of command included the prime minister, the Duke of Newcastle, and the head of the British Army, the Duke of Cumberland.[11] Braddock also had to cooperate with myriad agencies within the British and colonial governments to prosecute his campaign. On the opposite end, Vaudreuil had complete strategic freedom to prosecute the war, with his subordinates reporting to him and he to the Crown. Despite his control of French affairs in Canada, Vaudreuil had a difficult relationship with his allies. He had to bargain with the hundreds of tribes with many competing interests; therefore Vaudreuil often occupied the position of diplomat rather than leader.[12]

These two political systems supported different logistical systems. However political and bureaucratic the British system was, its extensive victualing, supply, and shipping system begat a consistent amount of combat troops and material for the war effort. Vaudreuil, by contrast, suffered from poor logistics support. This was especially true after 1756, when the Seven Years' War began in Europe and Louis XV turned his attention east, making Canada a low strategic priority.

GHOSTS OF FONTENOY AND CHAMPLAIN:
EUROPEAN LOGISTICS IN THE NEW WORLD

As the Seven Years' War in North America traced its origins to Europe and the global competition between France and Britain, so did the campaign for Lake George follow from the aforementioned Battle of Fontenoy. Most of the key military officers who fought at Lake George had faced each other at Fontenoy a decade prior.[13] As their most recent test of war, Fontenoy shaped their understanding of how to supply their armies and fight. What was the European understanding of logistics at battles like Fontenoy?

In *Supplying War,* Martin van Creveld sums up the attitude toward warfare and logistics during the eighteenth century: "The whole concept of supply from base was contrary to the spirit of the age, which always insisted that war be waged as cheaply as possible—an age, indeed, when wars could be launched for the sole purpose of making the army live at ones' neighbour's expense rather than one's own."[14] Supply was parasitic.

Thus, the scouting for forage areas, food, and lodging took on an important role in eighteenth-century European warfare—hence the infamous "Hussars" of Frederick the Great, who ranged for forage and food for the Prussian Army.[15] Long before Napoleon codified and perfected the army that marched on its stomach, eighteenth-century European warfare depended on supplies provided by means other than internal logistics. Under their internal capacity, with small wooden wagons and provisions carried by soldiers on their backs, armies could move about ten days before needing to stop for resupply.[16] Thus, extensive campaigns without external sources of supply were impossible.

Facing off against the European images of logistics were the North American wilderness and the musket. Unlike the armies at Fontenoy, which could depend on the local countryside to supply them with some manner of subsistence, the wilds of North America offered no such support. Armies had to bring supplies forward or take them from a defeated foe. In an isolated location such as Lake George, the logistics train, whether over land or water, gained foremost strategic importance because the line of supply was often the sole means to hold off starvation and defeat.

These strategic supply trains were at the mercy of the musket. The musket of the eighteenth century, even with a limited range of 125 yards, was deadly to massed formations in areas of open ground.[17] A wagon train with its methodical movement represented a similar massed-formation target in the steep terrain and wooded areas surrounding the roads of colonial North America, which hid attackers while highlighting the wooden vehicles. With much of their men and material having to move over land from the colonial cities to the contested regions of the conflict, British supply lines were under greater risk of attack than those of the waterborne French.

Besides the threat that the musket posed for land-borne transportation, the weapon was a critical component of the mobile warfare of the Native Americans. The introduction of the musket to native tribes by the French explorer Champlain in 1609, in a confrontation with the Iroquois near Ticonderoga at the north end of Lake George, transformed warfare in North America. Before this small battle, native warfare in northeastern North America followed the warfare of medieval European armies—mass armies with spears, shields, and arrows facing off to claim territorial grounds.[18] With the power of the musket, individual warriors gained primacy and used the lethality and range of the weapon to overcome their foes through speed and surprise. The narrow, steep, and wooded geography of North America well suited these methods.

While the Europeans brought musket technology to the Native Americans, the tribes taught the Europeans the effectiveness of rapid movement in the wilderness. Accustomed to centuries of far-ranging hunting and warfare, native warring parties had a much smaller logistical tail than any European army. Warriors could travel over fifty miles a day and subsist on little more than acorns and meat from smaller mammals, such as squirrels or skunks.[19] Native American speed and scarcity of supply came into direct conflict with European notions of logistics. With a larger contingent of native allies coupled with the speed of travel on waterways guarded with forts built to European standards, the French harnessed Native American warriors to great effect as a striking force. The British owned a small mobile force—Rogers' Rangers—that mimicked native raiding methods, but preferred their Redcoats and the requisite requirements for supply and transportation. Thus, the campaign for Lake George would be a test of Nathaniel Bedford Forrest's materiel axiom of war that the "fustest with the mostest" wins, the French the former and the British the latter.[20]

MONONGAHELA: BRADDOCK SUPPLIES
THE FRENCH FOR LAKE GEORGE

The campaign for Lake George began with Major General Edward Braddock's march to take Fort Duquesne from the French in 1755 (Figure 1.4). In February, Braddock sailed from England to Williamsburg, Virginia. The general took command and, through sheer force of will, impelled the colonies to support his operation with labor, supplies, and money.[21] Beyond his strategic correspondence, Braddock distributed his will downstream to the details of logistics preparation. He rearranged the debarkation plan for his troops into a single location at Alexandria, Virginia, using an easier sea route, saving a 300-mile land journey.[22] He bargained with the British Navy for thirty sailors to help him move the artillery over the mountains, since sailors knew how to use block and tackle to hoist cannons.[23] Braddock's hard work preparing his army to move overland from the seaboard of Virginia to the colonial outpost at Fort Cumberland, and march 110 miles through the wilderness to Fort Duquesne, also required the colonies to invest heavily in their own defense.

While Braddock worked with the navy, his quartermaster, Sir John St. Clair, worked on the basics of moving the army forward from Alexandria, Virginia, to the staging point at Fort Cumberland. No small task: moving the three-thousand-strong force 140 miles to the small fort on the edge of British civilization took all spring. St. Clair pursued this task with as much energy as his boss, winning few allies in the colonies. In a fit of frustration, after some supplies he needed did not materialize, St. Clair raged at a colonial agent and declared, "He would with his Sword drawn pass through the Province and treat the Inhabitants as a parcel of Traitors to his Master."[24] For his outburst, the colonists christened him "St. Clair the Hussar." St. Clair's moment of indiscretion reflected European understandings and long-regarded practices about who paid for war: those on whose land war was waged. Only in North America, it was British land. This incident was an indicator of the distance between American colonists and the Crown. Further afield in the contested

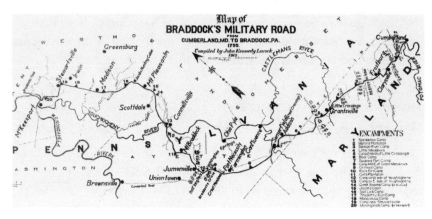

Figure 1.4. Map of Braddock's March. (John Kennedy Lacock, 1912.)

regions butting up against French territory, the wilderness demanded tribute and offered none.

WAGONS AND FOOD TO CUMBERLAND!
EARLY PROBLEMS OF LOGISTICS

For his land campaign, Braddock needed wagons to carry his army's food and war supplies, and the horses to pull them. Early in the spring of 1755, St. Clair promised Braddock he could get two hundred wagons and associated equine transportation numbering fifteen hundred horses from the area around Fort Cumberland, from Dutch and German settlers.[25] This promise of transportation never appeared, and the colonies were slow in getting Braddock the wagons. In exasperation, Braddock remarked, "the number of horses and waggons procur'd in these colonies do not amount to the tenth of what I was promis'd."[26] Braddock needed to march to Fort Duquesne, and the slower his transportation arrived, the more time the French had to reinforce the outpost.

In contrast to the other colonies' reluctance to act, Benjamin Franklin sent out a notice to Pennsylvanians, amassing wagons and drivers at Fort Cumberland. [27] Franklin's tongue-in cheek notice pronounced, "If this method of obtaining the Waggons and Horses [volunteering] is not likely to succeed, I am oblig'd to send Word to the General in fourteen Days; and I suppose *Sir*

John St. Clair the Hussar, with a Body of Soldiers, will immediately enter the Province, for the Purpose aforesaid, of which I shall be sorry to hear, because I am, very sincerely and truly your Friend and Well-wisher."[28] Franklin's jest toward St. Clair hints at the reality of supply in the wilderness: the Hussar had much to ask of settled property and nowhere to forage.

In a unique stroke of geographical luck, technological timing, and Franklin's interpersonal skills, 140 of the 200 wagons were Conestoga farm wagons, the predecessor to the larger famed Conestoga freight wagons of the American West.[29] The wagons were products of a unique combination of natural resources—timber for wood and rivers to power sawmills—and a German immigrant population skilled in blacksmithing.[30] The nimble wagons were ideally suited for traveling the long distances over rough roads needed to sustain western colonial communities near the Appalachians. By contrast, the British army used much larger wagons, which carried twice the cargo.[31]

Constructing a Conestoga wagon took significant effort. The lumber required four years of seasoning before any construction began. In addition, there was significant lathing and iron plate assembly needed to attach the wheels.[32] The effort the carpenters and smiths put into the wagons made them sturdy and light with a cargo capacity of two thousand pounds. The farm wagons' smaller size and weight gave Braddock the ability to transport his army over the unimproved roads to Fort Cumberland and along the woodland path to Fort Duquesne.

As the general gathered his transportation and forces at Fort Cumberland, he realized he had a food shortage. His first two days in camp focused on settling accounts related to food, ammunition, and the proper accounting of supplies.[33] Braddock backed up his concern for food with stern discipline. His first order at Fort Cumberland stated, "Any solider or follower of the army who shall stop any one bringing in provisions or forage to the camp shall immediately suffer death."[34] To expand his food procurement farther afield, Braddock sent messengers to neighboring towns and villages asking for more sutlers to serve the army, and raised prices for their services.[35]

Added to the human subsistence problems, a lack of forage threatened the horses. Fort Cumberland lacked the cultivated land or even rough open pastures necessary for the horses to feed, as was available to the east in colonial communities. Instead, the horses fed in the forest, eating "leaves and shoots of young trees"—resulting in many horses lost, scattered, or stolen by

Native American raiding parties or their former owners in the dense under-growth.[36] The forage became such a concern that, near the end of May, Brad-dock ordered several dozen men to encamp near a forage area for the cavalry horses—a day's journey by foot from Fort Cumberland.[37] Such expeditions required ever more security to protect the horses and their riders from am-bush or attack, further delaying Braddock.

Despite these trials of logistics, three thousand two hundred soldiers and over fifteen hundred horses had made it to Fort Cumberland by May. With this initial success, Braddock, St. Clair, and many colonial leaders grew more optimistic. Surveying the army at the remote output, Robert Dinwiddie, the governor of Virginia, wrote to Braddock, "I have no doubt the French will surrender on Sight of y'r Forces."[38] As a new British expedition trying to kill a nascent conflict in its crib, the army was a physical manifestation of logis-tics prowess and a strategic statement that the British had brought European warfare proper to North America. In a grand eighteenth-century spectacle of the materiel forces of war, Braddock had assembled the largest European fighting force of the time in North America.

THE ROAD-BUILDING MACHINE

On 29 May 1755, Major General Braddock ordered Sir John St. Clair and 600 men to cut a twelve-foot path 110 miles through the forest to Fort Duquesne. Braddock directed St. Clair to carry enough food for 3,200 men for eight days and set up a food depot magazine a five days' march up the road.[39] St. Clair and his men would cut the path, move the wagons, establish the supply depot, and then send emptied wagons back for use by the baggage train.[40] A few days later, Braddock's main infantry would follow, separated into three regiments.

In a foreshadowing of difficulty, St. Clair's force moved less than two miles on 30 May 1755, climbing out of the environs of Fort Cumberland. Captain Orme, Braddock's aide-de-camp, stated, "The ascent and descent were almost a perpendicular rock; three wagons were entirely destroyed, which were replaced from the camp; and many more were extremely shat-tered."[41] On the same day, Braddock also sent back the heavier "King's Wag-ons" to the fort.[42] These wagons could not manage the terrain as well as the lighter Conestoga wagons, being too heavy and requiring larger horses.[43] The rest of the journey was a continual logistical challenge as the army cut its way over the Allegheny Mountains toward the fort near today's Pittsburgh.

From the first perilous movement out of Fort Cumberland, St. Clair and Braddock transformed their army from fighting force to road-building machine. All infantry, artillery, or marine-specific jobs transformed into those of road builder, food supplier, or picket to move, sustain, and protect the convoy from attack.[44] Braddock ordered officers to release their best horses for duty as humble draft animals.[45] The general also subdivided the food, supplies, and wagons among the regiments to keep the back-and-forth movement on the narrow road to a minimum. To oversee this the synchronization effort, Braddock created the position of wagon master, in which capacity future pioneer Daniel Boone and Revolutionary War generals Daniel Morgan, Horatio Gates, and Charles Lee served.[46] Braddock spared no one in this logistics-forward effort, enticing men with an additional allowance as high as three shillings per day for officers down to nine pence a day for enlisted members for road building.[47]

As a road-construction crew comprising 3,200 men, two hundred wagons, fifteen hundred horses, and over two hundred cattle, the army cut a path through the white pine, beech, and oak forest with its thick undergrowth of brush.[48] In a region of Pennsylvania so dense that Native American tribes had to burn the forest during the dry season to plant food and mark travel routes, movement was arduous.[49] Beyond the concentrated flora, the hills and embankments were steep with significant rises in terrain over short distances.

St. Clair summed up the difficulties from his depot station on 12 June 1755: "The situation I am in at present *puts it out of my power to give you a full description of this country* [emphasis added] . . . tho our motions may appear to you to have been slow, yet I may venture to assure you that not an Hour has been lost. . . . The little knowledge that our People at home have of carrying on War in a Mountaneous Country will make the expence of our carriages appear very great to them, that one Article will amount near to £40,000 stir."[50] To put his expense in perspective, St. Clair's £40,000 was 1 percent of the total military budget for the burgeoning British Empire in 1750.[51]

Under such conditions, men became fatigued and required more food to continue the effort. Food was so precious, Braddock required more men to protect the columns, via pickets spread to the flanks, to ensure the army lost no supplies to French and Native American raiding parties.[52] The security worked well and protected the supplies, although French-allied native warriors scalped one soldier.[53] The heavy security sapped labor from cutting the path and further slowed movement.

With such slow progress, food supplies dwindled and the average solider went hungry. Following the privation, the prices on goods bought and sold in camp rose as much as 300 percent. An anonymous chaplain remarked, "Rum 20s a Gallon, the worst brown Sugar 4s a Pound, a Year old Calf sold . . . at 3 [pounds] . . . after the 25th of June a Dollar for a Pint of Rum, so you may judge of our Distress: The whole Country is a Wood."[54] In the same manner, the horses suffered without proper fodder. The animals ate whatever plants were available, including laurel, which the campaign books recorded as "certain death to them."[55]

For the exigencies of the mission, the food supply affected Braddock's strategy. Captain Orme recorded:

The General . . . found by his returns, that he had not above forty waggons over and above the hundred and fifty he had got from Pennsylvania, and that the number of carrying horses did not exceed six hundred, which were insufficient to carry seventy days flour and fifty days meat, which he was of opinion was the least he could march with without running great risques of being reduced to the utmost distress before the Convoy could be brought to him if he should meet with any opposition at the Fort.[56]

According to Braddock's calculus of logistics, his army lacked the transportation and food to prosecute the march and fight the French without resupply.

After twenty days of painstaking movement, with a dire but not deadly food situation, Braddock received word from his small contingent of native allies that French reinforcements would soon arrive at Fort Duquesne. With this new intelligence, Braddock sent a "flying column" of infantry troops armed with minimal provisions and the thirty wagons necessary to move the artillery forward.[57] The general left most of the baggage, heavier howitzers, and support personnel behind with Colonel Dunbar to follow and raced his French adversary to the fort.

RIVER WAYS TO BATTLE: FRENCH AND NATIVE MOVEMENTS

The Marquis De Vaudreuil, aware of Braddock's preparations all spring, ordered Captain Daniel-Hyacinthe Marie Lienard de Beaujeu and 240 French soldiers of European and colonial service from Montreal to intercept the British.[58] Beaujeu had fewer than thirty horses and no artillery pieces, relying instead on the small contingent of heavy weapons at Fort Duquesne.[59] Beaujeu began his journey from Montreal to Fort Duquesne on 23 April 1755. Although he left much sooner than Braddock, he had to travel five times the distance of the British march—over seven hundred miles.[60] Since Beaujeu's journey was via waterway, he challenged with a speed Braddock could not match and equaled Braddock's own feat of logistics.[61]

Besides Beaujeu, Vaudreuil sent out a call to his Native American allies. Between six hundred and seven hundred warriors joined Beaujeu at Fort Duquesne on 2 July 1755, one week before Braddock's arrival.[62] Many were from tribes far from Pennsylvania—including Wyandots from today's Detroit and Potawatomis from the western shore of Lake Michigan—lured by the promise of plunder.[63] Like Beaujeu, the Native American warriors used the extensive waterways of the old northwest to catapult themselves into the conflict.

Besides traveling light and fast and conjuring their allies from the far corners of their dominion, the French also had possession of the fort. Compared to Braddock and the British, they had a 146-year head start on the establishment of forts beyond the Appalachians in North America. These forts formed refueling outposts and protection in the wilds of North America. In addition, the forts established critical communication nodes with Native American allies, allowing the French to promulgate Catholicism, trade for fur, and call for military help when necessary. At the key intersection of the Ohio, Allegheny, and Monongahela rivers, Fort Duquesne fulfilled this task and thus became the object of Braddock's march. What the French lacked in firepower they made up in speed and possession.

DEFEAT AND DESTRUCTION: BRADDOCK MEETS BEAUJEU

On 9 July 1755, ten miles to the east of Fort Duquesne, Braddock's flying column of 1,300 met a lesser force of 254 French regulars and militia and 647 of their Native American allies.[64] The British marched their infantry into an open low area and collided with a French company, driving the French backward and gaining the advantage. As the British pressed ahead, they killed Beaujeu, and the French seemed to scatter in disarray. Taking up Beaujeu's position of leader, French colonial captain Jean-Daniel Dumas rallied his native allies, hidden behind trees and small hills at the start of the battle.[65] The French and Native Americans encircled the British and fired from the hillsides—surrounding the column for several hours, mortally wounding Braddock, and sending the British from the field in disarray. Although the British had artillery and fired almost one hundred shells during the battle, the French gained a lopsided victory from their advantageous position behind elevated cover. The French-led force inflicted 877 casualties on the British while losing only 44.[66] In follow-on action, the native allies of the French scalped the dead and wounded British soldiers, creating further panic among the stunned force.[67] Even with Colonel Dunbar and more troops in reserve at their back, with extra artillery and supplies, the sting of a heavy defeat in just three hours at the Battle of the Monongahela demoralized the British force.

As the beaten British scrambled back to Colonel Dunbar's position, they discarded every piece of equipment they could. A dying Braddock ordered his soldiers to destroy as much firepower and equipment as possible to lighten the load and hasten the retreat. Captain Thomas Ord, the artillery officer, recorded the demolition. At the start of battle, the British had twenty-nine artillery pieces—ranging from 12- and 6-pound cannons to 8-inch howitzers and several mortars. The French took thirteen pieces in the battle, while Braddock ordered the jettisoning of eight more pieces, which left the British with four 6-pound cannons and four mortars.[68] In addition, the French took most of the shot for the cannons, while Braddock's men destroyed 162 of 571 barrels of powder and 1,300 mortar shells.[69] All told, the British left 72 percent of their heavy weapons behind.

This waste rippled into Colonel Dunbar's force, which joined in the ordered destruction, though the reserves had one thousand men fit for duty, equal to the French and native forces. Despite the advantage in men, the British did not regroup or take stock of their situation—they fled.[70] Several officers involved in the defeat castigated their leaders for the chaotic and wasteful retreat, including Harry Gordon, an officer in the Royal Engineers, and Lieutenant George Washington. An anonymous officer wrote back to

Britain "in the General's name, was orders given to destroy everything . . . upwards of 150 waggons all the artillery stores of every kind . . . the confusion, hurry, and conflagration attending all this cannot be describ'd, but I can assure you it affected everybody."[71]

Braddock did not survive the march back to his source of supply, and Colonel Dunbar assumed command on 13 July 1755. In a final act of logistical ignominy, Dunbar ordered the general's body buried in the road, covered with soil, and driven over by the remaining Conestoga farm wagons.[72] This method of burial prevented the Native Americans from exhuming the corpse and taking Braddock's scalp. Few Conestoga wagons survived, and only one made it back to the British colonies intact.[73] Thus, the British had built "Braddock's Road" from Fort Cumberland to the banks of the Ohio River at the cost to the British of £40,000, 877 casualties, and the life of the highest-ranking British officer in North America. Braddock's final recorded words were, "Who would have thought it? We shall know better how to deal with them next time."[74]

PLENTY TO THE END: SUPPLYING THE FRENCH OVERLAND

The supply Braddock bequeathed to the French was handsome: four hundred horses, supplies for the artillery, food, and even one hundred head of cattle.[75] The French gain of logistical largess rippled through the rest of the campaign in North America in two major areas. First, the material success cascaded onto the psychology of the Indian tribes allied to the French. Braddock's supplies, lost in battle and left in retreat, made good on the French promise of the spoils of war for their fickle allies. Native American tribes rallied to the French cause, with hopes of more scalps and plunder. Warriors aligned with the French raided the British colonies between the Battle of the Monongahela and the summer of 1756, killing over seven hundred settlers. These incursions pushed the British frontier back from the edge of the Allegheny Mountains to the edge of Lancaster County and the home of the Conestoga—only eighty miles west of Philadelphia.[76]

Second, the British supplied the French with the most important combat weapons of the war—artillery. In the wilderness of North America, cannon dictated control of forts. As Edward Pierce Hamilton puts it in *Colonial Warfare in North America*, "It can be taken as a maxim in colonial warfare in North America that once an army had placed sufficient artillery before a frontier fort, and no relieving force arrived, the fort fell, and failing such artillery, the fort held."[77] Delivered from foundries in France and Britain across the sea to their colonies, artillery pieces were difficult to come by. Vaudreuil received from Britain what he could not get from the miserly and distant court of Louis XV. He wrote, "The corps was three thousand strong, under the command of General Braddock, they had considerable artillery, much more than was necessary to besiege forts in this country, most of which are good for nothing, though they have cost the King considerable."[78] British officers also understood that the loss of such a precious and powerful asset as cannon could alter the war's balance of power. An officer involved in the operations preparing to move north from Albany, New York, stated, "What's worst of all our train of artillery is left in their hands which ruins all hopes of doing anything this way."[79] The concerns of the British officer proved prescient: the French used artillery and ammunition they gained from Braddock against the British during the Lake George campaigns for the next four years.[80] In less than three hours, Braddock's logistical success turned to disaster and shifted combat power to the French, turning the Battle of the Monongahela into the first conflict in the campaign for Lake George. The French would use the speed and capacity of water transportation as a foundation for future operations vis-à-vis the slower land transportation routes of the British. It would take four more years of Braddock's "next times" for the British to wrest control of Lake George from the French.

FRENCH BY WATER, BRITISH BY ROAD:
IESKAU AND JOHNSON AT LAKE GEORGE

Braddock's overland journey and failure altered the British strategy for future campaigns. Back in London, the Duke of Cumberland penned a new strategy based on Braddock's defeat. Capturing Fort Duquesne using an overland route had involved "great tediousness, expence, and difficulties."[81] For the future, British operations would extend from Albany and either west to Niagara or north to Crown Point, seeking to control French waterways using shorter land routes to choke off Quebec and Montreal.[82] In addition, the British Navy would continue to attack French naval assets and work toward the capture of Louisbourg. Thus, in the later summer of 1755, the body of water standing between Albany and Crown Point—Lake George—claimed top billing in British strategy. On maps and in meeting rooms in London, the path to Crown Point from Albany looked like journey by water. However, there were two land movements required for the trip. The seventeen-mile movement by land from the Hudson River to Lake George and the one-mile movement overland from Lake George and Lake Champlain over the point of Ticonderoga proved tough lines of communication to sustain.

SUPPLY DEPOT AT ALBANY: OVERLOAD AND OAKUM

With Braddock's death, the governor of Massachusetts, William Shirley, took command of British efforts. While Braddock moved his force to Fort Cumberland in the late spring of 1755, Shirley had prepared his forces at Albany to attack Fort Oswego and move to Fort Niagara. Using the same supply base, William Johnson also worked to build up a force of colonials to take Crown Point as part of the original British plan. With the advantage shifted to the French after Braddock's defeat, Shirley and Johnson's efforts in upstate New York gained new urgency.

Because of Johnson's great cachet with the Native American tribes and his knowledge of the upstate New York frontier, Shirley recommended that Braddock make Johnson a major general and leader of the expedition against Crown Point in the spring of 1755.[83] Johnson was the consummate diplomat and salesman, who capitalized on the poor relationship between the Iroquois tribes and their previous Dutch interlocutors. Johnson became a trusted agent for the Iroquois in their dealings with the British and rose to superintendent of British Northern Indian affairs.[84] Although Johnson had no military skill, his mission to Lake George in 1755 set the basis of logistics for all future British operations.

New York lieutenant governor James De Lancey ordered Johnson to Albany to pick up his artillery and move with his force of colonial militias "clearing as you pass along a practicable road for the transportation of them and the other stores . . . and place of security to be erected."[85] The next order began, "Upon your arrival at Crown Point."[86] Although not mentioned, the plan required two modes of transportation for the army—land and water—increasing the complexity. While being vague about the difficulty of Johnson's future movement, the plan mapped out the French surrender. Johnson was to put his cannons at "the Rockey Eminence" of Ticonderoga, aim at Crown Point, and demand French capitulation.[87] As with Braddock's expedition, the expectation of easy movement and victory outweighed the reality of geography and a reactive enemy.

Through the late spring, Johnson hammered his vague directions into an operational plan. As part of the plan, Johnson assembled his army in Albany from several colonies including Connecticut, New Jersey, New York, and Vermont; then moved up the Hudson River to "The Great Carrying Place."[88] Johnson planned to construct a fort at this location and then move overland on a thin seventeen-mile trail that ran up a valley between steep hills to Lake George.[89] At the south end of the lake, Johnson planned to build another fort, then embark upon boats to sail up the lake to the Ticonderoga point. At Ticonderoga, Johnson would build a third fort and, after its completion, move the short distance north to Crown Point.[90] Thus, despite his lack of military experience, Johnson understood the critical importance of forts to sustaining the line of communication from the British colonies to French-held Crown Point. Johnson's challenge, however, was execution—not strategy.

Within the first month of his command in May of 1755, Major General William Johnson admitted to General Braddock that he was in a logistical morass. Johnson wrote to Braddock that he had few weapons, no transportation, no soldiers, no engineer or quartermaster to direct his efforts, and was financing the war himself.[91] Because of Johnson's concerns, Braddock dispatched Captain William Eyre, an engineer in the British Army, to help. Eyre arrived in late May and took stock of the transportation assets and the artillery train necessary for the campaign.[92] Braddock's reassignment of Eyre saved the captain from the defeat at the Monongahela and bequeathed to Johnson a capable officer. Captain Eyre was the only British soldier to serve in Johnson's army.

Eyre made sense of the logistical needs and soon immersed himself in the minutiae of the transportation requirements, from wagons to bateaux. A bateau, the French word for boat, was a "double-ended, flat-bottomed, chine-built small boat, much used on the St. Lawrence and on the American Lakes."[93] These boats ranged from twenty-four feet to as long as forty-eight feet, and were propelled by human rowing teams of four or six, although some had rigging for sails to provide extra power in favorable wind.[94] Much like Braddock's Conestoga wagons, bateaux required significant amounts of wood. Unlike the wagons, however, the wood required neither curing time nor significant work by blacksmiths. A carpenter could build a single bateau in just a few days.[95]

Because of a shortage of local artisans in Albany, Johnson imported carpenters from Massachusetts to build the bateaux. On 5 June 1755, the first few arrived in Albany and a colonial agent promised Johnson "50 or 60 Carpenders [*sic*] to be here in a Day or 2" and promised the craftsmen would build the boats quickly.[96] When Captain Eyre checked on the progress of the carpenters the next week he found they "cannot do above 6 or 7 a day, although he has been augmented in ye [the] number of his workmen lately."[97] Despite Eyre's disappointment, the simple construction methods of bateaux, coupled with the abundant lumber and ever-present timber mills of New York, enabled the carpenters to produce a transportation force of fifty boats per week. Captain Eyre's oversight was paying dividends in providing the information and expertise that Johnson needed to run his logistics.

By mid-June, the wealth of New York City, coupled with the capacity of water transportation moving up the Hudson River, relieved the material paucity Johnson suffered in May. While Braddock's supplies had to move ten days on rough roads from Alexandria to Fort Cumberland, Johnson was only a ten-day sail up the Hudson River from the commerce of New York City. On 9 June 1755, Shirley sent Johnson a list of supplies "provided, and providing per the Committee of War, for Crown Point Expedition, to be sent in 2 Transport Sloops of 80 tons each."[98] The cargo listed for sail on these two sloops included four artillery pieces, lumber for two hundred bateaux, four casks of nails to build the boats, and thousands of other items from hatchets to spoons.[99] By comparison, Braddock's wagons carried two hundred tons total and required fifteen hundred horses to move them.

By July, Johnson's shortages turned into largess, which became difficult to manage. The supplies kept flowing into Albany, as did colonial detachments of soldiers and militia bound for Johnson's campaign to Crown Point and Shirley's mission to Niagara. In July alone, Johnson's papers record over thirteen separate supply-store orders from differing merchants supplying the expedition.[100] These orders dwarfed the earlier amounts shipped on the two sloops and included labor costs for the taking apart, moving, and construction of goods.[101] Adding to the complexity, Johnson had to supply the Mohawk Indians joining the campaign and converging on Albany.[102] The growing supply depot at Albany and the land supply network to send the British north to Lake George, Ticonderoga, and Crown Point was just beginning its maturation.

The material and men flowing into Albany overwhelmed the space and stretched Captain Eyre thin in his multifaceted duties—getting the army supplied for the campaign, quartering incoming troops, and ensuring that the artillery worked.[103] Eyre also had to contend with his professional experience clashing with Johnson's colonial peers of higher rank. Because of Eyre's impatience at the lack of logistical support for Johnson's mission, he clashed with Shirley.[104] Eyre's experience with Shirley reflected the stress that the requirements for men and equipment were putting on Albany. The campaigns required too many supplies for competing units from both armies. A network of logistics to adjudicate need and supply did not exist—and would not mature until 1759. Shirley resolved the conflict in his favor, directing five hundred men from Johnson's Crown Point expedition to bolster Shirley's Niagara campaign.[105] Despite deferring men and supplies to Shirley, Johnson would face the French first.

Adding to the internecine strife over the Niagara and Crown Point campaigns came the news of Braddock's defeat. Losses of logistics from Braddock's mission hung heavy for Johnson's campaign—the cannons most acutely. Goldsbrow Banyar, the New York state secretary, urged on Johnson's action toward the French and remarked, "Where we can get Artillery time enough I know not"; and further opined, "some think you sho'd both [Johnson and Shirley] go to Niagara in order to retake the [artillery] Train & defeat them."[106] Banyar also recommended caution to Johnson as he prepared to move north, fearing he might lose supplies and treasure to the French.[107]

Albany to Fort Edward, Then Lake George: Seventeen-Mile Portage to Paris

On 1 August 1755, William Johnson issued orders to Colonel Moses Titcomb and his Massachusetts colonials to paddle up the Hudson and march to the Great Carrying Place.[108] Although easier than cutting a road through the wilderness, it was no mere paddle. The journey involved boat and land travel because of the influence of Atlantic tides for some distance north of Albany, which created shallow and swampy areas in the Hudson during low tide.[109]

After putting the boats in the Hudson River on the first day, the regiment's artillery boats leaked and sank because Titcomb's men had neglected to caulk the boats with oakum, a tarred rope-like material, to keep out wa-ter.[110] In an inauspicious beginning, Titcomb marched his force of one thou-sand back to his original camp and sent one hundred men to fix the bateaux before leaving for the Great Carrying Place on 3 August.[111] The lack of oa-kum plagued Johnson all summer. In late August, he lamented to Lieutenant Governor De Lancey that "I have been much retarded by the Battoes which were leaky and wanted to be re-caulked," and begged him for supplies.[112]

Despite this inauspicious beginning, Johnson left Albany on 9 August 1755 to join Colonel Phineas Lyman, his second-in-command, at the Great Car-rying Place with an incomplete force, an uncertain supply, and an unproven plan of transportation.[113] At the Great Carrying Place, Johnson christened the location Fort Edward, in honor of the Duke of York. Within a week of being at the site, Johnson assessed that the fort was taking too long to build, and the dis-parate militia forces that were supposed to meet him there had not yet arrived. To get to the lake before the French, Johnson needed to transport the forces he had forward without the finished construction of Fort Edward.[114]

At the same time, Johnson's negotiations with the Mohawk Indians had garnered him substantial numbers of native warriors converging at Fort Ed-ward. As in Albany, his native allies required food and shelter, further adding urgency to a campaign now four weeks from the first freeze. Johnson wrote many requests back "to the commissaries at Albany" urging them to "send up immediately the whole of the provisions allowed by your governments for that service."[115]

While Johnson called for supplies, his Mohawk scouts gave him intelli-gence reports of increased French activity at Crown Point. The French had bolstered Crown Point with reinforcements and sent scouting parties as far south as Ticonderoga, observing Lake George.[116] This intelligence added ur-gency for Johnson to move. After a council of war on 24 August, Johnson, Lyman, and the other officers, including Captain Eyre, decided that Johnson would take the two hundred warriors, fifteen hundred colonials, and the ar-tillery to the lake.[117] The rest of the force would stay and continue building Fort Edward.

Johnson's force left Fort Edward and followed an old hunting trail along a natural path between the steep hills of the southern Adirondacks. The jour-ney took two days to traverse the seventeen miles, as the colonial soldiers widened the path to the lake. The road was passable, but the journey was difficult. Wagon drivers threatened to leave the columns due to the rugged nature of the road and fear of attack by French and native raiding parties.[118] In addition, the rough course caused supply wagons to spill, and Johnson begged Lyman to use utmost care on future resupply missions.[119] Given the road's condition, Johnson told Lyman to send a working party of twenty-five men, with fifty men to guard them, to repair the road.[120] In retrospect, Johnson underestimated how much improvement the road from Fort Edward needed to support future British war efforts, but he had arrived at the lake with eighteen hundred men.

On 28 August 1755, Johnson named the water "Lake George, not only in honour of his majesty, [King George III] but to ascertain his undoubted dominion here."[121] Despite being less than a fortnight's travel from New York City, Johnson's men were the first recorded British subjects to see the waters—a testament to French control of the internal waterways of North America and the ruggedness of upstate New York. After unloading the supply wagons and sending them back to Fort Edward, Johnson set his force to clearing the forest around the edge of the lake and constructing a fort—Fort William Henry.

Although Johnson assured Shirley that he would soon sail on Lake George for Ticonderoga, by early September his army had not moved a single bateau from Fort Edward over the rough path to Lake George.[122] Rather than transport more boats forward, Johnson ordered his troops to dig new earthen works for the fort.[123] With his eye on defense, Johnson staked the northern British position for the campaign of 1755.

DIESKAU SAILS SOUTH: THE BATTLE OF LAKE GEORGE

While Johnson spent all summer moving a force of eighteen hundred a week's journey into the Adirondacks, and New France's native allies raided the frontier, Vaudreuil planned for further offensive operations against British territory. He first positioned Baron von Dieskau and his force of French soldiers, colonial militia, and Native American warriors to hold Fort Niagara. Fearing the greater threat from Johnson's force building in Albany, Vaudreuil ordered Dieskau to Crown Point in mid-August.[124] Moving via Lake Ontario and the St. Lawrence to Lake Champlain, Dieskau hoped to kill Johnson's young campaign on the shores of Lake George, driving the British back to Albany.

Unlike Johnson and his colonials, whose sole professional military member was Captain Eyre doing triple duty as quartermaster, engineer, and artillery officer, Dieskau had elite French military troops. He was also a decorated cavalryman who served under Saxe at Fontenoy. At Fontenoy, Saxe used unconventional warfare, striking cavalry into the heart of massed British infantry with speed and daring.[125] Dieskau hoped to use speed to defeat the British a second time.

On 4 September 1755, Dieskau's army rowed and paddled over three hundred bateaux and canoes south. His force numbered 1,500 troops—600 colonial French-Canadian soldiers, 680 Indians, and 220 Royal French soldiers.[126] Dieskau left many of his French regulars behind, brought no artillery, and carried eight days' worth of food.[127] His army rowed down Lake Champlain past Ticonderoga, paddled into Wood Creek, and rowed south until they hit land.[128] After leaving their water transportation, the army moved twelve miles overland to a point between Fort Edward and Johnson's camp.[129]

On 7 September 1755, Chief Hendrick, Johnson's Mohawk ally, alerted Johnson to Dieskau's movement and likely assault on Fort Edward.[130] Johnson sent a courier to warn Fort Edward and ordered a relief force to leave on the morning of 8 September to bolster the fort. Dieskau's scouts caught and killed the courier and took the message to Dieskau. With his native allies fearful of attacking Fort Edward, Dieskau turned his force toward Lake George and waited in ambush for the relief force.[131]

Three battles followed. First, Dieskau surprised the Lake George relief force, numbering one thousand men and commanded by Colonel Ephraim Williams, in "The Battle of the Bloody Scout"; and fought a chaotic retreat to Lake George, counting Williams as one of the dead.[132] In the second battle, the French chased the panicked colonial army back to Johnson's camp.[133] The British and French exchanged fire, with the British overturning wagons and pulling down trees to protect their encampment. With his Indian allies refusing to attack the British enclave since Johnson's army had artillery, Dieskau became impatient and abandoned his tactics of surprise and speed, ordering a fixed bayonet assault by his Royal French troops, and leaving his native allies to watch. Johnson's "raw country men" fired the artillery and cut Dieskau's troops to pieces, scattering his force.[134] The French soldiers and native-warriors force retreating in a long column back to their water transportation ran into a British regiment that had marched in relief from Fort

Edward to the sound of the guns.[135] In the "Battle of the Bloody Pond," the British inflicted their highest casualties of the day on the French.

The French left the field with 232 casualties and retreated to Crown Point, while the British suffered 262 casualties.[136] Leaders on both sides were counted in these numbers. Dieskau and Johnson were wounded, Colonel Moses Titcomb was killed, and the British captured Dieskau.[137] Thus, Johnson's artillery, manned by colonials under Captain Eyre's command, drove a force "bearing with them military reputation and traditions of Europe's greatest military power" from the battlefield.[138] Johnson and his colonials, however, were in no shape to pursue.

With French supplies limited to what they could carry in their small boats and Johnson's force limited by the few wagons they brought with them, both armies went hungry. When the French army arrived back at Crown Point on 12 September 1755, they were "worn out and dying of hunger," their eight-day rations exhausted.[139] For the British, the extra supplies Johnson demanded from Albany two weeks prior had not arrived, and he implored the mayor and the leadership of Albany to "impress Waggons, Horses, & Drivers."[140]

Per British victualing standards, Johnson's force required one pound of bread and three-quarters pounds of meat per day per soldier to keep starvation at bay.[141] Using these food rations, the force at Lake George needed 2,700 pounds of bread and 2,000 pounds of meat each day. Given the weight of food, the army encamped at Lake George needed a minimum of three wagons per day to keep the army fed.[142] Johnson's correspondence about his army's hunger corroborates this statistic. Post-battle, the first wagons came into Lake George on 14 September 1755, and Johnson lamented, "We have only 60 Waggons come . . . all we have had for near 10 days & if they had not arrived we should have wanted bread."[143] In those ten days, Johnson's force exhausted their food reserves. Based on the capacity of the wagons and the needs of the colonials at Lake George, Johnson required between three and six wagons a day, twenty-one to forty-two per week, to sustain his men at the camp. However, the British system of logistics could provide just enough sustenance for Johnson's army to sit and suffer.

Johnson's "victory" galvanized the British and their colonies. He garnered accolades from the British Crown and earned the title of Baronet and the honorific of Sir.[144] By contrast, camp diseases—so common in eighteenth-century warfare—ravaged his army. Whereas Braddock had avoided the dangers of camp life, the British at Lake George concerned themselves with sickness. Johnson wrote of his worry for the sick and demanded supplies and wagons to help move those too sick to fight back to Albany.[145] He had several councils of war to decide the garrison sizes of Fort Edward and Fort William Henry and how to feed them. The food situation was so dire that one council of war considered using horses, without wagons, to bring food as fast as possible—another testament to the difficulties of traveling by land during the era of wood, wind, and sail.[146] Johnson, who faced the prospect of needing forty wagons a week to feed his army, told the leaders of Albany that he needed all "Wagons & Horses in your county . . . to bring the remainder of the battoes from the Carrying Place [Fort Edward] *800 wagons will be necessary* [emphasis added]."[147] Although urged on by his superiors to prosecute an offensive across Lake George, Johnson could not keep his troops fed *and* have cargo space for his water transportation.

This sickness and food privation, and the shocks of their first battle, took a toll on the morale of Johnson's force. As the men starved and sickness spread, Johnson lost control of his ragged army. John Watts, a member of the New York City council, summed up Johnson's misery: "It is imagined Gen Johnson's chargeable army are stopt for this Season, the Troops are constantly coming & going ill arm'd, ill cloath'd, & worse disciplined."[148] Despite the grumbling and discipline issues, by November 1755 Johnson had willed his army to construct Fort William Henry at the south end of Lake George and left Captain Eyre in command.[149] After the trials of battle and supply, Johnson was all too happy to retire to his humbly named estate at Mount Johnson and remained in his role as Indian advisor for the next two campaign seasons.[150]

On the French side, Dieskau returned to France after the war. In the meantime, the British brought him down the Hudson to New York City and out to sea to London. The Marquis de Vaudreuil was apoplectic at Dieskau's loss. He felt Dieskau made the wrong choice in attacking Johnson's camp, the lightly defended Fort Edward being the better target. His passions cooled, however, when notifying his superiors, "M' de Dieskau's campaign, though not as successful as I ought to expect, has, nevertheless, intimidated the English who were advancing, in considerable force, to attack Fort S' Frederic [Crown Point], which could not resist them . . . and it would have required great efforts on our part to stop them."[151] Vaudreuil's summary was correct. The food and arms Dieskau's men carried in canoes and on their backs, whether for the actual battle at Lake George or Vaudreuil's preferred strike against Fort Edward, was not enough to hold territory. The retreating French force only just survived the trip back up the lake to Crown Point with the food they had. Any victory at Lake George or Fort Edward would have been fleeting—at best causing a temporary British retreat to Albany, at worst opening Dieskau's force to a reattack by the British. In either case, the French lacked the supplies and ammunition to hold the ground or repel an attack. Now the British had to hold the posts against French incursion, at the far reaches of their own line of communication from Albany.

To discourage further British movement across Lake George, Vaudreuil ordered the French to build a fort on the point of Ticonderoga.[152] French regulars and colonial troops built a sawmill at the falls descending into Lake George and cut wood for the fort. The new fort, christened Carillon, commanded the impressive heights of Ticonderoga overlooking Lake George and Lake Champlain. In late September, Sieur de Lotbiniere, the engineer of the fort, remarked that if he "could succeed in erecting at Carillon the fort I have projected, we shall be able to stop the enemy in the next campaign."[153] His foresight was correct, for with Fort Carillon built, the British needed a significant force of men, artillery, and supplies to dislodge the position, laying further requirements of logistics upon Johnson's aborted mission.

The British, after defeat and victory in 1755, well understood the herculean efforts required to wage warfare afoot in the age of wood, water, and sail while the enemy had control of the waterways. The logistics necessary to sustain a fort many days forward from Albany, like Fort William Henry, did not yet exist. Sir Charles Hardy, the governor of New York, wrote to Lord Halifax, president of the British Board of Trade, on 27 November 1755, detailing how the lack of wagons, supplies, and leadership doomed Johnson's and Shirley's expeditions. Hardy said:

It became impracticable for this Country to provide a sufficient number of Waggons & Horses to transport the necessary Quantity of Provisions & Stores for so large a Body of Men . . . but the principal articles wanted were a sufficient number of Battoes for transporting the Army thro' the lake, four hundred of which would not be carried from Fort Edward, with taking the Waggons from transporting the Provisions, which was so immediately wanted.[154]

The efforts at Albany to resupply the missions of Johnson and Shirley taxed the logistics abilities of the British. Supply problems swung between too much and too little. While large sloops of cargo from New York City overwhelmed the port at Albany, the first sixty wagons of relief supplied Johnson with only enough food to avoid starvation. In either case, the British lacked the capability to handle the needs of war during the first campaign season for Lake George.

1755–1757 STALEMATE

Despite moving sizable forces to Lake George in 1755, neither the British nor the French began another formal campaign until the summer of 1757. During this time, the British relieved Shirley of command and replaced him with the John Campbell, the fourth Earl of Loudoun, in March 1756.[155] Loudoun, a competent administrator with a keen eye for finance, assessed the logistics depot at Albany and found it lacking. Using London-backed companies to purchase items under one banner instead of relying on inefficient and thus expensive colonial sources, he revamped the supply system. Loudoun's efforts, which increased efficiency and drove down prices, were a source of irritation to colonial governments.[156] The British also moved eight thousand troops to Fort William Henry during the summer of 1756 to alight on Lake George for Fort Carillon. Just one day before moving north on 19 August 1756, however, Fort Oswego fell to the French. Loudoun directed the forces at William Henry back to Albany, concerned that a defeat in trying to take Crown Point would leave Albany open to attack.[157] With the Ohio River and the Great Lakes closed, the British strategy was defense. Again, the French ability to move via water overcame their wealthier enemy.

On the French side, their largess from defeating Braddock allowed them to attack and take Forts Bull and Oswego on Lake Ontario in 1756.[158] Added to their limited resources, the British supplies gave the French the material and the flexibility to move and distribute their forces as they saw fit. In addition, the spoils of war from the British encouraged the French's llies among the Native American tribes to stay in the fight. The Native Americans continued to harass British supply lines and forts at Lake George until the end of the campaign in 1759. While the British Navy tried to choke off the French from the Atlantic, the French sneaked one thousand men, and

Dieskau's replacement the marquis de Saint-Vera, Louis-Joseph de Mont-
calm-Gozon, through the British naval patrols.[159] Montcalm, although a
classic European general of the Enlightenment, would plague the British
in the wilds of North America until hostilities ceased. Although the French
had a dearth of supply from Paris, the British failed to capture Louisbourg
and close off the St. Lawrence River from the sea in 1757.[160] Thus, the French
line of communication to Europe was still open and the Great Lakes were
free of British influence.

In this static environment, the three new forts of 1755—Edward, William
Henry, and Carillon—were the map markers for the future battles of Lake
George. The winter of 1755 was difficult at all three locations. As the lakes
made ice in late fall and then froze solid by December, the prospects of relieving the forts from Albany and Montreal became impossible. Sleds and
snowshoes were the sole means of transportation on frozen roads, rivers, and
lakes. In addition, indoor confinement increased the spread of disease. By
December, the French moved all except one hundred caretaker troops away
from Fort Carillon and back to Montreal.[161] The British mimicked their presence with 250 men at Fort Edward and Fort William Henry.[162]

NATIVE LOGISTICS AND ROGERS' RANGERS:
SPEED, STARVATION, AND SCALPS

In the period of stalemate at Lake George, raiding the lines of communication to the forts took priority. The French relied on their Native American
allies, attracted by the plunder of 1755, who integrated the raiding of British
supplies into their established war-making and hunting cycles. The British
countered by building more forts and their own raiding parties led by Major
Robert Rogers, who co-opted Native American tactics.

Geography and weather patterns of colonial France and Britain yielded
short summers and long stretches of winter lasting from the first few weeks
in October until May. In such an environment, the Native American tribes
spent the spring planting, the summer hunting and war-making, the fall harvesting, and the winter with less activity.[163] With a lifestyle built on survival
and exercise, the Native Americans always impressed the Europeans with
their physical abilities and endurance.[164] Thus, when war called from Lake
George in the summer months, battle did not disrupt the normal cycle of

food procurement. Raiding the Europeans offered the ability to reap the spoils of war and add to the summer cycle of plenty through food, scalps, and prisoners.

Their pattern of sustenance throughout the year accustomed Native American tribes to periods of feast and famine. Hunger was a part of life and something to endure. When more food was available, feasting was encouraged. Often, this inconsistent attitude toward food flummoxed British and French officers at Lake George, when their Indian allies slaughtered cattle or demanded food beyond the clockwork eating patterns of the Europeans on campaign.[165] In addition, with a diet based on meat, Native Americans consumed three times the protein per day than Europeans of the time.[166] With such high protein in their diets, native warriors could stretch the energy they gained from carbohydrates longer, giving them the ability to move farther and faster than a European soldier could.[167]

In addition, their ability to adapt eating habits to the immediacy of the food supply—be it starvation, a gift of bread from European ally, or eating what animal was available—made the Native Americans the least in need of logistical supply during battle. Thus, Native Americans did not need the wagons or the thousands of bateaux that the French and British required for movement in the wilderness. Traveling light by foot or simple birchbark canoe, as they had done long before Europeans arrived, Indian warriors used the musket to great effect. Whereas British soldiers desired newer muskets with fine metalwork, the Native Americans wanted simpler trade guns, which required little upkeep and were lighter.[168] Given their speed and striking power, no sentry, soldier, or source of domesticated animal protein, whether at Fort Edward or Fort William Henry, was safe outside the walls. Because of this threat, during the summer of 1756 Loudoun had three thousand provincial soldiers stationed in various places along the supply line from Albany to Fort William Henry to protect the route.[169]

Harnessing their quick-strike and long-ranging abilities, Vaudreuil and Montcalm used native warriors to great effect to attack the British at Lake George. Alliances with Native Americans, however, came at great cost. Although they required little food or supply on campaign, coaxing them to fight often took many guns, wampum belts, and European trade goods.[170] In other words, the logistics and cost of having Native American allies occurred before the campaign, rather than on the march. In this strategic environment, Braddock's loss heartened the French, the promise of plunder from the British alleviating their crushing debts to the Indian tribes.

While the Native Americans were fast, they lacked the European cultural maxims of territorial control. Native Americans tied the value of land to the sustainment of life, rather than ownership.[171] When the food supply ran out, the tribe moved on to new territories. Land had function rather than form. As a result, tribal warriors did not remain after battle, leaving their allies to carry plunder back home and comply with elaborate social mores.[172] Besides their ranging after raids, Indian allies rarely attacked forts, and then only to plunder after a siege. Such a style made it impossible to hold territory. Since the French relied on native warriors to supplement their armies, permanent gains against British positions were fleeting.

This did not mean that native raids were ineffective. The threat of raids by Native Americans on supply lines and settlements invoked a great reaction from the British. In response to Native American raids from 1755 to 1757, the British built forts "every two leagues" from Fort William Henry to Albany.[173] These forts at Saratoga, Stillwater, Fort Anne, and Half-Way Brook gave the British protection from raids and respite for horses and men as they moved supplies by wagons.[174]

Underpinning all the fort-building by the British were vast amounts of forest and numbers of sawmills. The number of board feet to cover even a modest fort with cannon-resistant timber was massive; an average fort required fifteen hundred feet of timber wall-length.[175] Outbuildings and shelter within the forts also required more wood. Fortunately for the British, the colonies—especially New York, Connecticut, Maine, and Massachusetts—were teeming with sawmills. With abundant trees and moving water, these regions had the ingredients necessary for manufacturing lumber. According to a historian of the American forest, the mills were the first buildings erected in a town and "no mills meant no people."[176] While Western Europe had long been devoid of forests, the greatest concentration of trees and sawmills in the world existed in colonial America.[177] Further buttressing this culture of sawmills were British laws, notably the Naval Stores Act of 1705, that encouraged harvesting of trees for the British Navy.[178] The overabundance of sawmills and forests allowed the British to build so many forts in so short a time.

Besides building forts, the British also adapted their own striking force to attack the French lines of supply. Centered on colonial captain Robert Rogers, these Rangers first performed reconnaissance on Fort Carillon and Crown Point for William Johnson in 1755.[179] Rogers's missions became bolder over the next two years, at one point stealing away a French sentry from Fort Carillon and burning French barns near Crown Point.[180] When much of the British effort had been failure, Rogers's exploits kept the French security on high alert at Fort Carillon and Crown Point and made him the first colonial-American war hero.

Rogers used the same tactics as Native Americans—travelling light, striking fast, and stealing away back to British forts. Rogers's light logistics techniques and wilderness warfare became legend as "Rogers's Rules for Ranging," and his exploits became the basis for the future United States Army Rangers.[181] Much like the Native Americans, Rogers and his troops established an ethos of privation, moving great distances with little food.[182] Although successful on many of his raids, Rogers's tactics of moving light and vacating the field could not force the surrender of territory, much like the Native American raiding parties allied with the French.

1757: MONTCALM MOVES SOUTH

In 1757, with Fort Oswego in his control and the land routes to the Ohio River and Fort Niagara safe, Vaudreuil fixated on Lake George and directed Montcalm to lay siege to Fort William Henry that summer. Though the French held the advantage in the war, their supplies and manpower had dwindled by 1757. Montcalm and his superior both clamored for more supplies. Montcalm wrote from Carillon, "Our situation is critical; provisions are needed; the harvest has failed, and people are compelled to mix oats with the wheat. . . . Should supplies not be received early [from France], it will be impossible to effect anything against the enemy."[183] Vaudreuil also implored the French court for more troops, cannon, and food.[184] In contrast with the British reinforcing Albany and pushing manpower and supplies up the Hudson, Vaudreuil and Montcalm had to suffice with the supplies French transports sneaked through Britain's control of the Atlantic. While the French government sent only meager supplies over the sea as the British Navy held the French fleet in check, the overland logistics system of the British continued to bless Vaudreuil.

The first foray by the French to Fort William Henry came in March 1757, when Montcalm sent a fifteen-hundred-man raiding party to take the lightly manned garrison under the command of Captain William Eyre. Since Lake Champlain was frozen and ice floated on Lake George, the French surprised the British. After four days of fighting, however, Eyre and his cannons repelled the French.[185] Again, a fortified position with cannon held out against infantry without.

Although the French did not destroy the fort, they damaged the outbuildings and sawmill, which the British needed to turn the forest into water transportation and ramparts. Worse yet, the French burned a large British sloop, many of their smaller bateaux, and some canoes.[186] Without these craft, the British lacked the ability to reconnoiter the lake and view French movements, save for sending forces up the arduous steep trails to the west side of the lake.[187] The lack of boats proved costly.

As spring ended, Major General Webb was in charge of operations in New York with Lord Loudoun in charge in Albany as commander in chief of British forces in North America. They directed bigger garrisons for Fort William Henry and Fort Edward during the summer of 1757. About 5,500 British and provincial soldiers operated William Henry, while Fort Edward had 1,500 men inside its gates.[188]

During the summer, more frequent raiding parties of Native Americans and increased French activity on the lake alarmed Major General Webb and Lt. Colonel Monro, who now commanded Fort William Henry. On 27 July 1757, using all his boats and canoes, Monro sent a scouting party of about two hundred men to the western side of Lake George to watch French movements.[189] The party took many boats from Fort William Henry and rowed eighteen miles up the lake to Sabbath Day Point. In a ruse, a large party of French-allied Indians lured them onto land. As they were rowing ashore, Indian warriors hidden from beyond the point paddled in from behind, encircled them, and either drowned the British or took them prisoners.[190]

Montcalm began his preparations at the same time the "Sabbath Day Point Massacre" took place. In a bucolic scene of war preparation Frederick the Great would have recognized, Montcalm gave instructions to bake bread in the ovens for the journey and to load the boats. As the Lake George waters lapped against the shore and the warm summer weather showed blue skies, Montcalm ordered his officers to carry only the provisions necessary because "we have but few bateaux, and these are so filled with stores that a large division of the army must go by land. . . . Yet I do not forbid a mattress, Age and Infirmities may make it necessary to some, but I shall not have one myself, and make no doubt that all who can will willingly imitate me."[191] In stark contrast with Montcalm's refined classical European preparations for the war-summer camp of the Adirondacks, his native allies paddled in the captured colonials from Sabbath Point and began to eat three of them. When a French priest tried to intervene, an Indian replied, "Thou have French taste; me Savage, this meat good for me."[192] Montcalm's preparation for campaign in a European fashion—baking the bread for a ten-day campaign—contrasted with native cannibalism and illustrated the tension between the French strategy of territorial control and Native American preferences for plunder.

After the Sabbath Day Point Massacre, and a similar incident the same day at Fort Edward in which French and Native Americans attacked a colonial scouting party, killing and scalping over a dozen men, Webb sent for reinforcements from Albany.[193] Webb then rode to Fort Edward, leaving Lt. Colonel Munro in charge, and promising to send reinforcements. Instead of sending help, however, Major General Webb hunkered down at Fort Edward and called for help from Albany.[194] Citing his concerns for loss of the communications between Albany and the two forts, Webb let Munro face a European-style siege on his own.

Brigadier General Francios Gaston, duc de Levis, led the first French deployment of thirteen hundred Canadian troops, seven hundred French troops, and five hundred warriors overland to Fort William Henry, on the western edge of Lake George. Montcalm, embarked two days later with 250 batcaux carrying artillery and fifteen hundred warriors paddling in birch-bark canoes.[195] Montcalm's army totaled over 6,500, double the size of Braddock's force and the largest assembled in North America to that time. Compared to heavy-laden wagons or artillery carts, Levis's infantry moved fast. The journey for those French troops moving with the native warriors down the steep terrain of Lake George, covered with thick vegetation, was difficult. Two French officers almost died on the march.[196] When Montcalm arrived at Fort William Henry, it was a simple math equation of artillery and angles. As he had done in Italy during the war of Austrian succession, Montcalm had his force dig the entrenching lines and inch forward.[197] His overwhelming force of cannon claimed the fort. Munro gave a valiant defense, running out of shot and cannon balls before he ran out of will. With Webb stationary and his supply lines cut, he could not hold the fort.

Montcalm gave Munro generous terms, allowing his army to march back to Fort Edward with their colors. Denied the spoils of scalps and prisoners, Montcalm's native allies attacked the defenseless British train on its way out of the fort. This attack spawned a three-century debate about morality and the novel *The Last of the Mohicans*.[198] Despite the impact of atrocity committed after the siege, the lack of resolve by Webb and an insufficient supply line led to Munro's defeat.

Montcalm set his troops and remaining Indian allies—those not taking prisoners back to their tribes—to destroy Fort William Henry. In three days, Montcalm's army pillaged the firepower they could and demolished the rest. They carried as much powder, shot, and cannon pieces as they could back to Fort Carillon, including twenty-eight artillery pieces, seventeen swivel guns, and thirty-thousand pounds of powder.[199] They also burned some "boats and a woodpile" and drovewooden stakes into the other watercraft to sink them.[200]

Despite success in battle, Montcalm's logistics strained to maintain his army. He stated:

The extreme fatigue attendant on passing an army almost exhausted by fatigue and bad food over a portage, without oxen or horses, the want of munitions of war and provisions, the necessity of sending back the Canadians to their harvests already ripe, the departure of all the Upper country, and of almost all the domiciled Indians; such were the insurmountable obstacles which prevented our immediate march on Fort Edward.[201]

With a force that relied on water transport to move the heavier artillery, the roads proved a difficult impediment for an attack on Fort Edward. In addition, Montcalm's striking force of warriors had left with their spoils, depriving him of combat power. The French-allied Indians made it back to Montreal on 15 August. In only six days after the surrender of the fort, they had paddled 155 miles with captives in tow.[202]

In the loss of Fort William Henry, the British again both increased the combat power of their foe and gave Native American tribes reason to continue to side with the French. Added to the failure of Loudoun and Admiral Holborne to take Louisbourg in the fall of 1757, Fort William Henry was another mark of defeat for the British in North America. Again, the French used their power on the water to overwhelm British commercial, material, and manpower superiority in a localized instance. Unbeknownst to the warriors who attacked Fort William Henry, the garrison was suffering from smallpox. As the Native Americans took their plunder home, they spread the disease to the far western edges of the French New World. While their long range and speed had carried the warriors from the far western edges of the Great Lakes to the Adirondacks, these advantages turned against the tribes as they spread the disease far into Native American territory. Smallpox limited native participation in future conflicts—curbing the French's ability to fight and demanding more of their ever-dwindling supply line of troops and men from Europe.[203]

By the fall of 1757, the food supply of French Canada was reduced to critical levels. Crop failures and the scarcity of transport ships moving from France to Canada caused rampant inflation. To shock his superiors in Paris into action, Montcalm listed the prices of goods in Canada, many items showing 300 percent inflation in less than a year.[204] Depleted meat supplies reduced Vaudreuil and Montcalm to celebrating Christmas over horsemeat.[205] From now on, the French would play defense—battlefield successes in 1755, 1756, and 1757 fleeting in the face of their limited supply from the sea. Despite these challenges of supply, the French still had fight left.

1758: ABERCROMBIE'S ADIRONDACK ADVENTURE

Successive losses of life and treasure, coupled with the massacre at Fort William Henry, galvanized British legislative opinion against the Duke of Newcastle. While Newcastle remained the de jure prime minister, William Pitt now took over British strategy for the Seven Years' War. In doing so, Pitt changed course. He sacked Loudoun and put Major General Abercrombie in charge. The Duke of Cumberland also sent his favorite aide-de-camp from many years before at Fontenoy, Brigadier General Howe, to take charge of the operations at Lake George. More important for British logistics than the leadership change was Pitt's infusion of money.

While Newcastle tried to keep the costs of the war to a minimum, Pitt flooded British operations in North America with money. Before Pitt, Loudoun fretted to the dukes of Cumberland and Newcastle about the costs of war supply, from silver and gold exchange rates to price run-ups.[206] Pitt dispelled any notions that cost would impede victory, stating to General Amherst, the new commander designated to take Louisbourg, that military commanders in North America would get all the monetary support they needed.[207]

Pitt charged Major General Abercrombie to take Fort Carillon, then Crown Point, once again. Abercrombie, an ever-able administrator, spent the fall of 1757 to the summer of 1758 sending a furious correspondence to the colonies attempting to reinvigorate the expedition on Lake George.[208] Bolstered by the fear of French invasion and buoyed by Pitt's infusion of troops and money, the colonies responded with increasing numbers of men and a supply train to match. By the time his campaign set sail on Lake George in the summer of 1758, Abercrombie had amassed a force of sixteen thousand men and 1,035 lake craft ranging from individual bateaux to artillery barges.[209]

While Abercrombie ran the economic and political machinations of the campaign, Brigadier General Howe set to work on preparing the Lake George army and navy to take Fort Carillon and row to Crown Point. The first part of Howe's preparation occurred in Albany, and then he moved to the lake by early June.[210] Where Lord Loudoun had improved the logistic system in Albany but had difficulty organizing the transportation to the forts, Howe and his officers improved transportation for the army converging at Lake George.[211]

The biggest beneficiary of the improved transportation network on land was the capability of the British to travel by water. While wagons brought larger boats from Albany, the sawmill at the lake continued to churn out smaller craft for the operation.[212] The British also made the boats lake-worthy. Howe's first recorded command, in the army's books at Lake George, directed all available soldiers to caulk the boats.[213] With so many boats needed for the sail up Lake George, Abercrombie did what Braddock had done and made a special unit to transport his army. Where Braddock developed a team of wagon masters, Abercrombie designed a force of "bateaux-men" commanded by Lt. Colonel John Bradstreet to organize the boats for the mission and command the flotilla upon the lake.[214] The preparation for the water movement involved a week's-long effort to load the boats with their different supplies: some with flour and pork, others with artillery, and still others with medicine.[215]

Now that the British were moving via water, the food they could take expanded beyond the ten-day limit imposed by the technological limits of travel by land. While individual soldiers had six days of rations with them, the bateaux carried thirty days of rations in reserve for the army.[216] The amount of supply overland to support the British navy of Lake George was impressive. If Johnson required sixty wagons to provide enough food for 2,750 soldiers for ten days, then Abercrombie's army needed 1,250 wagon loads to give each soldier a six-day ration and provide for the thirty days of food in reserve for the journey to Crown Point. The 1,250 wagonloads were only for the food on campaign. Any additional day in camp required thirty-five wagons to maintain rations. In addition, these were wagons only for food, all the extra supplies of war—muskets, shot, powder, and boats— would have further increased the requirement for wagons.[217] Similar to Braddock's expedition, the longer the British sat at Fort William Henry, the more food they needed, thus impeding forward progress.

As Howe and other officers readied the force for Abercrombie's arrival, the contrast with Johnson's stalled logistics efforts was stark. British officers organized signals for the boats, established procedures for hospital ships to bring back the wounded, and issued detailed instructions for the army, from number of rations victualed per day to preservation of powder.[218] While the British made extensive preparation for the embarkation at Fort William Henry, they did not spend much time planning for the debarkation of sixteen thousand troops into the wilderness north of Lake George. This miscalculation cost them.

While Abercrombie and Howe planned under supply conditions of plenty in May of 1758, Vaudreuil could not start the campaign season or move troops for want of food. Luckily for the French, twelve of thirty-six transport ships slipped through the British blockade and arrived in June with twelve thousand barrels of flour.[219] This did not ease the food problems of French Canada—the British had caught twenty-four of the thirty-six relief ships— but it gave Vaudreuil the food he needed to send Montcalm to defend Fort Carillon. Montcalm and Levis arrived at the fort on 30 June 1758.[220] With three thousand troops, a split of French Royal troops and colonial Canadians, Montcalm ordered his force to defend the high area above Fort Carillon, rather than put so many troops into a fort designed for a tenth of their number. Over the space of three days, he ordered his army to build an abattis 150 yards in front of the French lines.[221] A classic technique of the time, the abattis was an impressive fortification of interlocking trees, as high as nine feet in sections at Fort Carillon, which could nullify any infantry charge. It was an easy target for artillery, however.

THE FIRST BATTLE OF TICONDEROGA

On the morning of 5 July 1758, the biggest army fielded during the French and Indian War alighted upon on the clear, calm waters of Lake George. Comprising forty-four pieces of artillery, over 1,150 boats, and 15,391 men, the armada was eight miles long and three miles wide.[222] Harkening back to the magnificence of Braddock's march into the wilderness, Robert Rogers declared, "The order of march was a most agreeable sight; the regular troops were in the center, provincials on each wing, the light infantry on the right of the advanced guard, the Rangers on the left with Colonel Bradstreet's battoemen in the center."[223] The British were coming.

Abercrombie's force spent the night twenty-four miles down the lake at Sabbath Day Point, and proceeded to Ticonderoga point on 7 July 1755. The British landed, sending Rogers' Rangers out first to scatter the few French pickets stationed by Montcalm on Lake George below Fort Carillon. Brigadier General Howe and a few regiments joined the Rangers in moving north and east from the landing point to Fort Carillon on Ticonderoga point. An equal force of French pickets, covered by the terrain, met the Rangers and Howe's force as they crested the steep hill. In the early volleys, the French killed Howe.[224]

With Howe flying up and away from the main body to catch the French pickets and meeting his death, the large body of troops behind him became confused in the dark, swampy, tree-lined floor of the forest. The sound of Howe's troops fighting the French for the less-than-ten-minute engagement further confused the army. Some units tried to move toward the sound of battle, while others moved away from it. In the disorder, many soldiers dropped provisions.[225] Major Moneypenny summed up the conditions of the pitiful army: "Part of the Army lay that night in the woods, the remainder lost themselves and returned to the landing place, on the 7th of July, the soldiers having lost their provisions, the whole troops returned to the landing place."

From a logistics perspective, Howe's plan to move a fifteen-thousand-

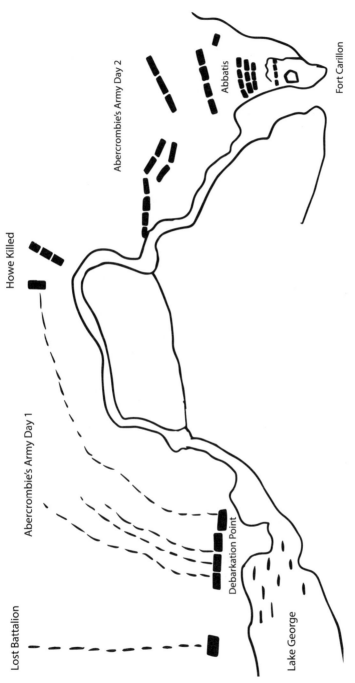

Figure 1.5. British Debarkation below Fort Carillon. Moneypenny wrote in a note below the map, "Abercrombie landed on the 6th of July and marched in four columns . . . columns soon in great disorder from the thickness of the wood. [Brigadier General Howe] fell in with the French Picquets." (Map by Avery Turner adapted from then–Capt. Moneypenny's hand-drawn map of debarkation of Abercrombie's army, "Copy of Map from Major Moneypenny: Sent with Report of Lord Howe's Death, Aug. 1758 From Westport House, Ireland." Reprinted with permission from the Curator, Fort Ticonderoga/Thompson-Pell Research Center.)

man army off the lake and into forested, swampy territory lacked the depth and vigor of his embarkation plan. Although he had spent time on raids with Rogers' Rangers, Howe had only led groups of a few hundred men through the woods.[226] These small movements were an order of magnitude easier than trying to move thousands of soldiers through dense forest with their equipment and artillery.[227] Although Abercrombie was behind Howe overseeing these efforts, it is clear from his dispatches to General Amherst after Howe's death that Abercrombie was an administrator and that battlefield command was beyond his abilities. Abercrombie recorded, "Having lost our way . . . we were perplexed, thrown into confusion."[228] The confusion cost the British twenty-four hours, while giving the French more time to build their defenses. With the confusion and the death of Howe, Abercrombie directed the army back to the landing place and saved the movement towards Fort Carillon for the next day. As with the forces of Braddock, Dieskau, Johnson, and Montcalm before them, the movement across the land of the North American wilderness proved difficult for Abercrombie's army.

The next morning, 8 July 1755, Abercrombie sent his British regulars into the teeth of Montcalm's well-built wood abattis. As Dieskau had done, Abercrombie attacked a well-defended position without artillery.[229] Although the famed Forty-Second Regiment, the Scottish Black Watch, attacked with vigor into the nine-foot-tall French defenses, the outcome was a complete defeat, with 1,936 casualties including thirty-four officers killed and eighty-four wounded.[230] Montcalm's army suffered fewer than three hundred casualties.

Although Abercrombie's plan called for placing artillery up Mount Defiance to range on Fort Carillon, Major Ord, the artillery officer, kept his cannons down on the lakeshore and never brought them forward.[231] The difficulties in moving artillery off the boats and onto land, while being bombarded by French artillery from above, stopped the big guns short.[232] In addition, Abercrombie received poor intelligence about the thickness of the abattis, thinking them easily penetrated by infantry without artillery support, despite having sent out two parties to reconnoiter the French defenses.[233] Added to these factors, the French had placed trees, rocks, and staves in the road leading from Lake George up to the fort, making it difficult for infantry to pass, much less artillery.[234] Nevertheless, Abercrombie believed he had an overwhelming firepower advantage and did not wait for Major Ord's men to emplace the artillery.

After the defeat on 8 July 1758, Abercrombie ordered his army to back across the lake to the British camp at the south end of Lake George. He ordered the retreat despite his superior numbers and firepower, and with his cannons' powder dry. The withdrawal was a chaotic rout. An anonymous British officer stated, "What could have occasioned the panic at headquarters the Lord knows. . . . But the whole conduct of the army after Lord Howe's death was equally madman-like."[235]

Much like Braddock's defeat, Abercrombie destroyed much of his combat power in the hurried retreat. The general had the troops lighten their load by discarding extra weight and starting a fire to burn extra provisions. Filling the boats with the wounded and dead, Abercrombie discarded what he could and directed his army to flee. Chaplain Caleb Rea, who accompanied the army, sardonically stated that his small group had to "stave 150 Barrels of flour and tow off a large number of Battoes that the occasion of our precipitate retreat cou'd not yet be discovered."[236] He also noted that in trying to hurry back to Fort William Henry the army used tents and extra clothing as sails.[237] With all the provisions lost in the confusion after landing, used up during the battle, or discarded in the mad rush to leave, Abercrombie's once well-supplied army went hungry.

The first recorded instance of Abercrombie's orders was on 11 July 1755, three days after the battle, when he decreed capital punishment for anyone caught stealing food.[238] In addition, Abercrombie's first transmittal of information was not to his own leadership in London, but a plea to a commissary supplier to buy or impress forty-six head of cattle because soldiers were under "great want of fresh provisions."[239] While the army was away, soldiers from other colonial regiments arrived late, and there was little provision left for latecomers or the retreating force.[240] Adding to their food misery, Native Americans attacked the supply line from Fort Edward. In the biggest such raid, a native raiding party of six hundred men led by French Captain St. Luc de la Corne killed over one hundred, destroyed fifty wagons, and alighted off with much-needed sustenance.[241]

With his force still camping on the ruins of Fort William Henry at the south end of Lake George and his supply lines under attack, Abercrombie faced a daunting task in rebuilding the fort. In the week after the battle, Abercrombie directed his force to build a large picketed entrenchment near the ruins of Fort William Henry. He hoped the defeated force, becoming sicker and hungrier as the season progressed, could defend itself behind the entrenched area, rather than in the open conditions of a tent camp.[242] This picketed area, however, could not protect Abercrombie's force during the winter. In addition, reconstructing a large fort such as William Henry would take significant labor, lumber, and time.[243] With the supply lines in jeopardy, the frost approaching, and the construction of a new fort impossible, Abercrombie set his carpenters and soldiers to rebuilding the Lake George navy.

A NAVY FOR TOMORROW

Abercrombie's carpenters built the new bateaux force in the late summer of 1758. Besides troop carriers, the carpenters built large radeaux, "flat-bottomed scow[s] with high angular sides containing portholes for cannons."[244] As the sawmill churned out lumber and his men constructed boats, Abercrombie waffled on a strategy of reattack for Fort Carillon. Back in London, Pitt replaced Abercrombie with General Jeffrey Amherst, who took Louishourg in June of 1758, a few weeks before Abercrombie suffered defeat.[245] By the time Amherst arrived at Lake George, in October, there had already been a freeze, and he and Abercrombie decided against taking the Ticonderoga peninsula.[246] Despite the clear indications that Amherst was now in charge, Abercrombie worked his force hard to improve the chances for success for the next year's campaign.

While his decision to attack a defended fortress at Carillon with a frontal assault and without artillery will always be subject to historical criticism, Abercrombie made a smart logistical decision for Amherst's future Lake George navy. With winter coming, Abercrombie ordered his army to sink the wooden boats into the bottom of Lake George and abandon the British position at the south end of the lake. For the last several weeks of the campaign, soldiers sank the boats into water to await their future home of ice.[247] By December, the British were gone.

With this stroke, Abercrombie solved five challenges for the British at Lake George. First, he eliminated any need to resupply the fort through the narrow road from Fort Edward, which made an inviting target for ambush. Second, he eliminated the need to occupy a fort, which would have further subjected his troops to disease. Third, he kept the boats from being stolen by the French or unallied native tribes. Under the water and ice, the French could not reach the boats. Fourth, there would be no need to transport boats over rough roads to the south, freeing precious space in wagons for other uses. Finally, the water and ice applied pressure to the wood planks, helping to seal the joints. With sealed joints, the boats were less susceptible to leaks and required less caulk, reducing the logistics burden for the next campaign.[248] In 1759, the boats were what the British needed—more than the fort at the south end of Lake George—to take Crown Point.

AMHERST: THE FINAL CHAPTER

When Major General Jeffrey Amherst assumed command of all British operations in North America, he brought a vast experience of combat and logistics. Amherst also had wide experience in Europe, ranging from commanding an infantry regiment at Fontenoy in 1747, to the supply of the British Army in Hannover buttressing Frederick the Great's western flank in 1757.[249] In 1758, a few weeks after Montcalm's defeat of Abercrombie, he and Brigadier General James Wolfe took Louisbourg in an amphibious operation, gaining him fame back home and assuring his leadership of the British efforts in 1759.[250] As 1759 moved apace toward the Adirondack campaign season, he used these experiences to expand on the logistical system the British had built in Albany and north to Lake George. Once again, the British would try to take Fort Carillon and then Crown Point.

While Amherst prepared for the campaign at Lake George, the French were in crisis. With the collapse of Louisbourg, the tenuous supply line from France was now little more than a smuggling route, and Quebec was open to invasion. In addition, the smallpox that the western tribes had contracted at Fort William Henry in 1757 had spread to the far west of the environs of French North America.[251] Whereas the tribes had been willing to supplement the French after four campaign seasons, they now stood apart. Lacking supplies and their Native American allies dwindling, the French would not last. With French weakness and limited access to the waterways, Amherst's campaign across Lake George to Crown Point was anticlimactic.

As Amherst prepared to take Crown Point in the summer of 1759, the British again upgraded the supply network from Albany to Lake George.

As an example of this improvement, Amherst made the journey from Albany to Lake George in two days.[252] Although he was moving only by horse and without a baggage train to inspect the lake, his quick journey illustrates how far the line of communication over land had advanced since 1755, when it had taken almost a week from Johnson to make his initial foray to the lake.

On 3 June 1759, Amherst left Albany to observe the transportation of supplies, men, and bateaux to the south end of Lake George. The general involved himself in every detail, from moving the army to Lake George, to sending out work parties to widen the roads in places, to repairing broken wagons.[253] Picking up his army at Fort Edward, Amherst marched into Lake George on 20 June 1759 with over six thousand men and began preparations to row, paddle, and sail up Lake George.

Amherst first charged his men to raise the boats out of the water. On 23 and 24 June, the British army brought up 232 bateaux and ninety-one whaleboats.[254] In addition, Amherst had his naval lake force commander, Captain Loring, working on the larger artillery boats.[255] While Amherst's men floated the lake boats from the depths of the lake, Colonel Bradstreet and his bateaux men moved more boats to Lake George from Fort Edward.

While Abercrombie delegated camp duties to Brigadier General Howe, Amherst put a higher level of personal energy into getting the army ready. Where Abercrombie busied himself with loading the boats for the last few days, Amherst's army felled trees for a field hospital, sent more men out to work on the road back to Fort Edward, and set the rest to work on rebuilding a fort near the ruins of Fort William Henry while also loading the boats.[256] Abercrombie had one page of directions in the orderly books for how to sail up the lake, while Amherst devoted four full pages discussing the embarkation, sailing, and final debarkation of the army at the north side of the lake.[257] Most important, Amherst had a plan to bring his cannon to bear from Mount Defiance.[258] Amherst would take the fort in the European way, by artillery siege instead of Abercrombie's failed infantry assault. These improvements were due to the monies provided by Pitt and the lessons learned over four years of campaigning in the wilderness.[259] Much of the effort and meticulous preparation of the campaign of 1759, however, was because of Amherst himself.

Even with Amherst's methodical planning and deliberate execution, the

British were still not immune to attacks on their supply lines at Lake George. On 10 July 1759, Native Americans allied with the French surprised a colonial party charged with gathering wood and scalped them.[260] Despite these small setbacks in Amherst's preparation, Montcalm would not come to oppose him. French Canada's existence was at stake with Brigadier General Wolfe on the move toward Quebec.

On 22 July 1759, Amherst's force of eleven thousand sailed toward Fort Carillon.[261] After debarkation, the general gave Major Ord, the unfortunate artillery officer for Braddock and Abercrombie, time to get the artillery in place, allowing him three days to move and emplace the pieces.[262] Once Ord's artillery fired at the small contingent of defenders, the French lit their own powder to assist in the fort's destruction, and fled.[263] Though Crown Point was less than ten miles away, Amherst took his time. Over the next three days, Amherst gathered his force, rebuilt Fort Carillon, and renamed it Fort Ticonderoga. After strengthening Ticonderoga, Amherst moved his army to take the deserted French fort of St.-Frédéric at Crown Point. With the French still in control of Lake Champlain and Amherst unsure of the success of the British attack, he paused again.

Inside both Fort Carillon and Fort St.-Frédéric, the British found many of their own cannon, lost during Braddock's campaign and the fall of Oswego, and more in the fall of Fort William Henry in 1757. Major Ord, who had to write the demoralizing report detailing the losses of his artillery at the Monongahela, now reported British success.[264] The British recovered twenty cannon and several howitzers, some pieces likely from Braddock's expedition.[265] Four years after emboldening the French at the Monongahela, the supply of combat power from the British to the French stopped.

Amherst first had his men build a sawmill to construct the bigger boats necessary to take control of Lake Champlain and bolster the works of the fort at Crown Point. The enormous undertaking kept the troops busy until Amherst ended the campaign in late October.[266] Knowing Quebec had also fallen to the British, Amherst left a small force to hold the fort and sent his provincials home.

Although historians criticize Amherst for his slow, methodical nature, he also understood how to conduct warfare given his tenuous supply lines.[267] Though he had moved fifty miles to Crown Point with relative ease, Amherst's line of communication still stretched back to Albany over water, land-portage, water, land-portage, and water again. By late fall, this supply line could not keep Amherst's army fed, his troops going several days at a time without food.[268] By reinforcing the forts from Fort Edward to Lake George, beginning a new fort where William Henry stood, rebuilding Ticonderoga after French destruction, and bolstering Crown Point, Amherst buttressed his army against retreats like those of Braddock or Abercrombie. Amherst ensured the British maintained control of Lake George and won the campaign. With Quebec taken, Crown Point in British hands, and defeats at Fort Niagara and Duquesne, the French surrendered at Montreal in the summer of 1760. Although the Seven Years' War was not over until 1763, the war in North America was over.

CONCLUSION: THE DOMINANCE OF WATER
AND THE FRACTAL LOGISTICS OF LAND

Water was the dominant mode of transportation during the campaign for Lake George. As a result, the French had the edge. Their vast advantage in access to waterways, which connected Montreal and Quebec to Forts St.-Frédéric and Carillon, coupled with the vulnerability and largess of the British moving overland, allowed them to stay in the war and keep their native allies engaged. This is not to say that the French did not have logistical challenges in these movements. They also overcame many difficulties of logistics at the tactical level, most notably Beaujeu's harrowing journey to defeat Braddock and Montcalm's quick moves to Fort Carillion in 1757 and 1758. With the advantage in reach and speed, the Marquis de Vaudreuil kept the war going for six campaign seasons, from 1755 to 1760, despite the strategic and economic indifference of Louis XV.

The campaign of 1758 epitomized French advantages of transportation. The starving French received twelve thousand pounds of flour through twelve ships, which made it past the British Navy in June 1758. With the small input of food, the Marquis De Vaudreuil could open the campaign and order Montcalm to Fort Carillon.[269] At the same time, Abercrombie required hundreds of wagons a week to keep his army fed at their encamped location on the ruins of Fort William Henry.

For the British, the internal waterways, unlike their advantage at sea, proved a hindrance. In a situation their French enemy would have envied, the British had a mismatch of supplies, men, and transportation during the buildup of Albany as a supply depot. In 1755, the capacity and speed of water transportation plagued the town with an overabundance of men and materiel streaming from New York City up the Hudson to the port. With each successive change in campaign season, and often leadership, the British improved the logistics network necessary to distribute and move the materiel of war to Lake George. Thus, even during an age of wood, wind, and sail, without a network to command and control logistics, too much was sometimes worse than too little.

In this Preindustrial Era, land transportation could not compete with water transportation. The difficulties of Braddock's 110-mile trek with 3,000 soldiers to Fort Duquesne stands in stark contrast with Montcalm's conjuring of an army of over 6,500 allies, from as far west as Lake Michigan, to converge on Lake George using vast waterways of the Old Northwest.

Even the much smaller seventeen-mile portage from Fort Edward to Lake George proved a tough task for land transportation. In 1755, with a chaotic ramble of wagons, bateaux, Native Americans, untrained colonial soldiers, a single British officer, and cannon, Sir William Johnson paved the first supply path from Albany to the lake. In a protoexample of what modern military forces label "hub and spoke," Johnson built up a major supply center, provided proper protection, and transported logistics to Lake George to construct Fort William Henry. Over thirty thousand British soldiers and colonial militia followed in his path.

By establishing lines of communication overland, the British built something anathema to European logistics: an "umbilical line of supply" that relied on internal funding to buttress wartime needs rather than living off an invaded region, as at battles such as Fontenoy.[270] The effort was expensive. Braddock's wagons, the series of forts from Albany to Fort William Henry on Lake George, and the thousands of bateaux for movement on the water, were consumptive of labor and treasure. Thus, even though the British had sawmills and a colonial culture based on timber, the technology could not overcome the advantages of water transportation in speed and cost. Nowhere was the technological advantage clearer than in the differences between the bespoke Conestoga wagon, which moved less than three miles an hour, and the simple bateau, which travelled as fast as the current flowed. After their defeat in 1758, Abercrombie and the British acknowledged by action the superiority of water transportation and sunk their navy into Lake George. The British could not hold the line of communication over the winter of 1758 without great expense. Clearly, the input of large sums of money to support the needs of logistics overland by William Pitt after 1758 was a key ingredient for British success.

For the British, land transportation was a cruel twist of Mandelbrot's "Lindy Effect" of fractal mathematics—a power law that postulates that the longer something exists, the longer it will exist.[271] For General Braddock, the longer his army took get to Fort Duquesne, the more the difficulty multiplied. The slower his army moved, the more it consumed the provisions in the wagons—requiring resupply, which lengthened the journey. Johnson suffered from a similar situation. Food delivered over the rough road to Lake George took up precious wagon cargo space needed to move other war goods—notably the bateaux. For each day Johnson's army stayed at Lake George, the requirement for provisions grew, diminishing the cargo available for the offensive toward Crown Point. Abercrombie faced the same challenge in 1758. Only with the abandonment of the fort and sinking of the boats were the British able to lessen their dependence on the inefficient line of communication from Albany to Lake George.

The French also had difficulty moving by land. Dieskau and Montcalm could fight a battle for a week's time, plunder, and retreat, but their movement stopped at the water's edge. Dieskau's army possessed only the food that could fit in canoes, and was starving after ten days of paddling to the Battle of Lake George and back. In 1757, despite an overwhelming victory and the British in full retreat, Montcalm lacked the wagons on which to load his cannons and attack Fort Edward.

Moving from land to water modes of transportation or vice-versa posed great challenges for both sides. In the aforementioned cases, the French lacked the resources to change modes. In the opposite case, the British had to build up logistics first, move on to the water, row or paddle, and move off the water again at the north end of Lake George. As illustrated by Abercrombie's failure and Amherst's success, planning for the transition from land to water, or in reverse, was critical.

In addition, harassing supply routes via raiding parties was an irritant but not sufficient to win the campaign. While French raiding parties did not win the war, they caused the British to spend much treasure and labor getting to

Lake George. On the other side, Rogers' Rangers were a distraction, rather than a strategic threat, to French operations.

Despite their material and vast advantage in population, the British had a difficult time driving the French from Lake George. Given the land transportation technologies of the time, the longest line of communication overland that the British held was the seventeen miles from Fort Edward to Lake George. The only action that assured this line of communication was Amherst's victory at the French port of Louisbourg, which eliminated French access to supplies from Europe and ensured his success in 1759 at Ticonderoga and Crown Point (see Figure 1.3).

Although transportation by water allowed the French to hold off a more populous and wealthier enemy for five years, the French reliance on waterways during the campaign for Lake George doomed them.[272] Because of the short growing season of their territories, their small population, and lesser wealth, the French required supplies and food from France. In turn, the British command of the seas choked the French source of supply and won, whereas the British efforts to attack from the land onto the water at Lake George stalled. Only the "mostest" of the British land transportation network from Albany, buttressed by the command of the sea of the British Navy, overcame the "fustest" of the French.

Geopolitical Impact—Lake George

The need to pay for the Seven Years' War in North America, especially expensive transportation by land, drove a political wedge between the British Crown and its colonies. After the war, the British tried to make the colonies pay for the victory and their own security; Parliament passed the Stamp Act of 1765, the Quartering Act of 1765, and the Townshend duties of 1767 to finance the debt of war.[273] One contentious restriction was a royal limit on timber felling. The mandates prohibited colonists from cutting down pine trees broader than twelve inches, their use restricted to construction of masts for British warships.[274] With timber in shorter supply after the war, many colonists resented this restriction and flaunted the cutting of large trees. When the governor of New Hampshire tried to enforce the law in 1772, colonists beat the local sheriff and his assistant, who came to collect fines during the "Pine Tree Revolt."[275] By 1775, with increased levies and restrictions on economic activity, the colonists began to see themselves as a nation apart and started armed rebellion against the Crown. Thus, the expense of logistics on land durng the Seven Years' War had in part cost the British their colonies.

During the American Revolution, following the wake of their French enemy, the British had their dependency on water transportation turned against them. The British relied on their transportation over the oceans and rivers as a critical part of their operational strategy. From their first sail out of Boston to avoid colonial siege in 1776 to their final defeat at Yorktown, with the French keeping Cornwallis's transportation at bay in the Battle of the Capes, British dependence on water morphed from tactical advantage to strategic vulnerability.

Despite the perils of being "too dependent upon water transportation" in North America during Mumford's Preindustrial Era, water was more efficient than the land for moving goods and services.[276] Thus, the nations that controlled the water prevailed on land during conflicts throughout the first half of the nineteenth century. No nation was more dominant on the water than Great Britain, which used its sea power to ensure the final victory over Napoleon at Waterloo, the Russian defeat in the Crimean War, and countless other engagements across the globe. After midcentury, the railroad leveled the contest between sea and land in moving the means of war, challenging the supremacy of the British Empire.

2

Steam on Steam in 1917
The Western Front

The ultimate outcome over this over-stressed power ideology and this constant struggle [of the Industrial Era] was the World War—that period of senseless strife which came to a head in 1914 and is still being fought by the frustrated populations that have come under the machine system.
—Lewis Mumford, *Technics and Civilization*

From the middle of the nineteenth century to the start of the First World War, the technological landscape shifted from apogee to apogee: Preindustrial to Industrial. Wood, wind, and sail yielded to iron, coal, and steam. Using weapons at the height of the Industrial Era—artillery, machine guns, and steam-powered dreadnoughts— and those of the nascent Late Industrial Era—airplanes and submarines—the Entente and the Central Powers fought in the Great War. To move these armaments to war, the belligerents relied on the power of steam—ships for the former, and trains for the latter. Across both land and sea, technologies of transportation delivered arms of war with great capacity and speed. The relationship between lines of communication over water and land, as at Lake George, underwrote this transformation of the geopolitical landscape. The great question of logistics on the Western Front remained in the balance in 1917: Had technology altered the dominance of water transportation over land?

GETTING TO 1917: TECHNOLOGY, LOGISTICS, AND TRENCHES

At full maturity in 1914, Industrial Era technologies of transportation and war collided. The era bequeathed to the ship the metal hull and the steam engine, which mitigated the effects of tide, current, and wind. Whereas a ship in the age of sail moved as fast as twenty knots, during unpredictable wind, and carried up to 260 tons, an ocean steamer with a coal-fired engine moved at a consistent eleven knots and carried up to 5,000 tons in 1917.[1] On land, iron and steam transformed the slow and diminutive wagon into the fast and expansive railroad. While the Conestoga farm wagon carried one ton and moved a maximum of ten miles *per day*, railroads carried up to fifteen hundred tons and moved as fast as thirty miles *per hour*. With such speed, capacity, and inexhaustible power, transportation to war in the Industrial Era ran ad infinitum.

Despite the lure of machines, the final delivery to the trenches from a rail-head or road involved the motive power of a solider or animal. In its postwar analysis of logistics, the Board of Allied Supply stated, "Although animal-drawn transport was generally used in conjunction with motor transport, the former was the only means of transportation which could be employed in the zones in close proximity to the front where roads were in very bad condition."[2] On the Western Front, the British had more horses and soldiers devoted to this "last tactical mile" of transportation than the rail-savvy Germans, but both sides relied on methods from a bygone era for final movement.

The Industrial Era bequeathed the same exponential improvements to battlefield firepower as it had to transportation. By 1917, the machine gun and the artillery shell had expanded killing power on the battlefield and across the water. While the musket at Lake George had a kinetic reach of 125 yards and its companion cannon ranged 1,500 yards, the machine gun had a range of 2,200 yards and standard-sized artillery flung projectiles 7,500 yards. The rate of fire quickened from a few times a minute in the eighteenth century to one thousand times a minute for a machine gun on the Western Front in 1917.[3] The firing rates, range, and destructive power of artillery made the weapon the king of the Western Front and World War I. While artillery accounted for 8 percent of German casualties during the Franco-Prussian War, the allied guns inflicted 58.3 percent of German casualties during the

Great War.[4] Under the hail of steel on the Western Front, mobility was difficult and belligerents measured successful operations in increments of hundreds of yards forward.

Besides the iron, carbon, and steam that powered weapons and vehicles on the Western Front, the internal combustion engine of the nascent Late Industrial Era made its debut.[5] The engine powered the airplane, the truck, the tank, and the submarine. During the war, the first three technologies fulfilled critical support roles for reconnaissance, mobile firepower, and logistics. The last, personified by the German U-boat, played a dominant role in 1917, threatening the primacy of water as the dominant form of transportation and a century and a half of British superiority at sea.[6]

LAND AND SEA: LOGISTICS OF THE BELLIGERENTS

In lining up the transportation technologies of logistics with the combatants, the Germans and French biased towards the railroad, whereas the British preferred movement by sea.[7] The development of the railroad was the "single innovation . . . vital for economic growth during the 19th century."[8] For Germany, led by Prussia, the railroad helped to create an economic powerhouse and unite a fractured region. The railroad also assumed a primary place in Prussian military strategy under Otto Von Bismarck and Helmut Von Moltke the elder.

Von Moltke noted, "Modern Wars will be carried on with armies of such strength that their provisioning can be accomplished only by means of railroads."[9] The railroads supported a larger strategy of flanking and encirclement called *Kesselschlact* in which "a skillful offensive . . . would consist in forcing a Prussian foe to attack a positions chosen by the Prussians, and only when casualties, demoralization, and exhaustion had drained the enemy of his strength should the Prussians take up the tactical offensive."[10] Integrating the power of steam and logistics into his theories of command and control, Moltke developed forces called *Eisenbahntruppe* (railway troops) to direct trains during war. Since the railroads were not solely a military operation, Moltke also programmed harmonization with civilian organizations, which ran the rails during peace.[11] Thus, under the guise of economic development, Germany prepared for war.

During the Königgrätz campaign against Austria (1866) and the Franco-

Prussian war (1870–1871), the Prussians rolled out their railroads. Freight trains allowed the Prussians to mobilize their armies at the borders with speed, a key to their success in both wars. Although an important part of victory, the railroads were not the juggernaut proposed by Moltke. Soldiers left their trains well behind after debarkation in both cases, and the Prussians burned through two thousand railcars held in reserve in less than three months in 1870.[12] According to Larry Addington in *The Blitzkrieg Era and the German General Staff,* "The 1866 and 1870 campaigns left him [Moltke] with an enlarged understanding of the relatively short striking range, the limited endurance, the logistical inflexibility of the German Army beyond the railheads, and the need to tailor doctrine and strategy to logistical limitations."[13] The Prussians gathered the lessons learned from Königgrätz and the Franco-Prussian War and used them to develop the Schlieffen Plan.[14] Moltke's insight would not prevail.

Whereas Moltke had learned caution and promulgated a strategy of more limited means based on the logistical problems of 1866 and 1870, his successor, General Alfred Von Schlieffen, planned a strategy of "total victory," and this strategy rolled into the German view of logistics for the next war.[15] For Schlieffen logistics placed no limit on strategy. Transportation and supply were tactical problems to solve.

Schlieffen planned on the infantry and cavalry extending well beyond the railheads, since he assumed his enemies, Belgium and France, would destroy the rails. One way to solve this problem was to increase the number of troops assigned to support and build railways, therefore he assigned twenty-six thousand *Eisenbahntruppe* to help move the trains.[16] A foreign observer in Germany in the spring of 1914 noted their work:

Never, I believe, did a country so thoroughly get ready for war. I saw the oddest spectacle, the building of a railway behind a battlefield. They had diminutive little engines and rails in sections, so that they could be bolted together, and even bridges that could be put across ravines in a twinkling. Flat cars that could be carried by hand and dropped on the rails, great strings of them. Up to the nearest point of battle came, on the regular railway, this small one. . . . It seemed to me that hundreds of men had been trained for this task, for in but a few minutes that small portable train was buzzing backward and forward on its own small portable rails, distributing food and supplies. . . . I've an idea that in time of battle it would be possible for those sturdy little trains to shift troops to critical or endangered points at the rate of perhaps twenty miles an hour. . . . A portable railway for a battlefield struck me as coming about as close to making war by machinery as anything I have ever heard of.[17]

The French learned from the Prussians, watching from afar at Königgrätz and watching the Prussian Army roll into their territory in 1870–1871. Responding in kind to the German developments of the late nineteenth century, the French military reorganized their transportation system first by committee, and then by the "creation under the law of March 13, 1875, of Field Railway Sections and Railway Troops."[18] As a result, the French were ready for their own mobilization by rail in 1914.

Germany and France were more land-centric in the makeup of their militaries, but they also had significant navies.[19] The British controlled the sea with a navy that dwarfed them both, and had a miniscule army by comparison. Britain owned the world's biggest navy with "just over 45 per cent of the world's steam ships" and "controlled in excess of 55 percent of global shipping and trade (80 percent when adding Allied vessels)."[20] Much more than guarantor of economic power, the British Navy had been a deterrent and projection platform for British interests since the defeat of the Spanish Armada.[21] The status of the British Army vis-à-vis the British Navy in 1914 reflected the preference. At the start of the war, the army had 476 artillery pieces, while the Royal Navy owned 1,560 guns.[22]

Command of world trade brought wealth and a necessity for rail systems within Britain to move goods. Thus, the British built their own rail network in the British Isles and their colonies in the Middle East, India, and Africa. Although not as plentiful as Germany's 39,439 miles of rail, the British had 23,441 miles of rail across the empire, much of it run by civilian companies.[23] These companies had no military ties, unlike in Prussia or even France; however, their motive for profit made time and efficiency their bottom line, concepts also valued in war. This civilian expertise provided critical knowledge and experience about modern transportation, much to Britain's advantage.

TRAINS AND SHIPS TO THE TRENCHES

As the war began in August 1914, Germany, a great land power which rode to the front on the rails, faced off against a lesser land-based power in

France and its sea-dominant ally, the British. The path to static warfare in the trenches began with the battles for Paris. In August 1914, the Germans started first, and using "war by timetable" executed the Schlieffen Plan, attempting to envelop the French capital.[24] The German railroads moved 1.6 million soldiers on more than eleven thousand trains and deposited them on the jumping-off points to Belgium and France in fewer than two weeks.[25] The mobilization was flawless.

Despite their initial success, the Germans outran the same trains supplying their food, fodder, and water at the First Battle of the Marne. The French used their own railways to stem the advance of the *Boche*. This first clash of armies proved that the steam engine as the motive force for the train had altered the geopolitical terms of war.[26]

As the two land powers ran into each other's rail line, the British used their control of the sea to land the British Expeditionary Force (BEF) in Boulogne, march into Belgium, cover the retreat of the Belgian Army, and stem the German tide. At the same time, the British Navy used all its might to hold the German Navy in check and build a blockade against German commerce on the sea.[27] In the First Battle of Ypres, the Germans and British raced each other to the sea in attempts to outflank each other. This contest reached the Belgian coast in late 1914. German supply and transportation by land stood against British transportation by sea connected to the land via French and Belgium railroads. This initial melee set the trench lines for the war.

The years 1915 and 1916 saw increasing numbers of soldiers, machines, and *le mort* on all sides. In the brutal calculus of the Western Front, artillery was king, churning the land into a moonscape. The range, size, and density of shells gave the defense a powerful edge, borne out in horrific losses for those nations undertaking an attack. From the German offensives at the Second Battle of Ypres in 1915 and Verdun in 1916, to the advance on the Somme led by the British in 1916, casualties expanded. In these big campaigns, the British suffered over 479,000 casualties, the French 710,000, and the Germans 835,000.[28] Besides the larger battles, continual artillery barrages, small raids, and reconnaissance patrols took their toll. Even small actions cost the British 7,000 men a day, what the bureaucracy of the BEF cynically termed "wastage."[29]

While the death toll was appalling, soldiers on both sides rarely wanted for food or ammunition. Steam power, in the form of railroads and ships, delivered supplies for sustenance and almost uninterrupted shelling. As in 1755, getting artillery to the battlefield was the key to victory, but the raw materials, manufacturing, and transportation necessary to produce munitions demanded much more of states and their economies. To keep up with ever-expanding requirements of war the Entente and Germany retooled their entire economic structures beginning in 1916, which required great sacrifices from the home fronts. In the Industrial Era, while the soldier with the full belly became grist for the artillery mill, the civilian populations suffered shortages.

With a grim past and a stark future in front, the belligerents raced to control the course of the war in 1917. Both sides understood that the "Americans and the tanks" were coming to alter the equation by 1918, but in the meantime 1917 became a contest of strength against strength: German rail power versus British sea power.[30] The Germans had a twofold plan in 1917. First, they wanted to use an unrestricted submarine campaign to halt the British supply lines and commerce before the United States could use its economic might to influence the outcome. The Germans well understood that the Americans would declare war because of the submarine's threat to ocean commerce. Second, the Germans needed to play defense on the Western Front, going on offense in the East to knock out a tottering Russia and return by rail to the Western Front to finish the British and French.

The nations of the Entente wanted to use their supplies from the sea, to include increasing amounts of artillery shells, which German submarines hunted, to bludgeon the German trench lines. In 1917, the Entente would take the offensive in four major campaigns—Arras and Aisne, Messines, the Third Battle of Ypres, and Cambrai.[31] After Arras and Aisne, the French would remain on the defense, with their army on the verge of revolt. Britain would take the lead on the final three offensives, while also continuing their sea blockade of Germany to starve their enemy and assist their Russian ally.

ALL IN FOR WAR: THE BELLIGERENTS,
SUPPLY, AND SOCIETY, 1914–1917

Two and a half years of stalemate and the demands the war placed on the manufacturing industries of the belligerents required both sides to retool economies and their logistics support systems to support their national strategies. To move their nations, both sides spent the latter part of 1916 and into 1917 revamping. The success or setbacks of these plans would play out long after the decisions made in response to the stresses of war, with their populations a crucial part of the equation. How each side arrived at the starting point of the battles in April 1917 is important to the story of war and logistics on the Western Front.

Germany

For the Germans the dangers of autarky, choked off from world commerce by the British Navy, showed up early in the war. German general Von Falkenhayn reported, "Only those who held responsible posts in the German General Headquarters in the winter of 1914–15 [understood that] . . . every single shot had to be counted in the Western Army, and the failure of one single ammunition train, the breaking of a rail . . . threatened to render whole sections of the front defenceless."[32] It was clear from the beginning that the railroad would be the German mule; their deft use of it held the Western Front.

The German offensives in 1915 and 1916, coupled with defense of the Somme, demanded ever more weapons. German machine guns numbered 2,450 at the start of the war and rose to 8,000 by 1915; and by 1916 German industry produced over 2,300 a month.[33] 105 mm howitzers followed the same trend, rising from 416 in 1914 to 3,000 by 1916.[34] The demand for manufacturing put pressure on the railroads, since both train and factory needed coal, and freight cars competed for power against the same munitions they carried from the factory to the front. Railroads and factories ran at full capacity with no hope of external economic support.[35]

With the demands of war, the Germans had to divert railroads from serving the population to serve the fronts. The situation was so severe in the winter of 1916–1917 that General Erich Ludendorff remarked, "The question of transportation lay at the root of all questions of keeping up the fight at home."[36] By 1916, the British naval blockade cut the average German caloric intake to fewer than 30 percent of 1914 levels.[37] By 1916, a poor fall harvest further depleted wheat and potatoes, and protein ceased as a component of the average German's diet.[38] In a cruel testament to the overtaxed transportation system of Germany, the trains continued to feed and supply the Western Front while home-front foods sat and spoiled, since the German economy depended on its railroads, rathen than cold storage, to move food to consumers.[39] To survive these shortages the German's ate turnips during the winter of 1916–1917.[40] These economic privations caused the German strategy to be one of defense on the Western Front in 1917, in hopes of knocking out their weak opponent to the east first.[41] Despite Ludendorff's exhortation about cooperation, the German population was all in for the war effort. While their nation supplied food and firepower to the Western Front, the German population starved.

In the fall of 1916, with severe shortages of transportation, artillery shells, and food because of stalemated trench warfare and the allied naval blockade, Germany reorganized its economy under both the Hindenburg and Auxiliary Laws. With the Hindenburg Laws, the chief of the army, General Paul Von Hindenburg, German industry, and army officials attempted to centralize many of the economic decisions of war.[42] Under the Auxiliary Laws, the Reichstag reworked labor rules to expand the workforce age range to all males between seventeen and sixty not serving in the war effort.[43] Under both laws, Hindenburg pleaded for German industry and society to transform itself from animal and human power to machines: "Men—as well as horses—must be replaced by more and more machines."[44] Despite the reorganization efforts, 1917 offered no relief for the population. The demands of war drove a rift between civilian and military rule in which General Hindenburg emerged as the undisputed leader of a militarized society and the trains held the front.[45]

Great Britain

The British Navy delivered the BEF across the channel without contest and helped stem the tide over the German attempt at Paris in 1914. As they had always done, the British came from the sea. With their sea lines of communication free, the British flooded the Western Front with troops and supplies. The demands of war, particularly the production of artillery shells, put a great strain on the world's most powerful economy.

During the German offensive at Ypres in 1915, the *Times* published a story detailing the loss of British soldiers at Auber's Ridge because of a lack of artillery shells.[46] A public firestorm ensued, and the Asquith government established the Munitions Board on 2 July 1915, headed by Asquith's future successor—David Lloyd George.[47] Reshaping the supply chain, the munitions program under Lloyd George's command sped up shell production from 368,000 per month in July 1915 to 5 million by January 1917.[48] So successful was the British program that the Germans modeled the Hindenburg and Auxiliary Laws along similar lines as those dictated by the British Ministry of Munitions in 1915.[49] Although a manufacturing success, the massive increase in war production filtered down as a demand signal to the transportation system supporting Northern France, which manifested itself in 1916 and, as we shall see, almost stalled British offensives in 1917.

As with the German population, the demands of war strained Britons. Rationing was a daily part of British life, and restrictions on meat, sugar, and bread bled over from the war into private life. The British government built an entire bureaucracy called the Food Controller's Department to regulate vast sections of the British diet to ensure food for the front.[50] Worse yet, the overperforming British economy was near failure. According to Alexander Watson, "The exertions of the past year [1916] had almost bankrupted the British. Paying for food and raw materials . . . as well as semi-finished or finished armaments, was costing the treasury two million pounds a day, and British gold reserves and securities were on course to be exhausted by March 1917."[51]

The British leadership of 1916 and 1917, led by Asquith and Lloyd George, understood well the impact of war on their society.[52] Although the situation was desperate in Britain, its people were not on the road to starvation as in Germany, but any further disruption in the food supply could have moved the nation toward hunger. Thus, when the unrestricted submarine campaign of the Germans began in 1917, starvation and loss of the sea lines of communications were at the forefront of British policy. Although to a lesser degree than their German cousins, the British population was also all in for total war, with their physical needs interwoven into national strategy.

As with Germany, the drive to reshape the economy for industrial war had political ramifications for Britain. Lloyd George's success in revamping the munitions industry was the crucial factor in his advancement. To solve the munitions crisis, Lloyd George reached out to industry for men of "push and pull" who would ignore standard convention.[53] One such man was Sir Eric Geddes, who got his start in business working on the railroads.[54] With his success during the munitions crisis of 1915 propelling him to 10 Downing Street, Lloyd George brought Geddes to the Western Front in 1916–1917.

France

While Germany and the British reworked their economies to support the war effort, France tried to recover. The Pyrrhic victory at Verdun had cost the French 377,321 lives; the battle combined with the Somme to account for 579,798 casualties in 1916.[55] Enduring most of the war on its soil, with some of its critical coal and manufacturing regions under control of the Germans, the French were losing their will. From a logistics perspective, they also suffered from overuse and misuse of their rail system and sought British help to fix their logistical challenges early in 1917.[56]

LOGISTICS GOES FIRST: LOGISTICS AND STRATEGY, 1916–1917

From 1916 to 1917, German leadership altered the course of the war in their attempt to starve Britain through unrestricted warfare. The Germans retreated to the Hindenburg line to buy themselves more time and space, falling back to their robust rail lines. The British hired Sir Eric Geddes to improve their system of transportation on the Western Front.

The British and Germans: Unrestricted Submarine Warfare

The British continued their dominance of the sea-lanes until 1917. As a result, their supplies and soldiers moved unimpeded from Britain and onto the Western Front. Britain's navy kept the global shipping afloat while holding the German capital ships in their ports.[57] This is not to say that the German U-boats did not have success. In the first half of 1915, they sank over three hundred vessels, representing eight hundred thousand tons of shipping.[58] The Germans had to walk a fine line in the realm of international commerce, however, to avoid bringing neutral nations—especially the United States— to the side of the Entente.[59] The German economy needed no more foes. Through the lens of logistics, with the BEF ensconced on the coast of northern France and southern Belgium, the British were fighting the ideal war of supply and transportation—near the front and protected by British control of the sea. The decision of German chancellor Bethmann-Hollweg and generals Hindenburg and Ludendorff to embark on unrestricted submarine warfare in 1917 changed the strategic calculus.

Table 2.1. German U-Boat Tonnage Sunk, February to May 1917

Month	Tonnage Sunk
February	499,430
March	548,817
April	841,118
May	590,729

Sources: Data adapted from Holger H. Herwig, *The First World War: Germany and Austria-Hungary, 1914–1918* (London: St. Martin's Press, 1997), 318; and Joachim Schröder, *Die U-Boote Des Kaisers: Die Geschichte Des Deutschen U-Boot-Krieges Gegen Großbritannien Im Ersten Weltkrieg* (Pegnitz, Germany: Europaforum-Verlag, 2001) as cited in Alexander Watson, *Ring of Steel: Germany and Austria-Hungary in World War I* (New York: Basic Books, 2014), 437.

After the winter of 1916–1917, when the British sea blockade had reduced the Germans to eating turnips, the debate within German political-military circles turned to submarine warfare—American entry into the war be damned. Besides the Hindenburg program and the Auxiliary Laws, the decision to turn the U-boat force loose on the seas reflected the German state's move to total war.[60]

On 9 January 1917, Bethmann-Hollweg approved the campaign, with the blessing of the German General Staff, the German Admiralty and Kaiser Wilhelm II.[61] With the U-Boat restrictions lifted, the Germans threatened the British populace, turning the British blockade on its head. Although there was no doubt in the minds of Germany's decision-makers that the United States would now join the Entente, they believed the submarines would cripple the British economy first.

To bolster this thesis, the Germans used detailed statistical analysis, newspaper reports, and the *Register of Ships*. German naval planners estimated they could bring Britain's imports—wheat the most important target—to a standstill by August if the U-boats could sink an average of 600,000 tons per month.[62] As the campaign began in February 1917, the U-boats seemed to make good on the mathematics, sinking 499,430 tons and then accelerating to 841,118 tons by April (see Table 2.1). The United States obliged the German action and declared war on 6 April 1917.[63]

For the Germans, the entry by the United States shifted the balance on the Western Front, but the material might of American industry would not reach combat readiness until 1918. In the interim, the U-Boat successes in 1917 bolstered internal morale and hope for the war in Germany. In addition, the submarines struck at British primacy of the sea and their logistics support for the war and home front. The belligerents remained equal in the West.

The Eastern Front, however, was in much more flux and presented a distinct advantage to the Germans. Although the Russian commitment in the East was in doubt for the first half of the year, by July the country was in the throes of revolution.[64] With the Russian state slipping, the Germans required a decreasing number of soldiers on the Eastern Front throughout the second half of the year, allowing them to ship soldiers and war supplies from the Eastern to the Western Front by rail to help hold back the Entente.[65]

Operation Alberich: The Hindenburg Line and German Rail

Alberich was a mischievous dwarf of ancient Norse mythology. Living and working in the mines, he was a metalworker. The daughters of the Rhine snubbed him and made fun of his rough looks. In return, he gave them a precious gold ring with a hidden curse. Thinking the ring a prize, the daughters accepted the ring and earned death. In early 1917, the Germans hoped to give the Entente the same curse, by trading ground for a better defensive strategy.

While German U-boats attacked British and allied logistics in January 1917, Hindenburg and the General Staff revamped their internal lines of communication. In 1916, the German Army learned some difficult lessons. During the British offensives at the Somme, the Germans discovered that infantry crowded into linear trenches were ideal targets for a "creeping barrage" of British artillery. Ludendorff said after the Somme:

The whole system of defense had to be made broader and looser and better adapted to the ground. The large, thick barriers of wire, pleasant as they were when there was little doing, were no longer a protection. They withered under the enemy barrage. Light strands of wire, difficult to see, were much more useful. Forward infantry positions with a wide field of fire were easily seen by the enemy. They could be destroyed by the artillery of the enemy, and were very difficult to protect by our own artillery. Positions farther back, with a narrower firing filed and more under the protection of our own guns, were retained. They were of special service in big fights.[66]

Reorganizing their tactics in 1917, the Germans sought a defense that could accept artillery and infantry assault and then follow with swift counterattack.[67] These readjustments yielded two new approaches: elastic defense and shorter lines of communication. The elastic defense contained deeper and thinner lines, with pillboxes of machines guns built with interlocking lanes of fire. In this way, fewer men covered more ground and avoided massing in one area as prey for artillery barrages. Reflecting Moltke's concepts from forty years before, the deeper lines gave German defenders the ability to fall back in small elements rather than massed formations and then regroup for counterattack.

To counterattack with the required troops and firepower, the Germans needed to shorten their rail lines extending into the Western Front. The lines from Cambrai and St. Quentin into the British and French sectors comprised four single-track lines with sixty miles of track.[68] The extended line overburdened the rails. Ludendorff reflected, "in consideration of the internal organization of the army and in the interests of the man, as supply, for both men and horses was suffering. . . . The reinforcements which were released for the battle could not be sent up to the front line in rotation. The railways were already considerably overtaxed by the ordinary traffic to and from the battle-lines."[69]

To shorten their lines and build their elastic defense, the German High Command ordered a retreat to the Hindenburg Line (see Figure 2.1). Falling back to St. Quentin, the Germans surrendered the single-track lines running east towest. In return, the Germans maintained the larger double-track rail lines that ran north and south and were behind the new trenches stretching from Lille to St. Quentin. Figure 2.2 illustrates the gains in capacity the Germans realized by retreating onto their larger rail lines.

Adhering to elastic defense, the Germans destroyed everything during their retreat in March 1917. An "average depth of nearly 20 miles, was to be made a desert: as far as possible, every town and village was to be destroyed, every tree cut down, the inhabitants were to be removed, and the wells filled up or polluted. It became 'the devastated area.'"[70] The Germans' destruction of private property and their removal of whole villages sparked outrage in the West.[71]

German army leaders cared little for morality but much for defense. They understood the barren place the army left behind would fill with mud during the rainy seasons to slow an advance and highlight any Allied movement to spotting balloons and aircraft.[72] Beyond making the ground they

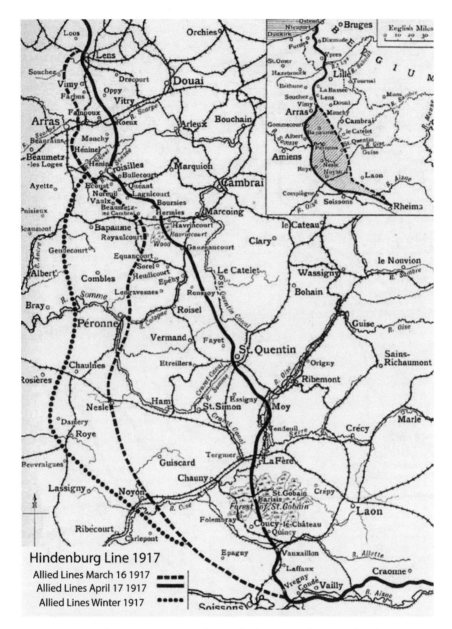

Figure 2.1. Map of German Retreat to the Hindenburg Line. (Reprinted with permission from Chris Baker, "Pursuit of the German retreat to the Hindenburg Line," accessed 23 April 2019, http://www.longlongtrail.co.uk.)

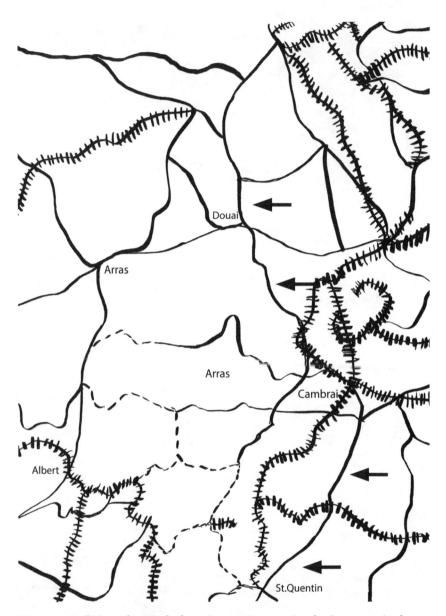

Figure 2.2. Rail Lines after Hindenburg Retreat. By retreating the Germans gained larger rail capacity. The hashed lines are the smaller single-track lines the Germans gave up by retreating. The arrows in the figure point to the larger double-track lines the Germans fell back on by retreating to the Hindenburg Line. (Map by Avery Turner. Adapted from "Map Showing Narrow Gauge Railways in France and Flanders, Chart 9, Chapter XVI," in *Report of the Military Board of Allied Supply* [Washington, DC: Government Publishing Office, 1924].)

relinquished difficult to own, the Germans reconstructed the lines from the French positions from Aisne in the south to Ypres in the north to reflect their new tactic of elastic defense. In 1916, those same defenses had been one mile deep, while the new lines were six to eight miles deep with interlocking avenues of fire for artillery and machine guns.[73]

The railroads were crucial to the construction efforts for Alberich. According to Herman Herwig in *The First World War: Germany and Austria-Hungary, 1914–1918*, "Operation Alberich became the war's greatest feat of engineering. . . . 1250 supply trains of 40 freight cars each hauled concrete and steel to the construction sites."[74] After Operation Alberich, the Germans waited—for their U-boats to starve the British, for the teetering Russian state to implode, and for the Entente to take the bait.

Entente Logistics Moves: Translating from Sea to Land

The logistics system the British built to supply the Western Front was inadequate by 1916. The success of the revamped munitions industry in 1915, which delivered increasing numbers artillery and machine guns to support the offensive at Somme in 1916, had overwhelmed the transportation system in France. In January 1916, 2,484 wagons moved per day over the railroad lines in the British sector. At the Somme, the number grew to 4,476, and by December the daily rate was 5,202.[75] In addition, the ports at Calais, Boulogne, Abbeville, Dunkirk, St. Valery, Dieppe, and Le Havre overflowed with cargo under an inefficient system of tracking and control.[76] Independent officers and staff ran individual rail lines with no integrated system of control, leaving supply subject to the vagaries of the chain of command.[77] Horses, men, and increasing numbers of trucks clogged the roads, while barges tried to break the gridlock by moving supplies up rivers to depots—all in uncoordinated effort. Added to this, the British sector of the Western Front, from the channel to the trenches, encompassed a scant 4,050 square miles.[78] With such crowded conditions, accurate movement of men and supplies to the proper location was essential, and the system in 1916 could not handle the problem of plenty.

Although the success of Lloyd George in producing massive numbers of munitions was the proximate cause of the difficulties of transportation the British suffered in late 1916, many of their problems originated before 1914. Before the war, the British and French negotiated a supply-and-transportation

Chart 3—Chapter XI.

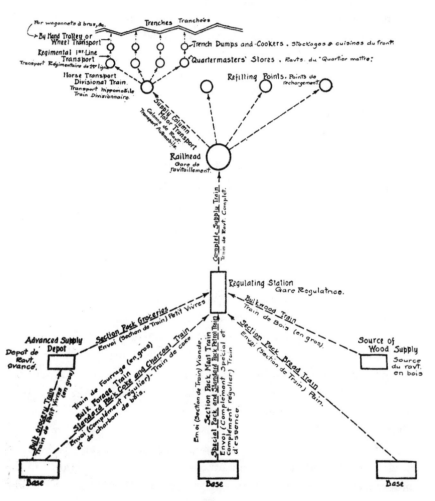

Figure 2.3. Transportation System of the BEF, 1914. (Reprinted from "General Scheme of Supply from the Base to the Trenches, British Expeditionary Forces, Chart 3, Chapter 11." In *Report of the Military Board of Allied Supply* [Washington, DC: Government Publishing Office, 1924].)

network. In this agreement, British cargo and men would move across the English channels to ports in France, forward to supply depots, and then to the front following a simple path (see Figure 2.3).[79]

As Figure 2.3 shows, the supplies all flowed in one direction in 1914—to the front. Ammunition, food, and supplies moved via rail, horse, or human; from base, to depot, to station, to railhead, to quartermaster stations, and finally to the individual soldier. The system resembled the one the British had built at Lake George from 1755 to 1759, and thus had the same ability to handle a steady supply stream to the front. While such a system moved cargo adequately in one direction from 1914 to 1916, it lacked mechanisms to adapt to the complexities of moving hundreds of thousands of soldiers across a front hundreds of miles long.[80] In addition, transportation by modern ships and railroads overwhelmed the one-way logistics of the British in 1914.

Added to the one-way transportation plan was a confusion about what went where. As much as the cargo flowed in one direction, so did information.[81] Without a proper flow of information, there was no method to stop, alter, or move cargo away from a congested railhead or toward a moving front, leading to further congestion and confusion.[82] Although the inadequate transportation network the of the British for the first three years of war is interesting as a case study in supply chain management, more important is that the faltering network hampered British strategy. Without the proper logistics network to move thousands of artillery pieces and millions of shells, any future offensive was doomed.

Into this morass of confusion stepped Sir Eric Geddes. Although Lloyd George had brought him along to help fix the antiquated munitions process in 1915 and 1916, Geddes's real experience was as a leader in the railroad industry. He had fixed the munitions program using industry practices of data collection and analysis, which searched for efficiencies to cut waste and improve the bottom line.[83] Geddes would translate these skills designed for profit to placate Lewis Mumford's great consumer—the industrial battlefield.

Before the Great War, the British military's procurement system was rooted in the eighteenth century. British generals and admirals bargained for food, supplies, and war armament with large bureaucracies in the British War Office. Even by 1915, the British system resembled the archaic process that Braddock, Johnson, and Abercrombie used to secure supplies for their campaigns. The British munitions office, before Lloyd George's overhaul in 1915, personified the style. For example, the Woolwich Arsenal had a system so Byzantine they nicknamed it "the Extract." The British war offices instructed Woolwich on manufacturing needs without establishing priority, artillery shell goals, or supervision to ensure completion.[84] Geddes had fixed Woolwich with data analysis and precise requirements, and now Lloyd George sent him to France to help the commander of British forces, Sir Douglas Haig, with his problems of logistics.

Recognizing his army's difficulty, Haig told Geddes, "Warfare consists of men, munitions, and movement. We have got the men and munitions, but we seem to have forgotten the movement."[85] Before delving into the details of the transportation problem, Geddes began his work by creating a cabinet-level position with "the right of direct access to the Secretary of State and of attending meetings of the Army Council when matters pertaining to his department were under discussion."[86] Assuming the title of this new office, Director-General of the Military Railways, Geddes cut through the balkanized logistics and created a system accountable to one boss.

With the command structure in place, Geddes then revolutionized the British logistics system by using his commercial methods. He built a team of military and civilian logistics experts and sent them to collect data on the transportation. In the fall of 1916, there was a lack of statistics on the Western Front; everything—port operations, rail usage, and traffic moved on roads— went unrecorded.[87] This was in stark contrast with the information the British kept on the location of soldiers, which they had tracked since August 1914. Reflecting the original plan before the war, the British concerned themselves only with men and munitions forward, and left the details unattended. With his work, Geddes recorded the first logistics data on the Western Front and started solving the problem.[88]

Geddes and his team took the data they collected and built a forecast for the planned offensives of 1917. They catalogued the transportation of ammunition and supply during the Somme offensive in 1916 and projected it forward for 1917, factoring in the increased munitions coming from Britain. This forecast was then placed on the British transportation system and divided into three segments: (1) unloading at the ports; (2) movements by rail, road, or barge to the front; and (3) final delivery to the trenches.[89]

The forecast estimated that the British needed to move 2,292 tons by barge and 21,601 tons by rail off the ports per day by mid-1917. At the port, this required a discharge rate of 198,662 tons of supplies per week, with a surge rate of 248,327 tons.[90] The port unloading system in late 1916 could deliver only 60 percent of the rate required.[91] To expand the throughput, the British and French increased the numbers of cranes to off-load ships from 121 in December 1916 to 314 by the end of the war—an increase of 259 percent.[92]

After the ports, Geddes and his staff revamped the scheme of movement to the front. They ordered more light railroads built and the roads improved, and reorganized how goods and information flowed to and from operational commanders at the front. In doing so, Geddes's reforms transformed the simple flows of the original system (Figure 2.3) to a complex, interactive system that considered movement in multiple directions and incorporated home-station manufacturing requirements (see Figures 2.3 and 2.4).

Besides revamping the transportation on land, Geddes also developed two innovative ideas to relieve congestion from the sea: the cross-channel barge and the channel ferry. Cross-channel barge service began in December 1916 and delivered goods by barge across the channel, then up the waterways of France to inland supply depots, without stopping at the ports.[93] The channel-ferry service directed a train full of artillery shells to proceed from the factory by rail to the ferry in Britain. With the train aboard, the ferry would sail to France, where cranes moved the train from the ferry onto the tracks for immediate dispatch to the railhead with the greatest need, eliminating loading and unloading at both ports and saving railcar usage in France.[94] Although the cross-channel barges carried only 7 percent of British cargo, the channel-ferries increased the numbers of munitions cars on the railroads from three hundred a month to over two thousand.[95]

Improving the final movement to the trenches was the most difficult task. Whereas the Germans had designed their attack through Belgium and France to include railroad-building on the move and harnessing existing rail lines, the British relied on roads, using horses and, in ever greater numbers, motor-powered trucks called lorries, by early 1917.[96] However, in the low-lying areas of Flanders, below sea level in places, wet weather saturated the ground and made the roads impassable. The solution to this problem was more track for the trains—both light rail and narrow-gauge track built closer to the front—to curtail dependence on lorries and horses. Geddes's efforts were impressive: in September 1916 there was no British light rail from the

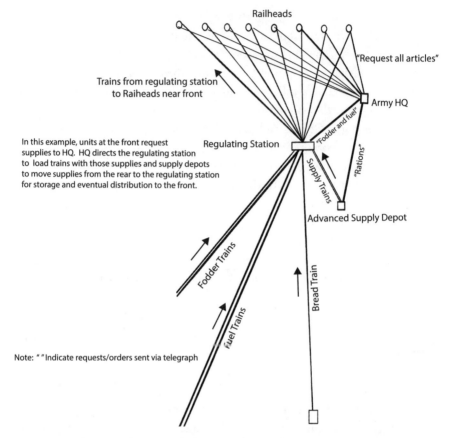

Figure 2.4. Adaptation from British Train Regulating Chart. (From "British Train Regulating Chart, Chart 1, Chapter XIV," in *Report of the Military Board of Allied Supply* [Washington: Government Publishing Office, 1924].)

railheads to the front, but by May 1917 "fifty-miles of track were being laid each week."[97]

Although the British efforts amplified allied rail capacity, they never matched the German network facing them on the other side in 1917. Figures 2.1 and 2.2 show the advantage the Germans had in terms of light rail in length and depth on the front. The retreat to the Hindenburg Line further pulled the Germans onto their narrow-gauge trench system.[98] Since light rail was the primary mover of artillery for both sides, this gave the Germans an advantage in speed and flexibility over the Entente.

THE NIVELLE OFFENSIVE: BRITISH SUCCESS, FRENCH FAILURE, AND FLANDERS

As the British fixed their transportation problems, they also faced a crisis of strategy in early 1917. General Haig favored an offensive in Flanders, around the Ypres Salient, to improve on the poor results of the Somme and pulverize the Germans with his growing artillery force. After two years of carnage, Lloyd George and others in the British War Ministry favored a strategy of moving forces to Italy to break the stalemate from the south.[99] French concerns about allied strategy in 1917 and U-boats interrupted the debate.

After the debacle of Verdun, Robert Georges Nivelle replaced Field Marshal Joseph Joffre. Taking command in December 1916, Nivelle tried to bring new life to the beleaguered French. He wanted to reinvigorate the famed French offensive spirit by using artillery across a large front, as he had done around the much smaller area surrounding Verdun to win Fort Douaumont. In January 1917 he visited London and impressed Lloyd George and the British civilian leadership with a plan to gather a massive amount of French artillery around the River Aisne and pulverize the German trenches. As part of his plan, Nivelle proposed that the British strike from Arras to the south, to push the extended German salient between the French and British back.[100] Although British officers including Haig were skeptical, Lloyd George was smitten, and the British supported the plan.

Nivelle's plan—called the Nivelle Offensive—required much of the Entente's logistics support. With the change in strategy, the British logistics system lacked the agility, while being recast by Geddes and the British army, to deliver the artillery pieces necessary to the proper locations near Arras.[101] In addition, the French lacked railcars for the same.[102] As the Allies prepared to meet at Calais in February 1917 to discuss the operational details, Haig brought Geddes with him to present the transportation problem to Lloyd George and French prime minister Aristide Briand.[103] In this meeting, Geddes explained, with agreement from the French generals present, that the Entente lacked the rail wagons and the transportation system necessary to prosecute the offensive. Geddes estimated that the French needed 490 more locomotives to move the artillery.[104] With the political backing of Lloyd George and Briand, Geddes arranged for the delivery of more British locomotives and trains to France, at the expense of railroad traffic in Britain, to solve the problem.[105] In the background, the U-boat successes of the year put even more pressure on the logistics of the Entente. Every munition or troop delivered to the front without waste diminished the requirement on the sea-transportation network from the United States to Britain.

Alberich Strikes Back

In February 1917, as the Allies debated their strategy, the Germans moved back to the Hindenburg Line. This forced a change in the operational plan for Nivelle. When the Allies learned that the Germans had retreated across the front in early March, they realized that the region they hoped to capture in battle was now bequeathed to them as a "no-man's land." Repairing roads and rebuilding rail lines into the new salient would take too long.[106] The only places to attack were those where allied troops existed before the German retreat—near Arras for the British and Chemis de Dames for the French. The German move eliminated the flanks and created the conditions for a future *Kesselschlact*—their loss in land traded for the advantage in position (see figure 2.5).

Under Nivelle's altered plan, the British would take the fight from Arras as scheduled, with the French moving from the Aisne toward Laon.[107] With the German salient disappeared, hopes of envelopment followed—the strategy was now force-on-force, and Nivelle believed the Entente could move the trench lines eastward with their growing arsenal of artillery. Thus, Nivelle's plan morphed from a strategy of encirclement to a plan based on the assets the British and French had in place, limited by the logistics needed to reposition the front between the Arras and Aisne.

As Nivelle's plan changed, so did internal French politics. Prime Minister Briand fell from power and was replaced by a temporary government under Alexandre Ribot, with a corresponding shift in the French cabinet. The new ministers of France were not impressed with Nivelle's plan. Haig noted, "I hear Nivelle had had trouble. Some of the French Government had wished to forbid the French offensive altogether. But Nivelle had gained. . . . And if anything goes wrong, Nivelle will disappear."[108]

British Success

Nivelle's plan to reinvigorate the French Army through "the stamp of violence, of brutality and of rapidity" and "in one blow capture the enemy

Figure 2.5. Western Front 1917: Major Offensives. The arrows to the south Cambrian front indicate the locations of failed Nivelle Offensive, which gained no territory. (Reprinted from T. Dodson Stamps and Vincent J. Esposito, *A Short Military History of World War I* [West Point, NY: USMAAG Printing Office, 1950], 58.)

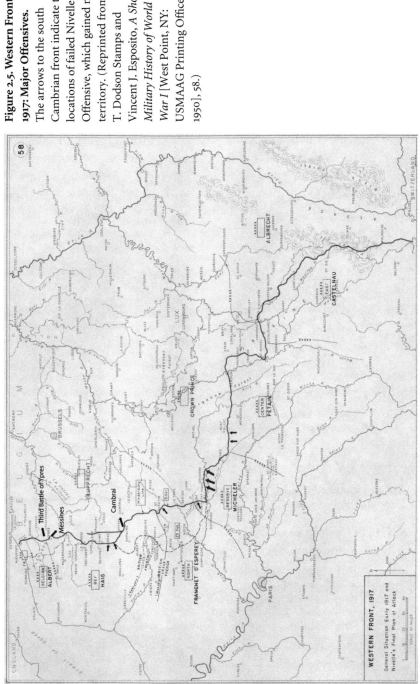

WESTERN FRONT, 1917

General Situation Early 1917 and Nivelle's Final Plan of Attack

positions and all the zone occupied by his artillery" began with the British shelling the German lines near Arras on 4 April 1917, followed by an infantry advance along a fifteen-mile front on the ninth.[109]

The array of artillery was impressive. Haig wrote, "Our concentration of our Artillery on the fronts attacked to-day was the greatest I have ever seen. The number of guns was as follows: First Army 1,106 on Vimy Ridge, Third Army 1,772 (astride the Scarpe), Fifth Army 519 (on St. Quentin front)."[110] The British amassed the guns thorough the expanded rail system, improved distribution system, and increased port throughput that Geddes oversaw. During the first month of the Somme in 1916, the British had delivered and used 11,784,435 shells of all types—from high explosive to shrapnel. At Arras, during the first month in 1917, the British used 14,562,219 shells, an increase of 23.5 percent.[111]

The most important update was the emphasis by Geddes and the British Army on narrow-gauge rail, which connected the larger railhead and supply depots to the trenches. The shelling in the first few days weakened the German defensive lines just as in 1916, but this time the British had a system of transportation system that could follow the offensive. Keith Grieves in *Sir Eric Geddes* avers that

the light railways were a crucial feature of a timetabled supply system. After the advance on 9 April, naval guns were moved forward on newly laid railway track and light railways were extended beyond Arras using resources stockpiled for the purpose. Field artillery units maintained a creeping barrage without fear of a failure of supply and were able to assist the Canadian troops in their capture of Vimy Ridge. At Arras the battle was followed by an infantry advance and transport followed more closely than ever before.[112]

As a result, the British opened a seven-mile-wide gap extending three and a half miles into the German lines near Arras in two days. In addition, the British captured over 180 artillery pieces and twelve thousand prisoners.[113] Ludendorff remarked that such a big hole in the lines "is not a thing to be mended without more ado. It takes a good deal to repair the inordinate wastage of men and guns as well as munitions that results from such a breach."[114]

Although a qualified success, the British did not break the code of maneuver warfare at Arras. Movement by rail had limits. Railroads took time to construct, and though they followed the offensive, it was difficult. The wet and cold conditions in April 1917, coupled with unimpeded German rail made it more difficult. On 12 April, Haig wrote:

Great efforts were made to bring forward guns, and, in spite of the difficulties presented by weather and ground, several batteries . . . reached position in rear of the old German line. . . . Our advance had now reached a point at which the difficulty of maintaining communications and providing adequate artillery support for our infantry began seriously to limit our progress. Moreover, the enemy had had time to bring up reserves and to recover from the temporary disorganization caused by our first attacks.[115]

The German defenses before and after Arras illustrate the limits of how far the British could push forward and the tenacity of the German defense supported by rail. Although the Germans lost territory, they maintained railroads within their internal lines of communication. Figure 2.2 illustrates the significant rail network the Germans possessed vis-à-vis the Allies, making it easier for them to fall back and defend in depth.[116] Even though the British followed the offensive forward with rail, they were not quick enough. The Germans bent but did not break. Their elastic defense—built in the winter of 1916–1917, strengthened by their retreat to the Hindenburg Line, and bolstered by their rail network behind—held.

Although it was a limited success and cost the British sixteen thousand casualties, it was the most significant movement on the Western Front by the Entente in two years of fighting. As the Germans learned in Austria and at Sedan in the previous century, the British realized the need to build railroads as the offensive moved.[117] Despite its positives, the movement by the British at Arras could not overcome French failure and German success to the south.

French Failure

With the British out of their trenches on 9 April, the French began their artillery preparation on a front stretching from Aisne to Champagne, with five infantry divisions standing behind the guns ready to push through the German lines. With the weather deteriorating, the French left their trenches on 16 April 1917.[118] Nivelle promised six miles in the first day. Instead, he faced defeat.[119] In an amazing feat ofélan, the French troops waded through the mud and sleet to attack the new German defenses with reckless abandon.

The Germans repaid them with 120,000 casualties in two days. The French medical service had prepared for "ten or fifteen thousand wounded . . . instead, on the first day of the offensive it received more than ninety thousand."[120] The French put the Germans' elastic defense to the test and failed. With such horrific losses, the French Army revolted and the French government fired Nivelle on 17 May 1917.[121]

With Nivelle's firing, the famed cult of the offense that had possessed the French Army since Napoleon died. General Petain, the hero of Verdun, took command. While Petain provided succor to most survivors and executed the more recalcitrant troops, Paul Painelvè addressed the French nation and admitted the failure in public.[122] The French still held their trenches, fought in the air, and made limited moves, but they ceded control of the railways to the British and joined their German enemies on defense for 1917.[123]

The efforts of the French and British at Arras proved two things to the Germans. First, the new strategy of defense on the Western Front worked. Whatever they had lost in land to the Hindenburg Line the Germans gained in tactical flexibility and reserves of men and ammunition to stem any allied advance. In the words of German general Von Janson, stationed on the Western Front during the Arras offensive, "This policy [Hindenburg Line] . . . enabled the Germans, though on the defensive, to impose their will on the attacking enemy and to keep their own freedom of decision of action, which practically amounted to a reversal of the usual relationship between the attack and defense."[124] Second, the growing armament, supplies, and soldiers of the Allies were worrisome. Von Janson remarked in his same memo after the Arras offensive, "The extent of the success is only fully apparent when one considers how much better able the enemy was to replace his exhausted troops with fresh forces."[125] To address the threat of allied logistics, the Germans hoped their submarines could save the day.

AN ISLAND ALONE: U-BOATS
AND BRITISH CHANGE IN STRATEGY

By mid-1917, the war on the seas seemed to favor the Germans. Although based only on their early projections of U-boat destruction, not what the British could withstand, the increasing tonnage sunk and their holding of the Western Front after the Nivelle Offensive gave Hindenburg and Ludendorff hope (see Table 2.1).[126] The crisis of supplying war while keeping their population alive, however, resulted in skepticism by Bethmann-Hollweg and the civilian leadership of the Reichstag regarding the war's progress.

Bethmann-Hollweg, in an interview after the war, stated, "Whatever happened, for 1917 we could not hope for a victory, either on land or at sea, which would mean a final decision. . . . The conviction that the U-boat campaign would not bring England to her knees penetrated even into those circles which had cradled themselves in such a belief."[127] Even Kaiser Wilhelm II, an ardent supporter of the war, had grown more passive by mid-1917.[128] Among many factors, the sense that the war was not winnable, despite recent success in the west and on the sea, led to the ousting of Hollweg in July 1917 and the capitulation of civilian rule.[129] Hindenburg and Ludendorff ran Germany until November 1918, the nation now a military dictatorship in function if not form.

With the disaster of the Nivelle offensive, the French on defense, and the German menace from the sea threatening British supply lines, General Haig pressed for a British offensive in Flanders. Long a historic region of British war-making on the continent—from Agincourt, Fontenoy, and Waterloo to the BEF stop of the German right wing in 1914—Flanders took on a new strategic meaning because it contained the German submarine bases of Ostend and Zeebrugge to the north and east of Ypres.[130] On 24 April 1917, Haig outlined his plan to shift the fight to Flanders, explaining to General Nivelle that he could not precipitate any attacks into the southern British sector without French help, and "in view of the submarine campaign, it was most necessary to clear the Belgian Ports soon, at any rate before autumn."[131] Haig was optimistic, after the victory at Arras, that the British were grinding the Germans down. For Haig, Flanders would be the final act, with a mass of 1 million British troops breaking through to the Belgian coast, cutting off the subs, and dashing forward through the German lines to victory. Through the rest of April and May, Lloyd George tried to steer Haig to Italy, while Haig pushed for Flanders. This debate within the British war cabinet reached a peak in June.[132]

At the height of the strategic discussion, Admiral Jellicoe, chief of the Royal Navy, announced to the war cabinet on 20 June 1917 that Britain would be out of the war in 1918 because of the success of the German U-boat campaign. Haig recorded in his diary, "This was a bombshell for the Cabinet and all present. . . . Jellicoe's words: 'There is no good discussing plans for next Spring—We cannot go on.'"[133] Jellicoe's biggest concerns were the ports on the Belgian coast—Ostend and Zeebrugge.[134] Winston Churchill later singled out Jellicoe's statement as "wholly fallacious"; however, the threat of the submarines to undermine British supply lines to home and the front clearly worried the British in the spring of 1917.[135] British leadership had further debates about the progress of the war, but Jellicoe's statement locked British strategy on Flanders in 1917. With Haig's plan approved to attack from Ypres north to the Belgium coast, the British poured men and material into the Ypres Salient for the Third Battle of Ypres.[136]

Messines: A Fleeting and Hidden Hope

While British leadership, civilian and military, debated the next offensive, Lloyd George gave Haig permission to break General Plumer out of his low-lying position in the village of Ypres in Flanders.[137] Haig hoped that a victory at Messines Ridge, to the south of Ypres, would give him the extra advantage to turn the strategy towards Flanders. The Ypres Salient was so flat that a height of just fifty feet could command an area. As a result of their "high" position surrounding the city, Ypres had become the German's favorite area for artillery shelling throughout the war.[138] For two years, General Plumer and his staff had studied the area while sheltered from the continual German barrage underneath Ypres. They determined that the best way to improve their positions was to take the Messines Ridge. The technology the British used to accomplish this goal was the same technology the British Navy deployed against German U-boats at the same time—the mine.[139] From January 1916 to 21 May 1917, the British dug nineteen tunnels under the German lines and filled them with 1 million pounds of explosives (Figure 2.5 shows the location of Messines).[140]

When the British detonated the mines on 21 May 1917, the explosion was so loud that a sleepless Lloyd George heard the blast from London.[141] Supported by 2,266 guns, British infantry poured onto the ridge and secured it from vaporized and stunned German soldiers.[142] With the front blasted open, the British moved the line two miles within the first two days and redrew the trench lines. The Germans lost the high ground around Ypres and suffered twenty thousand casualties and seven thousand prisoners lost, while the British suffered twenty thousand casualties.[143] Despite this marginal success, the British did not attempt to expand their gains, since Lloyd George and Haig were still locked in debate about the overall strategy.[144]

The limited goals at Messines gave no opportunity for the British to engage the transportation support necessary to move their artillery forward. Without a true test of logistics, the British assumed they could repeat the successful efforts of logistics at Arras at Ypres, a region located in coastal lowlands and water-soaked even in dry weather. Victory at Messines created a false sense of security for which the British would pay when they moved to expand the Ypres Salient to the north and east and into the teeth of the German defenses. The mud would swallow men and machines.

The Mine and the Airplane: Hide and Seek

At the Battles of Messines, the mine gave the British something they had heretofore lacked on the Western Front—secrecy. Although it took significant discipline to tunnel under the German positions for eighteen months, the mine gave the British the chance to avoid reconnaissance by air and land. Through the first two and half years of war, pre-scripted artillery barrages highlighted the areas that soldiers would assault, allowing both sides to adjust their defenses. Besides the tell artillery shelling gave to the Germans, the extensive logistical tail of the British made surprise impossible. The massive numbers of men and equipment that sailed into a small portion of France and Belgium, and then moved forward to the front, were hard to hide with German aircraft overhead.

Not only did the Germans hold the "high ground," they also had the advantage in the air over the local front until late summer 1917—making it easy to spot and report British movements.[145] While the British secured a victory at Arras on the ground, in the skies overhead Richtofen and his Flying Circus destroyed older British aircraft with their newer Albatrosses.[146] Their localized superiority gave the Germans the ability to see the movements of the British and direct the German guns on attacking troops.[147] While captured prisoners, maps, and the loose talk of Nivelle also doomed the French, lack of control of the air over the front allowed the Germans to detect and plan for the impending offensive.

On the opposite side, Entente losses to German aircraft coupled with terrible weather in early 1917 hid the huge German effort to prepare the front for elastic defense and move behind the Hindenburg Line.[148] The Germans moved and improved over three hundred miles of the front line unbeknown to the Allies.[149] German trains ran at such high numbers that German industry and civilian leaders had to meter them to supply coal and foodstuffs back to the homeland, yet all the rail movements went unnoticed by the enemy.[150] The secrecy of logistics allowed the Germans to retreat to the Hindenburg Line, thereby altering Nivelle's strategy and stopping the offensive in its tracks.

Buildup: Prelude to Steam on Steam

In 1917, Ypres personified the juggernaut of British logistics from the sea to the front. A commander in the Third Australian Division described it as "streams of men, vehicles, motor lorries, horses, mules, and motors of every description moving ponderously forward, at a snail's pace, in either direction hour after hour, all day and all night, day after day, week after week, in a never halting, never ending stream . . . pulsing its way slowly and painfully through the mud . . . a reek of petrol and smoke everywhere."[151] Moving on the transportation system improved by Geddes, the British delivered (see Tables 2.2, 2.3, and 2.4) [152]

The British could not conceal such a massive effort from aircraft of the *Deutsche Luftstreitkräfte*. The German high command had surmised even earlier in 1917 that a breakout from Ypres would be the focus of a British offensive, and bolstered their defenses in response. Ludendorff halted divisions bound for Italy as the Russians fell away on the Eastern Front. The Germans moved in sixty-seven fresh divisions to the area surrounding Ypres and

Table 2.2. British Port Activity to Support the Third Battle of Ypres, June–October 1917

	Ships Unloaded	Port Tons/Hour	Tons/Week
January	173	12.0	148,123
June	206	18.0	213,623
July	195	19.6	193,631
August	166	21.5	174,160
September	173	22.9	181,282
October	163	21.4	163,702

Source: Adapted from *Statistics of the Military Effort of the British Empire During the Great War: 1914–1920* (London: His Majesty's Stationery Office, 1922), 606.

Note: January is a baseline for reference in Tables 2.2 and 2.3.

Table 2.3. British Railroad Capacity and Track Miles, France, 1917

	Wagons (per week)	Standard Rail (miles)	Narrow-Gauge Rail (miles)
January	—	130	97
June	22,502	236	314
July	25,041	270	434
August	31,697	279	553
September	43,987	297	623
October	50,278	315	680

Source: Adapted from *Statistics of the Military Effort of the British Empire During the Great War: 1914–1920* (London: His Majesty's Stationery Office, 1922), 606–607.
Note: January is a baseline for reference in Tables 2.2 and 2.3.

rotated out fifty-one battle-tired divisions from July to November.[153] They stockpiled artillery shells in such great numbers that the effort negatively impacted the relationship between labor and the government back in Berlin during July.[154] The Germans also used more motorized transport trucks—though not in great numbers as the British did—sometimes putting them on rails and at other times using wooden wheels as a substitute for scarce rubber resources, choked for three years during the blockade.[155]

Thus, while Haig thought the earlier operations at Arras and Messines had worn down the Germans, the opposite happened. The slackening of German need in the east gave the Germans the capacity to move even more divisions

Table 2.4. British Road Building and Lorrie Activity, France, 1917

	New Road (square yards)	Resurfaced Roads (square yards)	Lorries at the Front
January	0*	0*	1,685
June	67,471	0	—
July	71,811	264,057	2,325
August	52,273	247,861	—
September	44,121	273,169	—
October	98,373	221,860	2,694

Source: Adapted from *Statistics of the Military Effort of the British Empire During the Great War: 1914–1920* (London: His Majesty's Stationery Office, 1922), 606–607.
*Winter weather

by train to the west. Haig thought his enemy had only 179 divisions when they had 210 on the Western Front.[156] By late summer, the Germans and their railroads were ready to fight the British strength from the sea.

SEA AND LAND: DEADLOCK

On 21 July 1917, 2,300 British guns fired on the German positions to the north and east of Ypres, beginning the Third Battle of Ypres, later called Passchendaele. For ten days, the guns fired, leaving in their wake thirty thousand German soldiers dead and nine thousand missing.[157] During the Somme, the British lobbed 1,227,131 shells per week at the enemy; in the fall of 1917, they sent 1,787,437 per week across the trenches, a 68 percent increase in rounds.[158] For the week ending on 23 September 1917, the British fired 3,279,276 shells—the most to date.[159] On the opposite end of the lines, the Germans struck back with 18 million rounds during the campaign, an average of 1,005,000 shells per week.[160]

Despite the barrage, the German lines held, due in part to the wettest weather in seventy-five years and their improved defenses. With the rain and shells falling in equal measure, the sea reclaimed the lowland of Flanders, turning the area into a thick soup of mud. One British observer remarked, "Through what might have been a porthole of a ship . . . saw as still a sea as any sailor gazed on . . . watched the blessed sun dawning on still another sea of mud."[161] Into this muck, the British infantry tried in vain for months to push the Germans back.

Timber resources were sparse, and the British could not build enough wooden duckboards to keep 1 million men above the water line. For this, the infantry suffered. In one example, it took a British division twelve hours to march two and half miles from Ypres to the jumping-off points.[162] Beyond the final trenches, offensives stalled in fatigue and mud, with no ground gained. All across the front, mud and water stalled the attacks and British soldiers were machine-gunned or, worse, drowned.[163]

For the British artillery units the story was no better, the pieces were too heavy to move without significant rail and horse support. For example, the 118 Royal Garrison Artillery unit diary recorded its attempt to move from 5 through 11 October:

5 October—Work continued at the new position. One gun in Zillebeke fired 200 rounds on various targets. One gun was dismounted and got ready to pull into the new position, apparently going up by rail.

7 October—Winter time comes into force. Very stormy wet weather. Arrangements were made to send a section of the battery forward by railway, but later on it appears improbable that the battery will move. Orders again canceled and one section ordered to move forward to the new position.

8 October—One gun taken out of action at Zillebeke and then taken down to Reninghelst to be entrained and run up on Decauville to new position. Another gun was made ready to be sent to the same position. This seems an extraordinary move. Reninghelst was several miles behind the battery position!

9 October—The 2nd gun for the new position was dispatched on the road at 5.30pm.

10 October—The gun had arrived at the new position, but owing to congestion on the railway could not be mounted. The other gun is hung up at Birr X [cross] roads.

11 October—One gun was dismounted and got ready to pull into the new position—apparently going up by rail.[164]

In Flanders, forward movement required significant effort, and there was neither enough rail capacity nor animal or human power to move the guns forward for resumed offensive firing. The British tried to overcome the lack of artillery support by using tanks, but they were far too heavy and bogged down in the mud as well.[165]

The lack of artillery support and the heavy mud added to the infantry's misery. Even when units made gains in territory, they found themselves stuck in shell craters or German pillboxes awaiting movement forward or rescue.[166] Men and animals suffered from food shortages and lack of water. By mid-October, the conditions were so severe that men wore backpacks to carry sustenance to the front.[167] In a cruel retrace to a century and a half prior, men were again going hungry and thirsty like their predecessors at Lake George.

THE SEA IS SAFE: STRATEGY AND THE U-BOATS

As the campaign ground on in fall of 1917, the U-boat threat became a lesser problem for the British. What had so concerned Jellicoe in June was a minor footnote by October. By using convoy tactics, the airplane, and innovative naval mining techniques, the Entente could cut losses below four hundred thousand tons per month, where they would stabilize for the rest of the war.[168] As with the support to the land campaign, the reconnaissance capabilities of the airplane had become critical to success at sea.[169] Haig's plan did not change. To the general, getting at the U-boat pens was much less important than decimating the Germans at their strongest point of defense on the Western Front.

The British gained on the German lines during the Third Battle of Ypres; however, by early December 1917, the movement was miniscule. The British pushed the Germans back only five miles at the deepest point, along the fifteen-mile front (Figure 2.5). In return, Haig's plan garnered 271,000 casualties while inflicting 217,000 on the Germans.[170]

THE ETERNAL LINE OF COMMUNICATION

Through the relentless British pressure, the German rail sustained the *Landwehr*. The punishing artillery barrages and the infantry assaults by the British pushed the Germans to the breaking point. Ludendorff remarked,

He [the British] was ready for our counter-attacks and prepared for them by exercising restraint in the exploitation of success . . . our wastage had been so high as to cause grave misgivings and exceeded all expectations. . . . In the West, we began to be short of troops. Two Divisions that had been held in readiness in the East and *were already on the way to Italy were diverted to Flanders* [Ludendorff's emphasis]. . . . These days were the culminated point of the crisis.[171]

The extensive German rail networks allowed Ludendorff to move his troops from Italy and other locations to the front. More important to direct support of the front, German trains outmatched the slow advances of the British in the mud. For example, in July 1917, before the battle began, the German rail line running from the north to the south between Lille and Roulers had few narrow-gauge or perpendicular spurs toward the trenches. Despite a few trenches to the north and the west of Roulers, the closest fortifications of the German trench system were eight thousand yards to the West, about four and a half miles.[172]

As the British moved forward during months of fighting, the German built a narrow-gauge spur to the north of Roulers to help erect a new defense and supply the front with troops. This spur allowed the Germans to load cargo on the outskirts of town and move supplies around the city to avoid clogging the roads.[173] As the front moved closer to Roulers, the Germans further used the railroad to reconstruct their elastic defense in-depth.

Before the British pushed the front back in September, the Germans had 6500 yards, 3.7 miles, of narrow-gauge track in the 60-square-mile area surrounding Roulers.[174] By the end of December, there were 135,000 yards, or 76 miles, in the same area.[175] This vast network allowed the Germans to pour men and munitions into the battle without pause. The British never stopped the railroads, and the Third Battle of Ypres ended.

CAMBRAI: HINTS OF THE FUTURE

The British operation against Cambrai in November 1917 was a harbinger of mobile warfare. Whereas all previous battles on the Western Front lacked mobility and employed only piecemeal use of airpower, at Cambrai the British coordinated tanks, artillery, infantry, and airplanes together. On the morning of 20 November 1917, 338 British tanks drove toward Cambrai without the customary registered-artillery barrage.[176] Using maps and scientific wind measurements, the British artillery fired in unison with the movement of tanks.[177] Royal Flying Corps aircraft did their part by strafing German positions to support the effort.[178] The initial effort was a success. The British advanced into the German lines, and moved as fast as three miles *per hour* (see Figures 2.1 and 2.2 for the location of Cambrai).[179]

Despite the initial success of British forces, the German railroads came to the rescue and enabled the Germans to counterattack. J. C. Slessor in his classic *Air Power and Armies* records, "altogether between November 20th and 29th 100 [German] trains a day brought in thirteen reserves divisions and 600 other units—batteries of artillery, engineer companies, and so on— to the German Second Army Front."[180] Ten days later, the Germans pushed the line back within two miles of the starting point; most British tanks were destroyed, stalled, or broken.

Just as Cambrai showed the potential for combined arms warfare, it also showed the potential for attack on the enemy's internal lines of communication far from the front. Slessor, writing from the perch of twelve years removed from the war, chided the British plan at Cambrai for its wasteful use airplanes for attacks on the direct front. He said, "Better results would have been obtained, and at less cost, if the assault aircraft had been used farther back; and in any case the story will serve as an example of the reason for using the air striking force against the enemy's rear communications and reserves, rather than against his forward elements on the actual battle-field."[181] War would have to wait, for the developments of the Late Industrial Era would provide the technological ability to pursue Slessor's vision

With their victory at Cambrai and the capitulation of the Russians in the east in December, the Germans achieved their operational goals for 1917. At the end of 1917, the stalemate on the Western Front remained. A breakthrough would not happen until the spring of 1918, when the Germans moved to the west with the Michael offensives, which faltered because of lack of logistics and heavy artillery support by rail.[182] Much as their British enemy had discovered in 1917, the German army found that advancing rail lines forward was too difficult and too slow in an era of machine guns and artillery bearing down from the other side. Despite being a close-fought series of campaigns in 1918, the United States arrived in full force in time to break the materiel parity of the war, and decided the contest for the Entente. The end of the war did not settle the conflict between Germany and her neighbors, but hinted at a more mobile and destructive warfare underpinned by Late Industrial technology coming in the next war.

CONCLUSION

By 1917, the Industrial Era of iron and steam had evolved kinetic weapons and land-transportation technologies. With its kinetic range, larger load, and rate of fire, artillery was the king of the Western Front in 1917. Neither side could move forward or hold a position without it. To quench the insatiable needs of artillery, the Entente and the Central Powers used steam-powered ships and trains to deliver to the sovereign its requirements with ever-increasing speed and density.

Propelled by the motive force of steam, the centuries-long dominance of water transportation over land transportation ended on the Western Front. In the Preindustrial Era, movement by land was inferior to movement by water. By the end of the Industrial Era, the autarchic and land-locked country of Germany competed with British economic and global dominance based on sea power using the strength of its railroads. To overcome German advantage in rail, the British spent an average of 7.2 million pounds per day in 1917 to translate their superiority at sea onto the land—the most spent per day in any year of the war, including 1918.[183] Thus, the relationship between land and sea transportation was a linear equation, but railroads changed the shape of the line, which now rose at a 45-degree angle from the origin. With the importance that rail power played on the Western Front, it is fitting that the Treaty of Versailles included as reparations from Germany to the Entente of "no fewer than 5,000 locomotives, 15,000 coaches, and 135,000 wagons for those lost in the conflict."[184] Land transportation had risen to parity.

Despite the equality of land vis-à-vis sea transportation, the comparison was qualified. Only by riding the rails did land rival the sea. As at the Third Battle of Ypres, and even the far more successful operation at Cambrai, movement on muddy roads or across open ground proved perilous with the transportation technology of the time. When tanks broke down, trucks stalled, or the rails stopped, the offense fell to the individual soldier, who fought the geography of Flanders—the mud—as much as he did his enemy. Thus, even in industrial-age warfare, supported by the might of the world's biggest economies and buttressed by thousands of ships and millions rail cars, all the supplies an individual solider could carry were all the logistics an army had.

Even more interesting than the rise of land transportation to rival sea, was how Industrial and Late Industrial technologies allowed belligerents to compete for the control of lines of communication, which were not their natural strengths. The Germans, a very recent naval power, used the submarine to threaten the basis of British power projection since the eighteenth century— sea-lines of communication. This threat influenced the operational strategy the British pursued on the Western Front, with the capture of the German submarine pens becoming a priority and thus shifting their fight to Flanders. The British also used command of the sea to deliver their supplies and equipment necessary to become a localized rail power in Europe and attack the Germans in four separate instances, delivering millions of men and thousands of guns to the front. In 1917, the world's great sea power became a great rail power.

Geopolitical Impacts—Western Front 1917 (Industrial Era)

The increased abilities of the modes of transportation and weapons had magnified the destructive power of the First World War. The war exacted a horrible price: 10 million dead and 5 million wounded.[185] With such a heavy loss,

World War I became the epochal event in human history by sweeping away the order of Westphalia. The Austro-Hungarian and Ottoman empires expired along with three monarchies—the Habsburgs in Austria-Hungary, the Hohenzollerns in Germany, and Romanovs in Russia. While the Windsors in Britain survived, war left their empire on a path to insolvency that was realized in the early stages of the next world war. France also suffered blows to her demography, finance, and psyche from which she would never recover. World War I left fertile ground for the Soviet experiment in Russia and the fascist regimes of Germany and Italy. The war also established the United States as a great power and Japan as an emergent challenger on the Pacific Rim.[186]

In Germany, the intoxication of almost winning was as bad as defeat. For many Germans, including a trench-runner named Adolf Hitler, who had been on the Western Front at the time of surrender, it was not the army that surrendered but the home front—the infamous *Dolchstoßlegende* or "Stab in the Back" myth. While the propaganda of the National Socialists proclaimed that Jews, Marxists, and cultural Bolsheviks caused the capitulation of 1918, in private the leadership of the Third Reich believed the privations of home broke the will of the Germans. In the Second World War, this led to a perverse system of logistics to follow their corrupt ideology, one in which the nation was not in full war-footing to well into 1943 and still provided luxury goods at home, while allowing the Sixth Army to be surrounded and starved by the Soviets at the same time.[187]

Those Late Industrial technologies which made their debut on the Western Front—the submarine, the tank, the truck, and the airplane—were harbingers of a more mobile, lethal, and material-needy war to come. While the Late Industrial technology of the submarine vaulted the Germans into a race for control of supply lines on the sea, the airplane showed its potential to influence logistics. Its ability to perform reconnaissance—for artillery, for hunting submarines, and for spotting the material buildup of an enemy—was crucial for both sides. It is telling that the bad weather and localized air superiority of the Germans over the Allies in the spring of 1917 hid the German pullback to the Hindenburg Line, ushering in the disaster of the Neville Offensive and the near-capitulation of France. In future wars, the airplane would take center stage in the interplay between land and sea modes of transportation, with a range and firepower capable of striking men and material far from the forward edge of battle.

3

Staving Starvation
The Battle for Guadalcanal, 1942–1943

A landing on a foreign shore in the face of hostile troops has always been one
of the most difficult operations of war. It has now become almost impossible.
—B. H. Liddell Hart, 1939

From 1918 until the Second World War, the Late Industrial Era subsumed the iron, carbon, and steam of the Industrial Era and replaced it with aluminum, oil, and the electromagnetic spectrum. The internal combustion engine, which debuted during the First World War in the form of the submarine, the airplane, the truck, and the tank, transformed the world economy in less than thirty years. With transportation no longer beholden to rail or ship, goods could be delivered to more areas of the world faster. Added to the growth in the physical effects of trade, the radio helped transmit information with increasing speed. With the ability to move material and information to the entire planet, the race for empire that categorized the run up to the First World War ended. The same Late Industrial technologies that affected the global economy and geopolitics also changed warfare, giving the belligerents greater mobility, lethality, and range. Into the middle of this seismic shift of the technological landscape, the Second World War began.

THE SOLOMONS: JAPAN, AMERICA, AND
TECHNOLOGY IN THE LATE INDUSTRIAL ERA

The exigencies of the Late Industrial world demanded that world powers master the resources underpinning the technologies of transportation and war. Oil was the most important recourse. It provided fuel for the internal combustion engine—cars, tanks, airplanes, ships, and all manner of motive transportation. Although many combatants of the Second World War were resource-constrained, Japan and Italy suffered the most. As a result, rather than projecting power from its industrial base outward via a line of communication, Japan had to project power to obtain resources. For Japan, an island nation with ambitions for power in the Pacific region, the war would always be about two intertwined issues: resources and China.[1]

The Japanese started the Second World War with their installation of a puppet regime in Manchuria, followed by four years of small-scale conflicts along the Chinese border leading to the full-scale invasion of China in 1937.[2] As the Germans started the European war in 1939, the incursions of the Japanese to western colonial regions in the Pacific put them at odds with British and American governments. Hoping to keep the Americans out of their dreams of the "Greater Asian Co-Prosperity Sphere," the Japanese attempted to destroy the US fleet at Pearl Harbor on 7 December 1941, and almost succeeded. After this stunning victory, the Japanese expelled General Macarthur and US presence from the Philippines, landed at Rabaul to threaten British primacy on New Guinea, and pushed south and westward into Java and Burma (see Figure 3.1). Although the Americans checked the Japanese at Midway and the Battle of the Coral Sea, and had carried out Jimmy Doolittle's morale boosting raid on Tokyo, the Japanese still mastered a good portion of the Pacific.

Underpinning the strategies in the Pacific were the larger concerns of the global war. In retrospect, the Second World War was preordained to Axis defeat. Once the manufacturing and combat power of the United States and the Soviet Union turned on Germany, Japan, and Italy, it was a simple and brutal math of logistics. In the summer of 1942, however, wherever the Allies looked they saw defeat. With its soldiers fighting Rommel in North Africa, the British needed their American ally to help protect Australia and help their limited forces hold on to Port Moresby. At the same time, the Soviets were on the ropes in Eastern Europe. While they had repulsed the Germans at the edge of Moscow, the Germans were planning a push south to Stalingrad and would soon throw the weight of the Wehrmacht on that city. While the United States planned for Operation Torch in North Africa for an invasion in late 1942, President Franklin Roosevelt and his military leadership also wanted to press the Japanese in the Pacific.

The Japanese hoped to keep the Americans at a distance and prevent any further incursion on their new gains while forcing the "sleeping giant" out of the war. In addition, they wanted to push the British out of New Guinea and isolate Australia. Japan also wanted to keep the Soviet Union at bay while holding China as their own; their blooding at the Nomonhan Incident in 1939 had taught them to stay away from the Soviet Bear.

These competing sets of strategic interests overlapped in a Venn diagram with Guadalcanal at its center. With their new port and runways in Rabaul on the north side of New Guinea, the Japanese could now project power to Australia. Looking from Rabaul to the southeast, the Solomon Islands, which also contained pickets on the front line of Japanese expansion, offered the potential for the Japanese to disrupt shipping to and from Australia and the United States, which ran through Nouméa, New Caledonia, and Espiritu Santo in the New Hebrides (see Figure 3.1).

To assert this control, the Japanese moved south beyond their staging base at Shortland, near Bougainville, and built an airfield at Guadalcanal in July 1942. For the Americans, the projection of Japanese airpower so far to the south threatened to cut off logistics to their Australian ally, who held on to Port Moresby in Papua New Guinea. At the suggestion of the commander-in-chief of the United States Navy, Admiral Ernest King, the War Department approved a plan to eject the Japanese from Guadalcanal and seize the runway.[3] Thus, before a shot was fired at Guadalcanal, airpower began to exert its influence on logistics.

Guadalcanal was as far from modern civilization as any island in the vast Pacific Ocean: 5,947 miles from San Francisco, 3,335 miles from Tokyo, and 1,737 miles from Sydney. Located just below the equator, the island had copious amounts of sunshine, rain, and deep tropical forest. Guadalcanal lacked any natural resources, save coconuts, but its geographic location put it at the center of the geopolitical battle for the Pacific between the United States and Japan in 1942.

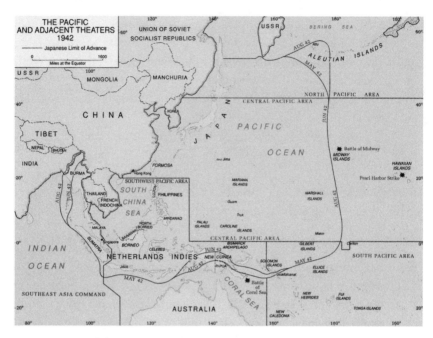

Figure 3.1. Map of the Expansion of Japanese Empire, 1933–1942. (Reprinted from Clayton R. Newell, *Central Pacific: The US Army Campaigns of World War II* [Washington, DC: US Army Center of Military History, 2003].)

With the strategy of both sides concentrated on sea lines of communication in the Pacific Ocean, logistics became the sine qua non during the battle of Guadalcanal. Guadalcanal was a siege for both sides and a race against the supply capacity of the enemy, with great distances from the respective homelands and the urgency of other wartime priorities looming in the background. In 1942, it was a contest between relative equals, the economic and manufacturing might of the United States not fully awake. Thus, the battle pitted similar levels of material supply and weapons of war against each other.

The Japanese harbored most of their army in China and the Americans had agreed to a Europe-first strategy, which siphoned off precious resources for both sides. The paucity of resources placed a high marginal utility on each ship, aircraft, armament, or soldier supplied to the fight. Guadalcanal was a fight against starvation that those combatants during the battles for Lake George would have well recognized—it was the tyranny of distance with its resultant suffering of supply that hit combatants in the belly.

Unlike the campaigns of Lake George or the Western Front in 1917, Guadalcanal had no linear phase to the operation. The requisitioning of supplies
and the buildup of troops and weapons happened in concert with ongoing
sea, land, and air battles. Unlike Braddock, who had months to garner his
resources, or even the British and Germans, who reworked their transportation networks in Western Europe over the fall and winter of 1916, battle
and logistics happened in unison at Guadalcanal. In a world of oil-turbine-
powered ships, long-ranging aircraft, and radio transmissions, the Pacific
Ocean, had shrunk. With less than two weeks of travel separating the belligerents and the distant island, the United States and Japan could deploy
their forces and supply them. Despite these benefits in speed and capacity,
both sides still had to fight their way to Guadalcanal through the other side's
combat power. That combat power, projected into the air by the internal
combustion engine, shaped seaborne transportation and supply.

As with the shift from Preindustrial to Industrial, the shift one era forward yielded great gains for transportation. On the ocean, the capacity of the
new technologies increased from capacities around five hundred tons to ten
thousand tons.[4] The airplane, as a method of transportation, increased cargo
capacity from a negligible amount in the First World War to the three-ton
capacity of the American C-47 Skytrain. In addition, the improved technologies of the Late Industrial Era allowed logistics vehicles to wield their own
firepower, yielding transport ships with machine guns, antiaircraft, and anti-
ship weapons to fight their way into areas of battle.

Artillery, king of the Western Front in 1917, yielded to all forms of mobile
firepower—aircraft, carriers, far-ranging ships, and torpedoes—in the Second World War. The internal combustion engine and lighter metals, such as
steel and aluminum, created a synergy of speed and power. Aircraft acceler-
ated from 130 knots with a four hundred nautical mile (NM) range in 1918, to
350 knots with upwards of a one thousand NM range by the Second World
War.[5] With newfound ability, the airplane, a critical tool of reconnaissance
in the First World War, became the basis for power projection over water
with the construction of aircraft carriers. Unlike the First World War or the
campaign for Lake George, both sides possessed similar transportation and
weapons of the age.

Added to the engine's motive power, the harnessing of the electromagnetic spectrum through radio transformed the world in the years after 1918.

In First World War, the radio was in its infancy and the telephone still subservient to the telegraph. By 1942, information passed great distances via radio and telephone and in full context—stripped of the need for telegraphic specialists. Radio added the benefit of wireless technology, increasing the command and control capabilities of Late Industrial weapons and transportation technologies with their greater ranges and speeds.

From the beginning of Guadalcanal, it was understood by the Americans and the Japanese that they could project power farther and move more supplies than ever before—but what did that mean for logistics? Had the internal combustion engine impacted travel on the remote island as well as the sea? Was the submarine a factor as it had been in the First World War? All these factors came to play in the Solomons, which would define the contest for the Pacific for the next three years.

7–21 AUGUST 1942: THE TEMPLATE
OF SUPPLY AND BATTLE

The invasion of Guadalcanal had a long history of planning for both the United States Marine Corps and the United States Navy. During the interwar years, the Marines revamped their amphibious landing strategy based on the lessons of the Great War—most glaring the failed British operation to take Gallipoli.[6] In doing so, the Marines incorporated the improved technology of the internal combustion engine to develop landing craft to move troops from transport ships to the beaches. The famed Higgins boat was the accomplice to this innovation in strategy. At the operational level, the Marines wed their amphibious assaults to the Navy's infamous War Plan Orange, which forecast a hypothetical war against Japan.[7] Despite the prescience of planning and war-gaming for the seizure of distant beaches, including the need for air reconnaissance and close air support to support, no one had foreseen the distant Solomon Islands as the first foothold of America's advance on Japan.

The Marines Arrive: Landing at Guadalcanal, August 1942

Led by a heavy barrage from cruisers, destroyers, and carrier aircraft, US Marines of the First Marine Division clambered down the nets from troop transport ships onto their landing craft on the morning of 7 August 1942.[8] Of the nineteen thousand Marines, eleven thousand landed at Red Beach on

Guadalcanal, four thousand rode their landing craft twenty-five miles across the sound to Tulagi, and four thousand stayed on the transport ships as reserves (see Figure 3.2).[9] Major General Vandegrift, the commander of the amphibious force, had 303 landing craft for troops, 116 dual-use boats for troops or trucks, and 48 larger cargo craft.[10] Moving at 10 knots the landing craft took nine minutes to traverse the 3000 yards to shore.[11]

As they approached landing area, the underwater undulations of volcanic rock and the sheer concentration of craft forced the navy drivers to stop the Higgins boats short of the beaches. They were new, but early, versions of the Higgins boat and many of the craft lacked internal ramps to allow for prompt exit.[12] As a result, the Marines piled over the side and, with the ocean reaching to their armpits, splashed, sputtered, and sloshed their way to the beaches.[13] Luckily for Vandegrift's men, the landing at Guadalcanal was unopposed and there were no casualties. Facing them on the island was a contingent of eight hundred Japanese engineers supported by twelve hundred Korean conscripts.[14] The Japanese beat the Americans to the island by a few weeks and had finished building the runway the day before. Recovering from a night of revelry after their successful construction, the Japanese grabbed their weapons and retreated into the jungle upon seeing the Marines.[15] In a stroke of luck for the Americans, the Japanese left their food rations behind, in addition to several trucks, small grading machines, and rudimentary tools. The most generous gift of all was the completed runway.

The Marines landing at Tulagi faced resistance, but they sustained only a few casualties on the beaches.[16] Vandegrift summarized the success in his final report: "The organization for landing, the technique of ship-to-shore movement, landing craft and special landing equipment developed in the ten years prior to the war were satisfactory to a degree beyond expectation."[17] The improved technology of the internal combustion engine had landed fifteen thousand troops on two separate islands with minimal losses; but the Higgins boats, with their lack of ramps, required improvement for future operations onto contested beachheads.[18]

Japanese sailors at the small naval base at Tulagi, which harbored seaplanes and submarines, sent a quick dispatch back to Rabaul—the Americans had landed. Admiral Yamamoto, commander of the Imperial Japanese Navy (IJN), directed an immediate response, and his commanders in the field wasted no time in execution.[19] On 7 August 1942, the navy staff recorded the

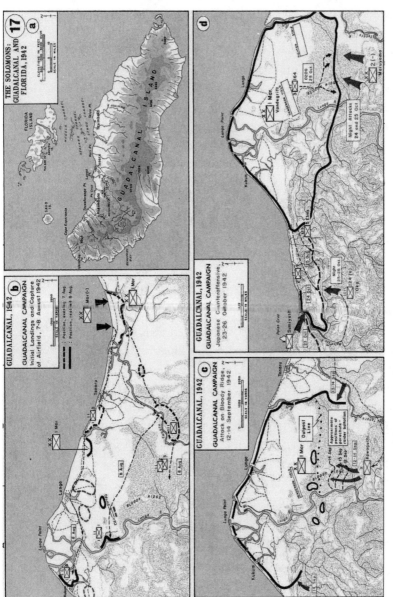

Figure 3.2. Map of Land Campaigns, Guadalcanal, August–10 October 1942. Red Beach is on the upper-left map. It lies on the far eastern side of the shore. The Japanese airstrip is six-thousand yards to the west. (Reprinted from Frank Martini, "The Guadalcanal Campaign, August–October 1942," Department of History, United States Military Academy.)

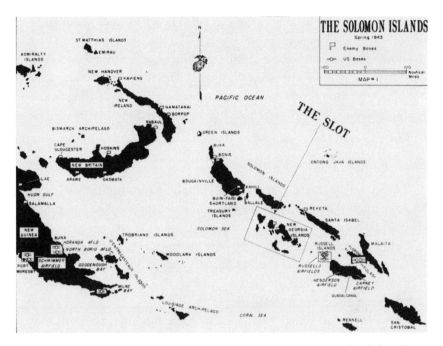

Figure 3.3. Map of the Solomons: The Slot, New Britain, New Guinea, Guadalcanal. (Reprinted from John M. Rentz, *Marines in the Central Solomons* [Washington, DC: Headquarters US Marine Corps, 1952].)

IJN's direction, "Should the enemy succeed in landing, he can immediately utilize the airfield just completed on Guadalcanal, thereby greatly influencing future operations. Therefore, the immediate recapture of Guadalcanal is very urgent."[20] The Japanese retaliation plan had three major movements— one by air and two by sea. Aircraft stationed at Rabaul would attack the landing force, a cruiser battle group led by the commander of the Eighth Fleet, Admiral Gunichi Mikawa, would steam to meet the US surface fleet, and the IJN would redirect army troops bound for New Guinea to Guadalcanal. In the background, the Japanese carrier force would seek to find and destroy the US carriers that had done so much damage to the Japanese fleet at Midway and were likely screening the landing.

Facing a daunting 1,120-mile round trip flight, twenty-one long-range A6M "Zero" Fighters and twenty-seven "Betty" Bombers launched from Rabaul in New Britain to strike the landing force (see Figure 3.3).[21] This was the longest mission the long-range Zeros had flown to date. About an hour behind them, the Japanese sent nine more "Val" bombers on a one-way trip to bomb the transports of the Marines and then point toward the west and ditch their short-range aircraft in the water.[22] This flight foreshadowed many one-way trips for aviators, sailors, and soldiers serving the Rising Sun. The Japanese hoped their fifty-seven aircraft would push the Marines back out to sea.

Red Beach: The Hardest Transition

As the Japanese planes alighted for their bombing runs and the lead units of Marines moved off the beach, the unloading situation at Red Beach turned chaotic. To assist with the movement on to the beach and then forward, Marine planners had assigned three hundred personnel from the First Pioneer Battalion to orchestrate the unloading.[23] Vandegrift charged the Pioneers with moving ten days of ammunition and sixty days of food onto the beaches to follow the eleven thousand Marines.[24]

After the combat units moved off the beach, the large transports moved closer to shore, shortening the distance landing craft traveled between ship and sand.[25] The increased flow from the close-in transport ships overwhelmed the Pioneers. Piles of water, gear, vehicles, and food filled the beach; and, with the combat units still pressing into the dense jungle, there were not enough personnel to assist. In addition, since many of the landing craft lacked ramps—requiring men to reach over the sides to move cargo—the unloading of the boats took significant labor away from the logistics of moving the supplies off the beach.[26]

More striking, however, was the lack of planning and aerial reconnaissance regarding the area needed to unload the supplies from eleven large-capacity troop transports. Red Beach was not big enough (see Figure 3.4). The supplies were too much, too soon, into too small of a space.

With the beach full, there was no way to move water or any other provisions forward to the Marines making their way through the jungle toward the Japanese airfield. From the rails of the transport ships, Guadalcanal appeared as a tropical postcard—calm waves, breezes, and palm trees. As the Marines moved ashore they discovered the opposite: Guadalcanal was "a hot humid hell-hole."[27] The vegetation began just off the beaches and was so dense that sunlight did not reach the ground, and the rivers seemed to

Figure 3.4. Red Beach, Marine Landing, 7 August 1942. Poor preinvasion survey and planning resulted in the Marines landing on the thin strip of land. (Reprinted from "Guadalcanal-Tulagi Operation, August 1942 [NH 97760]," United States Department of the Navy.)

run both toward and away from the sea. Into this dark, dank, and confusing landscape, the Marines navigated with inaccurate maps based on inadequate aerial survey (see Figure 3.4).[28] The infantry moved at a pace Braddock's or Haig's armies would have recognized when confronted with a challenging environment on land: "1/3 of a mile an hour." Thus, for both Marines at the beach unloading cargo and those moving to capture the airfield, improper reconnaissance led to slow progress.[29]

The slow progress in the heat caused dehydration and widespread thirst, and with the water supply brought to the beach not ready to move forward with the combat troops, the lack of water retarded the forward progress of the Marines. Past the initial difficulties with water dispersion, an efficient logistics system to clean and transport water forward would plague the Americans for the entire campaign.[30] As the United States Marine Corps and the

United States Navy were learning, amphibious operations comprised more than just a successful landing and required a closer integration of logistics and combat power than even the prescient leaders of the interwar years had envisioned.

As the cargo filled up on Red Beach, Japan's first strike force hit the Marines and navy from the air at 1230 local time.[31] Alerted to the incoming planes hours beforehand by coast watchers using telegraph and radio, the Americans were ready with thirty-four carrier aircraft to meet them. In a stiff fight, the Japanese claimed nine Grumman F4Fs in combat with six American craft ditching or crashing. The Americans claimed seven Bettys and damaged two others with two Zeros down.[32] All nine of the Japanese Vals ditched in the water and all their crews perished.[33] Stung by the resistance, the Japanese still damaged the destroyer *Mugford*, downing 50 percent of the Grumman F4Fs involved in the battle, and driving the US Navy transports to safe havens, interrupting the unloading of cargo for three hours.[34] This was the first day of an air war of attrition over Guadalcanal's sandy shores that claimed over six hundred aircraft from each side by February 1943.

The attack by Japanese planes sent shockwaves through the supply team on the beach. At 1449, only minutes after the final raid ended, the shore party radioed back to Admiral Richard Kelly Turner, the commander of the transport ships, that the unit was "badly in need of at least 500 men working party to unload boats, No troops available On Beach."[35] The urgent message echoed in the first lesson learned that Vandegrift posted in his summary of the landing phase: "A determined low level or dive-bombing attack on the landing beach may prove ruinous unless supplies are promptly cleared to dispersed dump areas."[36] Although Admiral Turner dispatched two hundred men from the transports to help, by 2330 that night the beach was full, and almost one hundred landing craft pregnant with cargo awaited unloading (see Figure 3.5).[37]

The naval commanders on the transport ships and overseeing landing craft pointed the finger less at labor and more on disorganization. The USS *Barnett* commander of the ships' landing craft reported, "Fifteen or twenty men unloading boats and about fifty others were swimming . . . started looking for the Beachmaster who could not be found. . . . I saw about one hundred men lounging around. . . . All of these men . . . should have been unloading boats."[38]

Figure 3.5. Cargo unloading at Guadalcanal, 1942. This photo is much later in the fall of 1942 and illustrates how cargo could overwhelm the supply system of the Marines at Guadalcanal. During 7 August 1942 the situation was much worse at Red Beach. (Marine Corps Historical Center, Thayer Soule Collection: Army and Marines on KoKum Beach, circa 1942.)

At daybreak on the second day, 8 August 1942, the Marines stuck in the jungle reoriented themselves and secured the airfield. On the beach, the Pioneers had made little headway and the haphazard cargo operations from the day before caused many food supplies—"sugar, coffee, beans, cheese, and lard"—to wash out with the tide.[39] In a technological irony, the lack of ramps on the older versions of the Higgins boats kept their cargo off the saturated beach and prevented the outgoing tide from pulling the cargo out to sea. Fortunately for the Americans, the Japanese did not strike the cargo on the beach that day, but aimed instead for the larger surface fleet and transport ships.

By midday, another Japanese raid interrupted the unloading. This time the navy had a more robust plan to defend the transport ships. Admiral

Turner sent the transport ships out of the narrow sound so the force of cruisers and destroyers could surround and protect them with the newest antiaircraft guns in the United States Navy, which used radar to perfect range.[40] In addition, the carrier aviation group put up twenty-seven F4Fs to meet the twenty-three Betty bombers and fifteen Zeros.[41] This time the Japanese damaged the transport *George F. Eliot* and the destroyer *Jarvis*, and bombed the airfield, creating several large craters.[42] With the *Eliot* on fire and listing, the Navy sunk the ship to avoid Japanese procurement. For their efforts, the Japanese paid a heavy toll—Turner's antiaircraft batteries hammered seventeen Bettys, and only five of the remaining bombers limped to Rabaul. As for the Zeros, US carrier pilots shot down five.[43]

With the transports out to sea and the unloading interrupted by the Japanese, the process at the beach stopped for the rest of the day. Marine second lieutenant Karl Soule remarked, "Crates and boxes took up nearly a mile of beach. Many near the water were partially submerged at high tide. Worst of all, the place was deserted. Supplies for the whole division, life and death in equipment, ammunition, and food, were inviting destruction from sea or air, and nothing was being done."[44] In the after-action report, Vandegrift noted, paradoxically and correctly, that too much cargo too soon during an amphibious operation was as dangerous as none, since the potential to have it destroyed in combat action or lost to ocean was great.[45] This failure of logistics haunted the Marines for seven more weeks.

Added to the problems of logistics and airpower was the scheduled departure of the carriers *Enterprise, Wasp,* and *Saratoga* on the evening of the eighth. The carrier task force commander, Admiral Jack Fletcher, who was the victorious naval leader at the Battle of Midway, made a promise for only two days of air cover for the landings at Guadalcanal. Admiral Turner and Major General Vandegrift disagreed with Fletcher, but the theater commander of the South Pacific, Admiral Robert L Ghormley, never overturned Fletcher. Fletcher's preference stood.[46]

Fletcher made the decision in part because of the threat of Japanese submarines, which coursed the Solomons frequently enough to earn the region the nickname "Torpedo Junction," and in part because of logistics. The naval force at Guadalcanal was not the US Navy of 1945; Fletcher possessed three of the five US carriers and could not afford to lose them to a submarine in the first days of the landing or run out of fuel on the five hundred NM journey to back to the refueling station at Espiritu Santo.[47] Added to this, the US buildup for the invasion of North Africa meant that the shoestring budget for the invasion of Guadalcanal also applied to the carriers. Fletcher had the resources he had and would receive no more. With these options, Fletcher ordered his carriers out to sea on the night of 8 August 1942, leaving the transports all alone to continue unloading. The US Marines on Guadalcanal were now alone, with only their logistics and no air cover. In less than twenty-four hours, the logistics would leave as well. The Marines would never forgive the navy for abandoning them and the US Navy would never forget the supplies swallowed in the tide at Red Beach.

THE BATTLE OF SAVO ISLAND:
JAPANESE PRIMACY AT SEA

While the Marines spent their second of many uncomfortable nights on Guadalcanal, the Imperial Japanese Navy executed Admiral Mikawa's second phase of the plan to dislodge them. The Japanese surface force of seven cruisers and one destroyer headed down "The Slot" to intercept the US landing force and its protective surface fleet of two US cruiser groups.[48] Despite the two-day transit time to Guadalcanal, US coast watchers, carrier-based airplanes, and a large contingent of PBY "Catalina" float planes, the United States did not properly perform reconnaissance against the Japanese ships.[49] In addition, despite owning the most advanced naval radar technology of the time—the high powered SG search radar—and individual sailors sounding the alarm because of the enormous electronic targets on their screen, the commanders of the two cruiser groups, Captains Howard Bode and Frederick Riefkohl, refused to believe the information. James Hornfischer summed up the mindset in Neptune's Inferno: "The unfamiliar power of a new technology was seldom a match for a complacent human mind bent on ignoring it."[50] As a result, the Japanese caught the much larger surface fleet of the US Navy unaware as they patrolled Savo Island to the west of Guadalcanal as a defensive screen for the transports.[51]

For their failures in air reconnaissance and radar interpretation, the United States Navy paid with four cruisers resting on the bottom of "Iron Bottom Sound," major damage to three ships, and the lives of 1,077 sailors. In less than two hours in the early morning of 9 August 1942 at the Battle of

Savo Island, the United States learned what the Russians had known since 1905—the Japanese were the ocean's best night fighters.

Despite the resounding success at Savo, the Japanese surface fleet never pressed the attack on to the transports. One Japanese destroyer captain fired several torpedoes at the great distance of thirteen miles and missed.[52] Another ship captain implored Mikawa to turn his victorious ships to the transports. Instead, Mikawa turned the fleet home.[53] In hindsight, Mikawa's decision was not much different from Fletcher's decision to remove the carriers, and largely one of logistics. Both men were at the end of their supply lines and had all the naval power in the region under their command.[54] Although victory was important, permanent loss could have meant a serious blow to strategy. By the next morning, the Imperial Japanese Navy was emboldened but also remiss. The reconstructed report of the Japanese Navy tersely stated, "[Mikawa's fleet] realized a great victory . . . thus raising the morale of all our forces. However, since attacks were not directed at the enemy convoys, the landings could not be checked."[55] Through their struggle to survive, with minimal supplies over the next few weeks, the Marines would prove the strategic importance of the logistics the Japanese left unharmed.

On the morning of 9 August 1942, the wakes of departing supplies, ships, and carriers tempered the success of the Marine landings on Guadalcanal. With an entire cruiser force at the bottom of "Iron Bottom Sound" and command of the sea in doubt, Admiral Turner ordered the transports to follow the carrier tracks from the night before and cruise back to Nouméa for resupply.[56] After the 9th, the only supplies the Marines had would come from the supplies on the beach and those rations taken from the Japanese.

HENDERSON FIELD: SAVIOR FOR SUCCOR

Without command of the sea and their seaborne air cover gone, the Marines' work to ready the airfield for operations gained new urgency. Vandegrift redirected the efforts to consolidate supply and make the airfield ready for aircraft by D+3—11 August 1942.[57] Reflecting the same serendipity that surprised the Japanese, the Marine engineer battalions took over the previously constructed runway. With much of their heavier equipment left on the transports—for example, graders and engine-driven tractors—the Marines turned to what the Japanese had left, including hand tools, a few 4 x 2 trucks, and miniature graders to improve the surface.[58] Working hard, the Marines had 2,600 feet of the airfield usable by the end of the day on 11 August 1942. The next morning a small PBY floatplane delivered Admiral John S. McCain to certify the runway for aviation operations, which he accomplished and promptly left.[59] The Marines did not have the perfect surface, but they had what they required—a permanent platform for airpower. Unfortunately, they would have to wait eight days for the airplanes.

While the engineers worked on the runway, the Pioneer battalion collected the supplies and spent ten days moving the cargo down the shore from Red Beach to Longa Point two miles to the west.[60] The Pioneers also took stock of their food. The food supply was less than thirty days, ten days' worth attributed to the rations the Japanese left in their drunken haze of retreat during the landing.[61] With the loss of their sea lines of communication and the small amount of food, Vandegrift ordered all Marines to a ration of two meals a day.[62] Beyond the debacle with lost sustenance, the sinking of the George Eliot became an even more serious blow to Vandegrift and his Marines. The transport had many heavy artillery pieces, most of the ammunition, and the aircraft search radar. The ten days of ammunition that Vandegrift had planned now stood at four.[63]

Without support from the sea, the airfield—christened Henderson Field for an aviator who perished at the Battle of Midway—gained a mythical quality for the Marines on the island. The defeat at the Battle of Savo Island severed the lines of communication back to US bases in Nouméa and in turn to the United States. As the Americans worked over the next several weeks to reestablish the supply line from Nouméa to Guadalcanal over one thousand miles of ocean, Henderson Field became the firewall against Japanese attack on their supplies.

While the carriers could screen the logistics out in open water, as the supply convoys reached the last several hundred nautical miles and intersected the reaches of Japanese submarines, surface forces, and airpower, Henderson Field was the only protector. Richard Frank, in his magisterial Guadalcanal, summed up the importance of Henderson Field: "Without local air cover, the regular movement of transports to Guadalcanal remained academic."[64] Henderson Field was food and combat firepower.

As if to underscore its importance, the first cargo resupply to the Marines contained 110 men and supplies to fuel, arm, and maintain aircraft.[65] The men and equipment disembarked off four older destroyers on 15 August with their equipment and no food. For the better part of week, these men joined the engineers working on the field. On 20 August 1942, nineteen F4F Wildcat fighters and twelve SBD Dauntless bombers landed on the primitive dirt strip.[66] The Marines at Guadalcanal had aircraft, and the Cactus Air Force was in business.[67] Vandegrift stated, "I was close to tears and I was not alone when the first SBD taxied up and this handsome and dashing aviator jumped to the ground. 'Thank God you have come,' I told him."[68] The importance of Henderson Field for Marine survival rippled up into the planning and strategies for both the United States and Japan, until its existence or elimination became imperative.

While the first aircraft arrived at Henderson, Admiral Nimitz fretted about food half an ocean away at Pearl Harbor. A distance of one thousand miles, with a two-and-a-half-day transport time, stood between food at Nouméa and the Marines on Guadalcanal. In mid-August, Nimitz noted, "The food situation there has not yet been cleared up. In fact since the initial landing not much of anything has been done by our Task Forces."[69]

Nimitz's frustration was not misplaced. In the quick and haphazard push to take Guadalcanal, both the US Navy and US Army forces operating in the South Pacific area of responsibility were in the early stages of building up their logistics network. The port of Nouméa, the critical link in the system, reflected the infancy. The few berths at the harbor gave Nouméa an unimpressive twenty-four ships a month discharge rate. In addition, the limited local labor supply coupled with a lack of cranes and lighters stalled loading.[70] The army recorded in postanalysis of the logistics in the South Pacific that "Amphibious campaigns required a larger proportion of service troop than was ordinarily provided—to man ports and depots . . . original task forces arrived with an extremely low proportion of service personnel."[71] In a scene reminiscent of the British ports in Albany in 1755 or France in 1917, the lack of equipment, organization, and labor left precious cargo in ships. In addition, the navy and army had duplicate lines of supply and did not coordinate to ensure that the correct supplies went to the right location.[72] Finally, the fast diesel ships with their large capacities and speed were overwhelming the port, leading to an inefficiency in delivering war supplies to Guadalcanal. With all these challenges, there were eighty-six ships waiting to discharge at the port by 30 September 1942.[73] Too much material delivered too soon at

Nouméa led to food crushed, supplies missing, and half-full ships. For the men on Guadalcanal, the supply problems translated into two meals a day of soup and tinned meat.[74] The great juggernaut of American economic power had not translated itself into victuals for the Pacific in 1942.

Despite these complications, Admiral Turner sent the cargo ships USS *Formalhaut* and USS *Alehna* with food and nonammunition supplies to Guadalcanal under the escort of three destroyers on 19 August 1942.[75] As they approached Guadalcanal, two of the destroyers took the lead and moved ahead of the formation to clear the area around Lunga point. Despite seeing a contact on radar, the destroyers proceeded. That contact was a Japanese destroyer, which launched a long lance torpedo and damaged the USS *Blue*. With the *Blue* listing the next day, 21 August 1942, the transport ships perched off Lunga Point and unloaded.

Unlike the unloading the weeks prior, however, there were few Higgins boats and little fuel for their engines.[76] As a result, the process plodded along, with the powerless destroyer a beacon for Japanese threats. As darkness approached, the USS *Alehna* was empty but the *Formalhaut* still had cargo aboard. Regardless, the ships' crews scrubbed the mission, unloaded the *Blue*, and sank the sinking craft. The Marines had increased their food supply by seven days at the cost of one destroyer, a disappointing and unsustainable result. The incomplete mission of supply reverberated back to Nimitz, and Ghormley's frustration as the theater commander boiled over into his message to Nimitz: "The Formalhaut is an example of the difficulties of unloading at places where facilities do not exist. Present AKs [transport ships] are built to unload at docks. The shortage of even elementary lighterage facilities results in being unable to unload any more than very limited cargo. . . . At present the logistics supply of captured positions is critical."[77]

Despite the grim picture, Ghormley offered a technological solution to protect future transports—PT boats.[78] The PT boats were small and fast but possessed enough firepower to harass destroyers and the underwater menace of submarines. The PT boats served a valuable fighting asset in the waters around the island and provided needed logistics support—everything from getting cargo to the beach to picking up downed aviators.

Ghormley's suggestion was one of the few correct decisions he made. The initial difficulty in supply for Guadalcanal, the mess at the Port of Nouméa, and the distance away from the conflict wore on Ghormley. His negativity and sense of hopelessness continued as the supply challenges and persistent enemy threatened the Marines on Guadalcanal. As if to signal the desperation of the geostrategic picture, Nimitz's staff summarized the grim picture for the Russians on 27 August 1942: "Press reports of the Russian situation are very gloomy. It looks like Stalingrad must fall shortly. . . . Nothing definite is known . . . however our difficulty in obtaining men and munitions of the Pacific can be traced to very large movements to Europe."[79] Along with desperation for the Soviets, Guadalcanal grew in importance if not priority as the Japanese responded with more aircraft, boats, and soldiers.

THE ICHIKI DEPLOYMENT: TEMPLATE
FOR JAPANESE LOGISTICS AND COMBAT

The final stage of the Japanese response to the Marine landings was the counterlanding of Japanese reinforcement to eject the Marines via land battle. As part of this operation, the Imperial Headquarters ordered local army commander Lieutenant General Harukichi Hyakutake to move several battalions' worth of men to Guadalcanal, a scant amount given the fifteen thousand Marines and navy personnel sitting on the two islands.[80] The lack of information regarding the size of the US forces at Guadalcanal reflected a technological blind spot of the Japanese.

While the US Navy had trouble with radar blips, the Japanese had trouble with the radio. When the Americans scattered the Japanese force on Guadalcanal, they left their radios behind. Thus, Japanese officers had to send messages by foot to submarines that alighted near the island in an uncertain schedule for relay back to Rabaul and the logistics base at Truk.[81] The Japanese restored radio service, but with reports of a full American division ensconced on the island, the Imperial Japanese Army (IJA) made no change in plans and left the invasion force at a size of nine hundred men.[82] This piecemeal commitment of Japanese troops, and an underestimation of the logistics necessary to sustain such a force, plagued their operations for the entire campaign.

The wrong conclusion about the number of Americans at Guadalcanal also reinforced early Japanese convictions that the larger strategic priority was kicking the British out of New Guinea and Burma, since the Americans were lesser foes. For Japanese leadership, the Americans were incapable of deploying that large a force to Guadalcanal; and even if they were on the island in great numbers, they could not hold given the prowess of the IJA. Logistically, this early calculus spelled doom for later Japanese efforts. Whereas the Americans struggled with too much too soon, the Japanese unwittingly settled their strategy on too little too fast—a prescription for defeat in a theater in which short distances were measured in hundreds of miles.

The IJN sent an initial support force of a transport ship and a few destroyers for those Japanese on the island, with food and ammunition, diverting them from the New Guinea operation. As the transportation convoy got underway, a US submarine sunk the cargo ship *Meiryo Maru* south of Cape St. George on 8 August 1942.[83] Unbeknownst to the submarine crew, this action prevented Japanese reinforcements from reaching Guadalcanal for ten more days.[84] In those ten days, US Marines and Seabees had the airfield ready for US aircraft.

Worried about the US carriers, after their aircrews had faced them over Guadalcanal on the seventh and the eighth, and now submarines, the IJN decided on a novel course for the initial deployment to Guadalcanal. Rather than use transport ships, which had slow speeds of nine knots and minimal defensive firepower, the Japanese chose destroyers to move the first reinforcing battalion to the island.[85]

The destroyers were fast and with plentiful torpedo tubes for the famed long lance torpedo. They were the ideal fighting vehicle for surface action. Destroyers, however, lacked the capacity and efficiency of cargo ships.[86] For example, a destroyer used four tons of oil per hour cruising at twenty-five knots and upwards of ten tons of oil an hour cruising at thirty knots.[87] A cargo ship consumed only one and a half to three tons of oil per hour cruising at the maximum speed of thirteen knots.[88] Thus, a cargo-ship run from the base at Shortland to Guadalcanal, a 620 NM round trip, used 53 to 106 tons of fuel to deliver two thousand tons of cargo. A troop transport could deliver seventeen hundred soldiers and two thousand tons of cargo for 192 to 298 tons of fuel. However, a single destroyer could deliver only 40 tons of cargo maximum at a cost of 104 to 217 tons of fuel, based on speeds ranging from sixteen to thirty knots.[89] For a nation that based its parasitic strategy of conquest on accumulating resources, delivering 2 percent of the cargo for as much as twice the fuel consumption seems counterintuitive in hindsight. At this early stage in the campaign, however, the Japanese had not lost a land battle since 1938 and had wiped the western colonial influence in Southeastern Asia off the map using the IJN to transport the army for amphibious operations. They called it *senshobyou,* or victory fever.[90]

Using the doctrine of speed, Lieutenant General Hyakutake chose the personification of their early victories in the war, Colonel Kinyonao Ichiki, to dislodge the green Marines with his battle-hardened troops, numbering nine hundred. Ichiki's aggressiveness helped precipitate the Second Sino-Japanese war when his actions as a company commander led to the "Marco Polo Bridge Incident."[91] When presented with the plan to lead nine hundred troops to Guadalcanal, he remarked, "May I retake Tulagi, too?"[92]

Ichiki's troops carried seven days' ration on their backs, a light load considering the remote location of Guadalcanal. Given the distances by sea from Shortland, or worse Rabaul or Truk, Ichiki was at a minimum two days from any relief. After the US submarine sank the transport on D+2, the Japanese matched Ichiki's minimal logistics with another quick trip in a destroyer with a follow-on force of an additional fifteen hundred troops to bolster his presumed victory.[93] Ichiki landed unopposed on the late night of 19 August 1942, nine miles from Henderson Field, using thirty-six small landing craft. Hoping to secure the airfield with speed, Ichiki ordered a direct march westward with no rest or food.

Like the Marines, the Japanese soon discovered the difficulty of land transportation on Guadalcanal. The rivers were deep and fast-running and required complicated fording to avoid loss of life, and the jungle was so thick that the troops had to walk on the beaches, a slow maneuver in their laden state. With the coming daybreak, Ichiki's soldiers had marched six miles in five hours.[94] His force exhausted and hungry, Ichiki retreated from the beach to hidden areas in the jungle and rested.

On the night of 20 August 1942, Ichiki's force marched out toward Henderson Field and met the Marines at Alligator Creek, just a mile west of the airfield at the Battle of the Tenaru River. Relying on a headlong assault, resembling those of the Western Front in 1917, Ichiki's force was stopped by the thin line of barbed wire the Marines had absconded from local farms and was then slaughtered by fire from US machine gunners.[95] On the morning of 21 August 1942, the Marines recorded over seven hundred Japanese dead with only forty-four lost on their own side.[96]

The four destroyers that unloaded Ichiki's army on 19 August shelled the

Marines on their way west passing Henderson Field, and then raced back to the port at Shortland (see Figure 3.3). With the unloading and the shelling, the destroyers tarried too long at Guadalcanal—a B-17 bomber from Espiritu Santo located and damaged the destroyer *Hagaikaze* as it ran full speed in the daylight to Shortland[97] Ichiki's follow-on logistics suffered a much worse fate on the open water. On 25 August 1942, a PBY reconnaissance aircraft spotted the destroyers screening the transport *Kinryu Maru,* a nine-thousand-ton cargo ship loaded with troops and supplies. The aircraft relayed the information to the new aircraft at Henderson Field; and seventy miles northwest of Guadalcanal, in a chaotic melee, the Americans scattered the convoy and sank the *Kinryu Maru.*[98] With the sinking, the destroyers skulked away to Shortland and planned for a delay in delivery to 29 August.[99] Admiral Matome Ugaki, chief of staff of the Japanese combined fleet, recorded in his journal from Rabaul, "It is apparent that landing on Guadalcanal by transports is hopeless unless the enemy planes are wiped out."[100]

As Ichiki marched along the shore and the first aircraft for the newly minted Cactus Air Force landed at Guadalcanal on 20 August 1942, the Japanese increased their attacks on Henderson Field. Japanese carrier aircraft began the first of these larger raids on 24 August 1942. The attacks lasted fewer than ten minutes, but effected a sizable crater in the runway.[101] In this attack, the carrier aircraft attacked Henderson only as a secondary target, since they were searching for Fletcher's carriers. In the future, the attacks on Henderson would come increasingly from Rabaul and other land-based runways. Whether by carrier or from runways, Japanese aircraft would be at their limit of range due to fuel considerations, and thus have limited attack time. The American aviators at Henderson, by comparison, were fighting overhead their own base, which gave them an advantage in range, time on station, and fuel efficiency.

THE BATTLE OF THE EASTERN SOLOMONS:
THE FIRST CARRIER DUEL

On 24 August 1942, the same day as the first Japanese air raid on Henderson, US and Japanese carriers sparred in the battle of the Eastern Solomons. Admiral Fletcher's carrier task force, with three flattops—*Enterprise, Saratoga,* and *Wasp*—maneuvered to the east of Guadalcanal to protect transport convoys and block Japanese attacks on the Allied bases of Espiritu Santo and Nouméa to the south.[102] A Japanese carrier task force under Admiral Ch ichi Nagumo with the three carriers *Shokaku, Zuikaku,* and *Ryujo,* met Fletcher's force on its way to set up for an air attack on Guadalcanal.[103]

Unlike the Battle of Midway, it was a tactical draw, with the *Enterprise* sustaining major damage and her planes sent to the *Wasp,* Henderson Field, and Espiritu Santo, while four destroyers escorted *Enterprise* back to Pearl Harbor for repairs.[104] The Japanese suffered the loss of the carrier *Ryujo* and thirty-one aircraft.[105] For the Americans, postbattle actions further hampered their efforts to secure Guadalcanal. Two submarine attacks by the Japanese followed the battle, on 31 August and 15 September. The former disabled the *Saratoga*—the ship's aircraft sent to Henderson Field, the *Wasp,* and Espiritu Santo. The second attack sent the *Wasp* to the bottom of the ocean, her planes dispatched to the *Hornet*—which had arrived in the theater to replace the *Enterprise*—and Henderson Field.[106] In less than two weeks, the Japanese submarines had sunk or damaged two of the five carriers in the US inventory.

During the battle of the Eastern Solomons, Henderson Field served as a critical platform to preserve aircraft; and unlike the carriers, submarines presented no threat. As the campaign wore on, Henderson Field continued this duty as an alternate landing location for both sea-based and land-based aircraft, a critical force multiplier for the Americans. The Cactus Air Force reflected the hodgepodge nature of aircraft destined for Henderson Field or diverted in a crisis, comprising units from the United States Marine Corps, United States Navy, and United States Army Air Forces (USAAF).[107] Unlike their enemy, the Japanese lacked land-based options close to Guadalcanal, a key tactical necessity they did not rectify for months.

For the Japanese, the tactical draw at the battle of the Eastern Solomons was a strategic loss. After a few weeks of bombing operations against Guadalcanal and the carrier battles, the island was demanding more aircrews than Japan could produce. In an age of industrial power, speed, and machine warfare, the Japanese still relied on a strict Preindustrial process to produce their aircrews—a bespoke process with a Bushido-like curriculum—yielding fewer than one hundred pilots a year before the war.[108] Under this system, losing nineteen aviators in the first wave of strikes during the battle of the Eastern Solomons was unsustainable.[109]

The initial exchange of airpower, sea power, land forces, and logistics set the template for the rest of the campaign for Guadalcanal. The Japanese would use fast destroyers, with their smaller capacity, to deliver their land forces at night, as they had done with Ichiki. Those same destroyers would bombard Henderson Field and race back home before the sun rose to avoid the US air threat. The Japanese called it "Rat Transportation," and the Americans named it the "Tokyo Express"—a dreaded system of supply that delivered men, artillery, and a nightly barrage onto the US defensive positions. The Americans would counter with airpower from Henderson Field, hunting Japanese convoys at sea while defending against Japanese attacks from the air. All the while, the carriers stood in the background, both assisting their own side while deterring the other. For the rest of the conflict, control of Guadalcanal oscillated between day and night, and diverged between air and sea power, with the Americans embracing the former and the Japanese the latter.

ICHIKI TO APOGEE: SUPPLY, BATTLE, AND ATTRITION

After Ichiki's demise, the IJA blamed bad leadership and poor tactics, while leadership within the IJN reasoned that the Americans were a much tougher foe on land. Both services agreed, however, that the Japanese needed to send another detachment to oust the Marines. On the American side, the victory over Ichiki illustrated the fierce and unrelenting nature of the Japanese soldier and brought with it a sense of foreboding about future battles. The erratic but functional supply line from Nouméa, which left the Marines with two-thirds rations and a tenuous water supply, coupled with the consistent delivery of Japanese troops over the next several weeks, did nothing to remove their dread. Regardless of nationality, soldiers suffered from malaria, fevers, disease, hunger, and dehydration in the humidity and heat of Guadalcanal. In the race to bring the most material and men to the fight, each side built on the template of logistics they had established in the first few weeks, while absorbing harsh lessons from combat on the island.

On 28 August 1942, the Japanese tested the first large delivery of a Tokyo Express convoy. With only one resupply force having made it to Guadalcanal since the Americans landed, other than Ichiki's self-sustaining unit, the desperate Japanese hoped to hide in poor weather over the ocean and thus avoid Henderson Field aircraft. Seven destroyers pressed towards Guadalcanal, and the Cactus Air Force intercepted them at sunset, damaging three vessels and sinking one.[110] Admiral Ugaki, Admiral Yamamoto's chief of staff, noted in his diary that the incident happened "because it got into the aerial attack range too soon [before dark] and proceeded at a slow speed."[111] The next night, 29 August, proved much more successful: six destroyers delivered over eight hundred Japanese soldiers and 180 tons of supplies.[112] After this success the Japanese official staff records stated, "Through the success of this landing, a tangible method for reinforcing Guadalcanal was established, and thereafter . . . became the standard method."[113]

The standard method delivered increasing numbers of Japanese troops onto the island in August and September. Between 29 August and 2 September 1942, over 4,700 replacements landed.[114] To the Marines, the Tokyo Express was a physical manifestation of their navy brethren's lack of engagement at Guadalcanal—the continuous transportation of supplies and men sent to push them off the island, coupled with an incoming shore bombardment, a reminder of their precarious hold on the island. Little did the Marines know that the destroyers were not a sign of Japanese strength in logistics, but rather a sign of weakness and evidence of the Cactus Air Force's dominance.

The Second Japanese Land Trek: The Battle of Edson's Ridge

Major General Kiyotake Kawaguchi's offensive to take Henderson Field on 12 September 1942 was the first demonstration of the growing weakness of the Japanese supply system. Kawaguchi landed with the reinforcements in early September and led his forces on another epic land trek through the fetid and dense jungle. The Japanese suffered another stinging defeat at Edson's ridge, losing 633 soldiers killed, 505 wounded, and several hundred missing in the jungle, for a casualty rate of over 30 percent of the original force of 5,000.[115] Their retreat foundered and faltered through the jungle in a scene reminiscent of Braddock's defeat. A Japanese private recorded, "They only had three days rations when they went into the attack and soon ran out. Four days they pulled their cannons over their trails but they had to give up and bury [75-mm artillery pieces]. It took around two weeks to make the trip and more than one-half of the men became sick and died on the way."[116] The Japanese had so little food for the return that some spent a week eating

jungle weeds and grass.[117] Kawaguchi's failure demonstrated the shortcomings of the Tokyo Express. Although the Tokyo Express could deliver men at
a brisk twenty-five knots from Shortland to Guadalcanal, the standard load
of fifteen tons of food per destroyer was insufficient to support a land-based
offensive on the island.[118]

Translating the limited capacity of the Tokyo Express onto their needs
for combat on land illustrates the stark supply situation of the Japanese. For
every one thousand men, the army staff estimated it needed 5.7 tons a day
of supplies, mostly food, to keep them ready for battle.[119] Even with the bolstered deployments that had delivered Kawaguchi and prepped him for his
offensive in the days leading up to 12 September, the Japanese already had
a deficit of food—their men four days behind in sustenance based on the
staff's standard of a combat ration.[120] Without food, Kawaguchi's offensive
through an impenetrable jungle failed.

Despite its limitations, the Tokyo Express was all the Japanese had. The
Cactus Air Force engaged in daily missions to scour the seas for surface traffic; after the first few weeks, the Americans had a working system of radar
control, which provided vectors toward enemy aircraft and air-raid warn-
ings.[121] In addition, US submarines sank four different transport ships bound
for Rabaul in September.[122] American airpower was dictating the terms of
Japanese logistics: they could deliver many men or some supplies but not
both, while US submarines were striking farther afield to limit the resources
available to move by the Tokyo Express.

While the Cactus Air Force hunted Japanese supplies on the ocean, the
Japanese continued their attacks on Henderson Field and American supplies. The air battle over Henderson Field raged during the first months—in
one span from 31 August to 18 September, the Japanese attacked the field
on eleven of nineteen days.[123] None of the attacks was fatal, but they often
resulted in significant damage, frayed the nerves of the Americans on the island, and delayed or shuttled unloading from the transports. On 30 August
1942, Japanese aircraft sent to attack Henderson Field spotted the transport
Colhoun driving between Guadalcanal and Tulagi and sank the ship, and
the transports *Little* and *Gregory* five days later.[124] In both these incidents
no cargo was at risk, since these three ships had stayed at Guadalcanal after
bringing supplies on 21 August 1942; however, the Japanese disrupted the
supply lines to Americans ashore. Postconflict, Vandegrift summed up the

Marines' supply situation through mid-October: "Ships arrived at irregular intervals with all categories of supplies, but were rarely unloaded completely, because of interference by enemy air, surface, and undersea attack."[125] Even an incomplete unloading of one cargo ship with a six-thousand-ton capacity, however, was more beneficial than what the Tokyo Express provided to the Japanese in an entire month. At a strategic level, the incomplete but consistent arrivals of cargo at Guadalcanal were an indication that the capacity of America's "Arsenal of Democracy" was beginning to accelerate.[126]

The air raids against Henderson Field piled up the losses on both sides. By 1 October 1942, the Japanese had lost seventy-one aircraft while attacking and the Americans seventy while defending.[127] Coupled with the resources required to supply themselves—oil, ships, men, food, and ammunition— Guadalcanal had become a major strategic battle and resource drain for both sides. With the math of logistics against them, the Japanese embraced a supply system based on calculated fatalism. The Imperial Japanese Staff recorded, "Plans were drafted for suicide shipments [Teishin Yuso, or "ant landings"] to Guadalcanal with sixteen large landing barges, supported by six destroyers and two submarines."[128] Persistent air efforts from both Cactus aircraft and other land-based aviation that United States Army Air Forces, under Major General Millard F. Harmon, and the United States Marine Corps and United States Navy under Admiral Aubrey Fitch, brought to bear prevented all but two of the barges from making the initial journey to Shortland.[129] Fortunately for any future transportation forces from IJN, the staff scrubbed these suicide missions.

For the Japanese, the oil the Tokyo Express had consumed, coupled with the air and sea losses and the shocking defeat of Major General Kawaguchi in his attempt to take Henderson Field, resulted in a strategic refocus. The Japanese army and navy stopped all offensive action in other theaters, including those against Port Moresby and Burma to support Guadalcanal.[130] In a strategic irony, the continuing efforts of their German ally at Stalingrad allowed the Japanese to feel confident enough to move troops from their Manchurian borders with the Soviet Union.[131] By the end of the month, the IJA agreed to move "five or six divisions in addition to twenty-five battalions of engineers and others to the Pacific Area."[132] The most important factor in this bolstered effort—named "Operation KA"—was to "gain control of the air at any cost so as to facilitate the transport of our own reinforcements and to check the arrival of enemy reinforcements."[133] The Japanese followed this commitment by sending eighty aircraft to Rabaul in late September.[134] As part of the revaluation of where to place airplanes, the Japanese constructed new airfields closer to Guadalcanal, including Buin in the Shortlands—which cut the flight distance from one thousand NM to six hundred NM.[135] With a closer field, the Japanese could hit Guadalcanal twice in one day and with longer loiter times. As the ships, men, and aircraft streamed from the other regions of the empire toward Rabaul and Truk for delivery to Guadalcanal, the Japanese went on the defensive on land and sea and waited for the proper concentration of assets and men to attack.

US SUPPLY: INSUFFICIENT BUT STEADY

Although the Japanese suffered more on the island, the supply situation for the Americans remained critical, and control of the island stood in doubt throughout August and September. Underscoring the role attrition was having on the course of the campaign, Admiral Ghormley wrote to Nimitz and King in late August that a "regular replacement program must be initiated immediately as one of the essentials necessary in order that present positions may be maintained and preparations made for a further advance. . . . Reference despatch [sic] is only definite information on front line attrition rate so far available."[136] Although the supply network from Nouméa was slow and interrupted from the sea and air, men and supplies flowed piecemeal to the island thanks to the work by the Cactus Air Force in protecting supplies. Major General Harmon summed up the lackluster but sufficient supply situation in a letter back to the War Department: "[We have to] try to get some definition of what the Navy can and will do so we will know what the Army has to do—and avoid duplication. Anyway some way it's moving along and no one has starved yet."[137] Harmon was right.

By 18 September 1942, Major General Vandegrift reported, "Full rations were restored, for all troops except headquarters units" due to "the high order of performance of our interception fighters which almost invariably were able to break up hostile bombing formations before the latter had opportunity for delivering a coordinated attack."[138] Although the food was not fresh, just a soup of warmed meat from tins, after seven weeks the Marines were in no danger of starvation—a vast caloric advantage over their enemy. Added to the improved food situation, the First Marine Division added an additional nine thousand Marines and US Army soldiers, bolstering their numbers to twenty thousand by October.[139]

By the end of September, Major General Vandegrift felt confident enough of his Marines, firepower, and food to attempt a major land offensive against the Japanese. He recorded in his memoirs, "With my forces numbering over 19,000, I felt an almost luxurious freedom of action."[140] His optimism was short-lived. During the last week of September, Vandegrift ordered two battalions of Marines to attack the Japanese at the Mataniakau River; both struggled to land on the shore near the Japanese positions and move inland through the jungle.[141] The jungle and stiff Japanese resistance swallowed the offensive of the Americans in the same way it had done to the two previous Japanese efforts. Vandegrift called off the ill-fated action on 9 October 1942. Movement by land, without roads, was as difficult as it had been in 1755.

THE AIR FROM EVERYWHERE AND NOWHERE: OTHER AIRPOWER AND LOGISTICS

While both sides bolstered their forces on the land, struggled to feed them, and tested each other with battle, US dominance in the air and under the ocean began to affect Japanese support operations farther afield. As the commitment to Guadalcanal grew, the War Department authorized more aircraft for use by Admiral Ghormley—even those precious few assigned to General Macarthur's forces in Australia and New Guinea. As a result, Major General Harmon's land-based forces grew in number, B-17s from thirty-three to ninety-four and fighters from twenty to forty-two, ramping up the ability to attack Japanese airfields and shipping.[142] In addition to the sinking of the aforementioned *Kinryu Maru*, which had been part of the force dispatched to bolster Ichiki's battalion, B-17s sank a Japanese tender ship near Rabaul and another cargo ship to the east of Port Moresby in early October.[143] B-17s also attacked destroyers and numerous surface craft as targets of opportunity.[144] More important, the B-17s possessed the range, defensive firepower, and navigation capabilities to patrol "The Slot" and notify Guadalcanal of an impending Japanese attack or supply run.[145] Using a bomber aircraft for reconnaissance was anathema to both Major General Harmon and the chief of staff of the USAAF, General "Hap" Arnold, but the desperate situation of the

Marines on Guadalcanal dictated the terms.[146] The remote nature of Guadalcanal, coupled with limited resources and airbases—including Henderson Field with its limited fuel, space, and short runway—left Admiral Ghormley with no choice but to use B-17s as eyes in the sky. He employed them to great effect, keeping the land and sea forces involved at Guadalcanal abreast of Japanese movements.

While the use of combat aircraft in the Pacific underpinned support for the Americans on Guadalcanal, so were transportation aircraft. To supplement the limited supplies from the sea for Guadalcanal, first Admiral McCain, then Admiral Fitch and Major General Harmon, established C-47 flights into the airfield just days after the Cactus Air Force landed. These military versions of Douglas DC-3 cargo aircraft brought in medical supplies with small shipments of food and evacuated the wounded. The C-47 began its first duty at Guadalcanal ferrying the sick and wounded off the island on 3 September 1942; by 1 October 1942, transport aircraft had evacuated 347 troops.[147] With the rates of disease eclipsing combat deaths on Guadalcanal for both sides, isolating and transporting the worse off led to greater rates of health for US service members versus their Japanese counterparts. In addition, the evacuations cut down on the medical supplies necessary to treat the wounded.

Whereas the Americans could evacuate their sick and wounded, the lack of airpower on the island afforded the Japanese soldiers no such comfort. Although Japanese aircraft could force Marines and US Army soldiers into bunkers and harass transport ships, they could do so for only limited time because of the great distance from Rabaul to Guadalcanal. By early September, the Marines harassed their Japanese enemy in ways the Tokyo Express and the Japanese air raids could not match.

The Marines adapted their P-400s—the export version of the P-39—into an effective close-air-support weapon. Not viable above fourteen thousand feet because of a lack of components for the oxygen system, a by-product of the convoluted logistics system in 1942, the P-400s fared poorly against the vaunted Zeros.[148] After the first couple of air raids and subsequent dogfights with the Japanese, the Marines kept the P-400s away from the Zeros and re-tooled them as a ground-attack weapon.[149] The P-400s forced the Japanese into the jungle and away from the beaches, furthering their misery and assisting in the spread of disease.[150] Thus, with the ability to evacuate their own soldiers on aircraft while driving their enemy into closer quarters, command of the air gave the US an advantage in medical support to land forces while taking the same away from the Japanese.

The firepower of American aircraft also made it difficult for the Japanese to offload cargoes on the beaches, bringing daytime operations to a complete halt and endangering nighttime operations during bright moonlight.[151] The local control of the air also allowed the US to turn the tables on the Japanese from the sea in specific instances. For example, on 8 September 1942, the Marine command post logs recorded that the "APDs [transports ships] have located Jap landing boats they will open fire to indicate locations [for] planes to destroy boats."[152] This creative use of a transportation asset to reconnoiter the enemy's logistics for an air strike typified the growing American superiority on the island. While the Tokyo Express harassed US forces with nighttime bombings and hurt morale, the American forces were bringing all the logistics they could to bear on the island and translating that material might into effective combat power.

RAIN AND DARKNESS: TECHNOLOGICAL LIMITS

While the control of the air around Henderson Field gave the US a distinct advantage, the Late Industrial technologies of the time could not overcome the environmental factors of bad weather and darkness. US fighter and smaller dive-bomber aircraft had only rudimentary turn-and-slip indicators and no navigation; therefore, flight through thick cloudbanks or even short distances away from island landmarks courted disaster.[153] Although certain PBY flying boats had radar, the systems were never attuned for weather detection. As a result, with bad weather or on dark nights, the Japanese could even the playing field and deliver the occasional destroyer with supplies, as they did in late August and early September.[154] In addition, overcast weather sometimes allowed Japanese air raids to slip past coast watchers and surprise the Americans at Henderson. The bad weather required to disguise a successful raid could also yield a treacherous flight—especially in large formations, since the Japanese lacked radios, giving no ability to avoid each other without visual reference. The Japanese staff lamented, "The weather changes completely enroute [from Rabaul], and pilots encounter unexpected weather over Guadalcanal, which hampers their operations."[155]

Although the Japanese pilots were more skilled at night fighting, like their Navy counterparts, flying one thousand NM at night with no radios and nothing but a compass to guide them made Guadalcanal a prescription for death. At night, carrier aircraft fared no better. Landing on a carrier at night was a hazard for plane and ship.[156]

For the Americans, their advantage in supply and transportation by mid-September delivered technological solutions to counter the dark. The US established a rudimentary lighting system and a navigation beacon for Henderson Field, expanding flight operations further into dawn, dusk, and moonlit nights.[157] After these upgrades to Henderson, the Japanese had to adjust their Tokyo Express to the lunar cycle.[158] By late September, a full moon meant no delivery.

APOGEE FOR THE RISING SUN: OPERATION KA

By mid-October, the Japanese were ready to execute, Operation KA. The plan had two phases. First, nighttime seaborne bombardment would destroy the Cactus Air Force while it sat on the ground, supplemented with daytime raids by aircraft and land-based artillery shelling. Next, with US airpower reduced, the heretofore-banished transports of the Japanese would supply Guadalcanal with the men and supplies necessary for an offensive thrust to beat the Americans.

Operation KA began with increased Tokyo Express runs in early October. The Tokyo Express disembarked as many as nine hundred soldiers three times a week—adding up to six thousand more soldiers between mid-September and mid-October.[159] These deliveries also included 160 tons of food (a two-day supply), thirty-nine artillery pieces, tractors, ammunition carts, and six antiaircraft pieces.[160] The Japanese delivered the last contingent of troops and Lieutenant General Hyakutake, who assumed direct leadership of the growing operation. On 9 October 1942, he took command from Kawaguchi.[161] The rapid influx of soldiers, however, exacerbated the food shortage; by Hyakutake's arrival, the Japanese had a food deficit of ten days.[162] With this lack of sustenance, the ability of the large transport ships to follow Hyakutake would determine Japanese survival.

For the Americans, by the second week in October, the logistics situation had improved: full rations for all and ninety aircraft sitting at Henderson

Field. The Marines had a strong defensive position on land and more men than ever. Although the *Wasp* and the *Saratoga* were gone, the *Enterprise*, back from repairs, and the *Hornet* still stood out to the east to block any Japanese carrier movement. Although the American leadership had intelligence suggesting a renewed Japanese offensive, the victory at Edson's ridge infused hope—reflected in more positive reports from the heretofore-negative Admiral Ghormley.[163]

To screen the slower transports and the follow-on heavy cruisers that were to shell Henderson Field, the Japanese sent a surface fleet to Savo Island on 11 October 1942. In another night engagement, the United States Navy fought to a win at the battle of Cape Esperance with four American cruisers and six destroyers facing three Japanese cruisers, eight destroyers, and two seaplane carriers in reserve.[164] This time Admiral Norman Scott had retrained the US cruiser group after the Savo Island disaster to follow a more prescriptive pattern for night fighting.[165] At the end of the battle, four Japanese destroyers and one heavy cruiser were at the bottom of Savo Sound, joining one American destroyer. The Japanese cruiser *Aoba* limped away along with two US cruisers and a destroyer.[166]

The battle of Cape Esperance was more significant for what stood behind the battle fleets than in them. Unbeknownst to the Japanese, Scott's cruiser force protected two US transports—the *Zeilin* and the *McCawley*—carrying the US Army's 164th Infantry Regiment to relieve the beleaguered Marines.[167] Unbeknownst to the Americans, the Japanese surface force was a screen for the sea-borne attack force that would bomb Henderson Field to open the beaches for Japanese transports to deliver their cargo.

The attack force, the Japanese battleships *Kongo* and *Haruna*, left the Japanese port at Truk on 11 October 1942, as the battle of Cape Esperance raged in Savo Sound. Screened by nine destroyers and fighters from the new runway at Buin, the force planned to arrive at Guadalcanal on the night of 13–14 October. The day before their arrival, forty-six aircraft bombed Henderson Field in the heaviest and most successful run since August, damaging twelve aircraft and hitting a fuel dump.[168] The bombing runs, coupled with Japanese artillery attacks, also put several large holes in the runway.[169]

That night at 0100, the Japanese battleships *Kongo* and *Haruna* placed 973 high explosive (HE) shells onto Henderson Field. The HE shells exploded dozens of feet in the air, spraying hundreds of shrapnel pieces several inches in diameter and one inch in width all over the airfield.[170] This was the epochal shelling of the campaign, and those Americans present would never forget it. The results were catastrophic.

As the Marines awoke the morning of 14 October, they took stock of their material. The bombardment reduced the ninety-plane-strong Cactus Air Force to forty-two aircraft.[171] Worse yet, the shells destroyed most of the aviation gas. Working all morning, the Marines scrounged fuel from destroyed aircraft and took stock of four hundred barrels of fuel, "about two days' supply for the planes serviceable at that time."[172] The desperation did not end for Henderson Field after the first night. Japanese aircraft hit the field on the fourteenth, and the IJN followed with another night bombardment by two Japanese cruisers—752 shells saturating the Marine positions.[173]

By the morning of 15 October, the Marines saw six full Japanese transports disembarking soldiers and supplies off Tassafaronga point to the west of the field—the first to make it to the island (see Figure 3.2—upper-right map). With their scavenged gasoline, the Marines put every available aircraft in the air to hit the transports and supplies on the beach, while countering the Japanese air cover for the same. Although the Japanese enjoyed air superiority, or at least parity, for most of the day, by 3 p.m. the Cactus Air Force, US carrier based-aircraft, land-based USAAF B-17s, and destroyers had set three transports on the beach on fire and forced the remaining three to withdraw out to open ocean.[174]

While defending their own transports ships, Japanese aircraft attacked one of Admiral Turner's fuel convoys as it approached Guadalcanal, which had set sail for Guadalcanal after the bombing on the night of 13 October. The convoy—two transport ships, a minesweeper, a tugboat, and three destroyers trailing three barges with two thousand barrels of gasoline each—was sighted by Japanese reconnaissance aircraft.[175] The sighting forced Turner to order all ships but the destroyers to return for fear of destruction from the air. In the ensuing attack, twenty-seven Japanese bombers sunk the destroyer *Meredith* and damaged the destroyer *Vireo*.[176] Incredibly, the transports retreated with only minor damage, and the crews salvaged the fuel barges.

For the Japanese, protecting the offensive movement ashore and attacking the American supply convoys cost them seventeen aircraft, while the Cactus Air Force lost ten planes.[177] With the efforts from the air, Japanese aircraft paved the way for the IJN to move on shore 4,500 soldiers and 65 percent of their cargo.[178] This raised the food supply of the hungry Japanese army from a deficit of seventeen days to a four-day reserve. In addition, they had turned back a much-needed fuel delivery for the aircraft at Henderson Field. From sunrise until 1500 on 15 October 1942, the Japanese had control of the air and dictated the supply deliveries of both sides at Guadalcanal.

For the Americans, the destruction of the three transports made the "breathing . . . a bit easier for all hands" since they had survived three days of sustained bombing from the air, land and sea.[179] Their confidence in their own supply situation, however, was shattered as the Japanese delivered two thousand soldiers on a Tokyo Express run with fifteen destroyers on the night of 15 October.[180]

SHOESTRING TO FIRST PLACE

While the Japanese had jolted to action after the failure at Edson's ridge in September, now the Americans awoke. General Harmon, the US Army commander of the South Pacific, sent a cable from Nouméa to General George C. Marshall, chairman of the Joint Chiefs, on October 17: "Situation Cactus Extremely Grave. . . . Air Operations from that base seriously curtailed . . . [situation] is vital as most important strategic position lines of communication south and southwest pacific and it is too lightly held for reasonable security until we are more secure in forward areas."[181] In other words, if Guadalcanal fell, then the Japanese could strike the ring of bases to the south, Nouméa and Espiritu Santo, and cut the Americans out of the Pacific. As if to help underscore Harmon's anxiety at the geopolitical level, the Soviets hung on by a thread at Stalingrad; and with the American preparation to invade North Africa close to completion, the Americans had to hold Guadalcanal. President Roosevelt, in a memorandum to the Joint Chiefs of Staff, stated, "My anxiety about the Southwest Pacific is to make sure that every possible weapon gets into that area to hold Guadalcanal. . . . We will soon find ourselves engaged on two active fronts and we must have adequate air support in both places even though it means delay in to other commitments particularly to England."[182] For these few weeks in the fall of 1942, Guadalcanal took the lead role in national strategy and concentration of resources. Europe would have to wait.

After the near destruction of the Cactus Air Force, Nimitz decided that the war had overwhelmed Admiral Ghormley. On October 16, Nimitz wrote to Admiral King requesting that Admiral Bill "Bull" Halsey replace Ghormley. King's reply was short: "approved."[183] Into this grim situation, Halsey provided much-needed vigor and used the strategic focus imparted by his president to great advantage, asking for as many men, ships, and airplanes he could muster.[184]

LOGISTICS FIRST: FIXING NOUMÉA AND SENDING FUEL FROM THE AIR AND SEA

Upon arriving at Nouméa and relieving Admiral Ghormley, Halsey surveyed the mess at the port and moved into action. Although integration of the army and navy supply routes from the west coast was an important as a long-term goal, Nouméa required clearing first, to expedite supplies to combat. With the supply of Guadalcanal preeminent, Halsey placed "definite responsibilities in the hands of each service" and let them work. Out of this decision, US Army Brigadier General Raymond Williamson assumed control of Nouméa and improved the monthly throughput from twenty-four ships a month to fifty-seven a month by late November.[185] The army soldiers and Marines on Guadalcanal noticed this improvement in short order.

The established routes of the C-47 aircraft paid dividends for the Cactus Air Force as the call went out for fuel. Major General Harmon's continued requests for more C-47s in theater resulted in the first deployment of additional USAAF aircraft to the South Pacific. The aircraft arrived just after the Japanese bombarded Guadalcanal in mid-October. The US Army and Marine C-47s brought in fuel to the field over the next few days, ten barrels at a time, each barrel capable of keeping a fighter aloft for about an hour.[186] Over the next two weeks, twelve to fifteen planes a day landed per week at Henderson Field, which put the range of fuel delivery between 840 and 1050 barrels for the first week.[187] Although this was not a large amount—the barges the Japanese pilots turned back carried two hundred C-47 loads each—the delivery by air kept the Cactus Air Force operating in their reduced status for a week until more fuel arrived by sea. The flights also bolstered morale. Pilots on Guadalcanal "were jubilant. They looked at the slow lumbering C-47s and felt a great tenderness for the flying boxcars and the pilots who were flying them."[188]

THE LAST JAPANESE OFFENSIVE:
LAND POWER AND LOGISTICS

While Halsey took charge of the theater, the accumulations of the fresh Japanese troops, food stocks, weapons, and ammunition delivered to Guadalcanal did not take long to materialize into a ground offensive. In another difficult march through the harsh jungle, Major General Hyakutake led his troops from the west toward Henderson Field on 15 October. A full thirty miles of jungle march sapped men, artillery pieces, and supply. By the time they began the attacks on the airfield on 20 October, Hyakutake's forces were exhausted, confused, and hungry. Despite their element of surprise "and a nine-to-one superiority" against the thin defensive positions Vandegrift posted, the Japanese were annihilated, suffering more than 2,200 casualties.[189] The Americans suffered fewer than 100. In one last effort, Kawaguchi, with the small forces remaining, attempted to take the airfield on 25 October 1942, but by this time the Cactus Air Force had enough fuel to assist and provided close air support.[190] Kawaguchi failed again.

Those Japanese who survived the battle had a harrowing march back thirty miles through the jungle. A captured Japanese journal noted, "The canteen I filled on the 24th of October was empty, I ate one of three [pieces of fruit] which were rotten. This gives an idea of the rations."[191] The offensive used most of the supplies that had landed with the transports. In their third successive land campaign, the Japanese had attempted to move through a jungle wilderness without the logistics to keep their men from starving, much less sustain their bodies to win.

RACE TO FEAST AND FAMINE:
THE AMERICANS SECURE GUADALCANAL

As the land battle ended, Halsey directed his carriers and surface force to strike. Down to the repaired *Enterprise* and the *Hornet*, with destroyer screens of nine and ten respectively, Admirals Kinkaid and Murray led their flattops into battle against two Japanese carrier groups. These two groups, led by Vice Admiral Nabutake Kondo and Admiral Nagumo, consisted of three regular carriers, one small light carrier, and several associated cruisers and destroyers.[192] On 26 October, the two forces met east of Guadalcanal at the battle of the Santa Cruz Islands. By the end of the day, ninety-seven Japanese aircraft and eighty-one US aircraft were lost; and two Japanese carriers, along with the *Hornet*, were sunk. The *Enterprise* had enough damage to require the carrier retire to Nouméa for repairs, while the remaining two Japanese carriers had to retire due to lack of pilots.[193] For the first and only time, the United States had no serviceable carriers in the Pacific.

Although Halsey's gamble with his only two carriers had been a tactical victory for the Japanese, once again the wastage of pilots was unsustainable. In addition, the strike kept aircraft away from Guadalcanal, allowing the Cactus Air Force to regroup and replenish its numbers, growing to seventy-six aircraft by the first week of November.[194]

WASH, RINSE, REPEAT: 11–12 NOVEMBER 1942—NAVAL BATTLES OF GUADALCANAL

After the *Hornet* sunk, and with the *Enterprise* in retreat, Admiral Yamamoto and the IJN believed the destruction of Henderson Field was imminent. In a rehash and resizing of Operation KA, this time the Japanese would use combined aircraft from carriers and land-based airfields, and a surface fleet of thirty-one ships, to escort eleven transports to Guadalcanal. These transports carried enough supplies for thirty thousand men for thirty days (about five thousand tons) and thirty-one thousand artillery shells.[195] In addition, the Japanese increased the firepower to clear the way. Two battleships, the *Hiei* and the *Kirishima,* were designated to shell Henderson Field along with the aforementioned aircraft and eleven destroyers. The eleven Japanese transports left Shortland on 11 November 1942, escorted by twelve destroyers.[196]

The Americans also had transports on the way. On the morning of 12 November, six US transports unloaded at Lunga Point. Alerted by their island warriors, the Japanese sent seventeen Bettys and thirty Zeros from long-distance Rabaul to attack the transports. Warned by coast watchers and radar, the Cactus Air Force and US surface cruisers shot down or damaged beyond repair fouteen of the Bettys and one Zero.[197]

Unlike the 8 August and 15 October bombing raids, the Japanese missed the US transports; and, by sunset, 90 percent of the supplies were unloaded.[198] That same day Henderson Field received a boost in aircraft, including twelve new P-38Fs, which provided significant upgrades in speed and power over the F4Fs, which the Cactus Air Force had relied on to fight the Zeros.[199] In addition, despite its injured state, Admiral Halsey ordered the *Enterprise* back in as a reserve station to launch aircraft, and redirected planes onto land-based runways surrounding the Solomons.[200] With the most airpower they had ever possessed at Guadalcanal, the US Marines, US Navy, and US Army stood ready for the Japanese transports.

The First Naval Battle of Guadalcanal: Trafalgar in 1942

Standing in the way of Japanese bombardment force was Admiral Callaghan with two heavy cruisers, three light cruisers, and eight destroyers. On the night after the US transports unloaded, the US and Japanese surface forces met in a battle reminiscent of Trafalgar but with Late Industrial weapons, firing at ranges less than one thousand yards. It was carnage. The US Navy lost two light cruisers and four destroyers, with two heavy cruisers and two destroyers damaged.[201] The Japanese lost two destroyers with a third damaged and, more importantly, the battleship *Hiei* sunk—its final sinking assured by bomber aircraft launched from the *Enterprise,* which then landed at Henderson Field.[202]

With the *Hiei* gone, the Japanese regrouped a second bombardment force under the *Chokai.* The *Chokai* and another Japanese cruiser sent 989 projectiles into the field, but they missed most of the aircraft—only destroying two.[203] As day broke on 14 November, USAAF aircraft, planes from Cactus, and the *Enterprise* arose and struck the departing cruisers and their destroyers out in the open water and damaged three Japanese destroyers, sunk another, and damaged the *Chokai.*[204]

Into this melee of airpower sailed the eleven Japanese transports and their thirteen supporting destroyers. Believing Henderson Field subdued, the army sailed with optimism aboard the IJN cargo ships.[205] West of Guadalcanal near the Russell islands, however, aircraft from all three sources—Henderson Field, *Enterprise,* and USAAF land-based runways—attacked the convoy. The IJN recorded, "Our convoy was attacked by an aggregate of 108 aircraft . . . seven of the convoy's 11 transports fell behind, only four continued ahead."[206] Aircraft sunk those seven. To support what was left of the landing force, the Japanese regrouped another bombardment force with the battleship *Kirishima* in the lead for the night of 14–15 November.

The Second Naval Battle of Guadalcanal

This time Japanese Admiral Nobutake Kondo faced off against US Admiral Willis Lee in the second naval battle of Guadalcanal. Lee, one of the early Pioneers of US naval radar, used his technological skill and knowledge to defeat the Japanese.[207] His force sunk the *Kirisihima* and one destroyer and damaged one cruiser, while sustaining three destroyer losses and damage to one battleship and one destroyer.[208]

As Admiral Kondo sailed away, he ordered Admiral Raizō Tanaka, the commander of the Tokyo Express destroyer force, to move the transports to the island and beach them to ensure delivery.[209] By the time Tanaka's crews beached the ships, it was 0400. As the sun rose, the Cactus Air Force hit the transports and spent the better part of the day attacking the burning hulks of the ships.[210] At the cost of eleven transports, the Japanese delivered just a four-day supply of rice and 2,000 exhausted soldiers to add to the 25,000 hungry men, while taking on a thousand navy casualties and dozens of ships sunk—including a battleship.[211] On the other side of the supply tally, the Americans delivered over 5,500 men and tons of supplies to Guadalcanal in the two days prior.

With the failure of supplies to reach the island, the Japanese soldiers now faced starvation. Given the dire situation, the Tokyo Express runs underwent one final innovation. Instead of delivering troops, ammunition, and food— the runs would deliver only the latter. During these missions, Japanese destroyer crews used the tops of their ships as extra stowage area for barrels of food. In this way, the Japanese could fit two hundred barrels filled with 330 pounds of rice each on top of the ship.[212] Instead of pulling up to a dock, the destroyers would push the barrels off the ship with ropes attached, so the barrels of food could float with the tide and then be pulled ashore. Not only would this increase the capacity of the destroyers, but it would also solve the unloading dilemma, which had been dictated by the Cactus Air Force. Japanese planners hoped this would require only 20 Tokyo Express runs, much fewer than the 150 runs a month needed to sustain the army.[213]

This plan withered under the threat of US airpower. In just one example of many failures, nine Japanese destroyers attempted to deliver twelve hundred barrels onto Guadalcanal, but only two hundred made it to shore.[214] The Cactus Air Force, and navy PT boats, destroyed most of the barrels and inflicted casualties on the Japanese soldiers trying to recover the supplies.[215]

If necessity was the mother of invention for the Tokyo Express and its variants, airpower killed the invention it in its crib.

The Japanese also delivered food by submarine during the end of November. Overall, sixteen submarines delivered twenty to thirty tons of food, about one-fifth of the food necessary to keep the Japanese army fed at full rations; with the food deficit the soldiers faced, the deliveries from under the water did little to stem hunger.[216] In the words of the Imperial Japanese Navy staff, "Under these supply conditions, it was impossible to meet even minimum requirements, much less supply them regularly."[217]

On 1 December 1942, the Japanese attempted one last time to deliver supplies to the island via surface screen. Unlike the two previous efforts, the Japanese had no bombardment screen planned, from the sea or the air. Instead, they planned to use destroyers to screen the Tokyo Express delivery.

With eight destroyers screening six Tokyo Express transport destroyers, Admiral Tanaka led the ships into Savo Sound to the west of Guadalcanal. A US cruiser force led by Admiral Carelton Wright, with five cruisers and one destroyer, was distrustful of radar returns and surprised by the Japanese at the battle of Tassafaronga. Using their long-lance torpedoes, the Japanese mauled the Americans, damaging three cruisers and sinking one. The difficulty and confusion of battle, however, forced Admiral Tanaka to turn the task force around, unable to deliver the food. Tanaka's last valiant try to supply his compatriots was on 11 December 1942; his destroyer force scattered by US PT boats and his flagship sunk by a torpedo.

By the end of November, the Japanese soldiers at Guadalcanal were desperate, sick, starving, and well below combat shape. Second Lt. Yasuo Ko'o wrote a macabre checklist categorizing life expectancy of the Japanese soldiers on the island at the end of 1942:

Those who can stand—30 days

Those who can sit up—3 weeks

Those who cannot sit—1 week

Those who urinate lying down—3 days

Those who have stopped speaking—2 days

Those who have stopped blinking—tomorrow.[218]

By stark contrast, the Americans on Guadalcanal received their first shipments of beer—and in no small quantity—in early December 1942. A large liberty cargo ship unloaded "thirty thousand cases"[219] the Americans did not want.

Admiral Halsey's reorganization at Nouméa had come through: from beer, to fire trucks, to equipment for building baseball fields. By the first of the year, Guadalcanal had grown from a forward-area combat base to a logistics hub, with five runways under construction.[220] Even more significant, the First Marine Division boarded transports to sail to Australia to reconstitute, Major General Vandegrift transferring command to Major General Alexander Patch and the US Army. Despite the initial victory and bountiful logistics, there were still twenty-nine thousand Japanese on the island.

GROUND WARFARE IN THE JUNGLE: A TOUGH MODE

With the supply situation overflowing and increasing numbers of aircraft, artillery, and soldiers at his disposal, Major General Patch planned to drive the Japanese off the island. In the first part of the offensive, Patch directed his force to push the Japanese off Mount Austen, six miles to the southwest of Henderson Field. The army would then consolidate firepower on the mountaintop and move west toward the bulk of Japanese positions. As with the Marine landing and the Japanese offensives before, logistics were a critical component.

After taking Mount Austen, which took three weeks, the army and Marines regrouped for an attack west toward the main Japanese positions. Major General J. Lawton Collins, who led the 25th Division in the sweep to the west, used jeeps, then canoes up river, then had mules shipped in on transports, and even directed B-17s to airdrop supplies to forward units.[221] In addition, aircraft from the army, navy, and Marines provided mobile firepower for the offensives.[222] Despite the impressive array of logistics support, like the offensive movements before them—American and Japanese—the jungle stifled US Army and Marine efforts.

The pressing need was water. According to Richard Frank in *Guadalcanal*, "Leaders became lethargic, and the led, ever more thirsty and exhausted, rapidly became fewer from heat exhaustion and casualties. In one platoon only ten men remained conscious."[223] Even the most advanced technologies of the age could not conquer the jungle.

The Japanese proved resilient defenders in the jungle, but they suffered greatly—entire regiments wiped out or missing. In one example, an entire company under the Japanese 124th Infantry Battalion executed a suicide attack since only 20 percent of their unit could walk.[224] After the month's long push to Mount Austen and then to the west, the Americans counted their gains and waited.

IN DEFENSE OF LOGISTICS: OPERATION KE AND THE SUCCESS OF THE JAPANESE

With their intelligence intercepts, the Americans noted the building up of supplies at Rabaul and Truk. Most leaders believed that this presaged another attempt to expel the US from Guadalcanal. They were wrong. The situation of the Japanese troops on the island had worsened to the point of ineffectiveness, without food and in the face of the American offensives over December and January. Admiral Yamamoto and Japanese leadership worried that the cultural shame of loss was so great that the entire twenty-nine-thousand-man garrison might commit ritual suicide by an all-out fruitless attack on the Americans. To avoid the tragedy, Emperor Hirohito placed his great political weight behind the plan named "Operation KE" to rescue the soldiers from Guadalcanal.[225]

In a final flight down the slot, to do what so many air attacks had failed to do—protect their lines of communication—thirty-one Betty bombers flew toward Guadalcanal on 30 January 1943 to begin the operation. This time, flying at night, the bombers caught a US cruiser group of three heavy cruisers, two light cruisers, and six destroyers out in the open water. In the ensuing bombing runs, and without interdiction by US aircraft, the Japanese wounded the cruiser *Chicago* and followed up with a torpedo run from Japanese fighters later that afternoon to sink the ship.[226]

At the same time, Japanese commanders on land marshalled their beleaguered troops from the jungle and out onto the beaches of Cape Esperance by the night of 1 February 1943. Those Japanese soldiers who could not move committed suicide. That night the Japanese navy flew eleven bombers overhead the island to keep the Cactus Air Force at bay. Although the Americans launched six bombers, they missed the fleeing Japanese, who had alighted on rubber boats and rowed to the six escaping destroyers.[227] The Japanese repeated this maneuver on the 4th and 7th. More than 10,652 Japanese made it off the island, with a cost of fifty-six Japanese aircraft to fifty-three American.[228] The Japanese left behind over fifteen thousand dead soldiers.[229] Lessons in integrating combat power that the Japanese had gained during offensive operations paid dividends during the successful evacuation. More specifically, the use of aircraft at night gave them short-term control of the air, keeping the Cactus Air Force away from the departing destroyers.

The first enemy of the Japanese at Guadalcanal, the First Marine Division, took eight months to reconstitute—most of its soldiers losing at least thirty pounds and Major General Vandegrift still underweight after five months of recovery in Australia.[230] The Japanese who left Guadalcanal never recovered. A Japanese officer on the evacuating destroyers stated, "All had dengue or malaria. . . . Their digestive organs were so completely destroyed; [we] couldn't give them good food, only porridge."[231] The naval forces that attempted to supply them suffered a worse fate—sixteen of nineteen transports, five submarines, and two destroyers sunk and nineteen destroyers damaged during the supply runs alone.[232] The Japanese lost the battle of supply and its twin brother, nutrition.

SUMMARY OF SUPPLY

We went to the Raiders' CP [Command Post] for breakfast this morning, and had a good time yarning over pancakes.
—Richard Tregaskis, United States Marine Corps, Diary, 24 September 1942

I am surprised by how food captures the mind to the degree that one is always thinking of it, I try to think of other things, but can't.
—Lieutenant Keijiro Minegishi, IJA, Diary, 30 October 1942

In looking back at the delivery of supplies to Guadalcanal, the ability of the Americans to deliver needed food to the island well outpaced the Japanese. Although in the first few days they suffered for the backlog of cargo on Red Beach, a subsequent loss of cargo due to Japanese air attacks, and the loss at sea at the battle of Savo Island, the Marines gained a huge advantage by capturing the Japanese food supply. Without the estimated ten days of Japanese supply, the Americans would have had only twelve days of food remaining by the time the first supply ship arrived.

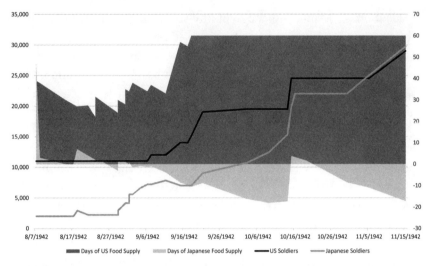

Figure 3.6. Numbers of Soldiers and Days of Food at Guadalcanal, US and Japanese, 7 August to 15 November 1942. This figure is an estimate. The exact amount of supply days for the Americans is from Vandegrift's postaction final reports. The supply days for the Japanese are based on 5.7 tons per day per one thousand soldiers from the Japanese staff estimates of the tonnage needed to sustain the approximately thirty thousand Japanese soldiers—180 tons—as quoted in Frank and Parshall in the source notes and then cross-referenced with the Tokyo Express Runs that were documented in the sources. The Americans had well over sixty days of supply by October; this is not listed to keep the figure in a scale to read the Japanese lack of supply. Data assembled from numerous primary and secondary sources: Frank, *Guadalcanal*; Jersey, *Hell's Islands*; Morison, *History of United States Naval Operations in World War II*, vol. 5; Ghormley, "COMSOPAC to CINCPAC" in *Chester A. Nimitz*; "Division Commanders Final Report on Guadalcanal Operations, Phase 4"; "Division Commanders Final Report on Guadalcanal Operations, Phase 3"; Ugakie, Prange, Goldstein, and Dillon, *Fading Victory*; "Japanese Monograph No. 98. Southeast Area Naval Operations. Part I, May 42–Feb 43"; Tregaskis, *Guadalcanal Diary*; Parshall, "Oil and Japanese Strategy in the Solomons: A Postulate." See bibliography for each source's full citation information.

The Japanese never recovered from the initial loss of food, nor did they ensure enough sustenance to win the battle on land. Figure 3.6 shows the supply situation and troop numbers on Guadalcanal for both sides, from the initial deployment of Marines on 7 August 1942 until the final attempted delivery by larger transportation ships of the Japanese on 11 November 1942.

The Japanese favored men over supply, in part because of their faulty assumption that the US Marines were fewer in number than they were and in part because of their chosen delivery mechanism—the destroyer. The destroyer could deliver men or supplies with speed but in only modest quantities. Using the destroyer as transportation vessel was not a choice of preference but rather of necessity. American airpower at Henderson Field, with its persistent interdiction of surface transportation, made the choice for the Japanese. By 14 October 1942, there were twenty-two thousand Japanese soldiers on the island with a similar number of Americans facing them.[233] Those twenty-two thousand soldiers would have required 110 tons of supplies per day to survive. Although the Tokyo Express averaged thirty-six destroyer loads a month to the island, the theoretical limit of cargo, without soldiers, was 1,440 tons—a seventeen-day deficit in sustenance per month.[234] Thus the Japanese improvised a system that could sustain five thousand soldiers, not twenty-five thousand.

The transport run of 15 October 1942—with a keen use of air, sea, and land power to blunt the Cactus Air Force—allowed the Japanese to go on the offensive. It was the apogee of their food supply. The offensives to take Henderson Field, however, sapped their reserves, and the Japanese were back in an emergency food situation by the first week of November. Although they attempted to innovate with barrel deliveries on destroyers, the ships were made to fight and thus insufficient for logistics.

While American food supplies decreased until 20 August 1942, the first day aircraft landed at Henderson Field they brought a steady increase in food. Moving that food and water forward during battles was difficult, and the Americans were on two-thirds rations for six weeks; however, by 18 September the Americans were back to full rations for front-line troops. In addition, the streamlined process, sparked by Halsey and delivered by Brigadier General Williamson, helped to increase the supply throughput to Guadalcanal from the port at Nouméa. By 1 December 1942, the island had excess beer. The Japanese fell down the other side of the starvation curve as the men on the island grew from five thousand soldiers in mid-September to twenty thousand by mid-October. After the failed delivery on 15 November 1942, the Japanese army at Guadalcanal was permanently debilitated, although valiant in the defense, as the Americans pushed through the jungle to their positions.

On 9 February 1942, Major General Patch triumphantly sent a dispatch to

Admiral Halsey: "[I] am happy to report this kind of compliance with your orders. . . . 'Tokyo Express' no longer has terminus on Guadalcanal."[235]

He was four months late. When the Japanese failed to dislodge the Cactus Air Force with the seaborne and airborne bombings of mid-October, the battle for supply was over. The Japanese had chosen speed over capacity, and although the Tokyo Express harassed the Americans and sent the Japanese soldiers that attacked them—all it brought was fleeting combat power. The Tokyo Express was never a transportation system with a terminus, but rather a makeshift logistics failure that ensured the death of almost two-thirds of the Japanese soldiers sent to Guadalcanal.

CONCLUSION

In a campaign to take control of an island, water transportation was the dominant mode at Guadalcanal for both sides. The capacities of the ship, transformed by diesel internal combustion engines for greater speed and size, delivered troops, supplies, and food in great quantities half a globe away from the US mainland and Japan. The moniker of dominance, however, brought a qualification for lines of supply from the sea during the Late Industrial Era. Transportation by water required control of the air.

Unlike previous eras, the ability to move men and material to battle depended on the control of another domain. In the Preindustrial Era, land power could affect water transportation and vice versa at short ranges—those of a cannonball or a musket. During the Industrial Era, the ranges expanded with long-range coastal artillery pieces and large-bore ship guns. In neither epoch was the success of one line of communication determined by control of the other domain. At Guadalcanal, however, the aircraft, with its speed, range, and firepower, dictated supply from the sea.

Since the Americans enjoyed control of the air for most of the campaign, they had a distinct advantage in supply. Control of the air also applied to the successful, but scant, Japanese supply deliveries. On 15 October 1942, the Japanese sea bombardment on Henderson Field, coupled with aircraft attacks, protected the biggest cargo run by the Japanese of the entire battle. The Japanese also deftly applied airpower to remove their soldiers from the island and avoid a complete loss—their most successful logistics movement of the campaign. In addition, both sides used airpower to attack ground forces. Japanese attacks affected American morale and sometimes slowed combat power, while US airpower limited the Japanese unloading operations and drove them into the disease-ridden jungle. This is not to say that surface fleets made no difference, but surface action could not control lines of supply as airpower did. Even in December 1942, the Japanese garnered a major surface victory at the battle of Tassafaronga, but this victory provided no lane for logistics.

Airpower was not complete in its dominance over sea transportation. Aircraft had primitive navigation and attitude-reference technologies. As a result, at night, in low-light conditions, or in bad weather, aircraft were in peril. While beacons and lighting set up at Henderson Field aided navigation, as did radar, technologies of the electromagnetic spectrum were new and needed significant improvement to make airpower effective at night and in the weather. This was akin to the issues surrounding the use of radar by the US Navy and the interpretation of radio reports by the Japanese during surface combat. New technologies were not a panacea, but rather a tool that took time to integrate. Even in the Late Industrial Era, both sides had their Fontenoy—an established pattern for conduction and supplying war—which demanded adaptation to the current conditions of war.

Land transportation on a remote island, without an established road network and covered in thick jungle, proved no easier for the belligerents during the Late Industrial Era than it was during the Industrial Era. Both had their supply challenges—water for the Americans and all manner of supply for the Japanese. The lack of logistics stalled units and pushed soldiers to the limiting capacity of the human body, stalling the combat power of the larger army, much as the mud in Flanders had stalled the British so completely that men wanted for water while caught in no-man's land. Late Industrial technology still had limits on land.

While movement overland was a struggle, delivery by air began to assume a role as a mode of transportation at Guadalcanal. The C-47 proved a valuable resource in evacuating sick and wounded American forces from the island. In addition, the navigational and operational rhythms established for medical relief helped pave the way for the critical fuel deliveries of mid-October. Although it is hard to determine how much the transportation of fuel raised stocks for the Cactus Air Force, it was enough to keep the aircraft active for a week. The small but significant amount likely contributed to the close-air-support missions flown to thwart the impending Japanese land offensive. Although it was not as dominant as the sea or land, at Guadalcanal the air mode of transportation offered a preview of how supplies could move with a speed unmatched by the former modes.

The technological limits of aircraft manifested in combat more than logistics, since airlift by C-47 was a small part of the overall deliveries to the island. At the Battle of Stalingrad, however, the case was different. With the German army cut off from its lines of communication on land, they attempted to supply themselves by air. Were the Germans able to adapt the technology of Late Industrial aircraft to deliver supplies in the winter, and to what effect? This is an important question for the next chapter.

If airpower dictated sea lines of communication—what happened to the vaunted submarine that had so gripped German and British imagination in the spring of 1917 in the fight for sea lines of communication? By comparison, the Battle for the North Atlantic seemed to repeat the template of the Great War—but in much greater scope with the improved technologies of the submarine, the cargo ship, the airplane, the radio, and the torpedo. The size of the Pacific, when compared to the Atlantic, may explain this difference, but the submarine was also part of the larger carrier- and surface-fleet battles that dominated the Pacific War. While Germany used its technological prowess to compete with the great sea powers of Britain and America, the Japanese and Americans were both great naval powers, and in 1942 equal in terms of capacity on the sea.

Thus, the Japanese focused their strategic gaze on the US carriers, and for good reason. With the success of Japanese submarines at the Battle of Midway and the subsequent sinking of the *Wasp* and damaging of the *Saratoga,* the underwater technology had done what the Japanese carriers could not— keep the American carriers at bay.[236] The problem with this strategy was that the airpower the Japanese needed to defeat was on the land, at Henderson Field, not on the ocean.

The Americans struck shipping targets with their submarines—critically the Ichiki reinforcement battalion—delaying the larger contingent of the Japanese soldiers from reaching the island until the Cactus Air Force had arrived. Like its enemy, however, the US Navy focused on the big targets, attempting to attack the carriers and capital ships more than shipping at this point in the war.[237] Only later in the war would the US Navy use submarines to great effect in destroying Japanese shipping.[238]

Geopolitical Impacts—Guadalcanal (Late Industrial Era)

If logistical planners understand the requirements and techniques of a major joint overseas amphibious invasion, they can handle lesser and simpler situations with relative ease.

—Henry Eccles, Captain, US Navy, *Operational Naval Logistics*

The lessons of logistics and combat power at Guadalcanal exemplified the Japanese mismatch between strategic priorities and logistics capabilities. In August 1942, with four years of unabated victory on land, many victories at sea, and the setback at Midway not quite realized, the Japanese thought they could continue their assault through Southeast Asia and the South Pacific unabated, while still holding their primary strategic objective of China. The initial tactical losses at Guadalcanal did nothing to change their direction. Instead, the Japanese seemed to embrace the counterfactual as a strategy and a logistics support plan: What if they had a few more soldiers, a few more artillery pieces, or a little more food? Then victory was certain. Only after two months of fighting and a significant drain on their resources did the Japanese readjust their operational priorities and shift forces from other regions, including China, to Guadalcanal. Paradoxically, the Japanese did so only when they were certain that the Soviets were tied up at Stalingrad rooting for a bogged down offensive for their German ally. By the time Japan refocused its priorities, however, the United States had solved its own logistics problems and cemented Marine positions on the island. This inability to change their strategic focus from China and the Soviets, along with failing to create a sufficient supply network to hold their gains, hurt the Japanese. Even after the loss at Guadalcanal, the insistence on another offensive toward Port Moresby and the Australians illustrated the Japanese lack of understanding of their own logistics' shortcomings and the strength of their adversary's.

The Japanese fixations on destroying the US Navy—both surface and carrier forces—did nothing to help this situation. Despite damaging or sinking all the US carriers in the region and adding thirty-five allied ships to Iron Bottom Sound, control of the sea did little to help them take the island of Guadalcanal. Had prewar planners, of either side, seen a war-gaming outcome in which the Japanese sunk or disabled three carriers, destroyed five US cruisers, and sent thirty other ships to the ocean floor, they would have likely concluded that it was a rout of the Americans. Instead, it was an utter Japanese defeat. US aircraft dominated.

For the United States, the lessons of Guadalcanal rippled through manuals, doctrine, and training. The exigencies of conducting an amphibious operation thousands of miles from the industrial base of supply helped to create a supply network, at first sufficient, and then evolving to a juggernaut of ships, aircraft, ammunition, and food by 1945. In 1942, the Japanese and Americans stood at parity in terms of naval power. By 1945, the United States Navy was bigger than all the other navies of the world combined, and the Japanese Navy was reduced to insignificance.

"Overgirding" this supply network was airpower. At the tactical level, airpower allowed the US to supply its Marines and soldiers on Guadalcanal and deny the Japanese the same. At the operational level, airpower gave the US a foothold in the Pacific and the ability to defend its own sea lines of communication from its ally of Australia to Hawaii and California. Airpower at Guadalcanal became the operational template for the rest of the war. Marines and army troops would land on distant islands to secure airfields or construct them. From these airfields, aircraft would attack farther and farther into Japanese territory. The projection of airpower gave the US control of supply from the sea, giving its submarines free reign to paralyze Japanese shipping—sinking a staggering 1,173 of Japanese merchant ships—and grinding the parasitic war economy of Japan to a halt.[239]

At the strategic level, control of the air and its byproduct, control of the sea lines of communication, allowed the Americans to connect their industrial might and supply networks to their ally, the Soviet Union, to defeat the Germans; while the Japanese, fearful of provoking the Soviet bear for the strategic priority of China, allowed this supply network to continue unabated and defeat their Axis ally. The United States used its control of the ocean and the air to deliver B-29s and atomic weapons by sea to the island of Tinian. The island, which Marines cleared of Japanese soldiers using the hard-won lessons of Guadalcanal, served as the platform to end the war.

4

Summer and Winter on Soviet Steppes
Stalingrad, 1942–1943

Who rules East Europe rules the Heartland; who rules the Heartland
commands the World-Island; who rules the World-Island controls the world.
—Halford Mackinder, *The Geographic Pivot of History*

The Late Industrial pull for resources drove the Third Reich, like its
Japanese ally, to expand the German Empire. The most important
of these acquisitions were to be land and oil. On the one side of
the equation was *Lebensraum* for the expanding German population, and on the other was the need to power the internal combustion engine for warfare, personified by the automobile and the airplane, symbols of German technological superiority and pride. To
get both, Adolf Hitler turned his forces from the west to the east, in
1941, and aimed for Halford Mackinder's *Heartland*, the resource-
rich and land-expansive region surrounding the Ukraine. Standing
in the way of the planned invasion—Operation Barbarossa—was
his erstwhile ally Joseph Stalin and the Soviet state.

During the interwar years, the association of the German nation with the older technology of the railroad had gravitated to the
faster and more mobile technologies of the airplane and the car.
The airplane was the ultimate technology of the Late Industrial Era,
with its construction of light alloys and a small-but-powerful engine, and the Third Reich used the Luftwaffe to great effect in the
Spanish Civil War and during planned state visits. James Corum, in
The Luftwaffe, notes that through these demonstrations, "The world

received the impression that the Germans had created a fearsome air force that could obliterate entire cities."[1] On the ground, Hitler's love of the automobile led to development of the Volkswagen car and the Autobahn.[2] The internal combustion engine and its requisite roadway personified a renewed German Reich, was a propaganda piece for Germans and visiting dignitaries alike, and represented a metaphysical rebirth of "harmony between technology and nature that Fritz Todt [Albert Speer's predecessor] believed the barbarous engineering of the railway age had destroyed."[3]

Despite an embrace of the Late Industrial technology under a utopian umbrella of harmony, the Germans needed rails to go to war. In 1941, and today, no technology could match the capacity of a train on land. The amount of rail used to perform the buildup for Barbarossa reflected this. The Germans moved the 141 divisions for Operation Barbarossa and their supplies to the front in over 33,500 trainloads between January and June 1941.[4] The resource-constrained Reich also had to reach back to the Preindustrial Era and recruit horses to do much of its heavy lifting. According contemporary author Chester Wilmot, "Because of the chronic shortage of oil, the Germans had never attempted to motorize their armies, as the Western powers had done. . . . Their panzer divisions were mechanized (though not on the same lavish scale as were the armored formations of the Allies) but in the infantry divisions two-thirds of the vehicles were drawn by horses."[5]

Not that the Germans did not have trucks and cars for the Eastern Front; in fact they had over five hundred thousand vehicles of all types for the start of Barbarossa.[6] However, the 33,500 trainloads of equipment and supplies now followed the panzer divisions in combinations of truck, car, horse, or human transports—all complicated by the primal state of Russian roads and the vagaries of weather in the Soviet Union.

While technological improvements from the Industrial to the Late Industrial Era increased the capacity of water transportation from hundreds of tons to thousands of tons, with only minor increases in speed, land transportation improvements reversed the equation. The railroad doubled capacity from fifteen hundred tons to three thousand tons, but increased its speed from 30 miles per hour to as high as 108 miles per hour. Although the Germans still used the power of an earlier era, coal-fired steam engines, the Soviets had some diesel-powered trains. The truck, still with a two-ton capacity, doubled its speed.

Melding the striking power of artillery and machine guns onto a mobile platform, the tank, first used in a large-scale operation by the British at Cambrai in 1917, formed the basis of the fast, mobile, and destructive arm of the German Wehrmacht—the panzer division. The Soviets, for their part, had superior armament in the T-34 tank: simple, effective, and capable of mass production. As at Guadalcanal, aircraft gained significant capability in both transportation and firepower to become a critical factor for both roles.[7] Despite the advances in combined arms, the German Wehrmacht had shown in Poland and France, the war to the east—with a harsh environment and massive enemy—would be the real test.

1941: LESSONS IN LOGISTICS

In the summer of 1941 during the first days of Barbarossa, as the German armies swallowed up hundreds of miles of steppe and forest, transportation vehicles struggled to keep up. Travel over the dirt roads of the Soviet Union, which turned to mud during summer storms and during the fall rainy season, chewed up tires and consumed fuel at a rate 40 percent greater than predicted.[8] Vehicles stalled, broke down, or were abandoned as the support units tried to keep pace with the panzers. At times, so many vehicles were stuck on Soviet roads that the Wehrmacht used the Luftwaffe to supply stalled columns of tanks and vehicles.[9] By November 1941, German vehicles numbered fewer than two hundred thousand.[10]

Despite the advanced technologies of the Luftwaffe flying overhead and the trucks moving down the road, the land forces of the Wehrmacht marched to war as they always had, on foot. In a bizarre mashing of logistics across all three eras of technology, the supply trucks sped ahead of the infantry, while planes flew overhead and struck Soviet rail and roads dozens of miles from the front, and *Eisenbahntruppe* struggled to extend German rail lines hundreds of miles to the rear.[11] The Luftwaffe guaranteed protection of the supply lines, but airplanes could build neither roads nor rails. Every mile the Germans moved forward was another mile the supporting logistics had to move as well—food, fuel, ammunition, vehicles, aircraft, soldiers, and supplies. In a situation Edward Braddock would have recognized, the fractal nature of logistics worked against the great distances the Germans covered. As a result, the Germans outran their supply lines eighteen miles from Moscow.

As they turned back to look west, their lines of supply stretched six hundred miles to the Polish border.[12]

Despite the tenuous supply lines and the difficulties of moving on Soviet roads and rail, the fall campaign was the most successful land operation in history. The Germans reduced the Soviets from five million soldiers to less than three million—with panzers encircling the Red Army in huge envelopments like those envisioned seventy years previous by Moltke—while the Luftwaffe flew ahead to interdict rails, roads, and men in retreat and attempting counterattack.[13] More important for German supply lines, the three-thousand-airplane-strong Luftwaffe destroyed over four thousand Soviet aircraft in the first week alone, keeping their logistics safe from attack.[14]

As the Germans stalled in the winter of 1941, straining against the Soviet weather and their overextended lines of communication, Stalin ordered his forces forward on the ice and snow. The Soviets pushed the Germans back; however, the Luftwaffe proved the deciding factor. German aircraft performed duties as front-line artillery, at first slowing the Soviet advance, then halting it. During these small but significant successes by the Soviets, Hitler ordered his armies to hold fast rather than move. As a result, the Soviet Army trapped one hundred thousand men of the Second Army in the Demyansk pocket in February 1943.[15]

At Demyansk, the transportation capability of the Luftwaffe saved the German land forces. According to the former head of Luftwaffe transportation forces, Generalmajor Fritz Morzik, "In four months of grueling work, marked by almost constant utilization of all the available personnel and material forces, the tremendous difficulties were overcome and the mission accomplished."[16] At the same time as Demyansk, the Luftwaffe also undertook the resupply of 3,500 men in the defensive pocket of Kholm through parachute drops alone.[17] Although successful, Morzik averred, "Demyansk, as it turned out, provided a rather dangerous illustration of the potential usefulness of air transport, for from this time on German military leaders were inclined to be indiscriminately enthusiastic regarding its employment."[18]

Mirroring his opponent, Stalin had also ordered his forces to hold at all cost outside of Moscow, throwing them unprepared, often without weapons, into offensive actions. For both sides, the commands of hold fast saved their armies and planted seeds of optimism within the minds of the dictators as to their strategic prowess. These perceptions of the winter campaigns of

1941–1942 set the stage for a bloody war of attrition at Stalingrad in 1942. By late spring, with Soviet advances exhausted and the freeze giving way to the late winter season of mud, the front stabilized.[19]

Operation Blau: Triumph of Hope over Logistics

After the brutal winter of 1941, which the Germans faced ill-equipped and under-supplied through tenuous lines of communications that stretched over hundreds of miles of mud, snow, and mud again, the warmth of spring brought a new hopefulness for the Wehrmacht.[20] The machinations of war in the Soviet steppes and forests claimed 207,000 horses, 300,000 vehicles of which 41,000 were trucks, and a staggering 917,985 human casualties, but the German lines held firm hundreds of miles into Soviet territory.[21] In addition, the Germans inflicted "just over six million casualties, with roughly 3.5 million killed, captured, or missing and about 2.5 million wounded or fallen ill."[22] Added to this operational achievement, significant efforts to revamp their logistics over the course of the campaign had resulted in more soldiers, horses, vehicles, and supplies moving into the front lines.[23] From July 1941 to the spring of 1942, the rail network supplying the *Ostheer* had grown to over 16,000 kilometers (9,760 miles) of single track and 5,922 kilometers (3,612 miles) of double lines with two hundred trains operating on the system each day.[24] Behind the German advances, millions of slave laborers poured back into captured territories and the Reich to boost production in armaments and other heavy industries through the gruesome ideological practice of *Vernichtung durch Arbeit* (Destruction through Labor).[25]

Thus, as the roads thawed, so did the bitter disappointments of lost opportunity to take Moscow. With a full complement of new tanks for his battalion, a German commander on the Southern Front remarked, "Morale was high again . . . we were in a good state."[26] The German high command felt that the losses of 1941 were mere setbacks—for the Soviets must be on the verge of collapse.

Nowhere was that optimism higher than with the Führer. Joseph Goebbels, the Reich's propaganda minister, recorded, "For the coming spring and summer the Führer has a clear plan. He does not want a boundless war. Its objectives are the Caucuses, Leningrad and Moscow."[27] As the talks continued with the German General Staff, the *Oberkommando des Heeres* (OKH), in early spring, the oil of the Caucuses became the prize for the new cam-

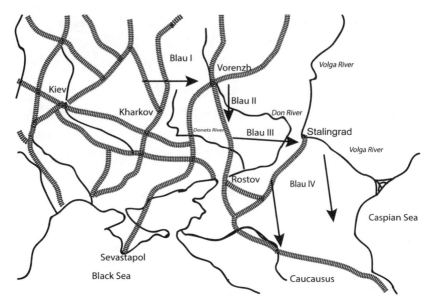

Figure 4.1. Blau 1-IV: German Drive toward Stalingrad and Caucausus, 1942. (Map by Avery Turner. Adapted from Max Bork "Comments on Russian Railroads and Highways," from the Historical Division, US Army Europe, 1957, e-book, http://www .allworldwars.com/Comments-on-Russian-Roads-and-Higways-by-Max-Bork.html; and Earl F. Ziemke and Magna E. Bauer, *Moscow to Stalingrad: Decision in the East* [Washington, DC: United States Army, 1987].)

paign, Operation Blau. Barbarossa had been costly in men and material, and Blau would reclaim resources, land, and prestige for the Germans. Hitler's optimism was so great that he promised the army would be in winter quarters by October.[28]

In the directive for Operation Blau, Number 41, Hitler first dictated Stalingrad's role. The directive ordered Army Group B to advance towards Stalingrad, with Hungarian, Italian, and Romanian Divisions holding the Northern Flank, and Army Group A moving forward on the Southern Flank, "To reach Stalingrad itself . . . or at least bring the city under heavy artillery fire to prevent its use as an industrial and transportation center."[29] Then, after isolating the city, Army Group B would secure the southern approaches to the city, while Army Group A moved south to take the Caucuses. An appraisal of the railroads and rivers of the Soviet Union in 1942, juxtaposed against the four-phased Operation Blau (Figure 4.1), reveals Stalingrad's importance to the logistics efforts of the Soviet Union and the oil-laden Caucasus.

By driving to the east first, the Germans planned to capture the key city of Voronezh, which was north and east of Kharkov where the two rail lines crossed east of the Don River, then push south to Rostov, and then east to Stalingrad. Through this movement, the *Ostheer* would cut all rail lines from the north and the interior of the Soviet Union leading to the Caucasus, guaranteeing the parasitic Third Reich its oil. After taking Stalingrad, the Germans could meet any attempted movement by the Soviets on the water, from the Caspian Sea up the Volga, with force. Once so situated, the Germans could fight forever.

Thus, much like Guadalcanal, Stalingrad was at the center of the logistics needs of the belligerents. Although taking the city was a subgoal of the German campaign in order to reach the Caucasus, isolating Stalingrad as a node of transportation was an important task. Unfortunately for the two million casualties claimed in the fight for the city, Hitler changed the strategy and Stalin followed.[30]

The optimism of Hitler and his subordinates belied a weakness in logistics offset by German ingenuity and hard work over the winter and spring of 1942. According to Generaloberst Erhard Rauss, "[In 1941] The Germans had no conception of mud as it exists in European Russia . . . after their first experience with mud, the Germans adopted the Russians' method of preserving roads through the muddy season. . . . Repair and maintenance of roads was assigned to engineer troops and to Organization Todt [paramilitary construction agency of the Nazi Party, auxiliary to the Wehrmacht]."[31] The Germans also used prisoners of war (POWs) to rebuild the rail gauges in the east to fit German trains, expanding the capacity and the speed of men and material moved to the Eastern Front, mitigating the need for more horses and vehicles at least early in the campaign.

The lack of capacity going forward for Operation Blau was the same in 1942 as it had been 1941. Whereas two hundred trains a day could move supplies to the front and slave labor to the rear, the capacity of the rails to the east of the German positions was twelve trains a day.[32] According to German General Max Bork, "One great disadvantage lies in the fact that all the traffic must pass through the Rostov bottleneck, so that either the troops advancing toward the Caucasus or those driving on Stalingrad will not receive adequate supplies. Even though the main line from Rostov to Baku does have sufficient capacity, numerous single-track stretches of the line slow up traffic considerably in view of the great distances involved."[33] With more limited rail capacity toward the direction of the Blau offensive (see Figure 4.1), the Germans would rely on roads to move, this time with a smaller corps of vehicles, leaning more on animals and men.[34]

After the experience of the mud in 1941, the Germans adjusted their scheme of transportation by shedding some of their Late Industrial technologies. Omar Bartov, in *Hitler's Army*, described this stripping away of elements of technology as, "The Demodernization of the Front."[35] Rather than rely on so many vehicles, the Germans placed even more emphasis on animal transportation in 1942. In 1941, during the summer invasion, the quaint Russian horse and cart epitomized the regressive Soviet mind. The Germans had even given the pair a derogatory name—*Panje*. After two seasons of mud and one of snow, the Germans held the humble method of transportation in high esteem. A German general remarked:

[In 1941] the tankers and truck drivers could not fail to notice the industrious little animals pulling heavily loaded peasant wagons cross-country whenever they were pushed off the road by the modern mechanical giants. They were looked upon sympathetically, but what was their performance compared to that of the steel colossi. . . . Any comparison obviously was out of the question. Many a man dismissed them with a disdainful gesture and the words: "A hundred years behind the times." Even next to the heavy cold-blooded draft horses and the tall mounts of the infantry divisions their dwarfish cousins seemed slightly ridiculous and insignificant. . . . A few months later the *Panje* horse was judged quite differently. It came into sudden demand during the muddy season when no motor vehicle could operate and any number of cold-blooded horses could not move the heavy guns and ammunition. How were the advance elements to be supplied when they were stranded without provisions? By *Panje* columns.[36]

In the same vein, the Germans stripped their trains of precision parts, which froze in the winter and required shipment forward from German manufacturing centers. They degraded their trains to match the crude machines of their Soviet enemy, running "stripped down locomotives until the severe weather receded."[37] Thus, despite the view of Blitzkrieg as fast-moving war, by 1942, logistics took a step back in technological sophistication, and those movements beyond railheads turned into *Pferd Krieg* (horse war).

Besides modes of transportation, tanks, armored vehicles, artillery, and airplanes were all in shorter supply in 1942 than they were in 1941. The Luftwaffe had 2,000 operable aircraft, down from 3,000 in 1941, with 4,903 aircraft destroyed in the year of war in the East.[38] In addition, the Wehrmacht lost "artillery, antitank guns, and mortars exceeded 13,600 gun tubes."[39] The German commander on the Southern Front, who felt his optimism surge after his unit received its full complement of tanks, did not know the weapons of war were moved from the North and Central Fronts—sixty-nine of their seventh-five divisions stripped of a third of their infantry and a quarter of their artillery to supply Operation Blau.[40]

Despite the wear of war and the need for replenishment in the East, Hitler and his Nazi leadership had yet to get the German economy on a full war footing.[41] The offensive in 1941 was too late for a fall harvest, and shipping conquered peoples back to manufacturing facilities to the west took up the bulk of train movements, making the Germans "land rich" but food and labor poor.[42] The fear of a food shortage at home and a return to the food crises of the First World War unsettled Hitler's dreams of *Lebensraum*. According to Adam Tooze, "For Hitler [control of the Ukraine] was *the* key priority, to be achieved prior to any other military consideration, the importance of which was only reinforced by the alarming decline in the German grain stocks."[43] Hitler wanted to avoid the food shortages Hindenburg had to attend to—the Führer was convinced the shortages of 1917 and 1918 had caused the capitulation of the German army.[44] As a result, the German government began severe rationing in captured lands by the middle of 1942.[45] Thus, the Germans began 1942 with an inefficient economy, political fears looming at home, and their forces extended hundreds of miles into enemy territory. By extension, the Wehrmacht's logistics were teetering on the edge. Despite the lack of material power and might of the 1941 offensive, Hitler stood fast on the knowledge that his army had almost finished the Soviets.

The Soviets: Loss and Logistics

Operation Barbarossa devastated the Soviet Union. Besides the aforementioned six million casualties, the Soviets ceded a "territory equivalent in U.S. terms to the entire region from the Atlantic coast to Springfield, Illinois."[46]

Added to this, the key agricultural region of the Ukraine was now in the hands of the Germans. Food production plummeted from 95.6 million tons of grain in 1940 to 26.7 million tons in 1942. The supply of farm animals, meat, dairy products, and other food staples followed the same precipitous path, and "by 1942 meat and dairy production shrank to half the 1940 totals and sugar to 5%."[47]

Despite these horrific losses, Stalin and the Soviet leadership accomplished a feat of logistics in their retreat. In the chaos of displacement, the Soviets moved Soviet industry east of the Ural Mountains and other regions, including the Volga River basin.[48] Despite competition for rail and road space with critical wartime logistics, the Soviets moved 1,523 industrial works and had over 1,200 of them back in operation by 1942.[49] In doing so, the Soviets moved their key manufacturing industries out of the reach of the Luftwaffe. While German aircraft savaged the Soviet Army and the roads and rails it traveled on, their manufacturing base was safe from aerial attack.

Stalin also secured manufacturing help from Britain and the United States. The Lend-Lease program began shipments in October 1941. By the end of 1942, Allied shipments totaled 2,500 aircraft, 3,000 tanks, 79,000 vehicles and "more important . . . were food supplies mostly shipped by way of Vladivostok [from the United States]. Food made up 14% of lend-lease tonnage, sufficient to feed over a million men for a year."[50]

By contrast, the Japanese and Germans never agreed to a strategy on how best to control the Pacific Ocean and link their own resources. According to Gerard Weinberg in *A World at Arms,* "The difficulties of establishing understanding between the partners in the Tripartite Pack make the frictions between Britain and the United States and even between either and the Soviet Union look minor by comparison."[51] Typical of this confusion, the Japanese allowed the Lend-Lease shipments to sail unmolested through their empire, at the expense of their German ally.

The Germans, however, did not sit still. From their Norwegian bases, the Germans sent two hundred aircraft in May 1942 to prowl the approaches to the northern port of Murmansk. With daylight approaching twenty-four hours, the Luftwaffe devastated Lend-Lease shipments. Between March and September 1942, the aircraft, with help from U-boats, sank sixty-one cargo ships.[52] The results for Lend-Lease shipments were devastating. In one particular attack in June 1942, the Germans sent 470 tanks to the bottom of the ocean.[53] Thus, as in waters surrounding Guadalcanal, shipment by sea to Europe required control of the air. This dominance over shipping waned as the war raged on in 1942, as the airpower requirements for Operation Blau thinned the ranks of the Luftwaffe in the north and allowed ships passage to Murmansk.

With the Axis unable to destroy Soviet manufacturing stationed deep into Central Asia, or choke off the Red Army from its Allied supply networks, the bludgeoned Soviets amassed their materiel. What Hitler saw as Soviet weakness—manifested by a year of tactical defeats—was rather a delay. While Hitler based the strategy in 1942 on an adequate, if diminished, disposition of material on the Eastern Front, hope of oil to the south, and a perceived frailty of his ideological enemy, Stalin had a positivity based on the growing economic output of his state, bolstered by his allies.

With the steady stream of trucks, aircraft, tanks, and foodstuffs reaching the Soviet Union, and industries ignited under the pressure of war, Stalin believed his materiel could destroy his overstretched opponent.[54] The winter of 1941 had given Stalin faith in his own military genius—he felt that his standfast order had saved Moscow and that the growing Red Army would overwhelm the Germans. In this vein, he pushed the Red Army staff, the *Stavka*, for a renewed offensive in the spring of 1942. Foreshadowing the coming campaign season, Stalin gave a speech to the Soviet population on May Day 1942, extolling Soviet strength and highlighting German weakness.[55] A week and a half later, his army surprised the Germans at Kharkov.

Kharkov: Soviets Strike First and the Luftwaffe Gets the Last Word

To begin Operation Blau, the Wehrmacht needed to reduce the salient surrounding Kharkov and capture of the fortress city at Sevastopol on the Crimean peninsula, the last remaining area of Soviet control. With these two moves, the Germans would cut off the Soviets from the Black Sea and allow buildup of logistics bases farther "east of the Northern Donets river" to support Blau.[56] While General Erich Von Manstein moved Army Group South's Eleventh Army to attack Sevastopol, with over six hundred Luftwaffe aircraft overhead, the Soviets attacked at Kharkov, surprising the Germans, on 12 May 1942.[57]

At Kharkov, the year-long materiel improvement of the Red Army and the manufacturing rebirth of the Soviet economy were in full display. The

Soviets arranged for five army groups to strike from the north and south to collapse the salient around Kharkov and ensnare the German armies protecting the city.[58] The force under Marshal Semyon Timoshenko had five hundred tanks, 750,000 personnel, and six hundred aircraft of the *Voyennovozdushnye sily* (VVS—the Soviet Air Force).[59]

From the beginning, the Soviets suffered from logistics missteps. In moving the massive force forward in the spring mud, the Red Army suffered the same logistical delays that their enemy had. The Soviet after-action reported stated:

The absence of a sufficient number of highways and dire roads, the presence of only one lateral railroad line with a traffic capacity of 10–12 trains every 24 hours . . . required army staffs to plan precisely for the arrival of forces in the regions . . . [and] regulate traffic precisely on crossing and organize reliable air cover over crossings sites and concentration areas . . . it was also necessary to expend a large quantity of material and employ a considerable number of people for repair, road construction and road maintenance.[60]

Besides the tactical issues of moving the army forward in battle, the complex logistics permutations of industrial warfare, heretofore unexecuted in Soviet operations, led to incomplete supplying of the front lines before the operation. The artillery units had only a two-day supply of shells versus a five-and-a-half-day planned allotment, and only seventeen of the thirty-two units were ready to move at the start of the offensive.[61] In addition, as the units moved forward, the complexity of positioning reserves and synchronizing movement forward to support battle caused several units to run into the supply lines of others.[62]

Despite their beginning difficulties, the Soviets were undetected and unmolested because of the Luftwaffe's concentration in the Crimea. With enemy aircraft absent, the Soviets' attack drove the Germans back in shock. The VVS performed an initial air attack lasting fifteen minutes, and the Soviet tanks followed with infantry in tow. During the first day, the Luftwaffe, with its miniscule complement, flew twenty-one sorties while the VVS managed over six hundred.[63] The commander of the German Sixth Army recorded, "being hit by 12 rifle divisions and 200 tanks in the first waves. Veteran troops, who had fought through the winter, were overawed by the masses of armor rolling in on them that morning."[64] With numerous tanks and air superiority for the first three days, the Soviets advanced as much as twenty-four miles into the German flanks.[65]

After the initial successes, Soviet transportation could not sustain the advances: "In conditions of the spring thaw motor and animal-drawn transport could not cope with the tasks of delivering material to the forces, and as a result, attacking forces, on the fourth or fifth day of the operations, were already experiencing acute shortages of munitions and fuel."[66] Added to the problems of moving their logistics forward, the Soviets had poor radios, which hampered their ability to coordinate offensive movement with follow-on logistics. After their advance, the Soviets held on to thin and uncoordinated supply lines stretching behind them.

Overhead this precarious situation, the Luftwaffe arrived. Oberst Anton Freiherr von Bechtolzheim recorded, "The army group hurriedly recalled the bulk of the Fourth Air Fleet from the Crimea—where fortunately victory was in the offing—to the battlefields around Kharkov."[67] The German machines hammered the two Soviet armies in the north while panzers under Generals Paul Ludwig Ewald Von Kleist and Friedrich Paulus counterattacked from the south. The Luftwaffe scattered the VVS, and so complete was Fliegerkorps IV and VII's domination of Soviet ground maneuvers that they "were often at the scene of action within 20 minutes of the army summoning help."[68] Over the next several days, as Kleist's army group enveloped the extended Soviets, German aircraft sealed off the defenders from their reinforcements and cut off all movements of supply.

By 24 May 1942, the Luftwaffe had cut out all bridges behind Timoshenko's forces, save one.[69] With limited transportation, the logistics of the Red Army imploded. The Soviet after-action report stated, "During the defensive battles, the small number of crossings over the Northern Donets River and the poor organization for their exploitation represented the worst bottle-necks in the work of rear service organizations."[70] Adding to the confusion, the German menace from the air prevented movement by day and relegated vehicle movement, whether tanks or logistics support, to hours of darkness—exacerbating delays.[71] In this confusion, the Luftwaffe wrecked Timoshenko's army. According to Fliegerkorps IV's battle reports, their aircraft destroyed "3,038 motor vehicles, 1,686 horse-drawn wagons . . . 6 complete trains . . . 14 munitions camps, 10 supply camps, and various other installations."[72] The deep-envelopment operations of famed Soviet marshall

Zhukov were still a year away, and the results were catastrophic in the nascent test at Kharkov: 270,000 Soviet casualties added to the 176,566 lost in the unsuccessful defense of Sevastopol.[73]

With the victories at Kharkov and Sevastopol, May through July 1942, the winter nightmare abated for the Germans. As Stephen Fritz states in *Ostkrieg,* "Victories in the Crimea and Kharkov had done much to restore German confidence and morale, while the shaky Soviet performance rekindled inflated notions of easy triumphs leading to the quick seizure of the Caucasian oil fields."[74] Although these victories resulted in fewer than twenty thousand casualties, they had come at a cost in war equipment. In attacking Kharkov and Sevastopol, the Luftwaffe had lost over three hundred planes.[75] Even worse, the lost pilots were a resource harder to replace, with months' worth of training necessary to build combat-ready aircrew.[76] Finally, the dependence that Operation Blau placed on the allied Axis armies of Romania, Hungary, and Italy to defend the northern flank illustrated that available resources did not meet the strategic appetite of the Third Reich. The Germans were at their limit before the push to Stalingrad, but did not realize it.

The initial Soviet and German maneuvers at Kharkov illustrated how important airpower had become to logistics on land. Offensive operations or beating a retreat required control of the air to prevent the destruction of supplies. Added to this, integration of the communication between combat arms and their supplying forces—perfected by the Germans after four campaigns and muddled by the Soviets in their first try—was crucial. Like the battle for Guadalcanal, Late Industrial technology, whether the aircraft or the radio, was no panacea for warfare and required integration and experience to hone its use.

For the Germans, the experience at Kharkov, in which the Luftwaffe saved the day, elevated the prestige of the air arm from expedient to expectant savior. In his study after the war, Luftwaffe General Hermann Plocher stated, "The Luftwaffe had become what might be called a firefighting force, which could speedily and flexibly brought to bear whenever and wherever a crisis arose."[77] This use of airpower as the salve for combat ills further stressed the supply lines stretching from the Reich to Stalingrad. As the Germans drew farther and farther east and fought more war in the summer of 1942, their airpower would complete for supplies and fuel with the panzers and ground forces. For the Soviets, airpower provided great help in the first few days of

Kharkov, but their pilots were no match for the Luftwaffe despite their numbers. As German General Paul Deichmann stated after the war, "[In 1942] the Russian Air Force was more annoying than destructive."[78]

THE BEGINNING OF THE END OF
THE REICH: OPERATION BLAU

On 28 June 1942, Operation Blau and the drive for Stalingrad began. With 1,635 tanks, 1,640 aircraft, 17,000 guns and mortars, and 1.25 million soldiers (three hundred thousand of them Hungarian, Italian, and Romanian), Hitler's army began the drive east toward the Don River.[79] Since the Germans needed rail to move the large amounts of supplies and numbers of forces of the *Ostheer*, they aimed to capture the two north-south railways east of Kharkov at the junction in Voronezh, just to the east of the Don River (see Figure 4.1).[80]

The initial operation was a success much like those enjoyed in 1939, 1940, and 1941—the mobile and combined arms formula of Blitzkrieg in full maturity. At any given moment, one hundred aircraft "were active against single Soviet divisions at the tip of German spearheads," according to Soviet General Kazakov.[81] The German tanks with motorized infantry behind them rolled up Soviet tanks and soldiers. Adding to the firepower in front of the panzers, Luftwaffe Generals Wolfram von Richtofen and Johann Pfulgbeil sent Fliegerkorps VIII and IV against railcars and ground transportation. The heaviest bombardment was at Voronezh, with its rail junctions and access to the Don River.[82]

On 5 July 1942, the Germans neared Voronezh. Stalin, convinced of the superiority of his materiel and personnel over the advancing Germans, ordered a full counterattack. He sent an order to Marshall Fillip Golikov, who commanded Soviet forces around Voronezh, "Remember well and truly—You now have more than 1,000 tanks, and the enemy, 300–350 tanks at the most. Everything now depends on your skillful employment and precise command and control of these forces."[83] The Luftwaffe interfered with Stalin's synopsis.

With the VVS providing only weak cover, *Stuka* and He-111 bombers hit Soviet supply columns moving into Voronezh by rail and road.[84] These attacks slowed the Soviets. They started late on 6 July 1942 and never caught up. Although there were specific tactical fights in which Soviet T-34s inflicted great damage on the German panzers, in one battle destroying thirty-eight tanks, the same could not be said for the movement of their reserves, supplies, and command-and-control facilities to the front.[85] Soviet command, steeped in secrecy, relied more on written orders than the radio, fearing German interception.[86] Without proper use of the electromagnetic spectrum, and with the Luftwaffe harassing and attacking lines of communication at will, the Soviets could neither reinforce nor control their forces.[87]

Although just one of many battles as the German forces raced across the steppes to Stalingrad, Voronezh was the archetype. German offensive with control of the air was followed by attempted Soviet counterattack without control of the air. Without control of the air, the Soviets could not reinforce or resupply themselves despite limited tactical success, spelling victory for the Germans. With Voronezh under their control by early July, the German results were impressive. An army of three panzer corps leading motorized infantry, foot-borne soldiers following at "10 Kilometer Tempo (six miles per hour)," and horse-drawn *Panje* carts plodding behind had advanced 120 miles in fewer than fifteen days.[88] With a balance of forces similar to Kharkov, the Soviets had more tanks, artillery pieces, and aircraft, but lacked the integration of combat arms and logistics required to bring them forward with coherence and purpose.

With Voronezh taken, the German armies to the south began their push to link with General Paulus, as his Sixth Army moved along the Don toward Stalingrad. Full of heady optimism in July, and with a worry about the oil resources the massive campaign required, Hitler changed the plan for Operation Blau. Antony Beevor remarks in *Stalingrad: The Fateful Siege 1942–1943,* "Hitler became increasingly impatient with delays that were essentially his own fault. *Panzer* divisions would streak ahead in sudden breakthroughs, but then came to a halt at a crucial moment when fuel ran out."[89] The Germans needed fuel to get fuel, and Hitler fretted that he had to get to the Caucasus sooner than on the planned schedule.

Rather than have Army Group B, under General Fedor Von Bock, push toward the East to join the Sixth Army as it moved south along the railway from Voronezh to Rostov for a drive to Stalingrad (see Figure 4.1), Hitler split the force in two, hoping to encircle the Soviets along two fronts.[90] In doing so, he pulled the Fourth Panzer Group away from the Sixth Army, leaving Paulus with the weaker allied armies of the Romanians, Hungarians, and Italians to protect his northeast flank and without tanks for the space of a few weeks.[91] The lack of railheads for the Sixth Army to follow made the situation even worse for logistics, forcing the Germans to rely more on trucks and roads. In exasperation, General Bock recorded, "sending all available forces ahead [to encircle the Soviets around Rostov] in the direction of Kamensk is impossible on the account of road conditions. Each motorized unit now needs its own road."[92]

Despite its voracious appetite for resources, Hitler's first change worked. By the end of July, the German war machine churned up 568,347 Soviet casualties, 2,436 tanks, 13,716 artillery pieces, and 783 aircraft, with Rostov and the route to the Caucasus clear.[93] Hitler, impatient and intoxicated with the optimism of summer, altered plans again, splitting the force for the last time. Hitler bolstered Army Group B—comprising Paulus' Sixth Army with two panzer divisions from Army Group A—for a planned conquest of Stalingrad, with the Luftwaffe concentrating on the city to avoid destroying the much-needed oil fields in the south.[94] Army Group A would continue the push south into the Caucasus.[95]

Thus, rather than the phased plans of the original Blau III to Blau IV (see Figure 4.1), Hitler directed the armies to conquer the oil fields and Stalingrad, with fewer available forces for each operation. As the armies split to take on these two daunting tasks, Hitler continued to shuffle tanks and men between them, devouring fuel, ammunition, and time.

While the Soviets suffered during the German drives east and south, they were also learning and amassing material strength. Starting with the significant resistance at Voronezh, the Soviets slowed the German army. The initial thrusts of Blau moved at 10 kilometers per day, slowed to 4–5 kilometers a day by 17 July, and as Paulus prepared to invest the city in mid-August the Sixth Army crawled at 1.5–1.75 kilometers day (1–2.2 miles)—a rate familiar to Braddock, Abercrombie, Haig, and the US Marines and Japanese soldiers at Guadalcanal.[96] Although their tactics reflected outdated frontal assaults and isolated unit attacks, versus the combined-arms tenets developed later in the war, the defenders continued to field enough soldiers, tanks, and planes to slow the Germans down, "reappearing, seemingly from Soviet graveyards."[97]

Rather than a graveyard, the Soviet manufacturing base and supplies of Lend-Lease made the Soviet armies reappear. The supply network that linked the two largest economies in the world manifested itself, even amidst German victory, as German officers relished the American-made Jeeps they captured from the Soviets.[98] Against this formidable resource, the Führer had split his army and stretched the logistics of the Sixth Army to the breaking point—its tanks and motorized divisions reduced to less than half their fighting strength by the middle of August.[99] In an ironic twist, it was the prowess of German airpower and the rapacious living off the fruits of the invaded Soviet countryside that helped conceal the material weaknesses of the Wehrmacht.

Luftwaffe and Logistics: The German Summer on the Steppes

During the race to Stalingrad, the only limits the Luftwaffe seemed to have were weather and daylight. As for the pilots who flew over Guadalcanal, flying aircraft in the weather on the Eastern Front was risky and borderline fatal. Neither the Germans nor the Soviets had a better solution to the technological limits of flying without a visible horizon during the night or in bad weather. On the German side, the Junkers Ju-87 *Stuka* dive-bomber had no navigational instruments, and its internal radio had a transmit range of only 50 miles and a reception range of less than 120 miles.[100] With limited instruments, *Stukas* flew only "1000 feet into a cloud deck," to be certain they could exit the weather and see the horizon for flying reference, making flight in rain, snow, or darkness rare.[101] Thus, the weather and the rotation of the earth dictated what airpower could and could not do.[102] The summer days with long hours and good weather hid the marked weakness of aircraft in the cold, dark weather of late fall and winter, less than three months away.

With their advantage during daylight, the Luftwaffe pummeled Soviet T-34s and approaching supply columns all while performing reconnaissance undeterred, reporting Soviet movements. With the limited rail lines, cities with junctions like Voronezh and Rostov were key centers for observation and attack. As Hitler changed the original Blau plans in July, Fliegerkorps VIII's staff reported daily on train movements south of Rostov.[103] If the Soviet trains were moving, then the army could determine where the most logical point for the next Soviet counterattack or defensive movement would occur.

For the logistics on the ground, motorized vehicles moved as long as the dry spells prevailed and the *Panje* carts plodded along behind. Summer rain

Figure 4.2. *Panje* **Cart Moving through Mud.** With the clothing the driver is wearing, this is probably in the spring or fall, but it serves as an example of what the Soviet steppes looked like after rain or thaw. (Reprinted from *Pamphlet, No. 20-20: Terrain Factors in the Russian Campaign* [Washington, DC: Department of the Army, 1951].)

showers, however, slowed the logistics moves, just as the fall and spring muds had during the first half of the war. While *Panje* carts were better than vehicles, they still suffered in the mud (see Figure 4.2).

As in the summer of 1941, with movement off the precious rail lines and over the primitive roads of the steppes to Stalingrad, fuel became a precious resource. As panzer units broke off from Voronezh to move south, they waited two days for fuel. Much as the Marines had done for their aircraft at Henderson field, the Germans did for their panzers, scrounging fuel from nonfunctioning vehicles and supplementing with fuel delivered by Junkers Ju-52 transport aircraft.[104]

The Luftwaffe's transportation fleet performed many emergency airlift missions in the summer of 1942 to rectify the fuel situation. The Ju-52s moved 4,600 tons of fuel and 1,800 tons of ammunition to armored divisions approaching Stalingrad in August.[105] This was a significant amount of support. At the Battle for the Don Bend, as the Sixth Army approached the city, the Germans had 290 tanks on the front.[106] A full fuel load for all 290 tanks comprised 125 tons; in theory, the 4,600 tons of fuel the Luftwaffe would have fueled up the tanks 37 times![107] However, a full German panzer division had three hundred vehicles attached in support, with an estimated fuel usage of 300 tons of fuel per day.[108] Placing this number onto the relative strengths of the Sixth Army, the Sixth Army needed 650 tons of fuel per day.[109] With the airlift missions, the Luftwaffe provided fuel for seven full days of the operation, pushing the Sixth Army forward in its final steps to Stalingrad.

In addition, the Luftwaffe moved 27,000 soldiers forward while evacuating 51,700 wounded to care behind the front.[110] Troop evacuation was critical. With their logistics straining under the weight, the Germans had to ensure that every ounce of food, fuel, and ammunition went to combat-capable soldiers versus the sick and injured. By the summer of 1942, building on their feats at Demyansk and Kholm early in the winter, the Germans had learned how to execute a robust line of communication through the air, the first in history.

Although this line of communication helped push the panzers of the Sixth Army to Stalingrad, the speed came at a terrific cost in aircraft fuel. A Ju-52 burned 1,240 pounds of fuel an hour compared with 20 pounds per hour for a supply truck—sixty-two times as much.[111] Yet, the Ju-52 was only ten times as fast, and the required downloading and maintenance upon landing reduced this speed to only four times as fast as a truck. Table 4.1 shows how much a delivery of cargo cost, in fuel, for a theoretical delivery of 120 miles to the front. An aircraft burned 50 percent of the fuel it could deliver in transit,

Table 4.1. Fuel Delivery by Air and Land, Luftwaffe and German Army, 1942

Mode (Technology)	Speed (mph)	Trips per 24 Hours	Fuel Delivered (tons)	Fuel Burned (tons)
Air (1 Ju-52 Aircraft)	120	4	8.0	4.5
Land (10 Opel Trucks)	20	1	18.46	1.9

Sources: Data compiled from "BMW 132," Wikimedia Foundation, accessed 5 February 2016, https://en.wikipedia.org/wiki/BMW_132; and Robert Forczyk, *Tank Warfare on the Eastern Front 1941–1942: Schwerpunkt* (South Yorkshire, England: Pen & Sword Books Limited, 2014).
Note: Transport aircraft did not fly at night and land at unimproved airfields like the roads and fields of the steppes. Daylight approached sixteen hours a day in the summer; therefore, four round trips—two-hour round trip plus an hour of unload and loading time on each end—were possible.

while a truck burned 10.5 percent of its fuel load travelling to the front. In bursts, the speed was worth it, and with roads clogged during rainy days and the panzers stopped without fuel, the Germans had no choice.

From June to August 1942, the fuel needs of the Luftwaffe competed with the same units its transport planes tried to supply at the front. This competition mirrored the fractious and bankrupt ideology of the leadership of the Third Reich. The Luftwaffe, long a favorite of Hitler, had its own supply line back to the Reich, including an entire manufacturing sector separate from other Wehrmacht efforts.[112] The rivalry between the services created competitions between the two systems of logistics—supply for the Luftwaffe and supply for the Landwehr—subject to the political machinations of Third Reich leadership, in which everyone clamored for the favor of the Führer. This tension created a system of supply out of touch with the realities of the front.[113] Such a race for top billing as political sycophant doomed the supply system to the east, which stretched to unimaginable lengths as the Germans approached Stalingrad in August 1942. In his postwar analysis, former Luftwaffe Generalmajor Hans Detlef Herhudt Von Rhoden summed up the transportation difficulties facing the front in the summer of 1942:

The quantity of available supply good was sufficient, but the transportation facilities suffered from the great distances and the low capacity of the three available one-track railroads running from Germany to the Taganrog (Black Sea)-Stalino-Charkow-Kursk Line. The difficulties may be understood when it is known that the following units had to be furnished supplies: A. Six (6) Armies. B. Two (2) Fliegerkorps C. Four (4) to Six (6) Flak divisions. D. Two (2) Rumanian Armies (second echelon). E. One (1) Rumanian Flying Corps. Including rear installations for them all. Distances Involved: From Stalino to Stalingrad—300 miles. . . . Length of the front line . . . by end of June 330 miles . . . by end of August 1100 miles.[114]

Thus, an ever-weakening line of communication supported Hitler's successes during the summer campaign. Airlift helped in the short term but required more fuel, parts, and supply as the offensive lengthened the long line of communication from the Reich. The weaknesses did not manifest itself until later, as the lessening daylight and cold weather impeded the Luftwaffe and thus protected the growing materiel of the Soviet army. As Paulus and his Sixth Army approached Stalingrad at the end of their supply line, the Luftwaffe was losing its lift.

While the Luftwaffe helped pull the Wehrmacht to Stalingrad with its mobile firepower and supply, the grassy steppes offered sustenance for the horses and camels pulling the bulk of the supplies behind them. For the human invaders, the Soviet villages became grocery stores and supply centers. Although many of the Ukrainians were yearning to break free of the Soviet yoke, the Germans cared not and focused on their own subsistence.[115] The rapacious living off the land reflected the racial ideology of the Third Reich and the brutality of war on the Eastern Front. The Germans came to conquer and exterminate—not rule.[116]

Parasitic living off the land gave soldiers a boost of confidence and, combined with the warm weather and battlefield successes, seemed to portend victory. A company commander in the 384th Infantry Division reported, "I've never eaten so much as here. We eat honey with spoons until we're sick, and in the evening we eat boiled ham."[117] This summer of success at the operational level was a fleeting moment, and there were signs that the supply lines, material, and labor that Hitler had committed to taking this region of the Soviet Union presented great risk to the grand strategy of the war. For example, as German soldiers drove closer to Stalingrad, the Soviets burned villages and, worse yet, poisoned the wells.[118] In another example, a German solider reported that Soviet night-bombing attacks had set part of the steppes on fire to destroy sources of fodder.[119] The Soviets, beaten and battered over a year of fighting, were learning to fight back and accumulating their supplies for war.

Soviet Lessons of Logistics: Deception and Determination

As the Germans culminated outside Stalingrad, using increasing amounts of firepower to gain ever-smaller stretches of territory, the Soviets revamped their logistics. The aforementioned strategic retreat of their industry was the first success. Their failures to break through in the winter of 1941 and at Kharkov in May of 1942, and their defeats at the hands of the Wehrmacht on the retreat to Stalingrad taught them more. With his state teetering on the edge, Stalin ordered a review within the military to digest the lessons learned from two seasons of defeat. In frank discussions within the *Stavka*, the Red Army recorded its failures.

From the perspective of logistics, the first lesson was the threat airpower posed to Soviet lines of communication. At Kharkov, German airpower

protected its own supply line while also inhibiting the flow of Soviet material and men to the front. In their review of the battle, Soviet officers recorded, "Having gained air superiority over the battlefield, the enemy was
able to protect its operations with strong tactical aviation support, concentrating its bombers on . . . second echelons, and on roads and river
crossing within the area of combat operations."[120] The effects of airpower
on Soviet supply and transportation in the retreat to the Don and toward
Stalingrad followed the same pattern. The Luftwaffe rendered two main
train lines that supported Stalingrad useless, and the Red Army scrambled
to have a supply of one day in ammunition and two days in fuel.[121] Without
planning for the effect of airpower on their transportation networks, the
Soviets were doomed.

The Soviets also understood and articulated the danger that aircraft posed
to their rear-area support and logistics. In a treatise on rear-area forces, the
Stavka stated, "The primary means of enemy pressures on the rear is aviation
used for the purpose of demolishing administration stations, bases (field and
fixed depots), supply stations, railroads, bridges, tunnels, and viaducts."[122]
To combat airpower, the staff reported that a "well-organized air defense of
the primary objects in the army rear has particular significance."[123] To defend their transportation and supply, the *Stavka* assigned centralized control
of the defense under the chief of the army rear area and dictated several overarching tasks for the chief to accomplish. These tasks included air defense
and observation, defining defense sectors, and planning for the defense of
important targets.[124]

Added to the need to concentrate firepower on the Luftwaffe was the
requirement to conceal Soviet supply movements from reconnaissance
missions. The *Stavka* directed, "In organizing the army rear, *maskirovka*,
[deception and concealment] should be widely used. The deployment of rear
units . . . should be dispersed and concealed from air observation. Mass work
on loading and unloading transports at the administration station, supply
stations, unloading station, and change point should be conducted at night
when possible. The massing of transports and trains at central railroad stations should not be allowed."[125] The reconnaissance of the Luftwaffe, which
combed the railways and roads for movement, had taken its toll over the
summer. For their future offensives, the Soviets would adapt their transportation by using concealment and movement during bad weather and the

night to counter the technology of the airplane and keep their combat materiel out of the vision and reach of the Luftwaffe.

Besides the threat airpower presented to Soviet logistics, the *Stavka* also
noted the improvements needed for their own transportation and supply.
They had to mimic the same improvements necessary to compete in modern Late Industrial warfare, improved command and control, and use of the
electromagnetic spectrum. Shoving supplies and men forward without synchronizing with the front slowed the advance and put the supplies at risk to
airpower. The logistics needs of industrial warfare demanded enough fuel,
food, and ammunition to support a breakthrough and advance. To organize
the front the Soviet staff defined boundary areas for the front line, the "immediate rear area . . . demarcation lines with rear areas of neighboring armies
and that of the rearmost boundary by the line of the rear support area of the
front."[126]

Within this geographic framework, the *Stavka* ordered a specific command and control system. While the Germans continued to rely on supply
companies assigned to individual divisions, the Soviets centralized their supply and transportation to avoid backlogs, delays, and uncoordinated operations, which often left logistics to the vagaries of the local commander rather
than the exigencies of the bigger operation.[127] In just one example of this
centralized control, the *Stavka* dictated:

The army railroad sector (or with a poorly-developed railroad network, automobile and water sectors) is the primary means of communication for the army.
. . . The dispatch of all railroad transport to an army address should be done *only
through the army administration* [emphasis added]. . . . The chief of the army
base is the head of the army administration station region . . . and bears full responsibility for the overall order, security and defense. . . . The chief of the army
base is subordinate to the chief of the army rear.[128]

The chief of the army rear also reported to the army commander with the
order to use "Telephone and radio communications . . . for communications and warning."[129] Such a network of information and material was one
Sir Eric Geddes on the Western Front in 1917 or Admiral Halsey at Nouméa
would have recognized as necessary for modern war. The volume of war material of the Late Industrial Era required strong centralized control to flow
and meter supplies to battle.[130]

While the *Stavka* applied the lessons of logistics to future operations, Stalin applied pressure on the Red Army. During the midst of the German advances in July 1942, Stalin issued NKO Order No. 227. In it he stated,

The enemy is throwing new forces forward to the Don, and despite increasing losses, is thrusting forward, bursting into the depths of the Soviet Union. . . . Therefore, we must radically nip in the bud the talk that we have an opportunity to retreat without end . . . if the retreat does not cease, we will be left without bread, without oil, without metal, without raw materials, without mills and factories, and without railroads. From all of this it follows that it is time to end the retreat. Not a step back![131]

This order galvanized the Soviet Army and changed how its leaders viewed the coming battle of Stalingrad. For logistics, this had great impact. The order gave precious time for the Soviet manufacturing base, transportation network, and the fruits of Lend-Lease to move men and material into the area for a counteroffensive. For those Soviet soldiers in the city of Stalingrad, the order doomed them to become means to an end—their dogged resistance provided the time necessary to amass resources for the struggle, but they received little sustenance.

THE BATTLE FOR STALINGRAD, AUGUST TO NOVEMBER 1942: MEAT GRINDER OF LATE INDUSTRIAL WAR

As General Paulus's Sixth Army, under Army Group B, arrived on the outskirts of Stalingrad in August 1942, the list of territory taken, from the Kharkov salient, to Rostov and the Great Bend in the Don, to the region between the Don and Volga Rivers just to the west of the city, was impressive. The Germans had expanded the Soviet defense zone from 360 miles to 1200 miles and in the process chewed through thirteen full Soviet armies.[132] To the south, Army Group A under General List was knocking on the door of Caucasus. Despite the successes, the strategic uncertainty of the Führer came to bear on the situation again in August, when Hitler made Stalingrad his all-consuming focus, pulling away significant men and material from Army Group A and pointing his forces toward the original goal of oil in the Caucus again.[133] Hitler based his reasoning on the assumed weakness of the Soviet Army and the ideological satisfaction of taking the city named for his nemesis. He was not at the front to watch the tenacity of the Red Army, as his generals were.

During the drive to Stalingrad, the Soviets fought with growing ferociousness. Fortified by Stalin's order to hold fast, their growing tactical expertise, and supplies from Lend-Lease, the Soviets were a formidable foe. XIV Panzer Corps, led by General Wietershiem, lost "up to 500 men per day" in their final push to cut the Soviet Sixty-Second Army off at the intersection of the Volga and Don.[134] Hailed as victory back in Berlin, according to David Glantz in *To the Gates of Stalingrad*, Weitershiem's operation "set the pattern for at best, victory in a deadly war of attrition, and at worse nothing more than a stalemate."[135]

In no area did the cost of summer war show more than in the German air arm. The Luftwaffe lost 1,224 aircraft in only three months: June, July, and August 1942.[136] Although German industry replaced these aircraft, reflecting improved logistics from the Reich to the Eastern Front, pilots could not be replenished overnight, cutting into the combat experience of the force.[137] In addition, rather than support one offensive as envisioned in Hitler's Directive No. 41, the Luftwaffe now had to prowl over a twelve-hundred-mile front supporting the operations at Stalingrad, the Caucasus, and the extended front stretching west along the Don to Voronezh.[138] The coming cold weather and shorter days would further reduce the capability of the Luftwaffe.

On 23 August 1942, over six hundred Luftwaffe aircraft performed sixteen hundred sorties, dropping one thousand tons of bombs on Stalingrad to open the way for the Sixth Army.[139] To boost the aircraft count, Hitler's staff ordered all aircraft to Stalingrad—even those from the Caucasus. In exasperation, General Richtofen, the head of Luftflotte 4, told the Sixth Army, "Make use of today! You'll be supported by 1,200 aircraft [Richtofen likely meant sorties]. Tomorrow I can't promise you any more."[140] The bombing devastated the civilian population that remained and turned the city to rubble.

The German Army followed the bombing into the city. After the first week, Soviet resistance stiffened. The Red Army kept reinforcing the city, Stalin's admonition of "Not One Step Back" ringing in their ears. The battle for the city devolved from engagements for blocks, then for buildings, and finally rooms.[141] As the battles drew into September and October, each industrial landmark became a prize to win, from the city's grain elevator to the tractor factory and the "tennis racket," a railroad loop in the center of the city. As the Germans slowly and with great loss—losing 38,700 casualties in August and September—pushed the Soviets back toward the Volga, Hitler continued to keep Stalingrad as the all-consuming objective.[142] This occurred even as the advance of Army Group A to the oil fields in the Caucasus stalled. On the Soviet side, the pressure was the same. To hold the city they needed time to amass their forces for an offensive counterattack: Operation Uranus.[143]

With the prestige of taking the city conflated with the honor of the Führer and the pride of the Third Reich, Paulus and his Army commanders turned to the Luftwaffe to pound the city into submission—and it did. While the initial bombing dropped one thousand tons of bombs over the entire city, later attacks focused hundreds of tons of bombs on individual targets. For example, in October the Luftwaffe dropped six hundred tons of bombs on just the tractor factory, to prepare the way for a ground assault.[144] For Von Richtofen, these close-in strikes were "less than a hand-grenade's throw from the German infantry" and wasted the firepower and flexibility of aircraft on fights better suited for infantry.[145] The Sixth Army commanders ignored Richtofen. Stalingrad was the prize.

Although the classic argument about the role of air and land forces in battle was interesting, more important was Richtofen's prescience. The Luftwaffe could not execute the tasks it had—bombing Stalingrad, reconnaissance, supporting the Caucasus, and more—with the assets on hand. This lack of resources had a grave effect on the ability of the Germans to stem the tide of Soviet logistics pouring into Stalingrad and its environs.

Transportation without Supply: Logistics across the Volga

The commander of the Soviet forces at Stalingrad, squeezed block by block to the edge of the Volga River, was General Vasili Chuikov. He was the right leader for the job. Antony Beevor describes Chuikov as "one of the most ruthless of this new generation. . . . His strong, peasant face and thick hair was typically Russian. He also had a robust sense of humor and a bandit laugh, which exposed gold-crowned teeth. Soviet propaganda later portrayed him as the ideal product of the October Revolution."[146] Chuikov would need every ounce of his strong-willed personality to supply his Sixty-Second Army from across the Volga River.

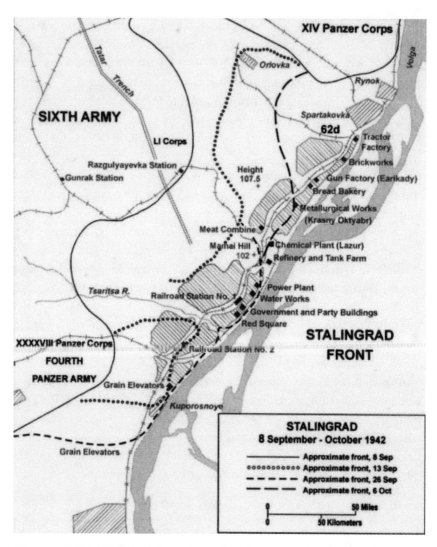

Figure 4.3. Map of Stalingrad, September to October 1942. (Reprinted from Earl F. Ziemke and Magna E. Bauer, *Moscow to Stalingrad: Decision in the East* [Washington, DC: United States Army, 1987].)

With the flanks of the city controlled by the German Sixth Army by early September, hope for resupply fell on the crossing of the Volga. Given the large size of Stalingrad, eighty miles long by as wide as twenty miles in certain sectors, the width of the Volga paled in comparison at one thousand meters (see Figure 4.3).[147] With the Luftwaffe controlling the skies over Stalingrad, however, and the Sixth Army advancing on the flanks to project firepower from land onto the river, the journey of men and materiel across the river to the city was dangerous.

Throughout the fall, Chuikov struggled with a precarious situation of supply, owned by German airpower during the day. His first taste of the failure of supplies to reach the front was during a counterattack by the Sixty-Second Army, which tried to attack across a fifteen-mile front in the city and failed. Chuikov stated in his memoirs, "It's also impossible to understand why this and subsequent counter-attacks were launched in the daytime (when we had no way of neutralizing or compensating for the enemy's superiority in the air), and not at night (when the Luftwaffe did not operate with any strength)."[148] This superiority in the air, coupled with closer artillery positions throughout the fall, made "the job of ferrying men and goods across the river for the 62nd Army . . . as difficult as it could possibly be."[149]

To counter this threat from the air, the Soviets turned to the night, much as the Japanese did at Guadalcanal, to supply themselves. Whereas the Japanese had hundreds of miles of ocean to cross in the night, the Soviets had a shorter commute to the front lines. The concealed movement to and across the Volga fed into the hard lessons learned during fourteen months of war against airpower—*maskirovka* was all-important. Chuikov recorded the difficult logistics operations:

Small units ferried across during the night to the right back had to be deployed and established in positions straight away, during the night, and supplies had to be distributed to the troops, otherwise they would have been bombed and destroyed. We had neither horses nor trucks . . . everything that was brought across the Volga, therefore, had to be distributed to the troops' positions on the shoulders of our men: during the day they fought off fierce enemy assaults, and at night, without sleep and rest, they had to carry ammunition, provisions and engineering equipment. The result was exhaustion, and of course, lower fighting efficiency.[150]

Despite a haggard force, Chuikov used the night to overcome the technology of the airplane and to lessen the amount of larger weapons moved. With such a premium of supply and the difficulty in transporting from the land to the water and onto the land again, Chuikov and Soviet military leaders stopped moving artillery pieces into the city. Not only was moving large pieces of equipment difficult across the open water, resupply of the shells would offer as much challenge. Chuikov averred, "It was much easier to bring ammunition fifty miles to the Volga than to carry it across the half-mile of water."[151]

Without heavy firepower, the Soviet soldiers themselves became the holding point of Stalingrad. To better move soldiers, the Soviets constructed three small footbridges across the Volga to move men to the front in early October. Although the bridges were less vulnerable than vessels to Luftwaffe or German artillery fire, it was a harrowing journey across the bridges avoiding German firepower.[152] Any accidental fall into the river as the days grew colder was certain death.

Once Soviet soldiers reached the city of Stalingrad, the prospect for survival was slim. With their thin supply lines that brought ammunition and weapons at the expense of food and water, the troops had few rations. Even during the anniversary of the October Revolution—the significant milestone of twenty-five years—many units inside Stalingrad did not receive their daily food ration.[153] As a result, soldiers scavenged what they could off German soldiers.[154] Fresh water was a precious commodity, sometimes funneled off shattered buildings during rain or sleet storms, since the Luftwaffe had destroyed the water treatment plant in August.[155] With little water, scant food, and living in dugouts and jumbled masses of shattered buildings, infection and disease were rampant.[156]

If the Imperial Japanese Army misunderstood the balance of supply at Guadalcanal, preferring firepower and men to food for the first few months, the Soviets understood the logistics calculations all too well. Backing the limited prospect of food or survival was Stalin's "Not One Step Back!" order and the secret police *Narodnyy Komissariat Vnutrennikh Del* (NKVD), who were always on the lookout for deserters or those soldiers lacking zeal for the cause. During the fighting for Stalingrad, the NKVD executed an estimated thirteen thousand Soviet soldiers.[157] Chuikov summed up Soviet leadership's view of their supply situation:

The Army Military Council had previously given our rear headquarters a strict time-table for deliveries to the units operating in the city, and had asked primarily for large-scale reinforcements of men and material to be brought up . . . the second priority was to be food, and the third priority warm clothing. We were deliberately going on hunger strike and were prepared to put up with the frost ... we could not do without men and ammunition. Shortage of ammunition in this situation meant certain death.[158]

At the time of the battle, Rifleman A. V. Bakshaeevoi did not share Chuikov's postwar stoicism: "They feed us once every three days in the rear and at the front, and we are never full. ... They give us 600 grams of bread [one-third rations by German standards], bad soup, and a little kasha."[159]

By November, the Soviet supply line of men and ammunition sent into the meat grinder of the *Wehrmacht* had paid a horrifying price. Using Soviet sources, David Glantz notes, "The casualty toll along the Voronezh and Stalingrad axes ... 1,212,189 men, including 694,108 killed, mortally wounded, captured, or missing in action and 517,811 wounded or sick by 17 November. ... This brought the gruesome tally of casualties the Red Army suffered along the Stalingrad and Caucasus axes to a total of 1,586,100 losses."[160]

The tenacity of the Red Army in the city worked against the firepower of the Luftwaffe and the mobility of German ground forces, turning the fight into a battle of attrition. Using airpower to attack first the city, then buildings and front line troops, German aviation turned Stalingrad into rubble. Ironically, this gave the Soviets more places to hide and more areas to attack from, while slowing the German advance into the city.[161] Targeted bombing of individual buildings increased throughout September, October, and November, growing with the Führer's rising frustration.[162]

The Luftwaffe also continued the pressure on the Volga River crossings. These attacks made a job in the "Volga Flotilla," delivering supplies and soldiers across the river to Stalingrad, one of the most dangerous of the battle.[163] Famed Soviet reporter Vasily Grossman recorded in an interview with General Alexander Rodimstev, "We've been collecting boats from all over the river. Now we've got quite a fleet: twenty-seven fishing boats and motor boats. ... We have enough supplies for three days."[164] The general's official optimism in the face of such a fragile supply and transportation line to the hold the city illustrates just how effective the Luftwaffe had become at slowing the supplies down. Grossman recorded more harrowing episodes; including the bombing of a barge filled with four thousand tons of ammunition, and the execution of a boatman who delayed in crossing the river for fear of attack from the sky.[165]

Such constant attacks on the city itself and the Volga crossings came at a cost. Although the Germans owned the air, close-ground-support missions put aircraft and pilots at risk to small-arms fire and ground impact. In addition, although not effective in any significant battle or operation, VVS aircraft and Soviet antiaircraft artillery still posed a threat. The cumulative effect of these impediments to the Luftwaffe chipped away at the aircraft available to attack the city. In a postwar interview, Major Paul-Werner Hozzel, a German *Stuka* pilot, added up the losses to his wing from July to November, "Four months, 120 days, 120 losses."[166] Continuing their attrition from the summer, the Luftwaffe lost 332 aircraft in September and 200 in October in the east.[167] The bomber force, composed of He-111s, suffered the worst, down from 323 in June to fewer than 186 operational aircraft by October.[168] As the German offensive ground to a halt in November, with 90 percent of the city under the control of the Sixth Army, Richtofen's Luftflotte 4 had "only 732 combat aircraft, of which a mere 402 were operational," a reduction of three hundred aircraft since the first bombardment of the city in August.[169] Added to the diminutions of aircraft was the need to move assets from Stalingrad to cover critical operations for Army Group A in the Caucasus, which had stalled short of its goal of the oil fields.[170]

From a climatological viewpoint, the seasons also effected the Luftwaffe. While the historiography of the Eastern Front points to the Soviet winter and the havoc it wreaked on man and machines, the length of the day was also important. As at Guadalcanal, the aircraft lacked sophisticated night navigation, and airfields lacked the robust lighting systems necessary for night operations.

Table 4.2. Hours of Daylight, Stalingrad, August to November 1942

Date	Daylight Hours:Minutes
8/1/1942	15:04
8/24/1942	13:53
9/30/1942	11:43
10/31/1942	9:57
11/19/1942	9:01

Source: Data compiled from "Sunrise and Sunset Times in Volgograd, August 1997," accessed 3 February 2016, http://www.timeanddate.com/sun/russia/volgograd?month=8&year=1997. *Note*: Table based on 1997 data. The difference over time equates to roughly one minute every twenty years. These times are within five minutes of 1942 daylight hours.

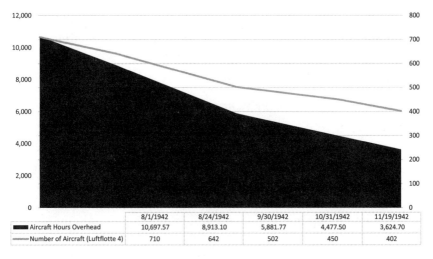

	8/1/1942	8/24/1942	9/30/1942	10/31/1942	11/19/1942
▬ Aircraft Hours Overhead	10,697.57	8,913.10	5,881.77	4,477.50	3,624.70
━ Number of Aircraft (Luftflotte 4)	710	642	502	450	402

Figure 4.4. Luftwaffe Hours Overhead Stalingrad versus Total Aircraft, August to November 1942. This is all the aircraft Luftflotte 4 had for the battles around Stalingrad and Army Group A's drive to the Caucasus. The exact number available for either front varied depending on the missions needed. Excepting the initial bombardment of Stalingrad on 23 August 1942 and the Tractor factory operation in October—when Stalingrad took priority for all airplanes—the aircraft used over Stalingrad would have been a percentage of this number. Although this percentage is unknown, Stalingrad was the priority once Hitler made the decision in mid-July to move from isolation to conquest of the city. Data compiled from "Die Staerke der Deutschen Luftwaffe an der Ostfront, 20.8.42," "Die Staerke der Deutschen Luftwaffe an der Ostfront, 20.9.1942," "Die Staerke der Deutschen Luftwaffe an der Ostfront, 20.10.1942," and "Die Staerke der Deutschen Luftwaffe an der Ostfront, 20.11.1942" in Karlsruhe Collection, United States Air Force Historical Research Agency, IRIS No. 468332, Slides 0604–0623.

With Luftwaffe sorties limited to the daytime, as the days shortened in the fall German airpower had less time to press its advantage (see Table 4.2).

Even if Luftflotte 4 had the same 710 aircraft from August until November, its combat power would have been reduced 40 percent based on decreasing daylight hours. Plotting the diminution of daylight against the decreasing number of aircraft in Luftflotte 4, the loss becomes starker. By November, the Luftwaffe had 67 percent less combat airpower over Stalingrad than it did in August (see Figure 4.4). Thus, while the technology of the aircraft dominated Soviet logistics moves, the technological limit of night operations gave the Soviets more time to supply themselves, as the days grew shorter in the fall of 1942. In addition to the dwindling daylight, the Luftwaffe contended with winter temperatures by early November, which drove reliability rates into dismal regions—sometimes below 35 percent.[171] Winter was coming and it would not be kind to aircraft.

The Luftwaffe and the Enemy Winter

Unlike trains, which could be retrofit with a lower level of technology, or trucks which could be replaced by horses to combat the cold, aircraft engines required more advanced technologies and procedures to combat the elements.[172] Generalmajor Fritz Morzik listed several of these improvements necessary in his postwar analysis of Luftwaffe flights on the Eastern Front, "Felt Screens for gasoline tanks, oil filters, and pumps . . . protective wrapping for all oil tanks . . . protective screens with which to cover aircraft wings in case of snow . . . antifreeze lubricants for, among others, starters, airborne armaments, instruments, and radio equipment . . . preparation of exact instructions for starting cold engines."[173] In addition, maintenance teams needed extra shelter and warming facilities to prevent frostbite and hypothermia.[174] Operations in bad weather and snow-covered runways required more plows, trucks, lighting, and fire pots to illuminate the landing areas, even in the daytime.[175] As Paulus inched toward the Volga in mid-November, the weather hampered the Luftwaffe to a great degree. On 11, 18, and 19 November, the air force did not fly, and had limited operations many other days because of cold and snow.[176] In addition, of the thirty days in November 1942, twenty-two of them had high temperatures below 32 degrees Fahrenheit (0 degrees centigrade).[177] Bad winter weather stopped the Luftwaffe cold.

German Logistics: At the End of a 2,000-Mile Tail

As the weather turned colder, the Sixth Army ground its way into Stalingrad and suffered declining combat power as well. Although food was in much better supply than for their enemy, ammunition, fuel, and the supply of soldiers were limited.[178] Six months of combat had hollowed out units. From September to October, the rate of "exhausted" units rose from 4 to 21 out of 540 total.[179] At the level of the individual German solider, the battle for Stalingrad was miserable. Diseases, including jaundice and hepatitis, did not heal in the unsanitary conditions of the cramped and dirty city, while food consisted of "dry black bread, canned meat, and dried vegetables"—though still far superior to Soviet rations.[180] After one hard-fought battle to eliminate a Soviet pocket of resistance in the tractor factory, an infantry soldier exclaimed, "Our battalion had 8 killed, 14 severely wounded, the rest medium and light wounded. . . . I was dumbstruck and couldn't utter a word. What had become of our regiment? Where were the replacements? If no experienced and battle-hardened men arrived—what use was the framework of staff and supply units, as well as units of heavy weapons?"[181] The Germans lacked men while their enemy lacked supplies.

With their manpower dwindling and their supplies stretched to the limit of what their land transportation could bear, the Germans attempted to save resources. With space on the trains at a premium, the German general staff relocated "some 150,000 horses, as well as a number of oxen and even camels," away from the front-line support in the city back to the rail lines.[182] This move allowed the Germans to cut down on the "supply trains required to bring forward the huge quantities of fodder."[183] In the same vein, the Germans positioned vehicle transport units to the rear as well to help conserve fuel.[184]

Through these conservation measures, the Germans doomed the mobility of the Sixth Army. Two examples from German divisions stationed in Stalingrad in mid-November 1942 illustrate how critical the horses and vehicles were to their mobility. According to reports on 16 November 1942, the Seventy-First Infantry Division had twelve artillery batteries with a mobility rate of 25 percent.[185] With their equine transportation, however, the division's mobility increased to 50 percent. Under the 100th Jäger Division, the Pioneer Battalion was 90 percent mobile with horses and only 50 percent mobile without them.[186] By mid-November, with the Luftwaffe degraded and their animal transportation stationed well behind the army, the Soviets had an advantage in mobility over the Sixth Army.

The Sixty-Second Army Holds

Chuikov and the Sixty-Second Army poured men into the shrinking pocket of Soviet-held Stalingrad. All the while, the Luftwaffe pummeled the ground forces, severing Chuikov's telephone links to his units fighting in the city and destroying Chuikov's own command post numerous times.[187] In the most harrowing incident, German Ju-87 *Stukas* struck fuel storage tanks just above the Soviet general's headquarters, which the Soviets assumed were empty. Chuikov reported, "The fuel tanks were on fire. A fountain of smoke eight

hundred meters high. . . . They dragged me out of the river of fire. . . . Up
to forty men were killed at the headquarters."[188] The attacks were relentless,
with the Germans averaging five to eight sorties per aircraft over Stalingrad
each day that the weather permitted.[189] Thus, Chiukov's army was on the
receiving end of somewhere between two hundred and nine hundred sorties
per day.[190] The totals on Soviet equipment equaled the appalling losses of
their men: "12,137 guns and mortars and 2,063 combat aircraft."[191]

After the grinding war of attrition in the fall, and with the Volga icing up,
Chuikov fretted, "So, for several days before the period of heavy drifting ice
and the beginning of the new enemy offensive, the Army laid in ammunition.
. . . In the same way we laid in reasonable supplies of provisions . . . about
twelve tons of chocolate. . . . I reckoned that in a difficult moment, by giving
out half a bar per man a time, we could survive a week or two, until the Volga
had frozen over and regular supplies could be delivered."[192] The desperate
supply situation and Chuikov's strategy of chocolate-victualing revealed was
well known to the Germans. With flowing ice, transition from land supply to
water supply and back to land went from difficult to impossible. Thus, the
chance for the Sixth Army to take the city was in November, while the mov
ing ice was a threat to Soviet water transportation and before the river turned
into a road. Richtofen lamented, "If we can't clear this situation up now . . .
when the Volga is blocked with ice floes and the Russians are in real difficulties, we shall never be able to. As it is, the days are getting shorter and weather
worse."[193] While German commanders worried about the tactical supply of
the city, the Soviets continued to prepare their logistics for counterattack.

Buildup to Operation Uranus: The Red Army Beats the Luftwaffe

The plans for Operation Uranus began on 27 September 1942, when Stalin
brought together General Georgy Zhukov, the deputy supreme high commander, and key staff of the *Stavka* to discuss plans for a counteroffensive at
Stalingrad.[194] In this plan, 1 million men, 22,019 guns and mortars, 1,550 tanks,
and 1,529 aircraft would encircle the Sixth Army on three fronts—the Southwestern and the Don front stretching one hundred miles to the west, and the
Stalingrad front south of the city. The bulk of the men and materiel would be
to the west and allayed against the weaker Axis-allied armies of the Romanians,
Hungarians, and Italians (see Figure 4.5 for Stalingrad airlift).[195] From a logistics perspective, the plan was a race to get to the Kalach railhead to "sever the

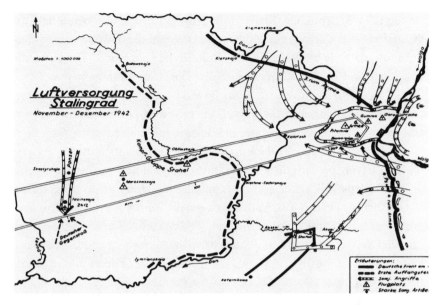

Figure 4.5. Map of Stalingrad Airlift, November to December 1942. Stalino not shown (airfield was to the west of the Sea of Azov). (Reprinted from Edward Milch, "Letter to Hermann Plocher, June 10, 1956," in Karlsruhe Collection, United States Air Force Historical Research Agency, IRIS No. 468335, Slide 1458.)

railroad communications of the German Army's Stalingrad grouping."[196] In addition, the operation also included directives to destroy aircraft and airfields.[197]

While the Luftwaffe tried to sever Chuikov's line of communication across the Volga and provide continual artillery support to Paulus's painful advances into the city, it could not also attack the logistics buildup of Soviet forces behind the lines and to the flanks. Hans Rudel stated in his memoir, *Stuka Pilot,* "At regular intervals we attack the northern bridges over the Don. The bridgehead is constantly being extended and every day the Soviets pour in more men and material. Our destruction of these bridges delays these reinforcements, but they are able to replace them relatively quickly with pontoons so that the maximum traffic across the river is soon fully restored."[198] One statistic that illustrates the lessening of German airpower against Soviet defensive positions are the width and depth of the fronts the Soviets could hold in 1941 compared to those at Stalingrad and the Caucasus in 1942. In 1941, the Soviets held a defensive position of 245–410 miles in width and

90–180 miles in depth near Kharkov. By November 1942, the Soviets held the Stalingrad front 300 miles in width and 90 miles in depth while also holding the 600-mile-wide by 480-mile-deep front in the Caucasus.[199] The Luftwaffe could help take the prized city or interdict Operation Uranus, but not both.

As Paulus directed the Sixth Army forward in the city in early November, Luftwaffe reconnaissance flights noticed increased Soviet buildup of men and material to the west of Stalingrad. Richtofen recorded in his diary on 11 November 1942, "Opposite the Rumanians on the Don, the Russians are resolutely carrying on with their preparations for an attack. Available elements of Fliegerkorps VIII, other fleet units and the Rumanian air forces continually hit them. . . . When will the Russians attack? I only hope that the Russians don't tear many large holes in the line."[200] The inability of the Luftwaffe to interdict the Russian buildup was a testament its lessening combat power— hastened by war, weather, daylight, and the Soviet use of deception to thwart the reconnaissance efforts of the German air arm.

The lessons learned about concealing their movements from German aircraft paid huge dividends for the Soviets during the buildup for Operation Uranus. Joel Hayward in *Stopped at Stalingrad* describes Soviet success: "In huge vehicle convoys and more than 1,300 railway cars per day, the pulled resources from all parts of Stalin's empire. . . . They ordered these movements to be conducted as stealthily as possible . . . in order to disguise the size and scope of their movements from the reconnaissance aircraft that Richtofen kept constantly overhead. . . . As a result of these deception efforts, German intelligence sections failed to deduce the scope and significance of Soviet movements, although they were carefully monitoring them."[201]

These efforts were hidden from their enemy and their own forces. On 17 November 1942, with ice floes thick on the Volga, the 138th Regimental Division of the Sixty-Second Soviet Army reported, "There are no bullets, mines, and food in the division. . . . During the last five days, 138th RD has fought chiefly with trophy weapons and ammunition, and in these difficult conditions, the division is holding on to its positions."[202] Members of the division had no warning that 1 million Soviet troops would relieve them in two days.

The Stalingrad Airlift: The Second Triumph of Hope over Logistics

Echoing the despair of the 138th Regimental Division of the Red Army starving in Stalingrad, the Führer believed the Soviets were exhausted. In a speech on 8 November 1942, at the Bürgerbräukeller in Munich to commemorate the founding of the Nazi party, Hitler stated, "I wanted to reach the Volga . . . to be precise at a particular spot. . . . By chance it bore the name of Stalin himself. . . . There are only a couple of small bits left. . . . No more ships are coming up the Volga. And that is the decisive point!"[203] With a bankrupt ideology and a strategythat his logistics could not match, Hitler had made the Sixth Army vulnerable to counterattack. With the Allied landings on 8 November 1942, the OKH ordered Richtofen to dispatch aircraft to help oppose the landings. This was a final blow to the army's combat power at Stalingrad. Richtofen's sacrificial lamb of three bomber groups to combat the landings, coupled with the losses at war, dropped Fliegerkorps IV's operational combat aircraft from 579 in October to 382 at the start of Operation Uranus.[204]

On 19 November 1942, in light snow and freezing temperatures, the Soviets began Operation Uranus. As their armies poured into the Romanian lines protecting the Sixth Army's flanks to the north and west, surprise turned into a rout. At first, Paulus misunderstood the gravity of the initial reports, which indicated a massive Soviet assault, and he did not maneuver his units to stop the advances. In addition, lack of fuel hampered the ability of many mechanized units to move out to meet the threat.[205] Worse yet was the decision made earlier in the month to move the horses and transport vehicles back to the railheads near Kalach, robbing Paulus of his mobility.[206] As the Soviets closed in around the Sixth Army, and with their ability to move depleted, the Germans destroyed equipment, food, and uniforms, and left animals behind to hasten retreat.[207] Ever cautious of his political master, Paulus anticipated an order to break out, but did not direct his forces to do so. In this melee of vast Soviet advances and chaotic German retreat, the Luftwaffe provided little help. Hans Rudel recorded during the chaotic first four days of Operation Uranus, "We are now flying in all directions over the pocket wherever the situation seems most threatening. . . . Our airfield is now frequently the target of Soviet airforce [sic] attack in low and high level raids. . . . Only now we are running so short of bombs, ammunition, and petrol that it no longer seems prudent to leave all the squadrons within the pocket. So everything is flown out in two or three detachments . . . our flying personnel moves back out of the pocket to Oblivskaja, just over 100 miles west of Stalingrad."[208] The weather hindered the air forces of both sides, rendering them obsolete for the first few days, a clear advantage for the Soviets.[209] Without dominance in the skies, the Germans were overwhelmed.

On 23 November 1942, Paulus sent a message to Hitler asking to break his forces out of the closing Soviet armies, "The inevitable sequel must be a break-through toward the southwest, since such a weakening of the eastern and northern fronts must make those sectors no longer tenable. It cannot be doubted that much valuable materiel will be lost, but the greater part of our valuable fighting strength will be saved as well as a portion, at least, of our equipment and weapons."[210] Hitler, with the successful winter defenses he ordered in 1941 on his mind, and his personal pride staked on Stalingrad, ordered him to stay. The Red Army had encircled "well over 250,000 Axis troops" by 23 November 1942, and for the Germans, the race to supply them by air began.[211]

As aforementioned, the decision to resupply the Sixth Army by air had several operational precedents. The Germans had supplied with success the Demyansk and Kholm's pockets. In addition, the transportation arm of the Luftwaffe had helped pull the advances of Army Group A to the Caucasus and Army Group B to Stalingrad, delivering supplies and taking out the wounded. While the operational concept of supply by air had a history of success, the reality of the situation surrounding Stalingrad was wholly different.

Rather than face an army, which had a neophyte understanding of combat arms and supplying its own armies as in 1941, by the late fall of 1942 the Soviets had better integration between their logistics and combat, meaning they could exploit and hold gains.[212] In addition, the loss of aircraft to North Africa and harsh environmental factors reduced the combat arm of the Luftwaffe to scant percentages of its former operational effectiveness. With the Soviets improved on the ground and the Germans reduced in the air, providing supplies to their trapped army was much more difficult. Finally, the scale of feeding and supplying 250,000 men inside an encircled pocket, with contested air above it and a hostile foe on the ground, was a daunting task.

The Sixth Army estimated that it needed five hundred tons of supply a day to maintain combat readiness and three hundred tons a day as a minimum to survive.[213] As the Soviets surrounded Paulus's Army, the debate about whether to supply the Sixth Army by air, or let them attempt a breakout of the pocket by land, raged back at the OKH headquarters. Into this debate stepped the head of the Luftwaffe. Göring settled the matter and promised the Führer that the Luftwaffe could pull as many Ju-52 transports into the theater as needed and deliver five hundred tons a day. As Joel Hayward remarks in *Stopped at Stalingrad,* the Reichmarshall "should first have consulted his air transportation experts, studied all available information on the situation at Stalingrad . . . and sought the opinions of Richtofen and the Fliegerkorps commanders involved."[214] Göring did not. He sealed the fate of the Sixth Army inside the pocket of the Soviet encirclement—or *Kessel*—to starvation and defeat.[215]

With supply by air the affirmed strategy, the Luftwaffe sent as many Ju-52 transports forward to the front as possible, including some of those used in training schools, with students and their instructors, and several from North Africa.[216] In addition, General Richtofen and Gerneral Martin Fiebig (the Fliegerkorps VIII commander) converted many He-111s from bombers to transports. These efforts bolstered the transportation force. When the first airlift sorties began into the surrounded pocket on November 24, Richtofen only had thirty operational transports to put to the task. By 5 December, the airlift force had two hundred Ju-52s and several dozen He-111s.[217] In addition, the Luftwaffe added a motley group of other aircraft: "two wings of converted Ju-86s; a converted He-177 wing; and even a long-range formation equipped with FW 200 Condors, Ju-90s, and Ju-290s."[218]

In theory, this large contingent of airlift aircraft seemed sufficient to meet the five-hundred-ton promise of Göring, even with operational capable rates squeezed by maintenance and poor weather. In 1971, the former leader of the Berlin Airlift—United States Air Force lieutenant general William Tunner—postulated that 768 tons a day was feasible.[219] Theory did not match reality. The *Kessel* had an active enemy in the Soviet Union, with the VVS bombing runways and Soviet artillery hammering German positions. Added to the firepower arrayed against the *Kessel,* the bad weather hampered all segments of the resupply effort from loading and unloading aircraft to takeoffs and landings.

Given the position of Soviet forces and the Sixth Army, Richtofen organized his force to operate from three general fields to fly into the pocket: the Ju-52s out of Tatsinskaya, He-111s out of Morozovskaya, and the other groups of aircraft out of Stalino (see Figure 4.5).[220] Inside the *Kessel,* Pitomnik and Bessargino were the most suitable.[221] Major General Fiebig would subsume his duties as commander of Fliegerkorps VIII to direct the airlift.

As the lift began on 24 November 1942, the continual threat from Soviet antiaircraft artillery, aircraft of the VVS, and the weather took their toll. The He-111s were better suited to cold weather and needed fewer fighters to help them into the *Kessel*. Ju-52s, however, were built for transportation. The cargo aircraft struggled in the cold and against Soviet air defenses.[222] In the first month of operation, the airlift did not meet the promised 500 tons per day or even the scaled-back 300 tons a day. The most delivered during this time in one week was 1,162 tons from 18 to 24 December 1942, very different from 2,100 tons minimum needed or the greater 3,500 tons promised.[223]

In mid-December, Hitler ordered an attempt to break into the *Kessel* while counterproductively ordering the Sixth Army to remain fixed in place in the vain hope the beleaguered army could still capture Stalingrad. He also redirected Army Group A from the Caucasus to support, the Soviets now threatening to cut it off as well in the wake of Operation Uranus. The plan, called Operation Wintergewitter (Winter Storm), directed General Hermann Hoth's Fourth Panzer to strike toward the center southwest corner of the pocket. Begun on 12 December 1942, Hoth came as close as eighteen miles to the Sixth Army, but Hitler's stand-fast order still stood for Paulus. With Paulus frozen by order and the Fourth Panzer losing one thousand soldiers a day in the efforts to reach the Sixth Army, Hoth's advance failed.[224] After 23 December 1942, there were no more ground-relief operations planned for the Sixth Army. Across the lines, the Volga froze solid just as Winter Storm fizzled, allowing Chuikov to use the Volga as a highway: "In the course of the next seven weeks, travelled vehicles, 18,000 lorries, and 17,000 trucks crossed over."[225]

With the unsuccessful breakout in late December, the Luftwaffe was the only method left to supply the army. Despite the installation of General Erhard Milch in early January to remedy the situation—and he did improve operations with forced cold-start procedures and better conditions for the maintenance troops—the toll of bad weather, short daylight hours, and persistent ground and air attack by the Soviets further collapsed the pocket.[226] Milch's efforts were more window dressing than substantive change to airlift operations. In addition, the Germans lost their critical base of Tatsinksaya after a covert tank attack by the Soviets, which destroyed forty-six Ju-52s.[227] As a result, the operations shifted further afield to Salsk in the Caucasus—lengthening the trip and lessening the potential tonnage into the pocket.[228]

As the pocket succumbed to increasing Soviet attacks on the starving and ill-equipped Sixth Army, Pitomnik airfield fell on 16 January 1943, shifting operations to the inadequate Gumrak airfield.[229] By 26 January 1943, Gumrak was useless, under constant Soviet attack with aircraft wrecks taking up all the space on the field. After this date, Paulus ordered only airdrops of food.[230] The airlift failed.

To supply any small pockets of German soldiers still fighting, Richtofen, Fiebig, and Milch decided that "for as long as German soldiers remain alive and can be located, they will be supplied."[231] On 31 January, the Luftwaffe put up 85 aircraft and followed up with 116 aircraft two days later, attempting to find pockets of German resistance and supply them. On the ground, a signals officer led a heroic effort to establish a proper zone with lights and radio beacons to ensure delivery. With this improvement, "supply containers were dropped in the right place."[232] Many airdrops failed, however, their containers lost in the snow, unrecognizable with white parachutes.

Surrounded by the Soviets, Paulus surrendered on 3 February 1943. His army had suffered 60,000 dead since the Soviet counterattack and over 130,000 captured, including 91,000 in the final days.[233] Of these 130,000, only 5,000 ever saw Germany again, with Paulus himself confined to East Germany until his death in 1957. For their efforts, the Luftwaffe lost 1,000 aircrew members and 488 transport aircraft during the attempted relief of the Sixth Army.[234] From February 1943 onward, the Reich was on the road to defeat.

Translating Airlift to Ground Power: The Failure of the Stalingrad Airlift

The historiography of the Stalingrad airlift rightfully focuses on the tonnages, the sorties, and the strategy leading to the decision to supply the Sixth Army by air.[235] An examination of the airlift within its historical and technological contexts, however, yields a different perspective. While the airlift failed, the Germans still delivered a significant number of supplies by air, even though the amount was insufficient. In his postwar analysis, Generalmajor Morzik recorded that from 26 November 1942 to 2 February 1943 the Luftwaffe delivered 1,235 tons of gasoline, 1,122 tons of ammunition, 2,020 tons of food, and 129 tons of "miscellaneous supplies" into the Stalingrad pocket.[236] In addition, the airlift saved 24,910 wounded by removing them from the surrounded Sixth Army, which Richard Muller states was "impressive given the dismally low serviceability rates for the transport aircraft supplying the Sixth Army."[237] Given the fate of those German soldiers taken prisoner by the Soviets at Stalingrad, the operation saved their lives. Despite the tonnage delivered and the success of the medical evacuation, the resupply efforts from the air could not meet the challenge. The attempt to supply 200,000 soldiers, surrounded and under attack, from the air had no historical precedent. Even the much easier efforts to supply the pockets at Demyansk, Kholm, and Army Group South as it ate up huge chunks of the Soviet steppes in the summer of 1942, paled to the needs of the trapped army.

What Stalingrad did resemble were the efforts to supply China "Over the Hump" by the Americans during the next three years of war, and the Berlin Airlift of 1948; large operations, with significant numbers of aircraft, which required a continual operated line of communication through the air. Unlike these two operations, however, the Stalingrad airlift suffered from a compressed timeline. In took years, during the Hump, and months, during the Berlin Airlift, to build the proper networks of supply to the airfields, landing and unloading operations, and farther movement onward to the front. In other words, the story of the attempted resupply by air of the Sixth Army was more than the need, three hundred to five hundred tons of supplies, on one side, with the capability of the Luftwaffe on the other, and subtracting the impact of the weather and the Soviet military—VVS, antiaircraft artillery, or Red Army—as well.

A more probing analysis examines whether the Sixth Army could have fed itself even if the airlift had met the cargo delivery amounts. Although there were many operations needed to execute such a large airlift, from weather forecasting to engine heaters and loading equipment, the Sixth Army had to accomplish three basic tasks in coordination with the Luftwaffe. First, the Sixth Army had to transmit information about the supply needs inside *Kessel* to the outside, and then the German support units and the Luftwaffe had to translate that information into actual supplies for airlift missions. Second, the Germans had to receive, unload, and dispatch aircraft at the airfields inside the *Kessel*. Finally, the Sixth Army had to distribute the supplies off the airfield to 250,000 soldiers.

The communication of needs from the Sixth Army to the Luftwaffe was never smooth. Weather, always a hindrance for aircraft in the winter, also put a damper on the electromagnetic spectrum. The technology of the radio was not robust enough to overcome freezing rain or heavy precipitation, or even dense cloud decks. On 27 November 1942, General Fiebig noted in his diary, "Ice-rain has broken all communications to the rear."²³⁸ Under these conditions, information about supplies the Sixth Army required was often misinterpreted or unsent.

The most glaring example of the information gap happened in the first few days of the encirclement, at the same time that General Fiebig noted the difficulties in communication. While General Paulus noted on 22 November 1942, "Food supplies are available for a further six days," General Fiebig wrote just a few days later in passive and uncertain voice, "it is told that food will be sufficient for a month."²³⁹ With the fog and friction of Operation Uranus, coupled with the havoc that weather played on the radio, some miscommunication was inevitable. The difference between thirty days and six days delayed food deliveries to the Sixth Army at the expense of ammunition and fuel.

At the lower levels of the operation, the lack of clear communication channels resulted in haphazard or ill-advised cargo for the airlift. For example, on 28 December 1942, General Arthur Schmidt, the Sixth Army's chief of staff, sent a message General Schulz, the chief of staff of Army Group Don, in a teletype: "In spite of urgent requests, we received no fuel today. Instead we got 10 tons of bonbons, even though pilots reported there is fuel available at Salsk."²⁴⁰

The communication back to the Reich on what the front needed from the massive airlift was even worse. Determining which units had priority between the Luftwaffe and the German Army on the overtaxed rail lines leading to the eastern front was Byzantine, and fraught with the political machinations that defined the corrupt ideology of the Third Reich.²⁴¹ With such an inefficient and complex system that yielded poor results, the Sixth Army leadership expressed growing frustration over the airlift. Paulus dressed down a Luftwaffe major sent by General Milch to examine logistics operations at the airfields in the pocket: "Here you are talking to dead people. On order of the 'Führer' we have stayed here. The Air Force has left us in the lurch and did not keep what it promised."²⁴²

The second problem the Sixth Army needed to overcome was the reception and onward movement of supplies. Airplanes had to land, unload cargo, load the wounded, and take off again. The German experiences in emergency airlift of supplies throughout the Eastern Front paid off at first. Major-General Wolfgang Pickert, commanding the airlift operations inside the pocket, had Pitomnik well established in late November. With little fuel and many pieces of equipment lost in the encirclement, Pickert relied on human power to clear runways, move wrecked aircraft, and execute unloading and loading.[243] For the first few weeks, the situation on the ground was adequate. At first, the ground crews had strength, but as the food ran thin, the unloading of cargo and loading of wounded expanded from a two-hour process to over four hours. By the end of January, it took ground crews seven hours to unload each aircraft.[244]

Had the cargo amounts, which never reached three hundred tons for two days in a row, approached the desired five hundred tons per day, the cargo load might have overwhelmed the logistics and supply networks in the *Kessel* and the surrounding airfields. An instructive example to illustrate the difficulties of organizing large amounts of cargo was the Marine landing at Guadalcanal (see chapter 3). It took the three hundred pioneers of the United States Marine Corps a week to move twenty days of supplies for eleven thousand Marines off the beaches and take a full accounting of its stock. This number of pioneers was so insufficient to the task that Major General Vandegrift recommended one thousand Marines for a similar amount of cargo in future operations. Although it is difficult to compare exact tonnages, the twenty days of supplies for eleven thousnad would have equaled one day of supply for 250,000 German and Axis-allied soldiers trapped in the *Kessel*. The Sixth Army required a system of thousands of support troops to help manage and control the cargo process, an impossible labor requirement given the need to fight back against the Soviet encirclement.

Added to the physical handling of the cargo, the aircraft also required much effort to receive them safely. The most critical piece in the reception process was ensuring a clear runway, or at least level surface for aircraft to land. This was backbreaking work requiring machines, which Pickert and the Sixth Army lacked. By comparison, the modern United States Air Force requires a full snow-removal plan for each base that receives "over 150 millimeters [6 inches] of average annual snowfall per year."[245] At Stalingrad, the airfields often received this amount of snow in one day. The Sixth Army never had enough personnel to maintain the runways in the pocket.[246] The result of large amounts of snow and ice, improperly packed down for aircraft operation, was dozens of crashes.[247] In his postwar analysis, Morzik estimated that 50 percent of the aircraft lost were because of weather and not hostile fire. None of the Luftwaffe's aircraft had the cargo capacity to load the vehicles necessary to keep the runways clear or packed. Thus, more sorties would not have improved the Sixth Army's ability to keep the runways safe.

From a technological perspective, there were strong radio beacons in the pocket for navigation, which helped planes arrive at the airfield even in bad weather.[248] According to Morzik, however, "The direction finding equipment at Pitomnik was excellent, but it was so overburdened by the number and frequency of landing approaches that not every aircraft was able to make contact and some had to turn back without landing."[249] A larger sortie rate might have overwhelmed the navigational capabilities even more.

The third problem the Sixth Army had to solve was distribution. After the Soviets closed around the Sixth Army, the Germans needed to move food, fuel, and ammunition from the airfield to the front lines of the *Kessel,* an area thirty-five miles long by twenty miles wide.[250] As much as it was difficult to move artillery pieces to shift firepower as the pocket collapsed, the same held for logistics. With the horses moved back far from the front lines, transporting food would have required human power. After the start of Operation Uranus, numerous unit histories and reports documented the efforts of human transportation. Hauptmann Löser of the Seventy-Sixth Infantry wrote on 28 November 1942, "Some 300 men . . . with field kitchens pulled by teams of men drag themselves along: a terrible sight."[251] Many of these "terrible" duties fell to *Hiwis,* Soviet soldiers who joined the Germans or were prisoners of war.[252] Antony Beevor states: "'When the retreat stated on 20 November,' reported one Russian prisoner of war, 'we were put instead of horses to draft the carts loaded with ammunition and food. Those prisoners who could not draft the carts as quickly as the *Feldwebel* wanted were shot on the spot.'"[253] The more physical exertion required, the more food the soldiers needed. Larger cargo loads would have required more transportation, either men or horses, and more food. The Sixth Army lacked all.

Thus, a greater delivery of cargo, toward the five-hundred-ton requirement, would have overwhelmed the system. The Germans lacked the network of logistics necessary to translate a line of communication through the air to supply a huge army during the extreme winter weather and under the hostile threat of the enemy. In fact, all these difficulties in getting supplies and distributing them within the *Kessel* hits at the largest issue of the Stalin-grad airlift—hunger. Without proper sustenance, the army could not function in defense of the *Kessel* while also supporting its logistics needs.

SUMMARY OF SUPPLY: STALINGRAD *KESSEL*

While Paulus understood that he had only six days of food, by the second day of Operation Uranus, he and local army leadership were much more concerned about Hitler's order to stand fast, defending against the Soviets, and planning for a breakout rather than immediate feeding. Much like their Japanese ally at Guadalcanal, the Germans chose combat power first. As a result, the logistics that followed was ammunition and fuel for machinery, and for this, men suffered. Table 4.3 shows the amount of food lifted in the first eleven days, and the amount of food required to keep soldiers in war fighting health—282 tons per day.[254]

Table 4.3 highlights the outrageous nature of the claims by Göring that the Luftwaffe could sustain 500 tons per day or even the more modest 300 tons. Most important, the table shows how little food the Germans supplied to the Sixth Army, 30 tons versus 3,102 tons at full rations, a scant 1 percent of the food needed in the first eleven days. From then on, the Sixth Army was in an insurmountable hole for food rations. (See Figure 4.6.)

How bad was the food situation? To translate the food supply of the Sixth Army to perform operations—whether defensive, breaking out of the *Kessel,* or even conducting loading and unloading of aircraft, Guadalcanal provides a useful rubric. For the Japanese, in two separate instances, mid-October and late November, food supplies dropped below a fifteen-day deficit. In both these cases, this food deficit prevented them from conducting offensive operations. Without the heroic effort in mid-October to supply their troops, they could not have attempted the last attacks on Henderson Field by land (see chapter 3).

The internal reports of the combat strength of the Sixth Army's battalions show similar declines in performance. On 16 November 1942, the Sixth Army had 44 of 113 battalions listed as "weak or exhausted"—less than 30 percent full strength. By 15 December 1942, that number grew to 71 of 134 battalions. This was an increase from 39 percent to 53 percent in only a month.[255] Anecdotally, the Sixth Army weakened in early December. Cargo unloading

Table 4.3. Food Required/Food Airlifted Compared to Ammunition Fuel/Airlifted (in Tons), Stalingrad, 24 November to 5 December 1942

Date	Food Airlifted	Food Required	Ammo/Fuel Airlifted
11/24/1942	0	282	84
11/25/1942	0	282	66
11/26/1942	0	282	72
11/27/1942	0	282	28
11/28/1942	7	282	94
11/29/1942	0	282	46
11/30/1942	0	282	129
12/1/1942	0	282	85
12/2/1942	4	282	116.1
12/3/1942	3	282	0
12/4/1942	16	282	127.8
Total	30	3102	906.3
Half Rations		1551	
Quarter Rations		775.5	

Sources: Data compiled from "Diary of General Pickert, C.G. 9th Flak Division: Air Supply of the Sixth Army from 25 November 1942–1 November 1943," in The Papers of Lt. Gen. William Tunner (Maxwell Air Force Base, AL: Air Force Historical Research Agency, IRIS No. 1038188); and Richard R. Muller, The German Air War in Russia (Baltimore: Nautical & Aviation Publishing Company of America, 1992), 96–98

Note: The ammunition and fuel delivered are an estimate. Pickert's information for the food delivery in the Kessel was subtracted from Muller's total tonnage to arrive at the ammunition and fuel delivered. Muller's primary data came from General Milch's daily reports (outside the Kessel).

times expanded from two hours to four, soldiers refused to move, and many younger soldiers perished from malnutrition brought on by a lack of fat in their diet and the calorie-consuming cold weather.[256] Thus, using a fifteen-day deficit, which occurred about 15 December 1942, also appears to be an appropriate measure for the inability conduct offensive operations. After 15 December 1942, the Sixth Army required an external army to break them out of the encirclement, as it lacked the combat strength in healthy men to conduct offensive operations or perform logistics. Operation Winter Storm, which began on December 12 and fizzled out by 23 December 1942, was the last real chance to save the army.

The decision to send food, above all else, into the Kessel as operations were just beginning would have been a tough adjustment for the Germans.

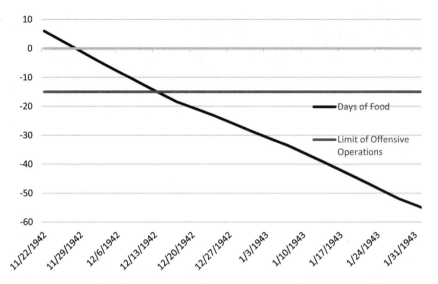

Figure 4.6. Days of Food Remaining, Sixth Army in the *Kessel.* Data compiled from Paulus, "Funkspruch an Heeresgruppe B, Armee-Oberkommando 6, Abt. la. A. H. Qu. 22.11.1942, 1900 Uhr"; "Diary of General Pickert, C. G. 9th Flak Division: Air Supply of the Sixth-Army from 25 November 1942–1 November 1943," in *The Papers of Lt. Gen. William Tunner.* United States Air Force Historical Research Agency, IRIS No. 1038188; and Görlitz, "Paulus and Stalingrad: A Life of Field-Marshal Friedrich Paulus, with Notes, Correspondence, and Documents from his Papers."

For an army accustomed to mobile warfare and a culture of logistics, which outran supply lines as a matter of standard practice and then extricated itself through airlift, it was unlikely that German leadership would have made that decision early enough. In addition, the Sixth Army had hoped ground action would save it, versus support from aerial resupply. As a result, by the time the Sixth Army reached a crisis stage for food, it was too late to save them.

Much like the Japanese, when the Sixth Army was past saving, the Germans then shifted their supply operations to food. Based on the airlift records in General Pickert's diary, there was a decided shift to food after 18 December 1942; the daily tonnage of food jumped to 245 tons on 19 December 1942 and was often in triple digits until mid-January.[257] This was the same time that that the Sixth Army staff communicated to Army Group Don and the OKH the dietary needs of the army, about 282 tons of food a day for combat.[258] In addition, significant discussions took place regarding the slaughter of the remaining horses for food. Over several days, General Schmidt, out-side the *Kessel,* and General Schultz discussed how many horses were in the pocket and directed the Sixth Army to slaughter the animals for food.[259] If their transportation at first, it was non-xistent with the death of the horses. By late December, the only hope for the Sixth Army was the Luftwaffe, and it could not deliver.

CONCLUSION

In the contest to control a critical transportation node, Stalingrad, land transportation was dominant. Within this mode, the railroad, its capacity and speed increased from the Industrial to the Late Industrial Era, brought most of the cargo of war to the battlefield for the Germans and Soviets. Just as with transportation by sea at Guadalcanal, however, there was now a qual-ifier. Lines of communication on land depended on control of the air.

As the Germans pushed off for Stalingrad and the Caucasus in the sum-mer of 1942, the Luftwaffe, from Kharkov and Rostov to the Great Bend in the Don, to Stalingrad, stopped Soviet logistics and reinforcements from mov-ing to the battlefield. In addition, the range of the airplane gave the Germans a significant edge in reconnaissance about Soviet movements. The Luftwaffe protected the German supply lines, although stretched to their limit at 2,400 miles from the Reich.

The Soviets understood what a threat the airplane was to their logistics. They adapted techniques to protect their supply lines: by deception and night movement, by increased antiaircraft artillery in rear areas and on railroads, and by abandoning the supply needs of their soldiers in the city of Stalingrad. The Soviets also learned that as Germans lost more aircraft to the war effort, the ability of the Luftwaffe to interdict Soviet logistics waned. By the time of the Soviet counterattack on 20 November 1942, the Luftwaffe could sup-port the Sixth Army in the city, fly interdiction against the thirteen hundred railcars that were moving per day into the areas surrounding Stalingrad, or support the stalled efforts of Army Group A in the Caucasus; but only one at a time and not all three as the Luftwaffe attempted.

While the railroad dominated land transportation, especially on the So-viet side where their growing manufacturing base bolstered by Lend-Lease overwhelmed the capability of the overextended Luftwaffe, travel on the simple roads of the Soviet steppes bogged down vehicles in wet conditions and could stop any offensive or retreat in its tracks. As at Guadalcanal, undeveloped road networks stalled Late Industrial technologies and required other methods to move men and supplies. After the lessons of 1941, the Germans reached back into the Preindustrial Era and bolstered their loss of vehicles with native horses and *Panje* carts. The Germans also retooled their engines to make them simpler and less susceptible to failure during the Soviet winter. The "Demodernization of the Front," the Soviet environment forcing the Germans back onto more primitive technologies, was less an innovation and more a necessity.[260]

Unlike land transportation and weapons, aircraft could not be demodernized. Instead, the German flying machines required advanced technical solutions such as special blends of fuel, complicated starting procedures, and portable heating equipment to operate in the cold. The Soviets timed the counterattack to take advantage of the Luftwaffe's vulnerability in cold weather. As at Guadalcanal, the inability of the Luftwaffe to fly at night, due to the primitive navigation and instrumentation of their fighter aircraft, limited the combat power of the German air arm. With the farther north latitude of Stalingrad, the daylight shrunk from fifteen hours in August to nine hours by November, a critical reduction as the cold weather also affected flying. With the Luftwaffe grounded, the Soviets moved unmolested into the snow-laden plains to the west and south of the Sixth Army and exploited their initial gains with timely supplies and reinforcements. On 1 December 1942, Colonel Robert Hurley, a US Army colonel sent to observe the battle remarked, "One Soviet officer asked where the German air force had gone; another asked what the Germans were preparing to do with their airpower. In the resultant discussion, the Russians said the Germans have been using far less air force than previously employed on the Russian front . . . these conclusions left unanswered in the minds of the Generals the question, expressed in Army slang, 'What's cooking?'"[261] By then, the Luftwaffe did not resemble the dominant force of the summer of 1942.

While the combat capability of German airpower decreased over the course of the campaign, the transportation arm of the Luftwaffe showed modest improvement. Without airlift of fuel and ammunition to stalled panzer divisions, the slowing pace of the German advance to Stalingrad would have decreased to a stop before the city, theoretically moving the tanks backwards seven days. With the successes of Demyansk, Kholm, and the summer offensives, the utopian idea that the Luftwaffe could supply an army of 250,000 surrounded by a 1-million-man-strong Soviet army gained traction and stuck as the strategy to save the Sixth Army. While the extraction of twenty-four thousand wounded was a miracle, the Luftwaffe never met the needs of the trapped army. In part, this was because of a lack of control of the air—thwarted by the severe winter weather or Soviet attacks, including the surprise taking of the airfield at Tatsinskaya by Soviet tanks. The airlift also struggled due to the lack of an integrated network to receive, deliver, and transport the supplies to the soldiers in the *Kessel*. Even if the Luftwaffe had delivered, the capability to move the large amounts of cargo required a robust system to support it, which the Sixth Army lacked.

The British at Le Havre in 1917 and the Americans in Nouméa supporting Guadalcanal had time to develop and improve their methods of distribution. By contrast, the Germans required a robust network for aerial delivery in days, not months or years. The Soviet enemy denied them the time. Thus, air transportation of the Late Industrial Era, when compared to the land and sea modes of the Industrial Era, required a significant logistics network, in place or established post haste, to harness its speed and capacity.

Although the German efforts to supply Stalingrad were a failure, the air mode of transportation had come into its own on the Eastern Front. After the war, Lieutenant General Tunner of the United States Air Force wanted to compare the success of the Berlin Airlift, not to his efforts organizing the "Hump" missions supporting China, but rather to Stalingrad.[262] Tunner's homage was a recognition of Stalingrad's scope rather than its failure.

Geopolitical Impacts—Stalingrad

At Stalingrad, the Germans, buoyed by victories in the summer, well outstretched what their supply line could handle. In addition, they had allied themselves with a nation whose strategic appetite was also more than it could handle. Thus, while the Germans struggled to take Stalingrad, the Japanese saw an opportunity to keep their strong Soviet neighbor from incursion into their Pacific sphere of influence. As a result, while the Germans racked up miles of land, destroyed Soviet armies, and pushed the Soviets on the defensive for sixteen months, the manufacturing goods of Lend-Lease passed through the Japanese-controlled Pacific without interference.

Although it is hard to argue with certainty what the goods sent from the heartland of America to the heartland of Europe meant for the Soviet Union, without it their ability to feed themselves would have been in doubt. While Hitler hoped the Japanese would keep the Americans at bay, the attack at Pearl Harbor only intensified the efforts of the United States and connected the supply networks of the world's two largest economies to bear on the Reich, ushering in the defeat of Germany.

The outcome of Stalingrad and the wider war mirrored the methods each side used to command and control their logistics. After their failures in 1941 and most of 1942, the Soviets realized that a more centralized command-and-control system was necessary to move large armies in Industrial Era warfare. By Operation Uranus, the Soviets had learned from their failures and adapted a more centralized system of logistics. This dovetailed with the secretive and autocratic ideology of Stalin and the Soviet state, which allowed them to move masses of men and machines forward in coordination and without notice from German aircraft or their own soldiers. Although later generations of Soviet generals in the 1980s criticized such a top-heavy approach, with the complexity of thousands of tanks, aircraft, trucks, and men on the move, it worked. As one German general remarked well after the war, Soviet logistics on the Eastern Front were "crudely effective."[263]

The Germans chose a different approach to handle their logistics needs. Blitzkrieg demanded a more flexible and mobile logistics than any centralized system could handle; therefore forces split logistics rather than shared them. While such a system allowed for tactical flexibility and garnered much success from 1939 to November 1942, it was also subject to the vagaries of the ideology of the Third Reich. With the focus of the Third Reich attuned to the favor of Adolf Hitler, the various commands of the army and the Luftwaffe fought over supply and transportation to the Eastern Front, which exacerbated the poor condition of the overstretched lines of communication to Stalingrad.[264] The most egregious example of the sublimation of logistics to the political corruption of the Third Reich was the promise of Göring to supply five hundred tons per day to the *Kessel*, rooted in his desire to court favor with the Führer.

The same ideology that corrupted their own supply systems had also left a wasteland of burned and plundered villages behind the *Heer* as they advanced forward in the heady days of the summer of 1942. Rather than co-opt locals who opposed Soviet rule, the Germans treated the conquered peoples as slaves. As they retreated to the west, the Germans discovered that their harsh treatment of the proceeding summers had turned the population into a vast network of Soviet-aligned partisans who attacked trains, trucks, and vehicles headed to the front. In the summer of 1944, over one hundred thousand Soviet partisans "launched an extensive, coordination aimed at nothing less than crippling supply into all of Army Group Center."[265] These attacks sapped German offensives and further threw the inefficient German lines of communication into chaos. Yet, Hitler continued to commit forces to battle, preferring a noble slaughter than a negotiated peace. As Stephen Fritz records, Hitler "left some of his intimates under the impression that he had no illusions about the outcome of the war, they made it equally clear that he would not capitulate. There would be no repeat of 1918; his strength of will— or obstinate refusal to face reality—remained intact."[266] The Wehrmacht followed their Führer, destroying the German economy and state.

The Luftwaffe, so critical in early German success and later defeat at Stalingrad, would never be as powerful as it was in 1942. After that, its fighter force would pay a heavy price in defense of the Reich against the Combined Bomber Offensive of the Allies. By the summer of 1944, the famed German menace from the air had little of its combat capability left. Without this threat, the Allies brought transportation of supplies to the Normandy peninsula to a halt before 6 June 1944, and interdicted all German shipments by rail and truck attempting to respond to Operation Overlord. In the east, the Soviet VVS learned and gained experience; and, by 1945, the famed deep battle of Zhukov would be on full display. The Allies took the lessons learned from the Luftwaffe and turned airpower back onto the German state— ensuring its defeat.

After the Late Industrial Era, the status of great power fell to those nations with great air forces—the United States of America and the Soviet Union. Through airpower, these two nations legislated which supplies moved where, whether at sea or on land. With the Soviet detonation of their first atomic weapon in 1949, both sides had the ability to hold each other—and their manufacturing bases—hostage. The nuclear weapon bridged the transition from the Late Industrial to the Modern Era and changed how nation states used logistics in warfare much as the transitions from Preindustrial to Industrial to Late Industrial Eras had done over the previous two centuries. At Khe Sanh, during the Tet Offensive of 1968, the Americans would discover the impact of the nuclear weapon and the technology of the Modern Era on logistics.

Khe Sanh, 1967–1968
The Triumph of the Narrative

*Hence the closed world is not simply the proliferation and imposition of the
discursive framework of superpower confrontation but also an understanding
of the world that defines the latter as finite, manageable, and computable.*
—Antoine Bousquet, *The Scientific Way of Warfare*

In 1945, the Soviet Union and the United States of America, their
supply networks connected through Lend-Lease, crushed the Axis.
The massive amounts of trucks, tanks, airplanes, artillery, and weapons churned out by modern industry and fueled by the resources
of the two economic behemoths overwhelmed the parasitic nations
of Germany and Japan. The atomic bomb, the ultimate weapon of
the Late Industrial Era, ended the war and ushered in a new era of
technological advancement—the Modern Era. On top of the oil, the
internal combustion engine, and the electromagnetic spectrum of
the prewar world, the Modern Era staked its claim to technological dominance with nuclear power and the computer. In the 1930s,
Lewis Mumford hoped that the Late Industrial Era, with its emphasis on the abstract physics of Bohr, Plank, and Einstein in opposition the linear world of Newton, would usher in an era in which the
organic overcame the machine.[1] Instead, the opposite happened.

Nuclear weapons, simple machines that required a vast industrial
base for support, controlled the affairs of not just of men but nation
states. If the Late Industrial Era made the earth a closed system—
all areas reachable by transportation, communication, and weap-

ons—through deterrence the Modern Era networked the nations of the earth through threat of their own extinction. As Thomas Schelling states in *Arms and Influence,* "deterrence rests on the threat of pain and extinction, not just military defeat."[2] After the Soviet Union tested its first atomic weapon in 1949, the Cold War personified the threat of annihilation.

Under the logic of nuclear deterrence, the two former allies of the Second World War, the USSR and the United States of America, fought the Cold War. Weapons of warfare followed suit. Jet aircraft delivered bombs, missiles, and rockets. Both sides even converted tactical-range ammunition to wield nuclear attack. Under the threat of extinction, the United States and the Soviet Union danced the dance of deterrence, seeking allies and alliances while using the same to fight proxy wars with conventional weapons in Latin America, Africa, the Middle East, and Asia.

According to Paul Edwards in *The Closed World,* the existential threat of the nuclear weapon required information processing and data analysis to provide "total oversight, exacting standards of control, and technical-rational solutions to a myriad of complex problems."[3] Computers, improved radar sensors, and communications gear gave the United States and the Soviet Union the ability to expand the usable portions of the electromagnetic spectrum, from radio and infrared to the visible waves of television, to monitor each other. In warfare, these technological improvements made it easier to guide missiles and weapons toward aircraft, while also making it tougher for machines run by internal combustion engines to conceal their location, giving off returns of heat and noise for computers to process and locate.

The computer also helped promulgate mass media by underpinning the space race, itself a battle for nuclear supremacy, and the launching of satellites. In this postwar world, news about international affairs did not wait for the newspaper, the telegraph, or the radio. Satellite networks broadcast information for visual consumption to televisions each night and sometimes in real-time. This visible realm of media, the ideological battle—the ebb and flow of communist versus capitalist—played out for the world to see. In this environment, the United States and the Soviet Union courted world opinion for their share of the winning narrative.

For logistics, the postwar brought booming economies and consumers ready to purchase goods from around the world. The same computer technologies that helped to rationalize the logic of nuclear deterrence and Cold

War planning helped to develop supply chains into more efficient methods for profit. For example, the large cargo ships of the Second World War grew bigger and accommodated containers, which filled up large holds better and were easier to move on and off ships than lose cargo. From a military perspective, the experiments with containers resulted in the Containerized Express (CONEX) for the Americans, while the Soviets developed a system of large and small containers to ship cargo for war.[4] With improvements in containers, efficiency, and communication, the cost to ship goods fell 90 percent from $5.16 per ton in 1945 to fewer than twenty cents by 1960.[5]

While the capacity and efficiency of the sea mode of transportation increased, so did the prospect for transport by land. Land transportation, still dominated by train, expanded into an era of trucking and the personal automobile. Nations paved well-built roads all over the globe, including the interstate system in America, championed by President Eisenhower. As a result, more goods and more people moved farther and faster on land than ever.

Similar advances occurred in aircraft travel. Improved during the war, aircraft expanded civilian travel opportunities while the militaries of the Cold War era built ever-larger aircraft to fly farther and with more cargo to support allies and wars all over the globe. The Americans, who championed the growing industry of civilian airlines with the jet-powered Boeing 707, led the way.[6] While Stalingrad personified the failure of airlift, the Berlin crisis personified the technical prowess and the logistical capabilities of the United States in the postwar world. Rather than supplying a 250,000-man army, however, it supplied West Berlin and its 2 million people with eight thousand tons per day of food and supplies.[7] This was a fifteenfold increase over Göring's most boastful estimates of how much cargo the Luftwaffe could deliver to the Stalingrad *Kessel.*

The bipolar contest of the Cold War kept in check by nuclear weapons was not equal across all aspects of international competition. The ability of the US military to supply Berlin from the air reflected an economic capacity that no nation, not even the Soviet Union, could match. From 1945 to 1970, the US share of the world's gross domestic product pegged between 30 and 40 percent.[8] As the undisputed economic leader, and with the transportation networks and technologies to reach anywhere, the US flexed its muscles in the Cold War, propping up the militaries of allied nations while providing the bulwark for the economic system of the world. Whether it meant bullets or beans, machines guns or the Marshall Plan, the US used its power to combat the influences of the Soviet Union. In turn, the president of the United States took on the moniker of leader of the free world.

VIETNAM: COMPETITION OF THE COLD WAR

With the two superpowers keeping score over which countries fell within the communist or capitalist fold, civil wars across the globe attracted interest, monetary support, and arms from both sides. Vietnam was part of this rubric. The Japanese invaded Vietnam, a French colony, during the war, turning rule over to Vichy France until 1945 when the British took Saigon. Although rebel groups who fought the Japanese, including the Viet Minh led by Ho Chi Minh, advocated an independent state, the French regained control after the war.[9]

Ho Chi Minh's vision of an independent nation stretched back to the end of the First World War. As a young representative to the postwar treaty process in Paris, President Wilson's Fourteen Points and the utopian promise of freedom of independence for all people captivated Ho. He hoped to meet with Wilson but never got close. Instead, he fell into the orbit of international communism, drawn to Lenin's more practical promise to eradicate colonialism.[10] Although Ho Chi Minh aligned his movement with the Soviet Union and Mao's China, he hoped the United States would support the Viet Minh and used the American Declaration of Independence as a source document for his revolutionary thinking.[11] In a slow-burning geopolitical irony, the seeds of freedom promulgated by the Americans in the first half of twentieth century would come back to haunt the nation in the second in Vietnam.

Just a year after the Second World War ended, Ho Chi Minh led his forces to attack the French, beginning an insurgency that lasted until 1954, when the Vietnamese surrounded the French at Dien Bien Phu, choked off their supplies, and forced the French to resupply the fortress by air.[12] The airlift failed, and Ho Chi Minh's forces, commanded by General Vo Nguyen Giap, took Dien Bien Phu.

Despite the Viet Minh's victory over the French, not all Vietnamese followed Ho Chi Minh. After Dien Bien Phu, the world powers split the country in two under the Geneva Accords of 1954, aligning Vietnam with the bifurcation of the Cold War. Ho Chi Minh's Communist Party consolidated power as the Democratic Republic of Vietnam, with Hanoi as the capital.[13] The US bolstered Ngo Dinh Diem in the south of the country at Saigon. They hoped Diem could keep the Republic of Vietnam out of the communist fold.[14] Between both states stood the demilitarized zone (DMZ) across the Seventeenth Parallel, designed to keep Vietnam from civil war. Despite the DMZ, the two sides were in continual conflict for the next two decades, North Vietnam seeking to overthrow the South Vietnamese government and unify the country.

During France's struggle to maintain its colony in the early 1950s, the United States provided economic assistance. The United States sent $25 million in equipment in 1950, expanding to $150 million in 1952.[15] With the Soviet detonation of its atomic weapon in 1949, the loss of China to Mao's communists, and the Korean War, it seemed to the Truman and Eisenhower administrations that Asia was slipping under communist control.

During a press conference in the spring of 1954, as Dien Bien Phu was under siege, President Dwight Eisenhower first referenced the intellectual underpinnings of the domino theory. At the center of this theory was Vietnam. A reporter asked Eisenhower to comment "on the strategic importance of Indochina to the free world." Eisenhower's response put the Vietnam conflict in an economic and geopolitical context:

First of all, you have the specific value of a locality in its production of materials that the world needs. Then you have the possibility that many human beings pass under a dictatorship that is inimical to the free world. Finally, you have broader considerations that might follow what you would call the "falling domino" principle. You have a row of dominoes set up, you knock over the first one, and what will happen to the last one is the certainty that it will go over very quickly. . . . We come to the possible sequence of events, the loss of Indochina, of Burma, of Thailand, of the Peninsula, and Indonesia.[16]

The fall of Dien Bien Phu and the troubles between the nascent governments of Vietnam seemed to portend dark times as former colonial subjects rose to declare their independence from the war-weakened British and French empires. Not only had colonial subjects in Vietnam overthrown a former great power, they had achieved victory under the auspices of communism. By 1954, the US funded "80 percent of the French war" in its defeat and continued to prop up Diem and the regimes that followed as a backstop to hold the domino of South Vietnam.[17]

The Uncertain Trumpet of Logistics: The Doctrine of Flexible Response

Beginning with the second Eisenhower administration and accelerating under the tutelage of President Kennedy, involvement by the United States in the civil war of Vietnam increased. At first, the US confined support to the Central Intelligence Agency, assisting the Diem government in its fight to pacify a growing insurgency in the south run by the National Liberation Front (NLF). The NLF was the political and military organization supported by the North Vietnamese in the south, and their solders were part of the People's Liberation Armed Forces (PLAF, also called the Viet Cong by South Vietnam).[18] Although Eisenhower wanted to keep South Vietnam in the sphere of American influence, he did not want to inject many American troops. His doctrine of the New Look, articulated in 1955, advocated a large nuclear arsenal to keep the Soviets at bay, while holding to a modest defense budget for conventional forces.[19] In an era of nuclear weapons, Eisenhower did not trust that war between the United States and the Soviet Union would stop at a nuclear threshold, and thus wanted to limit options for conventional war.[20]

After President Kennedy's election in 1960, US involvement in Vietnam grew to include ground troops as part of the doctrine named "Flexible Response."[21] General Maxwell Taylor articulated this strategy in his book *An Uncertain Trumpet*, which critiqued the Eisenhower administration's strategy for its inability to respond to Soviet incursions.

Under Flexible Response, Kennedy espoused the need to deter Soviet aims through nuclear deterrence, economic assistance, and military means, using special operations and conventional forces designed to carry out the promises of his inaugural address to "pay any price, bear any burden, meet any hardship, support any friend, oppose any foe to assure the survival and the success of liberty."[22] The Kennedy administration wanted to stop the dominoes from falling and fight a war using ideological, economic, and military options against communist governments, wherever competition occurred— including Vietnam.

Much of the strident optimism of Flexible Response came from the technological leaps that gave the US military the capacity to transport forces anywhere in the world in weeks if not days. Taylor listed transportation to hot spots across the globe as a "Priority 1" requirement for Flexible Response. He stated that air and sealift forces must be "progressively modernized through introduction of cargo jet land and sea planes and roll-on-roll-off shipping."[23] Undergirding the technological improvements that Taylor sought was an implied ability of the United States to move its forces uncontested by air or sea anywhere in the world. A robust defense of international airspace guaranteed freedom of navigation in the air from the routes over Iceland to airways in the Pacific. At sea, the United States Navy protected transportation lanes, continuing its dominance after 1945 and replacing the British as guarantors of freedom of the seas for international commerce. Instead of men-of-war, the navy turned to carriers and airpower to protect the lines of communication running over the oceans.

To transport the forces necessary for such a robust strategy, Flexible Response required that the US Air Force and the US Navy open their transportation arms for planning with the US Army in peacetime, instead of movement to war dictated by "The Joint Chiefs of Staff in an Emergency."[24] The buildup to deployment for war could no longer be an ad hoc affair that waited for crises to begin. Deployments for battle, which took five years at Lake George, a year on the Western Front in 1917, and several months for the push Stalingrad and Guadalcanal, were scheduled for weeks under Flexible Response.

With advances in technology and a strategy that favored quick and bold action, transportation to a conflict anywhere on the earth was a planning factor for the United States by the mid-1960s. As part of the robust and time-sensitive network of logistics, airlift was a critical component rather than a support function, underpinning the concepts of national strategy and rolled into operational and tactical planning at all levels of the US military. For the Vietnam War, this meant that the United States would never want for the materiel forces of war.

After President Kennedy's assassination in 1963, President Johnson did not alter Flexible Response. In fact, he hired General Taylor, since retired, back to work for the administration as a military advisor as the Vietnam War escalated in the mid-1960s. With North Vietnam making incursions along the DMZ, growing US troop presence under the Johnson administration, and increasing battles between US forces and the NVA and Viet Cong—notably the battle of the Ia Drang in 1965—the undeniable prowess of the United States in military power and logistics would be tested by a determined foe in North Vietnam. Although it was a nation of poor farmers, North Vietnam had carried the war into the south for two decades, delivering supplies by bicycle down the Ho Chi Minh Trail since the days of the French. By 1968, the strategic goals of the North Vietnamese and the United States and their lines of communication ran into each other at Khe Sanh. Unlike Guadalcanal, where the Japanese and US met undersupplied for the battle that ensued, the soldiers and material for both sides were in plenty when the fight began in 1968.

TRANSPORTATION AND KINETIC TECHNOLOGIES:
MORE, FARTHER, FASTER

Just as with the transitions between previous eras, transportation vehicles and weapons of war gained great strides in range, power, and capacity from the Late Industrial to the Modern Era. For the Americans, ocean-going ships with increased capacity that accompanied containerization grew from ten thousand tons to forty thousand tons tons by the mid-1960s. In the air, C-130 cargo aircraft carried twenty tons, compared to the C-47s and Ju-57s of the Second World War, which had capacities of two tons. The helicopter, which did not exist in the Second World War, could now carry upwards of eight tons without needing a runway or even a prepared surface for landing.[25] For the North Vietnamese, the 2.5-ton truck was the mainstay of their transportation efforts down the Ho Chi Minh Trail. Although it still had the same cargo capacity and speed as the Late Industrial Era, its efficiency, improved reliability, and lower cost made the truck viable as transportation for the third-world nation.

The jet engine thrust aircraft into the Modern Era. F-4 Phantom II fighters traveled at speeds 300 percent greater than those of the Second World War and carried upwards of nine tons of armament. The B-52 bomber had a range of ten thousand miles on its own fuel and an unlimited range when refueled by another aircraft, a massive increase in performance over bombers of the Late Industrial Era, which had less than a four-thousand-mile range. In addition, the B-52 carried twenty-five tons of bombs, much more than the two to four tons of the B-17. Married to the modern invention of the computer, these aircraft became more accurate and more devastating.

Although the North Vietnamese had aircraft, they did not use them at Khe Sanh. Artillery was their great weapon. Both sides had guns with effective ranges eclipsing ten miles and calibers as high as 152 mm.[26] In addition, machine guns, mortars, rockets, and antiaircraft artillery all graced the battlefield at Khe Sanh.

AIRPLANES VERSUS BICYCLES: ROLLING
THUNDER AND THE HO CHI MINH TRAIL

As the war between North and South Vietnam escalated in the mid-1960s, the United States pressured North Vietnam by bombing the country from the air in an operation called "Rolling Thunder." The genesis for the campaign began in 1964 with President Lyndon Johnson's direction to give "Particular attention . . . to shaping pressures so as to produce the maximum credible deterrent effect on Hanoi."[27] After drawn-out negotiations in Washington throughout the year, aircraft bombing raids under Rolling Thunder began in February 1965.

Reflecting President Johnson's initial direction of "shaping pressures . . . [and] deterrent effect," the strategy for the air campaign called for graduated response. Under graduated response, US bombing would increase until Hanoi backed off its support for an insurgency in South Vietnam. Logistics hubs and transportation networks were targets: "bridges, military installations, and lines of communication."[28]

The Cold War, with its ever-present threat of nuclear war, constrained President Johnson and put limits on the bombing. For example, under Rolling Thunder, the president forbade bombing north of the Twentieth Parallel to avoid incursion into Chinese territory, and directed a safe zone around Hanoi to minimize civilian casualties.[29] While Johnson wanted to pressure the North Vietnamese into stopping their attempt to unite the two Vietnams under northern rule, he did not want the conflict to risk nuclear war. A democratic South Vietnam was important, but it was not worth an exchange of missiles with the Soviets or Chinese.

Thus, Rolling Thunder had political limitations that neither Guadalcanal nor Stalingrad had. The two earlier campaigns were part of a wider global war and were contested in distant regions. The battles unfolded in near-obscurity, and the results were relayed after the fact. With the improved telecommunications of the late twentieth century, an errant bomb that struck a civilian target, or was propagandized as such, was fodder for international condemnation on the evening news and the next day's newspaper.[30] As Mark Clodfelter reports in *The Limits of Air Power,* "France, Britain, and India officially denounced the 1966 raids on oil storage areas in Hanoi and Haiphong. The spring 1967 raids on power plants drew similar responses."[31]

Despite these restrictions and political restraints, Rolling Thunder rained an impressive amount of destruction on North Vietnam. Air force and naval aircraft dropped over 643,000 tons of bombs and "destroyed 65 percent of the North's oil storage capacity, 59 percent of its power plants, 55 percent of its major bridges, 9,821 vehicles and 1,966 railroad cars."[32] This destruction, however, failed to stop the flow of munitions and supplies into South Vietnam, including the large buildup of forces around Khe Sanh by late 1967. The coercive campaign came at a high cost of operating expensive aircraft against a third-world nation that had only a modest amount of industry. From 1965 to 1966, the cost required for the United States to achieve $1.00 in damage rose from $6.60 to $9.60.[33] The aircraft the US lost over North Vietnam followed a path similar to rise in cost: "171 in 1965 . . . 280 in 1966 . . . 326 in 1967."[34]

Besides the steep costs, Operation Rolling Thunder did not stem the flow of material from the Soviets and Chinese to North Vietnam. US Defense Secretary Robert McNamara reported to the US Congress in 1967, "The North Vietnam seacoast runs for 400 miles. . . . The mining of Haiphong or the total destruction of Haiphong port facilities would not prevent . . . foreign shipping . . . even if the inevitable damage to foreign shipping were to be accepted, would only lead to total reliance on land importation through communist China. The common border between the two countries is about 500 air miles long."[35] Under the threat of nuclear escalation, striking Chinese or Soviet shipping to get at the supplies sent to arm the North was too risky a gamble. Moreover, keeping the coastline of North Vietnam free of shipping was impossible.

If the supply side of the logistics equation was difficult for airpower to address, the demand side of the war in South Vietnam was even more daunting. The war in the south was a counterinsurgency and not a conventional war. Ho Chi Minh relied on his guerrilla army of 245,000 Viet Cong already living in the South Vietnam to prosecute the majority of the war. These guerrillas fought infrequently and relied on the North for ammunition—versus the food, fuel, or any number of supplies that a large conventional army required. The miniscule needs of the Viet Cong dropped the needs to "34 tons a day from sources outside the South. Seven 2 1/2 tons trucks could transport the requirement."[36] Although airpower could destroy much, cutting deliveries below this small amount of logistics was impossible. Ironically, the only weapon capable of such destruction was a nuclear device, an option not available in the bipolar landscape of deterrence in the mid-1960s. Thus, without elimination of all lines of communication from the North, the insurgency in the South could have continued indefinitely.

1967: THE YEAR OF CHOICES

By 1967, the Johnson administration had increased US troop strength in Vietnam to 480,000, with the trucks, tanks, aircraft, and all forms of armament increased to match.[37] With the surge of forces and the steady, if uneven, progress in the political situation of South Vietnam, Maxwell Taylor stated in January 1967, "I have a feeling that the Vietnamese situation may change drastically by the end of 1967."[38] Although military leadership at the lower levels was much less optimistic, General Westmoreland, the commander of Military Assistance Command Vietnam (MACV) in Saigon exuded the same confidence.

The long supply lines from the United States ran unabated and undeterred; and, by 1967, Westmoreland had the men and supplies to prosecute the war on his terms. General Westmoreland planned to use this large force in Vietnam to "militarize the pacification program," centralize pacification under his MACV command in Saigon, and end the insurgency in the South.[39] On the home front in the US, the war was increasingly unpopular; and, by the fall of 1967, President Johnson had "initiated an intensive public relations campaign" to shore up support at home, even bringing Westmoreland back to the States for interviews and speeches.[40]

The logistics capacity of the United States helped give Westmoreland an optimistic outlook—the United States could send enough soldiers and weapons to Vietnam to end the conflict through military means. By 1967, the American population saw the increase in troops and materiel with uneven progress as cause for pessimism. Opposite Westmoreland, the North Vietnamese Army (NVA) and its leadership was embroiled in a political battle for control of the strategy of the war.

After twenty years of conflict, the burdens of war had taken a toll on the internal unity of the North Vietnamese government. Although the Rolling Thunder campaign did not stop the flow of logistics and soldiers into the South, as the Americans hoped, the campaign drove massive relocations of the North's population into rural areas and required the diversion of entire industries.[41] Besides internal struggles, the war put the North Vietnamese at odds with the Soviets and the Chinese. In a protoexample of the future Sino-Soviet split, the Soviets urged caution with North Vietnamese war aims to avoid escalation from the Americans, while Mao Tse Tung urged a higher tempo of guerrilla warfare.[42]

With the North's limited economy, even before Rolling Thunder began, Ho Chi Minh and General Giap wanted to keep the war in a guerrilla stage. From a logistics perspective, both leaders well understood that undertaking a conventional war in the South would sap and strain North Vietnam's industrial base. The short hit-and-run battles fought in South Vietnam, with their minimal supply requirements, typified the revolutionary ideology of guerrilla warfare set forth by Mao and adopted by Ho Chi Minh and Giap.[43] According to Mao, guerrilla warfare passed through three phases: "Phase I: organization, consolidation, and preservation . . . Phase II: progressive expansion . . . Phase III: decision, or destruction of the enemy."[44] In theory, through each of these phases the guerrilla armies aimed to rally the local populace to their cause, build support, increase attacks, and eventually form a conventional army to defeat the ruling government.[45] General Giap and Ho Chi Minh were content, much like Mao, to accommodate action on a continuum—moving from guerrilla to conventional and back again, when the time permitted. The massing of the North Vietnamese Army to overwhelm the French at Dien Bien Phu and then shifting back to an insurgent war against the government of South Vietnam typified Giap's strategy. According to Phillip Davidson in *Vietnam at War,* "Giap believed that the form of combat must be chosen by an analysis of strategic effects actually existing at any given moment. . . . [Giap] strayed from Mao on the 'man versus arms' question. To Mao, power of the human will was supreme. To Giap, human will was important but weapons played an equally significant role."[46]

From the opposite political view, General Secretary Le Duan and his ally,

Le Doc Thou, analyzed the situation in 1963 and believed that attacking cities in the south would undermine Saigon and lead to revolution. The local uprisings in Hue and Saigon in 1966 against the government of South Vietnam reinforced this view.[47] Ho Chi Minh and Giap's view of protracted struggle lost out to the political machinations of General Secretary Le Duan and Le Doc Thou. As Lien Hang T. Nguyen states in *Hanoi's War*, "Le Duan steamrolled over his adversaries in the North as well as in the South. . . . Rather than continue the policy of paying equal attention to northern economic development and the southern liberation struggle, Le Duan subordinated the former to promote the latter."[48] Le Duan and Le Duc Tho's rise resulted in purges within the party and required turning the nation into a police state from 1963 onward to keep power.[49] At the highest level, Ho Chi Minh and Giap, although revered and feared internationally, became mere figureheads and supporting officials to Le Duan's party. Within the communist bloc, Le Duan pulled North Vietnam away from the cautious Soviet stances, setting in motion the plan to attack the south. From a military context, Le Duan shifted North Vietnam's strategy from Giap's patient view, who worried that the North could not long support a large conventional war, to call the for the "General Offensive, General Uprising," which would manifest as the Tet Offensive, with the siege at Khe Sanh as a key site of battle, in January 1968.[50] From a material and logistics view, the internal purges silenced dissenting voices, placing ultimate faith in Le Duan's path and requiring a large buildup of forces.

American involvement in the war tested Le Duan's strategy from its inception. The Johnson administration escalated American troop levels in 1965 with Secretary of Defense McNamara arguing for "approximately 600,000 additional men" by 1966.[51] By 1967, the combined air arms of the US Air Force and US Navy struck North Vietnam and the Ho Chi Minh Trail while the increased US troop presence in the South thwarted North Vietnam's efforts. While Rolling Thunder had failed to stop the North, as mentioned it displaced the North's industry and hamstrung NVA support to the Viet Cong. As a result, the insurgency in South Vietnam suffered as did Le Duan's hopes for the "General Offensive, General Uprising."[52]

In January 1967, a Viet Cong council meeting in the Chau Thanh district, south of Saigon, reported, "As for the masses, they are afflicted by fear—fear of hardships, difficulties, illnesses, lack of work and pay, the back and forth movement in weak areas, and enemy terrorism."[53] The Chau Thanh Viet Cong attributed the low morale to the disruption of their logistics by the US military and ARVN, who had "captured all three of our food procurement and supply centers" and "furthermore, the enemy carried out its economic blockade plan through encirclement and the use of poisonous chemicals to spoil our rice and other crops."[54] Though the insurgency only needed seven trucks' worth of supplies a day to survive in the South, this did not equate to an easy life for the Viet Cong. According to William Allison, "under such conditions, then, a decisive victory [for the North Vietnamese] was needed sooner rather than later."[55]

With increasing American pressure from 1965 onward and increased side-lining of those in the North who favored the more pragmatic path of Ho Chi Minh and Giap, the Communist Party set itself toward conventional warfare.

To pursue a definitive victory, the North Vietnamese built up their forces for an offensive in January 1968, designed to take advantage of the Tet holi-day—an agreed ceasefire for the past several years. The North Vietnam-ese planned to use the Tet Offensive to flood the cities of the South with NVA troops and Viet Cong, evolving the war from its guerrilla roots and beginning a conventional battle. Tet had three objectives: first, "Annihilate and cause the total disintegration of the bulk of the puppet army [ARVN]"; second, "Annihilate a significant portion of the American military's troop strength and destroy a significant portion of his war equipment"; and third, "Crush the American will to commit aggression of force."[56] The campaign to besiege Khe Sanh was part of the bigger plan for the Tet Offensive. Khe Sanh fit squarely within the second objective of the NVA, which supported the third.

Was Khe Sanh a diversion or main thrust for the Tet offensive? The ques-tion still resonates within the historiography of Tet, with viewpoints ranging from General Westmoreland's postwar synopsis that Khe Sanh was to be a "catastrophic Dien Bien Phu," to Giap's postmortem that "Khe Sanh was not that important to us," to scholar Lien-Hang Nguyen's insight fifty years after Khe Sanh that the battle "was to really tie down the United States and have them focus on Khe Sanh when really the main target were the cities and towns across South Vietnam."[57] Alternatively, and even more provocative, as Edwin Moises asks in *The Myths of Tet*, was the North much more capable of sustaining a conventional campaign?[58] As the underpinning of combat, an examination of the strategy and execution of logistics at Khe Sanh will help answer these questions.

End of the Line: North Vietnam's View of Logistics

With their supplies and war effort stretched thin under US military pressure from the air and land, the North Vietnamese took comfort in the belief that they were wearing out their adversary. In 1966, the United States captured documents outlining the North Vietnamese assessment American weaknesses:

1. The (war) waged by US imperialism in both zones of our country is entirely unjust and illegal. 2. The US cannot devote all of its strength and money to war in Vietnam because of its role as an international gendarme and because of its preparations for a nuclear war. . . . 3. The aggressors cannot solve their logistical problems . . . everything must be transported to South Vietnam from the United States and they cannot meet their logistical needs when they step up the tempo of war. 4. They cannot meet . . . the (techniques) of a people's war, which is a multiform war in which the enemy . . . is compelled to deploy his forces everywhere, divide his forces into many parts, each part of which then is encircled.[59]

These NVA planners believed the United States did not possess the economic means to be a nuclear police officer, send its men and material to Vietnam to bolster the South, and prosecute an offensive against the North. In an article in 1967, Le Duan echoed the assessment:

For the past few decades the market and raw material problem has become a thorny one for the imperialist capitalists as the successes of the socialist and national liberation revolutions in a series of countries have narrowed the imperialist markets and spheres of influence. . . . Imperialism has been under attack everywhere, chiefly in Asia, Africa, and Latin America, and it is American imperialism that has suffered the most setbacks. . . . They have been militarizing their economy and frantically speeding up the arms race. . . . In particular, U.S. imperialism has been most urgently preparing for war, a fact that is proved by the considerable increase in its annual military budget.[60]

Khe Sanh, a remote US outpost closer to the Ho Chi Minh Trail in Laos than to the nearest US base at Dang Ho, seemed to fit into the image of an overextended America for the North Vietnamese. South and west of the

DMZ and only thirty miles from the border with Laos, Khe Sanh was at the end of two lines of communication (see Figure 5.1). The first line of communication ran from the manufacturing and population centers of the United States over the ocean to Hawaii, then to the Philippines, and then to the ports or airfields at Saigon, Cam Rhan Bay, or Da Nang; and the second line ran from either road or air to Dong Ha for final airlift to Khe Sanh. Given such extended distances, if the NVA and Viet Cong struck in the cities of South Vietnam during Tet and besieged Khe Sanh, the North Vietnamese reasoned that the US could not fight in the cities and the countryside with enough men and materiel to succeed on two fronts. With Khe Sanh's close location to North Vietnam, it also tilted the geographic and distance equation in favor of the NVA. Basing their strategy on the perceived logistical weakness of their enemy, the North Vietnamese moved increasing numbers of men and supplies down the Ho Chi Minh Trail during the second half of 1967.

While Khe Sanh and Tet fit into the ideological struggle of communism versus capitalism, the North Vietnamese underestimated the economic largess and logistics network of the United States. Not only could the United States transport men, material, and supplies to Vietnam, but the country had the technological capability and the network of logistics necessary to keep its soldiers supplied indefinitely by air, land, or sea.

As much as the North Vietnamese underestimated the largess of American logistics, they overestimated their own capability to transport and supply. Much of this misdiagnosis can be attributed to Le Duan's ideological cleansing of dissenting voices within political and military circles.[61] Those officers aligned with Giap were also the most seasoned with conventional fighting in battles such as Dien Bien Phu and Ia Drang. With such experiences, they also had a better understanding of the support they needed to sustain such fights. As the planning for the Tet Offensive wound into 1967, local commanders in South Vietnam echoed Giap's caution about moving from a guerrilla campaign to conventional battle. Dang Kinh, a Viet Cong commander, told Giap, "You will all starve to death! . . . Sir, our military region cannot handle another regiment. . . . I'm a guerrilla commander, if you give me too many troops, I will not be able to command all of them."[62] Despite the misgivings of military leaders, Le Duan and Le Duc Tho were certain of victory, much as Westmoreland was convinced of his superiority in firepower and material.

As Mark Bowden states in *Hue 1968,* "When the plans for the Tet Offensive were drawn up . . . Westy's [Westmoreland's] ramrod optimism paled next to the party's. . . . Over the objections of more realistic politburo members, Hanoi had convinced itself that victory was within its grasp."[63]

The tension between ideological certainty and pragmatic planning appeared in the final directive of the Fourteenth Plenum. Published two weeks prior to the Tet Offensive, the directive of the Fourteenth Plenum acknowledged the certainty of victory up front: "Even though the American imperialists, the impetuous leaders of imperialism . . . possess massive material and technological power . . . they have encountered ferocious resistance from a nation of more than 30 million people who use the peasants and workers. . . . The American imperialists are now at as strategic dead end."[64] From a logistics perspective, the North Vietnamese Communist Party was also optimistic, "The South Vietnamese revolution also has a large, direct rear area of support, the socialist North, which is in turn linked to an even larger rear area, meaning the socialist camp." Thus, the North's material support, bolstered by Soviet and Chinese aid, would serve as the lifeline for the Tet Offensive and Khe Sanh.

As the directive wound into an evaluation of the North's conventional combat capability, it veered from the overt optimism about the coming victory against the Americans to uncharacteristic realism: "We still have a number of weaknesses in logistics, supply, and transportation, and in our enemy proselyting and puppet proselyting operations. We need to strive to overcome these weaknesses and difficulties during the course of the development of the revolution."[65] This blunt assessment of weakness echoed the concerns of those military leaders at strategic levels of the party, such as General Giap, to tactical leaders who would carry at the offensive such as the aforementioned Dang Kinh of the Viet Cong. Supplying a large conventional army while directing local uprisings over the cities of South Vietnam would be no easy task. Given Le Duan and Le Duc Tho's ruthless purge of dissenting voices in the North and their own denigration of American's capability to sustain the war, such a frank acknowledgement of shortcomings was almost subversive.

The Fourteen Plenum, however, did not dwell on the underlying weakness of logistics for long. Reaching a crescendo of optimism as the document discussed operational goals, "Our policy is not simply to launch a general

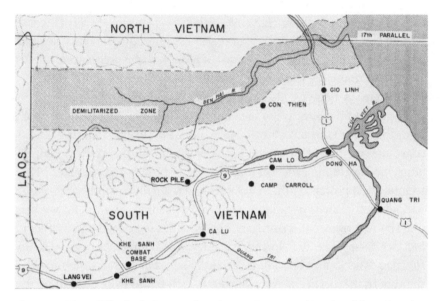

Figure 5.1. Map of Khe Sanh, Route 9 from Laos to Dong Ha. (Reprinted from Captain Moyars S. Shore II, *The Battle for Khe Sanh* [Washington, DC: US Marine Corps Historical Branch, 1969].)

offensive but simultaneously launch a general insurrection . . . which will enable millions of people . . . to rise up in insurrection, coordinating with our armed forces to annihilate and disintegrate the enemy army . . . turn the enemy's rear area and his strategic stockpiles into OUR rear area and OUR strategic stockpiles, rapidly change the balance of forces in our favor and against the enemy, and secure a decisive victory for our side."[66]

Thus, the North Vietnamese hoped to create an insurrection involving millions, while also seizing the supplies and rear areas of the Americans for their own use. The unrealistic expectation belied historical norms of industrial and postindustrial warfare: capturing the enemy's logistics and using it for your own supply had not been a staple of warfare for over a century. As if to put an exclamation point on the triumph of hope over reality, General Giap was sidelined in the final planning for Tet and "left for Eastern Europe and did not return until well into 1968. The defeated Ho Chi Minh followed suit."[67]

Begging for Dien Bien Phu: Khe Sanh and US Strategy in 1967

As the presence of more soldiers, sailors, airmen, and Marines from the United States increased in South Vietnam into 1967, Westmoreland possessed the forces to counter any North Vietnamese incursion. To stop the flow of men and supplies from the North, both Secretary of Defense McNamara and Westmoreland championed a "strong point obstacle system" across the DMZ.[68] At the end of this system in the west lay Khe Sanh. Although the strong-point obstacle system failed under the weight of its own logistics requirements and bureaucratic infighting between the US Army and Marines, the significance of Khe Sanh remained. The outpost occupied a critical location, close enough to the DMZ to monitor the North Vietnamese and help stem the flow of men and supplies into South Vietnam.[69] Besides its key geographic position, General Westmoreland also had Khe Sanh in mind as "an eventual jump-off point for ground operations to cut the Ho Chi Minh trail."[70] Westmoreland always hoped for a widening of the war deep into Laos to allow his ground forces to cut the lines of communication from North Vietnam, and Khe Sanh was his starting point for any future approval to attack the trail. At the geopolitical level, carrying the war into Laos was no easy matter. Westmoreland had sent small pockets of ground forces into Laos; it was in secret, however, with few troops before 1968. For the Johnson administration, expanding the war into other nations was a precarious consideration, for fear of Soviet or Chinese nuclear retaliation against the United States in support of North Vietnam.

In early 1967, with increasing NVA movements near Khe Sanh, Westmoreland's MACV and the III Marines, which controlled the region, sent increasing numbers of troops to the base to protect the small communications battalion at the base as they monitored NVA radio traffic across the DMZ and down the Ho Chi Minh Trail. Marine leadership, first under General Walt and then General Cushman, was never sanguine about the prospects for holding on to Khe Sanh. Their pessimism was founded on two factors: first, the Marines felt the strategy for the Quang Tri province, in which Khe Sanh was located, should involve quick-offensive operations and not holding onto fortified positions; and second, the supply route over Route 9 was tenuous.[71]

Ground travel over Route 9 to the base was difficult. Although Khe Sanh was only twenty-four miles from Dong Ha, Route 9 (see Figure 5.1) was a dirt road with several bridges in various stages of disrepair. The poor road made for challenging travel during the wet season from May to September. In addition, the road was close to the DMZ, and with steep mountains rising over fifteen hundred feet above a dense jungle canopy as high as ninety feet off the ground. In such an environment, US military movements were easy targets for enemy patrols. With the ground line of communication unreliable, the airfield at Khe Sanh was the only way to supply the base. In 1967, Marine staff officers set up a war game to simulate resupply of the base by air while under siege from NVA forces. The Marines discovered that without supplies transported by land over Route 9, the Marines could not hold Khe Sanh under sustained attack.[72]

Despite Marine misgivings, Westmoreland continued to advocate for Khe Sanh and ordered the Marines to stay in 1967. In February, to bolster their position, the Marines sent US Navy Seabees in to improve and lengthen the runway to hold up better under the wet weather and provide a longer landing surface for larger cargo aircraft, specifically the C-130 Hercules, which had a capacity of up to twenty tons. Marine companies sent to protect the Seabees encountered increasing North Vietnamese resistance on roving patrols. Concerned about the base, the Marines sent a second company to Khe Sanh in early spring. In April and May, the Marines fought a series of heavy engagements for hills 861 and 881 North and South (see Figure 5.2) against the North Vietnamese. The US military later named these the "Hill Battles of Khe Sanh."[73] The Marines were victorious, but at a steep cost of 155 killed and 425 wounded for an engagement that involved only a few companies. For the North Vietnamese it was much worse—1,000 dead.[74]

The victory was significant for the future supply of Khe Sanh. Unlike Dien Bien Phu, where the French had ceded the high ground to the Viet Minh, "the Marines held the hills . . . thus hampering communist observation and fire on the vital airstrip through which supplies and replacements flowed."[75] While keeping the high ground away from the North Vietnamese helped the Americans supply the base, those Marines on the hills would also require replenishment. Much like their brethren on the base, their supplies would come by helicopter, with travel by land blocked by the NVA.

After the hill battles, the war game that predicted the difficulty of logistics at Khe Sanh seemed prescient. The monsoons during the summer of 1967

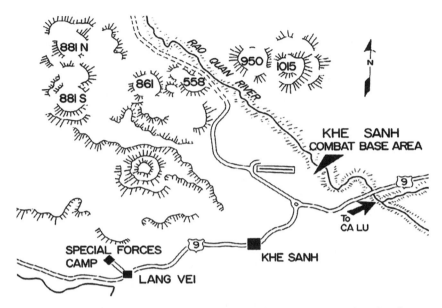

Figure 5.2. Map of Khe Sanh Hills, Combat Base, and Rao Quan River. (Reprinted from Captain Moyars S. Shore II, *The Battle for Khe Sanh* [Washington, DC: US Marine Corps Historical Branch, 1969].)

washed away the runway, requiring major construction and leaving the surface unusable to heavy transport aircraft until November. During these repairs, engineers brought in new metal matting for the runway and put down a new foundation of crushed rock to assist with drainage.[76]

While the runway was down, III Marine Headquarters reinforced supplies and artillery from Dong Ha over Route 9 with a convoy of eighty-five vehicles and long-range 175 mm artillery pieces.[77] On 21 July 1967, the NVA ambushed the convoy and forced the Americans to stop short and deliver the supplies to Camp Carol (see Figure 5.1).[78] With the threat to land transportation and the runway down, the Marines relied on helicopters as the sole means of resupplying Khe Sanh from August to November. During this time, the NVA also increased the men and supplies moving down the Ho Chi Minh Trail to besiege Khe Sanh and prosecute the Tet Offensive.

All the activity at Khe Sanh in the spring and summer of 1967 reinforced Westmoreland's view of the base. While the Marines wanted to abandon the base in the summer of 1967 before it became a focal-point battle with a

vulnerable line of supply, Westmoreland saw the increased attention at Khe
Sanh as evidence that the North was building toward a conventional fight.
In the general's view, indications that the North was building toward an offensive was good news. Instead of having to fight an insurgency bolstered by
the North in South Vietnam, the US could defend the border areas, like Khe
Sanh, to prove to "the world that this war was an invasion. By forcing the
enemy to fight on the borders, from his sanctuaries, we bring frontier defense into sharp and realistic focus."[79] More important, defending the frontier would allow Westmoreland to apply the full effect of modern American
firepower onto the North Vietnamese Army without the "causalities and ref-
ugees" attendant with fighting guerrilla warfare in the more populous areas
of South Vietnam.[80]

In defending his strategic thinking about holding Khe Sanh, Westmoreland turned to the battle that loomed large in circles of American policy
makers: Dien Bien Phu. While the French had suffered a humiliating defeat
at a similar outpost at Dien Bien Phu, the American general saw no parallel,
given the superiority of US airpower and logistics. He stated, "The French
had limited airpower; American air support; including B-52s, was massive.
. . . The airstrip at Dien Bien Phu was inadequate, and French lacked aerial
resupply capability other than by small parachutes . . . the airstrip at Khe
Sanh could handle C-130 transports . . . they could resupply the base both by
huge cargo parachutes and by specially packaged items disgorged from the
rear of low-flying C-130s. The French had no helicopters; ours were plentiful, including cargo helicopters."[81] In his memoirs, Westmoreland stood by
the belief that "Khe Sanh will stand in history, I am convinced, as a classic
example of how to defeat a numerically superior besieging force by coordinated application of firepower.[82]"

Besides Dien Bien Phu, Westmoreland also interjected answers to questions about whether the US could defend Khe Sanh while also covering the
rest of South Vietnam. Although unaware of the belief of the North Vietnamese that the United States could not bring materiel and men to the defense of the cities and Khe Sanh, Westmoreland seemed to answer them in
absentia. In a message to the General Wheeler, the chairman of the Joint
Chiefs of Staff, Westmoreland stated, "The idea that we can't fight the enemy
along the borders without seriously diverting forces from the populated areas is not entirely sound. . . . In general, I keep my reserves in populated areas

(along the coast in II Corps) where they can be productively employed to grind down the enemy while awaiting other missions."[83] To get to these missions, the US used army helicopters—a tried-and-true delivery system that had provided near-limitless mobility throughout Vietnam—proving itself in everything from medical evacuation to moving troops across the battlefield.[84] Far from being limited, as his North Vietnamese adversaries thought, Westmoreland could execute any battle required of his forces in Vietnam with superior airpower and air mobility. Thus, Westmoreland wanted another Dien Bien Phu, not with the same outcome, but rather with the same concentration of enemy forces, so his army could use firepower and maneuver to destroy it. The historical precedent of Dien Bien Phu and Westmoreland's preference for concentration and conventional battle would lead to a blinding focus on Khe Sanh during Tet.

With the importance of Khe Sanh cemented, Westmoreland ordered the Marines to hold the base after the summer of 1967. As the NVA moved more forces into the area, the Marines decided they now needed two battalions to hold the base and reinforced the garrison on November 1967.[85] According to Major General Thompkins of the US Marine Corps, the Marines were "not at all excited about the idea," fearing they would be undersupplied and overrun.[86] Whether Khe Sanh would be a post overrun or a siege lifted depended on the forces, armaments, and supplies that the North Vietnamese could bring to bear against base. While Westmoreland was exhilarated by the chance to make Dien Bien Phu anew with American technical and economic might, neither he nor any American leaders understood the size of the force that would invest Khe Sanh. The two battalions isolated at Khe Sanh, as if surrounded by water, would face two full divisions of the North Vietnamese Army.

Against Air Supremacy: Down the Ho Chi Minh Trail in 1967

Although Rolling Thunder did not achieve strategic objectives for US policy makers in Washington, DC, its impact on the North Vietnamese line of communication stretching down the Ho Chi Minh Trail was significant. The NVA constructed the trail and geared operations to mitigate the ability of US airpower to interdict their logistics. In the early 1960s, with US presence in Vietnam consisting of advisors and special-operations forces, there was little need for heavy artillery, associated ammunition, and the transportation technologies to transport them. Thus, porters and bicycles sufficed to sustain the insurgency in the South.[87] By 1967, with the North Vietnamese strategy transitioning to conventional warfare, the NVA needed a more robust network of logistics and with it improved methods to counter US airpower.

While the images of the army being and pushed and pedaled down the Ho Chi Minh Trail formed an important part of the narrative—the militarily superior Americans out-supplied by the primitive North Vietnamese—this was not reality by 1967. The NVA possessed a robust system of trucks, drivers, maintenance personnel, and over twenty-five thousand members of the NVA in Laos.[88] The Seventh Air Force Intelligence Directorate described the trail:

The North Vietnamese have a considerable logistics system, manned by a relatively large number of personnel along the corridor routes to render assistance and to man way stations. . . . Generally vehicle shelters and supply storage areas are located at intervals varying from 10 to 30 kilometers. . . . Each shelter area is commanded by a North Vietnamese officer who controls truck convoy moments and provides assistance to disabled vehicles. Normally, convoys arrive at shelter areas prior to sunrise. After arrival, each truck's cargo is unloaded at one of the supply shelters and then the truck is parked in a vehicle shelter. Drivers sleep in hammocks located in the jungle nearby. After sunset, the trucks are reloaded and the journey continues.[89]

Rather than have the supply columns—six trucks in size—move in one unit the length of the trail, the NVA had the trucks move between "three and seven shelter areas [30 to 210 kilometers (18 to 125 miles)] and return to their point of origin."[90] In this way, they kept the drivers familiar with the roadway and operation of the same truck.[91] The familiarity lessened the need for light at night—a critical requirement to avoid detection from the air. This system of logistics required much labor, however, to load and unload the cargo at way stations. What the NVA lacked in technology they made up for in sheer numbers of soldiers and support troops.

The biggest deterrent to airpower was the location of the Ho Chi Minh Trail itself—Laos (see Figure 5.1). Movement through Laos, allowed the North Vietnamese to travel parallel to the South Vietnamese border for easy movement of supplies in and out of South Vietnam, thus avoiding the DMZ. The terrain of Laos also allowed the NVA to take advantage of the small roads that wound through jungle canopy at the bottom of steep terrain. Added to this geographic advantage, weather wreaked havoc on air operations. Although the fighters and bombers of the era had far superior navigational instruments than their predecessors of the Second World War, the tactical aircraft of 1967–1968 could not target through clouds. This left only USAF B-52 bombers and "two A-6 squadrons" of the US Navy with the ability to bomb without visual contact.[92] Despite the B-52s' ability to bomb targets in any weather, due to political constraints of using the nuclear-capable aircraft, the US military excluded the aircraft from the interdiction campaign.[93]

The North Vietnamese used bad weather and darkness to blunt the technological superiority of their foe's airpower, much as the Japanese at Guadalcanal, the Soviets at Stalingrad, and the Germans before their pullback to the Hindenburg line in 1917. As in the Second World War, transportation during a clear day with aircraft present was hazardous. Low cloud cover helped shield truck convoys during the day, while at night the NVA preferred a full moon. With steady moonlight, trucks, in standard convoys of six vehicles, turned off their lights to mask movement. On darker nights, the lead truck was the sole vehicle with standard lights on, while the following trucks used red lights on the bottom of the truck to provide some ambient illumination.[94] To better mask the light signature, the NVA fashioned special hoods to focus the light forward and down.[95] The sight or sound of aircraft brought the convoys to a stop and the drivers would exit the vehicle and move as far from the road as possible.[96]

Weather and darkness were not panaceas for the North Vietnamese. The wet season, May through September, stopped most movement down the trail with flooded roads and impassable river crossings. In addition, the United States had infrared radars and photographic equipment mounted on reconnaissance aircraft to track movements down the Ho Chi Minh Trail.[97] With the interplay between weather, combat power, and logistics, the movement down the trail followed a pattern similar to the movements to Lake George, the trenches on the Western Front, over the water to Guadalcanal, and in the Eastern Front. Seventh Air Force officers recorded, "The war exhibited ebb and flow characteristics. Almost traditionally, during the dry season from November to April, the enemy moved to the offensive and expanded his holdings. Pushing back the friendly forces, he tried to consolidate newly won regions. But, as the wet season came on, from May to September, the communists were forced to pull back."⁹⁸

More important than the physical environment of Laos were the political constraints placed on the United States by North Vietnamese logistics movements through Laos. While MACV wanted to stop the flow of men and materiel to support the insurgency in South Vietnam, the command also wanted to support the Laotian government, which had its own communist insurgency to attend to. An internal report on the interdiction campaign by the USAF stated, "The increased tempo of air operations over Laos in 1966 had caused a correspondingly rising number of inadvertent strikes [destruction of Laotian property and people]. The tragic trend continued into early 1967. This was an extremely sensitive issue to the Laotian Government, which was struggling against a stubborn enemy who was attempting to win adherents to his cause. . . . The USAF did not treat . . . the incident[s] lightly."⁹⁹ In addition, the Johnson administration worried that the US widening the war into neighboring countries, even in secret, might attract more attention from Soviet and Chinese foes and thus raising the specter of nuclear conflict.¹⁰⁰

These political concerns filtered down as Rules of Engagement (ROE) for the air interdiction efforts of the United States. For example, the ROE in 1967 stated, "Any target of opportunity could be struck, day or night, provided it was located within 200 yards of a motorable trail or road"; and, "It was mandatory that aircraft, which carried out strikes without FAC [Forward Air Control] . . . assistance, confirm their position by radar or TACAN [Tactical Air Navigation beacon] beforehand. If any doubt existed concerning his position, the pilot was not to expend his ordnance."¹⁰¹ US pilots had to strike targets on or near roads to avoid innocents; and, if they were unsure of their position, they would not bomb.

With these political limitations put upon US airpower, the North Vietnamese adjusted tactics. As the NVA moved supplies down the trail, they positioned shelters for trucks "500 to 1,000 meters from the edge of the road."¹⁰² In addition, the North Vietnamese lessened their logistics to support transportation efforts by minimizing the maintenance done to trucks once they were moving down the trail. According to US intelligence reports, "Repairable vehicles were towed to the next area for repairs; non-repairable trucks were stripped of parts and moved off the road. Generally, only minor maintenance—welding or parts replacement—was performed on the trail."¹⁰³

Besides their passive means to thwart US airpower—by geography, logistics processes, or technological solutions—the NVA also provided their own offensive counterweight using antiaircraft artillery (AAA). By early 1967, the USAF estimated there were 185 AAA pieces operated by the NVA in Laos.[104] The system was effective, especially against slower-moving propeller aircraft such as the A-1 Skyraider.[105] With the increased AAA presence and activity on the Ho Chi Minh Trail, the USAF took fire on 14 percent of its sorties in the first half of 1967. As the weather dried in September and the NVA moved the logistics down the trail to support the future siege at Khe Sanh and the Tet offensive, the rate jumped to 22 percent.[106] Combat losses followed the same pattern. From January to June 1967, the USAF averaged the loss rate of about three aircraft per month over Laos. The last three months of the year, the rate of loss increased to five aircraft per month, with eight downed aircraft in December 1967 alone.[107]

Even if their efforts to fend off airpower did not work, the NVA could always scrap movement by machines and use people and bicycles as they had during the early days of the trail. The system of human-powered transportation—harkening back to the Preindustrial Era—was a credible backup. Seventh Air Force reported in 1968, "This allowed them to counter even the most severe interdiction efforts."[108]

The increased losses of USAF aircraft corresponded to the higher rates of soldiers and equipment the NVA moved down the Ho Chi Minh Trail in the fall and early winter of 1967. According to Vietnam War scholar John Prados, in the fall of 1967 the NVA moved "212 weapons, among them eight 152 mm guns [with an effective range of more than ten miles], sixteen 130 mm guns, thirty-six 122 mm guns, eight 105 mm howitzers, twelve 100 mm guns, 120 rocket launchers, and assorted other pieces."[109] In addition, the NVA emplaced 184 antiaircraft weapons ranging from machines guns to larger-caliber 37 mm pieces.[110] By comparison, General Giap's forces that surrounded Dien Bien Phu fourteen years prior had sixty artillery pieces, fifty mortars, and about seventy-five other heavy weapons, including recoilless guns and mountain guns.[111]

Added to this static firepower, the NVA also moved nine tanks down the trail, a logistics move the US did not detect until the siege began on 20 January 1968.[112] Using a convoluted route, the NVA sent PT-76 amphibious tanks down the Ho Chi Minh Trail and through small rivers and overland to avoid detection from the air. In *The Valley of Decision,* Prados and Stubbe describe the journey:

Simply advancing down Route 9 with tanks would have been foolhardy. . . . The NVA armor made a wide circuit to the south, traversing the new road they had built and then following a trail the last few kilometers to the Xe Pon river. The tanks entered the river eleven kilometers south of Route 9, swam a kilometer or two, and then mounted the west bank of the river. For about six kilometers the tanks apparently drove overland up the Laotian side before entering the river once more to swim perhaps four more kilometers to the Vietnamese village of Lang Troai [a few miles west of Lang Vei—see Figure 5.1].[113]

Thus, when the battle began in late January, it saw the first use of NVA armor in the Vietnam War.[114]

In addition, the NVA poured food into the area, hiding it in large storage areas of cave complexes throughout the region. By the start of the battle in early 1968, US reconnaissance aircraft recorded "6 Bivouac areas, 7 storage areas, 16 probable base camps, 250 Bunkers, 636 Fox Holes."[115] The total of the food supplies of the North Vietnamese Army at the start of the battle was sixty days' worth.[116] In addition to the stashed food, the 325th C and the 304th Divisions had nine hundred tons of supplies built up for the first phase of the offensive—representing an additional three days of supply.[117]

Despite the impressive logistics infrastructure, for the soldiers of the NVA the journey pushed them to their physical limit. The march down the Ho Chi Minh Trail took four to ten weeks and was fraught with danger from the ground and the air.[118] Colonel Biu Tin recorded his remembrance of the hardship: "Quite a large numbers of deaths occurred. At each military staging post . . . there was a cemetery for those who had sacrificed their lives on the Trail. They died from a variety of causes. Some soldiers lost their way in the jungle and died of starvation. . . . What we really lacked was vegetables and fruit. . . . Occasionally we would find an orange tree. . . . We became so thirsty we began to see stars and had to drink very slowly whenever we reached a stream."[119]

Despite the hardship and casualties of the journey, the NVA kept up the psychological pressures on soldiers to keep moving. Much like their Soviet brethren at Stalingrad, North Vietnamese officers and political officials had a sophisticated system to ensure compliance. The narrative of the struggle

against the enemy, this time capitalists instead of fascists, was more important than material subsistence.[120] Nguyen Trong Nghi, a communist political
cadre member assigned to NVA troops marching down the Ho Chi Minh
Trail, stated,

On our way to the South we often met groups of wounded who were going
north. Some had lost their arms or legs, some had been burned by napalm. . . .
They all looked like skeletons. . . . We told each other that some day we would be
like that. . . . Sometimes the men asked the lower-ranking cadres questions. The
answer was that war always bring death and that we shouldn't bother ourselves
with morbid thoughts. *No one argued with the cadres* [emphasis added]. But everyone was frightened, especially when we met those men for the first time. It
was horrifying. It was like looking at our future selves.[121]

The result of the labors of NVA cadre and soldiers was the emplacement
of two full divisions—the 325th C and 304th Infantry—at Khe Sanh by January 1968, ready to attack the US Marines.[122] All told, twenty-eight thousand
soldiers with nine thousand support or logistics troops and two hundred
artillery pieces made the trip down the Ho Chi Minh Trail to besiege the
Marines.[123]

TRACKING LOGISTICS: MUSCLE SHOALS, THE AIRPLANE, AND THE COMPUTER

If the results of Rolling Thunder were unsatisfying for the Americans, there
was a positive technical outcome for the interdiction campaign at Khe Sanh.
As the need to identify, track, and bomb logistics targets grew throughout
the air campaign, the United States Air Force turned to its research labs to
design a method to track movements. Aerial photography and side-looking
radar were in use from the beginning of Rolling Thunder. The former allowed
precise detail of logistics movements but with a significant time delay, while
the latter peered beneath weather and the jungle canopy to provide gross electronic signals of vehicles. In both cases, forward air controllers had to provide visual confirmation to ensure it was a vehicle from the NVA. Although
the system worked, its slow analysis time and uncertain information blunted
the ability of airpower to thwart the logistics of the NVA moving down the
Ho Chi Minh Trail. Thus, the Americans needed a solution that could track

smaller movements while also providing information to attack targets faster and with more confidence during the day and the night, and in any weather.

Beginning in 1966, the United States Air Force experimented with pressure sensors designed for drop by aircraft or helicopter onto a ground line of communication.[124] By mid-1967, the system—named "Muscle Shoals"—showed promise during initial tests.[125] Muscle Shoals was a complicated system. First, helicopter or aircraft had to drop the sensors on the battlefield with the locations recorded for future map plots of seismic and aural data. Once in place, the sensors then transmitted data to airborne EC-121 surveillance aircraft. The aircraft then transmitted this data to a computer-processing center for analysis; the information was then sent back to the battlefield as coordinates of latitude and longitude.[126]

As the Vietnamese moved more men and materiel around Khe Sanh in November 1967, Westmoreland and Secretary McNamara asked to use the system to protect Khe Sanh.[127] The computer processing system was in Thailand and run by the United States Air Force under the code name "Dutch Mill."[128] Dutch Mill processed the information and transmitted the coordinates of the NVA movements to the fire-control cell at Khe Sanh.[129]

Dutch Mill had the secondary benefit of dovetailing with Secretary McNamara's penchant for data and information, which smoothed the bureaucratic path to using Muscle Shoals on the battlefield.[130] The rationality of war in the nuclear standoff between the United States and Soviet Union demanded vast stores of information that, according to Paul Edwards in *The Closed World*, could provide "confrontation with limits."[131] Muscle Shoals personified the rationalist and "Closed World" mentality of the nuclear age and exemplified the rational thinking of the Cold War, reducing the battle to a precise and finite application of firepower.

KHE SANH: THE BATTLE JOINED

In the fall of 1967, Colonel David Lownds, the commander of the Marines at Khe Sanh, limited ground patrols outside the confines of the base because of increased NVA presence, ordering just two patrols a month from September to December 1967.[132] With the highest hills held by individual companies of Marines, this order changed their method of resupply. After August 1967, the hill outposts required supply through the air, much like the base itself.

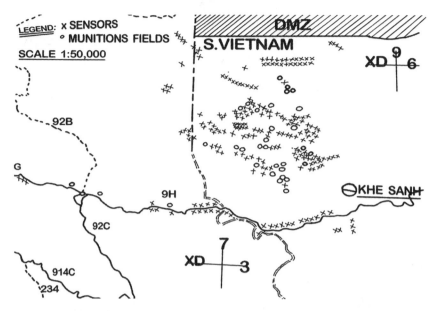

Figure 5.3. Map of Sensor Locations, Muscle Shoals System at Khe Sanh. (Map by Layton Barney from "Muscle Shoals Six Month Summary Evaluation Report, 31 May 1968." United States Military Assistance Command Vietnam [Air Force Historical Research Agency, IRIS No. 1000577, 1968].)

The first deployment of sensors from the Muscle Shoals system dropped by US aircraft over Laos along the Ho Chi Minh Trail in early December 1967 detected an uptick in traffic moving toward Khe Sanh.[133] In addition, the Marines at Khe Sanh detected enemy presence near the base, notably NVA probes of the special forces camp to Lang Vei located just a few miles to the west of the Khe Sanh base and airstrip. USMC leaders worried enough about Lang Vei's relief during an attack; they simulated a relief effort under combat conditions. In a trek that Marines at Guadalcanal or Braddock's men would have recognized, it took a small team of men nineteen hours to make the six-mile journey.[134] By the end of 1967, Lang Vei joined the hill outposts in isolation.

With the build-up of NVA forces in December, General Westmoreland received permission from President Johnson to use B-52s to interdict NVA logistics moving toward Khe Sanh under Operation Niagara.[135] The first missions flew on 14 January 1968, with the first large package of aircraft flying on

21 January, when eleven B-52s, sixty-one USAF Fighter-bombers, seventy-two USMC tactical support aircraft, and twenty USN aircraft struck NVA positions around Khe Sanh.[136] The same day, US helicopters dropped the first Muscle Shoals sensors around the base (see Figure 5.3).[137]

Overwhelming Firepower: A New Western Front 1968

Twenty-one January 1968 was auspicious for the siege of Khe Sanh. Just after midnight, the NVA ranged artillery fire against the outpost on Hill 861, and 250 troops from North Vietnam attempted to take the position. After a few hours of fighting, the Marines held the hill, but the NVA responded with a three-hour bombardment of the Khe Sanh combat base.[138] So began the seventy-seven-day siege of Khe Sanh, pitting twenty-five thousand NVA soldiers and artillery against seven thousand US Marines supported with US airpower and land-based artillery.[139]

The shelling of the main base and the hill positions by the NVA and the bombing of NVA positions by US aircraft and artillery became a daily affair. NVA units put upwards of "1,307 rocket, artillery, and mortar rounds on or near the base" on any day, with the weekly average of shells hitting the base surpassing twenty-five hundred.[140] The US, on the other side, flew 5,100 sorties in the first ten days of the siege of Khe Sanh and followed up with an average of 2,750 sorties per week for the rest of the campaign.[141] B-52s flew from 24 to 39 sorties per day, as part of the overall effort.[142] Each B-52 sortie could deliver fifty thousand pounds of bombs—making the total of bombs dropped from the bomber at from six hundred to twelve hundred tons per day.[143] The issue for the United States was not whether they had enough airpower, a problem faced by both belligerents at Guadalcanal and the Germans at Stalingrad, but deconfliction of hundreds of sorties per day.[144]

Besides airpower, the US used artillery at Khe Sanh and army long-range guns twelve miles to the northeast at "The Rockpile" and at Camp Carroll (see Figure 5.1).[145] The US fired 158,981 rounds of artillery, mortars, and re-coilless-rifles rounds at NVA positions around Khe Sanh.[146] With the massive firepower arrayed against each other, the belligerents resorted to the time-honored formula of digging deep trenches and tunnels.[147]

The NVA developed ingenious methods to hide their heavier artillery pieces (130 mm and 152 mm) which they had placed across the border in Laos. According to the USMC account of the battle:

The NVA gunners fired only a few rounds every hour so that continuous muzzle flashes did not betray their positions and, after each round, quickly scurried out to cover the guns with protective nets and screens. Some pieces mounted on tracks, were wheeled out of caves in Co Roc Mountain [in Laos], fired, and returned immediately. Though never used in as great a quantity as the rocks and mortars, these shells wreaked havoc at Khe Sanh because there was very little that they could not penetrate; even duds went about four feet into the ground.[148]

The firepower of the NVA pinned the Marines down so completely that the grunts created a term for hitting the ground and running for cover with incoming bombardment: "The Khe Sanh Shuffle."[149]

At the opposite end, the NVA soldiers faced the same hardships under a severe artillery and airpower bombardment form the Americans. The B-52 sorties—called "Arc Light"—had the most significant effect of the campaign on the morale of the NVA and the Marines at Khe Sanh. The heavy bombardment of a B-52 attack produced psychological and physical effects. One NVA solider reported, "The whole area was filled with fire and smoke. . . . I felt as if I were sitting in a metal case which someone was pounding on with a hammer. I was sure I was dying."[150] Because of the risk of fratricide, US leaders kept B-52s three thousand meters from US Marines. As the command, control, and coordination of firepower improved, this line moved as close as five hundred meters from friendly positions. These near strikes "served as a morale booster for those who flocked from their bunkers to watch, what the Marines called, 'Number One on the hit parade.'"[151]

Added to their heavy firepower, both sides also used snipers to hit men careless enough to be on open ground for too long.[152] Khe Sanh resembled the Western Front in 1917, with enemies entrenched and attempting to break through the wall of each other's firepower. For the logistics of both sides, getting through the firepower was a tough task, especially for the 325th and 304th Divisions of the North Vietnamese Army.

The Computer and the Airplane: Stopping NVA Logistics

Coupled with computers, the airplane became an even more deadly weapon against logistics. As the NVA rained long-artillery shells from Laos and mortars near Khe Sanh, the Marines and the airpower of the USAF, US Navy, and US Marine Corps put the Muscle Shoals system to use. At first, anytime a "string" of sensors detected movement by men or trucks of the NVA, the fire-control center at Khe Sanh directed artillery fire or the roving aircraft overhead to attack the targets.[153] Such quick action proved premature due to the time necessary, thirty minutes in December 1967, to relay the information back to Khe Sanh from the computer stations at the Dutch Mill facility in Thailand.[154] Used in this way, Muscle Shoals proved no better than firing at visual movements or aural detections of NVA by human means.

Luckily for the Marines, Captain Mirza Baig, an intelligence officer, built a heuristic of how the NVA moved in conventional battle based on attacks he had witnessed at Con Thien in 1967. He based his model on observations that the local commanders of the NVA were tied to a plan sent by the NVA staff, which demanded rigid compliance; and, the plan "would reflect the classic siege tactics of Dien Bien Phu."[155] With this knowledge, Baig extrapolated the information from Muscle Shoals.

With Baig's inputs, the Marines began a more in-depth use of Muscle Shoals as an overall predictor of NVA movement and logistics, adding the systems inputs to observations from aircraft and land-based reconnaissance. In addition, the information kill chain grew shorter as the Marines and pilots learned how to use the system.[156] In postmortem, the USAF reported the success of Muscle Shoals in the detection of marshalling of men and equipment by the NVA:

At Khe Sanh, the enemy could not move up against the wire because of the small arms fire and mortar coverage. He would move his logistics bases within 3 km [three thousand meters] of the lines because he felt we would not bomb that close to our lines with B-52. . . . For his attack, he would build trenches radially toward the base, and when as close as he felt safe in coming, he would dig trenches parallel to our lines. The troops would go through the trenches and attack on a line front. Sensors located on the trails to the bunker and trench complex would tell when his reserve forces were being moved into position for an attack. . . . Air and artillery would strike the reserve forces coming to join the attack. . . . Five times he tried this kind of attack, and five times he suffered tremendous casualties. A number of times, the sensors gave all the indications of an impending attack and the artillery and air barrage was started but the attack never came.[157]

The most striking example of the success of the system was the detection of NVA troops against Hill 881S (see Figure 5.2). On one night, the system recorded two thousand to three thousand NVA soldiers amassing for an assault on Hill 881S.[158] US Marines concentrated all available artillery on the base of the hill for thirty minutes. When the firing stopped, the fire-control center at Khe Sanh reported hearing "screams, yells, orders, and general panic," and as a result "the attack never came off."[159] Just thirty minutes later, the NVA attacked Hill 861, which lacked sensors, without notification. Although caught by surprise, because of the way the NVA arranged their forces for the attack on Hill 881S, the Americans were able train their artillery to the same positions around 861 to "halt the initial wave of troops."[160]

By adding computing power, Muscle Shoals took the advantage away from NVA during bad weather and darkness. It allowed aircraft and artillery to train on targets unseen, just as the NVA troops surrounding 881 South. A III MAF intelligence officer stated that Colonel Lownds, "gets immediate readout in the CP [command post]. We can hear people moving. We fire artillery and hear the screams. It's just beautiful. . . . They're really blood-curdling. And we can pick up tracks. We can tell if it's artillery or tanks. So it's really great."[161]

In addition, the system allowed the Americans to hone the precision of their target tracking by supplementing radar-controlled strikes with accurate data. The radar system, similar to those installed in USAF B-52s and US Navy A-6s to strike targets in weather, allowed ground controllers to direct tactical aircraft onto targets. The radar locked onto the US aircraft, and the ground controller programmed in the coordinates and information about the ordnance onboard. A computer system then selected the best release point for the aircraft and sent information for airspeed, altitude, and heading adjustments for relay by voice to the pilot. The controller "called a 'Mark' to the pilot, who 'Pickled' his bombs."[162] Although not as destructive as their B-52 brethren, Marine ground commanders prized these strikes by tactical aircraft for their accuracy.[163]

Artillery, airpower, and the computations of Muscle Shoals doomed not just the NVA offensive against Hill 881S but every offensive. As the siege wore on, the Americans shortened the time from notification by the Muscle Shoals system to striking a target from thirty minutes to sixteen minutes by March 1968.[164] The ability of the Americans to find, fix, and finish targets prevented the NVA from moving their logistics forward to capitalize on any offensive.

Even the one success the NVA had at overrunning a Marine position, the assault on Lang Vei on the night of 6 February 1968, was a pyrrhic victory. As predicted by the Marines the previous year, the NVA isolated the camp with ease. Using three infantry battalions and nine PT-76 tanks they had moved down the Ho Chi Minh Trail, the NVA overwhelmed the 850 defenders—Laotian soldiers, local Bru tribesmen, and twenty-four American Special Forces soldiers.[165] The NVA inflicted grievous casualties: 316 killed, 75 wounded, and 253 captured. The NVA themselves suffered 200 casualties, a stark admission in the NVA accounts of the battle. In addition, US aircraft rendered the tanks useless by destroying the majority of them.[166] According to Shawn Callahan in *Close Air Support at Khe Sanh*, after Lang Vei the NVA battalion used in the attack had "such severe morale problems (manifest in desertion and self-inflicted wounds to avoid combat) that the parent command doubted the battalion could be used again."[167] Thus, the situation for the NVA at Khe Sanh resembled the Soviets at the Kharkov salient in 1942, where German airpower had halted the offensive gains of the Red Army.

Through the Gauntlet: Supply of the Marines by Air

While the NVA had to work for six months to bring their firepower and food forward to Khe Sanh, the US forces had a clear advantage in their ability to transport goods through the air daily. Like the NVA, however, their logistics had to pass through the gauntlet of hostile fire. With their outposts on the hills isolated from ground resupply because of NVA presence, the Marines had to supply the combat base and the hills from the air.

When the NVA surrounded Khe Sanh on 21 January 1968, the Marines relied on fixed-wing aircraft—larger C-130s and smaller C-123s and C-7s transport planes—to supply the main base. In addition, there were helicopters at the base to supply the hill positions and hundreds of helicopters at Dang Ho, including the large CH-46 "Sky Crane" that could carry larger cargo, including lumber and four-hundred-gallon water containers.[168] For the first twenty days of the siege, C-7s, C-123s, and C-130s moved steady amounts of cargo into Khe Sanh.[169] USAF aircraft moved 250 tons per day for the first eight days and reached "a single-day high of 310 tons for the entire campaign" on 27 January 1968.[170] The Marines used up not only food and water, but also thousands of artillery shells a day.

Undergirding this effort was a robust system to load cargo at the out bases (Da Nang and Cam Ranh Bay, South Vietnam), control and receive the planes at Khe Sanh, and offload the cargo at Khe Sanh. The system of logistics, which Maxwell Taylor envisioned in *The Uncertain Trumpet* in 1960, bloomed at Khe Sanh in 1968. Air force ground-loading units sustained twenty-four-hour operations at Cam Ranh Bay to keep moving the cargo onto Khe Sanh.[171] For control of aircraft into Khe Sanh, Seventh Air Force had extensive air-traffic control and prioritization systems to deconflict cargo missions with strike sorties from fighters and bombers.[172] The Marines also had a Ground-Control Approach (GCA) radar, which helped direct transport aircraft onto the airfield in ceilings as low as two hundred feet.[173] This technological capability was important at Khe Sanh, which often had significant periods of morning fog because of its relatively low elevation compared to the surrounding terrain.[174]

Once the aircraft landed, USAF cargo handlers had separate bunker locations and a myriad of forklifts and cargo-handling equipment to discharge the C-130s as soon as possible.[175] The sick and wounded were then loaded for quick transport back to hospitals in South Vietnam. This was a marked contrast to the lack of care for the wounded by their enemy.

With the transportation of supplies by the Americans increasing in early February, NVA artillery regiments homed in on the airfield and the aircraft. The first casualty was the GCA radar facility that the NVA damaged on 7 February 1968.[176] Without the radar, approaches in weather less than one thousand feet in ceilings, a frequent occurrence, were impossible.[177] After hitting the radar facility, the NVA targeted aircraft as they slowed for the final approach and then rolled out upon landing. On 10 February, seven USAF C-130s received small arms or shrapnel damage. The following day NVA artillery hit a USMC C-130, carrying bladders loaded with fuel. The explosion destroyed the plane and killed two crew members.[178] After these incidents and the danger of losing the bigger and more expensive transports, Seventh Air Force halted C-130 missions into Khe Sanh. The smaller C-123s continued missions into the base for the next week while the USAF, USMC, and US Army worked on a technological fix.

The first solution to the airlift problem was a system called "Low-Altitude Parachute Extraction System" (LAPES), developed in the fall of 1967 to supply Khe Sanh while the runway underwent repairs. LAPES involved deploying a drogue chute from the aircraft near the runway. As the aircraft leveled a few feet off the runway at 150 miles per hour, the C-130 crew released the cargo-lock mechanism, allowing the chute to pull the cargo onto the runway. In this way, the LAPES system enabled the C-130s to maintain their speed and avoid touching down, placing the aircraft under the threat of NVA artillery for less time, while also delivering bigger loads than the C-123s.[179]

Although effective, LAPES was risky.[180] In several cases, cargo pallets careened off the runway, injured or killed Marines, and shattered the supplies.[181] LAPES deliveries accounted for only fifty-two cargo loads during the siege at Khe Sanh.[182] Although the deliveries by LAPES were only a fraction of the total, they provided a critical bridge until Seventh Air Force, the US Army, and the US Marines could work out a new radar-guided airdrop procedure.

While the military designed C-130s to airdrop cargo, the ability to do so in the weather and under hostile fire was unproven until Khe Sanh. Using the GCA radar at Khe Sanh, since repaired after one week, the C-130 crews could align over the runway at five hundred feet. Then, using an internal Doppler computer, the crew measured their actual movement over the ground and steered the aircraft to the Computed Air Release Point, based on winds, cargo and parachute data, to drop the cargo.[183] Accuracy was crucial because of the small drop zone of three hundred square yards. Its size, dictated by the heavy NVA presence, made the parameters for an accurate airdrop a narrow three-second window.[184]

Much as they had the system to onload and off-load aircraft at Khe Sanh, the Americans had the logistics capability to keep the massive airdrop effort afloat forever. The airdrop and LAPES delivery adaptations at Khe Sanh required several US Army companies of aircraft "riggers" to fasten the cargo to airdrop parachutes. The US Army stationed an entire company, the 109th Quartermasters, at Da Nang airbase to prepare the loads of cargo for airdrop.[185] By the end of the seventy-seven-day siege, the USAF delivered 8,100 tons by airdrop, twice the amount of the 4,200 tons delivered by traditional landing and cargo off-load.[186] In addition, USMC aircraft transported over 1,800 tons bringing the total delivered during the siege to 14,430 tons.[187]

Supplying the Hills: The Toughest Transition

Supplying the base by aircraft was difficult, but supplying the hill outposts was the most dangerous job at Khe Sanh. At first, helicopters stationed at Khe Sanh provided the food, water, and ammunition to the outposts. After a few days of intense NVA shelling, the transportation efforts shifted to other bases. Most of the cargo missions by helicopter to the hill outposts originated out of Dang Ho. As with the fixed-wing missions, the critical points were the transition periods between air and land, off-loading cargo and evacuating the sick and wounded.[188]

Given the importance of the resupply missions, the Khe Sanh fire-control officers homed in on NVA AAA attacks directed at the helicopters. According to Shawn Callahan, the fire-support command center "gave antiaircraft positions a very high priority in targeting, and once a 37 mm position was identified, it was repeatedly attacked until it was destroyed or abandoned. By the end of the siege, the Marines claimed more than 300 had been destroyed."[189]

Despite the capability of land-based firepower, the weather, instead of the NVA, threatened to halt the resupply missions in February. Bad weather had cloaked the hill outposts in clouds for a week during the first week of the month. The low ceilings made the helicopters easier targets for the NVA, since they had to fly lower to the ground to avoid the clouds. Without the helicopter missions, the Marines on the hill outposts could not survive long, especially without water, and without the hill outposts the Marines would no longer control the high ground overlooking Khe Sanh. The loss rate of the helicopters during the siege testified to the importance of the hill outposts to both sides. By the end of the battle, thirty-three helicopters had been shot down or rendered nonoperational upon return to base.[190]

To help thwart the NVA's advantage during bad weather, Marine commanders devised a system called the "Super Gaggle," which involved the massing of twelve A-4 Skyhawk attack aircraft and four UH-1 Huey gunships to escort the resupply helicopters to the hills. In a complicated maneuver, the A-4s first dropped conventional bombs, napalm, and tear gas to clear the way, the UH-1s followed with a smoke screen to cover the landing zone, and then the CH-46 helicopters landed to off-load cargo and upload casualties.[191] Although the maneuver was complex, it increased the success of the resupply missions for the hill outposts. With a better success rate of cargo delivery, the Super Gaggle continued after the low weather lifted in February. A company commander remarked after the siege that "if it weren't for the gaggle, most of us wouldn't be here today."[192]

COMPARISONS OF SUFFERING: SUPPLIES
OF THE NVA AND US MARINES AT KHE SANH

Thrust into a cauldron of firepower, the two divisions of North Vietnamese and the two battalions of United States Marines held on in miserable conditions. While the logistics of the United States were superior, the soldiers of both sides suffered. For the average NVA soldier, Khe Sanh was a nightmare.

The food situation for the US Marines was not ideal, but it was sufficient. Food consisted of unappealing C-rations and precooked and canned meals, but it met their subsistence needs. Sometimes the hill outposts had to ration food, cutting C-rations to one meal a day. At the height of the supply crisis in early February, First Lieutenant Crenshaw wrote in a letter home, "The food situation here is critical. The only food we have is C-rations. We have had to restrict our Marines to one meal per day to ensure we have enough food if this battle goes on for months."[193]

By late February, the situation, even for the outposts, was much better. One Super Gaggle helped pave the way for ice cream deliveries to the hill positions.[194] Despite the vast improvement in food delivery, hot food was a luxury, and many Marines would not have a warm meal during the seventy-seven-day siege. Thus, much like their brethren at Guadalcanal who suffered food shortages at first, the food situation for the Marines at Khe Sanh continued to improve as the fight continued. The US military possessed more than adequate logistics to transport unabated the subsistence of the Marines.

North Vietnamese sources on the effects of the bombing in men killed, weapons destroyed, or logistics lost are limited, but there are indications the attacks devastated morale and materiel. The USMC History of 1968 estimated that the Americans killed 10,000 to 15,000 NVA during the siege.[195] Recent research of NVA documents suggests that the casualties of the two divisions were 33 percent, a still-severe 9,320 killed or wounded out of the original 28,000 soldiers arrayed around Khe Sanh.[196] In either case, these losses were horrific. Hoai Phong, an NVA cadre member at Khe Sanh, summed up the situation for the average soldier in his diary, "Fifteen days after the siege began, things turned about to be more atrocious than ever and even by far fiercer than . . . Dien Bien Phu. We retreated to our trenches . . . B-52 bombers continually dropped their bombs in this area with ever growing intensity and at any moment of the day. If someone came to visit this place, he might say that this was a storm of bombs and ammunition which eradicated all living creatures and vegetation whatsoever, even those located in caves or in deep underground shelters."[197]

For the sick and wounded of the NVA, the situation was even more appalling. In their trek down the trail to Khe Sanh, a member of the 325th Division lamented the situation of the sick and wounded. He stated, "Treatment was not sufficient with two medics for 120 patients . . . these two medics were sent to battle to give aid to wounded soldiers. No one took care of the patients. Thus the moderately sick patients looked after the serious ones."[198] This misery for the sick harkened back to the Soviets at Stalingrad, the Japanese at Guadalcanal, and both belligerents at Lake George. The adjectives sick or injured equated with death.

The same misery for the wounded was also in store for the healthy. If the Marines suffered, with tons of supplies delivered daily to the base and weekly to the hill outposts, how bad was the food situation for the NVA? At the end of the siege of Khe Sanh, the Marines discovered 13,500 tons of food dispersed and hidden in various caves and underground complexes used by the NVA.[199] Given the food situation of the North Vietnamese Army throughout the war, this decision seems illogical on three fronts. First, the aforementioned difficulty in transporting that much food down the Ho Chi Minh Trail made it a precious commodity. Second, the shortage of food throughout the war, in the North and South, made sustenance a constant priority. According to Jon Van Dyke in *North Vietnam's Strategy for Survival,* even those soldiers assigned to provide food to their units spent "most of their time searching for food. There [was] never . . . enough," and many units noted theft "from the central rice supply."[200]

Most important was the evidence provided by first-hand and official accounts regarding the poor food situation of the NVA. A soldier in the 324th Division at Khe Sanh remarked in his diary, "Rice is almost depleted and so is our salt. Dissension rose between the unit's soldiers and the political cadre. The situation is becoming worse due to lack of food, sleep, and worries. I feel too weak."[201] The NVA combated the lack of supply the same way that the Sixty-Second Army at Stalingrad had—through a narrative backed by force—the NKVD replaced by NVA political party operatives. As in the ruins of Stalingrad, it was miserable for the average soldier.

Marines noted the poor food situation of their enemy. A Marine stationed on Hill 861S remarked, "A lot of chopper pilots got scared when they caught a lot of fire [while delivering supplies]. They often released their external loads a little too soon or a little too late, and a lot of the food landed . . . in enemy territory. We had to send out patrols at night, secure the area, and get our food. Sometimes, we had to fight for our food, because the enemy wanted it, too."[202] Another Marine on a separate outpost recorded a scheme to trick the NVA into thinking artillery canisters, used for waste removal, were full of sustenance.[203] By the end of March, soldiers of the NVA "lived on a half a pound of rice a day" and soldiers captured by the Marines during the final days of the siege in April reported "no food at all for three days."[204] The lack of food hampered the operational effectiveness of the NVA surrounding Khe Sanh. In their history of the Vietnam War, the NVA recorded that "main force divisions were unable to achieve the goal of fighting a battle because of limitations in our battlefield equipment and weaknesses in our command and supply arrangements, etc."[205] While an insurgency could subsist on a few tons a day across all South Vietnam, conventional war required a supply system, which the North Vietnamese lacked. Thus, the decision of the NVA to abandon thousands of tons of food at Khe Sanh was not by choice but by necessity.

At Khe Sanh, the ability of American aircraft and artillery to pin down the NVA blunted their offensives, halted their logistics, and kept the NVA from their food. The coordination of firepower, radar, and computers to track movements of vehicles and large troop concentrations would have made feeding NVA troops a tough task. If the Muscle Shoals system had tracked two thousand troops moving in one area around Hill 881S, any organized or controlled feeding process of units approaching five hundred troops would have likely tripped the system. Rob Brewer, a Marine working at III MAF headquarters, summed up how difficult food rationing was for the NVA: "I knew that getting food to the assembly areas would be an enemy problem. . . . In comes the Marine intelligence officer from Khe Sanh with a question, 'Why are the villagers around Ca Lu being ordered to make hundreds of paper cones?' Elementary! So the NVA can put them on their flashlights as diffusers when they go for their forced march!"[206]

Besides the food caches left, the Marines found "over 200 crew-served weapons, 12,000 rounds of large caliber ammunition, 5 wheeled vehicles, and a tank."[207] The abandonment of such large amounts of combat weapons, vehicles, and food illustrates how airpower, artillery, and the computing power of the Muscle Shoals system had circumscribed NVA transportation. Placing the map of the location Muscle Shoals sensors next to a view of the Khe Sanh base shows how difficult NVA logistics movements were. The US had sensors well placed surrounding the hill locations and those roads and areas well in the rear to see NVA movement towards Khe Sanh. While the Marines controlled 881S, 861, 558, and 950, the NVA had artillery spotters on Hill 1015 and commanded Hill 881N. From these positions, Marines or aircraft would have spotted any transportation or troop movements in the flat of the Rao Quan River just as the NVA pinned down the Marines at the Khe Sanh base.

For the Americans, the sensors covered the rest of the battlefield. As the Muscle Shoals map shows, it well covered movements crossing the DMZ to the north or coming across roads from Laos. Thus, the Americans would have detected the feeding of over twenty-eight thousand soldiers in any coordinated effort by trucks or people. While it is tough to gauge how hungry the NVA were, like the combatants at Guadalcanal and Stalingrad, their supply situation was dire.

Water, Water Everywhere but Not a Drop to Drink

If the Marines enjoyed a tolerable but miserable existence with poor food and constant shelling, access to water was a serious deficiency. The struggle and success with keeping water flowing to the Marines encapsulated the logistics superiority of the Americans over their adversary. For the combat base, Marine engineers connected a pumping system to a small stream near the base, which was a tributary of the Rao Quan River.[208] Out in the open, the hoses and storage bladders suffered from NVA shelling and needed continual repair.[209] As a result, water shortages were common for the base and for the hill outposts. Although the base had the water supply system, the artillery and sniper fire from the NVA kept individual units so immobilized that transportation across the base was impossible. According to Bruce Geiger, a Marine 1Lt. at Khe Sanh, moving the water "500 meters across the runway wasn't an option. . . . The NVA FO's [Forward Observers] would invariably wait until our gun truck pulled up to fill water cans, and walk a barrage of artillery rounds across the area."[210] Instead of walking across the runway, resupply helicopters delivered water buffaloes (four-hundred-gallon water containers) to areas of the base that needed them.[211]

The men on the hill outposts suffered the worst, as they did with food rations. During the bad weather of early February, the Marines of 861S rationed their water down to half a canteen per day. With water scarce, beards were common and washing was nonexistent. Hill 861S suffered through almost ten days without a helicopter delivery, during which the officers at the position discussed abandoning the hill. Glenn Prentice, a Marine sergeant on Hill 861S stated:

I was standing radio watch in the command bunker, and I listened to Captain Dabney and other officers discussing plans to leave the hill because without water and food fighting ability can be compromised. Some had the idea of leaving and fighting our way back. . . . Captain Dabney's idea was to fool the NVA and set out for Laos. Once over the border, an LZ could be set up and evacuation by helicopter could begin. Luckily, for all of us, the next day we received a major resupply of food and water, and the battle continued as it had been.[212]

Given the impossibility of sneaking through the twenty-eight NVA soldiers surrounding the men of Khe Sanh, the water situation on hill 861 S was dire.

The situation on Hill 950 was just as bad, and the Marines at the main base devised a method to deliver water via old 155 mm shell casings and "filling them with plastic bladders that were used in milk dispensers . . . and dropping them on the hills."[213] With the improved Super Gaggle procedures to the hill outposts and water brought in by helicopter to the main base, the situation stabilized by late February, but the Marines still rationed water until they left in April.[214] As American firepower dominated the battlefield, so it also ensured delivery of logistics.

The US Marines at Khe Sanh were fortunate. The NVA never attempted to cut their water. Not only was the unimpeded flow of water into the Khe Sanh camp a mystery to Colonel Lownds and USMC leaders, but it is still a question within the historiography of Khe Sanh.[215] The answer lies in the source of water and the ability of US firepower to cover the battlefield.

The Rao Quan flowed from the north, south towards Khe Sanh, and then tracked east to the ocean (see Figure 5.1). Since, the NVA were scattered around the hills that the Marines occupied north of the base, the NVA required use of the Rao Quan as much as the Marines downstream at Khe Sanh did.[216] If the NVA poisoned the water or diverted its flow, their soldiers would have perished. Therefore, to poison or cut the water required a method to transport the water forward to NVA troops. As illustrated with the transportation of food, the movement of water would have been difficult under the threat of US firepower.

Just as US firepower kept the NVA from their food, command of the Rao Quan River prevented the NVA from blocking the river's flow. The Marines would have stopped any efforts by the NVA to block the water from the hill outposts or the base itself, if the NVA had attempted to do so near Khe Sanh. Further upstream, the US had coverage with airpower and artillery to hold any incursion near the river at bay. In fact, the US Air Force built the Muscle Shoals system with the Rao Quan as its eastern boundary. The river was a natural open area, making for easy reconnaissance by US aircraft to spot NVA units without the need for the sophisticated system.

OPERATION PEGASUS

In early March, NVA attacks lessened against the hill outposts and the base at Khe Sanh. On 7 March 1968, the NVA reported in its history that the 325th Division vacated the area, leaving the 304th Division in place.[217] This movement coincided with US military planning to open the land route to Khe Sanh, Route 9, to relieve the Marines who had been under siege for almost two months. General Westmoreland approved the plan on 10 March 1968, and MACV/III MAF planners christened it "Operation Pegasus."[218]

The planning staffs at III MAF and MACV recognized the difficulty of supplying Khe Sanh by air and wanted to guarantee access to the base over land by the time the monsoon rains came in early summer. They set the start date for Operation Pegasus in early April, before the monsoon season began.[219] The plan involved using the entire contingent of army helicopters of the First Air Cavalry to transport US Army soldiers and place them east of Dang Ho on Route 9, while several Marine regiments moved along Route 9 with trucks, vehicles, and artillery. Pegasus involved three hundred helicopters, 148 artillery pieces, and over thirty thousand troops, including an ARVN airborne regiment.[220] In addition, Seventh Air Force and USMC air planners allotted ten B-52s for on-call close-air support for the duration of Operation Pegasus, and allotted 1,625 attack aircraft sorties.[221]

In this massive show of airpower, land-based firepower, transportation, and logistics, the forces from Operation Pegasus linked with Colonel Lowds and his Twenty-Sixth Marines, declaring Route 9 open on 11 April 1968. The NVA put up stiff resistance and suffered eleven hundred killed as part of the operation, while the Americans had ninety-two killed in action and 667 wounded.[222] During Pegasus, NVA prisoners reported supply shortages and thus could not "coordinate anything larger than a company operation."[223]

On 15 April 1968, "wave after wave" of helicopters lifted most of the Twenty-Sixth Marines out of Khe Sanh.[224] Three days later the hill outposts were relieved. During the seventy-seven days of the siege, the Americans suffered almost three thousand casualties with 271 killed; a large number for a force of seven thousand men.[225] For the hill outposts, the casualty rates reached nearly 100 percent because of "daily bombardment and harassing sniper fire."[226] Airpower played another critical role as the savior of over twenty-five hundred wounded Marines.[227] Their NVA enemy suffered a slightly lower rate of 33 percent casualties out of the twenty-five thousand men deployed to Khe Sanh—with no hope of rescue.[228] For the Americans and NVA, the battles of Khe Sanh continued, but in decreasing interactions until the last Americans left Khe Sanh on 11 July 1968.[229] The siege of Khe Sanh was over.

TET: WHILE KHE SANH WAS WON, THE WAR WAS LOST

For both sides, preconceived notions of what their logistics could and could not do to meet larger strategic goals were shattered at Khe Sanh The overconfidence in Le Duan's writings before Tet regarding the material weaknesses of his opponent and the belief in North Vietnamese strength was crushed under the weight of American firepower and logistics. Rather than fighting an enemy who he believed had a "market and raw material problem," Le Duan's countrymen faced a nation with the capacity of logistics to move anywhere and supply its forces under any condition, even the thousands of artillery shells the NVA launched into Khe Sanh each week.

Despite the impressive feat of moving two divisions of the NVA to encircle Khe Sanh and supply the battle for weeks, the logistics of the North Vietnamese was no match for American technology and firepower. The schizophrenic nature of how the Party addressed logistics in the Fourteenth Plenum—realistic about their own weaknesses to supply under fire, while hopelessly optimistic about their own ability capture American supplies and bases—proved remarkably prescient. Resupplying and moving their forces at Khe Sanh became impossible under the threat of American firepower, and the noted weakness of their own logistics held true for North Vietnam. The utopian belief that the NVA and their allies could capture and turn the logistics of the Americans into their own never came to fruition. Such a preindustrial view of logistics in war had not existed for over a century and lacked a realistic understanding of logistics and warfare in the Modern Era.

For Le Duan and the party's overconfidence, the NVA and Viet Cong suffered over twenty thousand casualties with huge losses in equipment.[230] As William Allison in *The Tet Offensive* states, "In a purely military sense, Tet appeared to be a resounding victory for American and South Vietnamese forces, as the communist gamble to concentrate forces for mass assaults against defensive positions allowed American firepower to lay waste to the PLAF's [Viet Cong] most experienced forces."[231]

General Westmoreland was ecstatic over the victory at Khe Sanh, believing he could now use the base as a launching pad to expand the war into Laos and defeat the NVA in total.[232] As if to underscore his success compared to the French debacle at Dien Bien Phu, he ordered MACV to conduct an in-depth comparison of both battles, citing the advantages and disadvantages of both sides during both conflicts.[233] For Westmoreland the battle went as planned: the North Vietnamese had concentrated their soldiers and logistics and the Americans had destroyed them.

While a stunning tactical success that destroyed two divisions of the NVA, Khe Sanh also diverted Westmoreland and his subordinate commands away from the larger operational and strategic concerns of the Tet Offensive. With Westmoreland's focus on Khe Sanh, American leaders were slow to realize how successfully the NVA and the National Liberation Front had infiltrated many of the cities of South Vietnam. The most glaring example was in the city of Hue, where US Marines and US Army soldiers asked for support and reinforcements to hold off the takeover of the city by the NVA and southern partisans.[234] In numerous examples during the Battle of Hue, higher headquarters failed to realize how grave the situation was for the Americans on the ground and just how strong the North Vietnamese were in terms of firepower, personnel, and supplies. Mark Bowden sums up the fight for the city this way: "The takeover of Hue was so unexpected that, even during the month it took to wrest the city back, the MACV seemed reluctant to believe it had actually happened."[235] In turn, the ability of the North Vietnamese and allied forces in the South to infiltrate the cities also shifted US public opinion from skepticism of the Vietnam War in the fall of 1967 to disapproval by the spring of 1968.

The breaking of preconceived notions from the belligerents about logistics before Khe Sanh under the weight of actual combat circles back to the question posed earlier in this chapter: Was Khe Sanh a diversion? From the North Vietnamese perspective, the focus of the Fourteenth Plenum right before the Tet Offensive was on the uprising in the cities with conventional battles elsewhere as the catalyst. Thus, using Khe Sanh as a diversion fit naturally into the overall strategy for the Tet Offensive, and as aforementioned, the strength of NVA forces around Khe Sanh did divert General Westmoreland and MACV from other concerns.

From the perspective of logistics, however, the diversion theory appears less certain. The logistics required for Khe Sanh was tenfold greater than the six tons a day needed to support the insurgency in the South before Tet. North Vietnamese efforts to move almost thirty thousand men and their weapons of war to the remote area of Khe Sanh, under constant threat of US airpower and artillery, was a success of the first magnitude. The hundreds of crew-served weapons and the 13,500 tons of food left behind at Khe Sanh was a testament not only to US airpower during the siege, but also to the supply and transportation network of the NVA.[236] Not only did the NVA move soldiers just across the border to surround Khe Sanh, they moved thousands of soldiers into South Vietnam with enough equipment and supplies to threaten US and ARVN forces for weeks, to include besieging Hue for a month.[237] The logistics needs of Khe Sanh and Tet and the ability of the NVA to get them in place bolster Edwin Moises's argument in *The Myths of Tet* that the North Vietnamese were stronger militarily before Tet than the American military wanted to admit.[238] More important, such an effort of logistics to move the NVA around Khe Sanh points less to a diversion and more to Le Duan's overall view of the campaign.

Given Le Duan's optimism about his own nation's prowess and the near-exhaustion of his capitalist enemy, Le Duan believed the North would win. He was so determined that he purged those from the Communist Party who advocated a more cautious stance toward the growing conflict in the South suggest not a diversion but rather a plan for victory. And despite crushing tactical and material losses, the greater narrative become one of strength rather than weakness, echoing Le Duan's overoptimistic assessment of the North's chances to defeat the Americans and the government of South Vietnam.

The hoped-for turning of American logistics and bases into North Vietnamese support stated in the directive of the Fourteenth Plenum was short-lived. The North Vietnamese and their allies in South Vietnam were not the French at Fort Duquesne. Much like the Japanese at Guadalcanal, the ideology of victory won out over pragmatic concerns of the material needs of battle and the reality. For those North Vietnamese soldiers traversing the Ho Chi Minh Trail in 1967 as part of the buildup for the Tet Offensive and the siege of Khe Sanh, this strategic mistake would cost many their lives. Paradoxically, this mistake also delivered them the narrative to win the conflict.

Although the NVA lost the battles of Tet and Khe Sanh—all of them—they won the war. Back in the United States the images of Tet—the US Embassy attacked and under siege, the destruction of Hue during the fighting for the city, and the Marines besieged at Khe Sanh—turned the population against the war. The small, industrial-limited nation moved enough soldiers and supplies to South Vietnam to put up stiff resistance for weeks and in some cases months. It was not that the NVA had to move the logistics necessary to win the battle, only enough to convince their enemy of their strength. It worked. The American people saw the television broadcasts and could only conclude that a nation of peasants was winning against the half-million personnel and thousands of weapons of war the nation had sent to bolster South Vietnam. From January 1968, the unpopularity of the Vietnam War rose from 47 percent against to 62 percent against by the end of March.[239]

The incongruence between how Westmoreland and the military viewed the conflict compared to the political mood of the nation was most evident in the actions of Westmoreland as the NVA egressed the area around Khe Sanh in early March 1968. As his planners worked on Operation Pegasus, Westmoreland met with key military leaders in Washington, DC, to plan a campaign to close with the NVA, including launching into Laos from Khe Sanh to attack the Ho Chi Minh Trail. Westmoreland stated in his memoirs, "If I could execute those moves fairly rapidly following the heavy losses the enemy had incurred in the Tet offensive, I saw the possibility of destroying the enemy's will to continue the war."[240] Westmoreland was correct regarding the heavy losses and the sagging morale of his enemy. North Vietnamese General Tran Van recorded in an article in 1988 that "we also sustained the biggest losses in military and political forces, especially the high-ranking and local cadres. . . . These losses, both in troop strength and materiel, caused us untold difficulties in coping with the enemy's frenzied counterattacks."[241]

With his optimism buoyed, Westmoreland floated a proposal for an additional two hundred thousand troops to pursue the NVA to their defeat. The *New York Times* broke the story on 10 March 1968 of Westmoreland's plan; and, by 23 March, President Johnson had relieved Westmoreland of command in Vietnam and installed him as the new chief of staff of the US Army.[242] President Johnson himself announced his decision not to seek a second term eight days later.[243] After the strategic imperative to hold Khe Sanh throughout 1967 and the first half of 1968, the Americans abandoned the position on 11 July 1968. While Westmoreland got the battle he wanted at Khe Sanh, and won it, the victor lost the war. In 1975, the domino fell.

CONCLUSION

At Khe Sanh, the effect of the technological advances of the Modern Era— computers, sensors, jet engines, helicopters, to name a few—allowed the United States to project a force forward into a remote area and supply it in total by air. No longer was delivery by air an emergency or a stopgap for other modes, as it had been at Stalingrad and Guadalcanal. The air was now an equivalent mode of transportation in war.

At Khe Sanh, transportation by air had two advantages. The foremost was speed. The Americans put their second Marine battalion with their full complement of equipment into Khe Sanh by air in six days. By comparison, the NVA built up their logistics for over six months to invest Khe Sanh using ground transportation. The two divisions the NVA emplaced around the Marines at the base comprised four times the number of men that the Marines had. Moving thousands of soldiers of NVA and their supplies down the Ho Chi Minh Trail took weeks, all under threat of US airpower.

The second advantage to air transportation in the Modern Era was the ability to perform a full range of operations. These operations were not expedients as at Guadalcanal or Stalingrad, but normal mission sets. From standard cargo missions to helicopter supply, airdrop, and aeromedical evacuation, air transportation provided a decided advantage for the Americans over the North Vietnamese.

Critical to this flexibility was the C-130 cargo aircraft. Coupled with computing technology and radars, the Americans used the C-130 to perfect an airdrop system in the weather, a procedure never tried but proven reliable enough within a few days to deliver cargo in sufficient amounts. Besides airdrop, these aircraft had the capacity for standard cargo missions or LAPES cargo-releases for delivery to the Khe Sanh base. Much like Braddock's Conestoga wagons, the "Herks" were the ideal technology for the job.

Added to the fixed-wing mission, the US used helicopters to supply their outposts on the hills surrounding Khe Sanh to maintain the high ground while also moving thousands of men forward in Operation Pegasus to open the ground line of communication to the base. Air transportation could also evacuate the wounded, preserving life and bolstering morale for the Marines stuck at Khe Sanh. Thus, the capabilities of the Americans to deliver cargo as needed was a vast improvement over the rigged parachutes of the Germans to supply the *Kessel* at Stalingrad or the awkward loading of fuel barrels onto C-47s to help provide gas for the Cactus Air Force at Guadalcanal. By comparison, the Americans delivered fourteen thousand tons of supplies into Khe Sanh by air for 7,000 soldiers over seventy-seven days, while the Germans delivered three thousand tons of supplies for 250,000 soldiers over sixty-nine days.[244]

Undergirding the logistics at Khe Shan was a proper system designed to receive aircraft, load, unload, prepare for airdrop, and prioritize cargo. The system of logistics, articulated almost a decade earlier in *The Uncertain Trumpet*, came to fruition at Khe Sanh.[245] In a vast and complex network, the US military moved cargo into Khe Sanh via aircraft, helicopter, and parachute with a speed and capacity unmatched in any previous conflict. From US Army riggers at bases afield, to USAF ground handlers at Khe Sanh, to enlisted Marine radar operators who guided aircraft toward the airfield and drop zones, the US brought its logistics to bear on Khe Sanh and kept the Marines alive.

So complete was the supply victory at Khe Sanh that a debate ensued between the US Marine Corps and the US Army after the battle whether the garrison was ever under siege and thus requiring the relief of Operation

Pegasus.[246] Pegasus further built on the successes of supply during the siege. While suppled via airlift, III MAF and MACV could open a road with a division's worth of US Army helicopters and follow with hundreds of trucks over Route 9—all at the same time.

Despite its effectiveness at Khe Sanh and its potential to be an equivalent mode of transportation, moving goods by air and stopping those of the enemy was expensive. For example, the fuel for only the C-130 missions eclipsed $5 million dollars, and the transport planes burned fuel at a miserly three miles per gallon. [247] Although the amounts are uncertain, the helicopters and fighter and bomber aircraft necessary to pave the way for transportation burned much more fuel than that. In addition, postwar estimates put the cost of running the Muscle Shoals system at $18 million per week—about $200 million for the seventy-seven-day siege at Khe Sanh.[248] Coupled with the transportation costs including fuel, supplies, and aircraft lost, the resupply of Khe Sanh cost well over $300 million. At this cost, the line of communication established through the air at Khe Sanh was available only to the United States, with its 35 percent share of the world's GDP. Even supported by the Chinese and the Soviets, North Vietnam could not have afforded such a system.

Thus, for the Americans, the opening of Route 9 by land was an acknowledgment that land transportation still outpaced aircraft in capacity and efficiency.[249] Technological improvements in trucks allowed even the third-world nation of North Vietnam to possess and operate thousands of vehicles and move almost thirty thousand men and their equipment down the Ho Chi Minh Trail to attack Khe Sanh. As during previous eras, vehicles required a usable road network. The vast improvements the NVA made to the Ho Chi Minh Trail, transformed from a path for porters into a logistics system of truck routes and way stations, supported the massive movement to Khe Sanh. Without the established road network and the 2.5-ton truck, the NVA would have struggled to move the supplies they needed at Khe Sanh. Yet despite the benefits of land transportation, airpower still held sway over ground lines of communication in combat.

While the NVA thwarted airpower by moving during bad weather and at night, and using their AAA to shoot down aircraft, by 1967 the US caught up—aided by the integrative power of the computer wedded to the airplane in the Muscle Shoals tracking system. When fielded at Khe Sanh, Muscle

Shoals allowed aircraft and artillery to train on vehicle or large troop movements, ending any NVA massing of men or material in battle. US firepower was so accurate and dominant from land artillery to B-52s that the North Vietnamese left large caches of supply and subsistence behind when they vacated the battlefield in March 1968. Khe Sanh illustrated that in the Modern Era the advantages that weather and cycles of sun and moon once held against airpower were waning.

Geopolitical Impacts—Khe Sanh (Modern Era)

Westmoreland and Le Duan got the battle they wanted at Khe Sanh—a conventional fight resembling Dien Bien Phu. The earlier battle had sent shockwaves into the geopolitical contest of the Cold War. The French defeat shook the West, bringing strategic doubt as to whether or not its nations could hold back the tide of revolutionary fervor breaking forth over the world in the wake of the British and French empires weakened by two world wars. Despite a tactical victory by the United States, Khe Sanh and its companion, the Tet Offensive, brought the same sting of defeat as Dien Bien Phu had for the French, with the American population turning against the war.

With the ability of the world to watch the drama of battle play out and hear of its effects on the radio and TV, a win on the battlefield was not as important as winning the war of ideas. The air superiority and logistics capability of the Americans, which gave them a tactical victory and from which the NVA did not recover for years, was a resounding defeat in the world of public opinion. Computing technology, battlefield analysis, precision firepower, all borne of the age of nuclear weapons, were useless against the narrative. The view of the North Vietnamese soldier standing and challenging the Goliath of the American military was a victory in the war of ideas even though it was a loss on the battlefield. The immense effort the North Vietnamese spent in supplying and transporting soldiers for that offensive surely earns a piece of the success.

For the American military, Vietnam was a watershed—an example of hubris and failure not to be repeated. The younger American officers who suffered the defeat of Vietnam turned the failure into a cause, exploring new and better ideas for the use of force. USAF colonels John Boyd and John Warden redefined the technological and theoretical uses of airpower, while US Army general Powell redefined US strategy and political-military relationships during wartime. As for logistics, the US military viewed Khe Sanh not as a success, but more as an example of the improvements required to supply troops in wars of the Modern Era and how best to combat the Soviet foe.[250] Eventually, the debates about how best to transport forces to war resulted in the creation of the US Transportation Command in 1987 to oversee all the transportation of the US military to war. These concepts of airpower, strategy, and logistics led to in the victories of Desert Storm in 1991 and Allied Force in 1999.

Conclusion

We came to Landlord Frasers and there went to breakfast. . . . We ate milk and this was the first milk I had since summer. . . . Then we came to Lyman's and could not get anything. . . . Then we came nine miles and there got some victuals.
—Robert Webster, travel from Crown Point to home, 21–23 November 1759

Logistics represent well the technological shifts from the Enlightenment to the dawn of the twenty-first century. Modes of transportation manifested the great change. The increased capacity for transport across the sea, land, and air domains is astounding. As Figure C.1 illustrates, the cargo capacity—across all modes—expanded 165-fold over three centuries.

Control of the dominant mode of transportation augured well for the possessor, regardless of era. At Lake George, in the Preindustrial Era, water transportation dominated movement over land. The French, at a decided disadvantage in numbers of inhabitants, wealth, and political support from their sovereign, held off the British by using their native allies and moving to war via water. The French defeat of Braddock at the Monongahela is a fitting example of the power of water transportation over land. Despite months of effort, tens of thousands of pounds, and an army of three thousand, a less equipped but speedier force commanded by the French equaled Braddock's journey and bested him in battle. A complex wooden wagon was no match for the speed and capacity of simple bateaux.

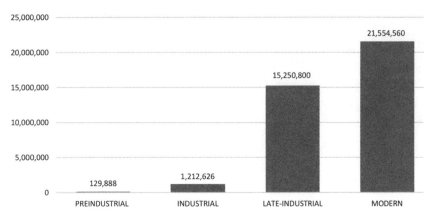

Figure C.1. Ton-Miles per Day per Technological Era (All Modes). The cargo capacity of the era is based on the highest amount of cargo delivery capable for a representative technology in each mode (e.g., railroad and ocean steamer in the Industrial Era). Ton-miles per day represent the theoretical cargo capacity a given technology can deliver within a twenty-four-hour period, without stopping. The above numbers account for the maximum capacity for all modes available during the era—sea, land, and/or air.

The seventeen-mile portage from the Hudson River to Lake George, on wilderness roads, was also a tough line of communication to hold. The British began by building two forts—Edward and William Henry—and designed their logistics to include way stations with protective garrisons, ensuring that the food, ammunition, and boats arrived at Lake George. After Montcalm's victory over Abercrombie at Fort Carillon in 1758, the British acknowledged the superiority of water transportation to land, sinking their freshwater navy and abandoning Lake George to the French for the winter. Keeping soldiers supplied, fed, and disease-free via the roads of the eighteenth century consumed too much treasure and human life.

While the capacity of the French on inland waterways, rivers, and lakes was fifteen times as great as British over land to Lake George, the capacity of the sea transportation dwarfed both (see Figure C.2). As a result, the British victory at Louisburg in 1758 assured Amherst's victory in 1759 at Fort Carillon. While the British spent much to establish a presence at Lake George, only victory at sea preserved their line of communication over the land.

The Western Front in 1917 illustrated the changes the industrial revolution had bestowed upon logistics. The supply lines of the allies, carried over the

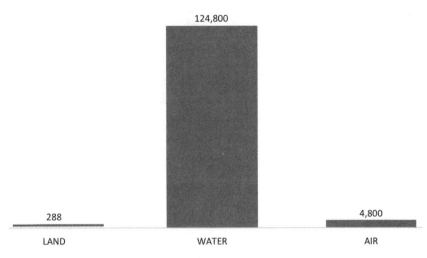

Figure C.2. Ton-Miles per Day, Lake George (Land and Water). See appendix for source data. The following technologies are representative of the modes: Conestoga wagon (land), transport sailing ship (water), large bateau (inland water).

sea, met the supply lines of Germany carried on rail. They tied. The capacities of the railroad and ocean steamer reflect the evenness (see Figure C.3). In this uniform contest of logistics, a massive war of artillery defined the conflict with hundreds of thousands of shells lobbed over the trenches. Each lacked the mobile firepower to break the deadlock. The internal combustion engine, making its debut in the First World War in the form of the submarine, tank, truck, and the airplane, held promise, however, for a more mobile future.

While the airplane impacted logistics on the Western Front in 1917, first as a reconnaissance platform, the technology grew into its own during the Second World War. At Guadalcanal and Stalingrad, the aircraft legislated the delivery of supplies across land and water. The Marines used Henderson Field to great effect, aircraft launched from the runway interrupting Japanese supply deliveries to the island while guaranteeing delivery of American supplies. Despite Japanese dominance of the sea for most of the campaign, including the sinking of three US carriers, they failed to resupply their soldiers due to the constant pressure of American airpower.

Much as in the Pacific in 1942, airpower legislated the logistics of Stalingrad. For the Soviets, only when the Germans had frittered away their airpower through attrition, environmental factors, and the fortuitous Allied invasion of

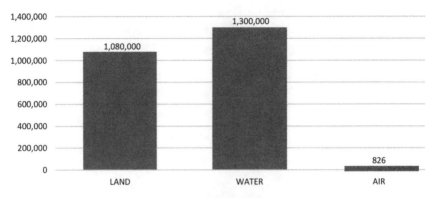

Figure C.3. Ton-Miles per Day, Western Front, 1917 (Land, Water, Air). See appendix for source data. The following technologies represent the modes: train with fifty freight cars (land), ocean steamer (sea), large bateau (inland water). Air transportation was in its infancy in World War I and not a factor in logistics. For comparison only.

North Africa could the Red Army turn the tables of encirclement on the Germans. German domination of the air early in the conflict enabled the Luftwaffe to range far beyond the capabilities of their land power, interdicting Soviet soldiers and materiel sent to the front and almost severing the Soviet line of communication across the Volga. The Luftwaffe pulled the *Heer* forward, through firepower and transportation—to the edge of Stalingrad. However, once their airpower diminished, the Germans had neither the combat power to take Stalingrad, nor enough to stem the Soviet advances of Operation Uranus. Thus, while the capacity to move cargo across water and land had increased exponentially since the Industrial Era, this technological leap was not germane to logistics (see Figure C.3). Control of the air was the deciding factor.

Air transportation also came into its own in the Second World War. Airlift performed admirably in both campaigns, especially as an aeromedical evacuation platform removing sick Americans from Guadalcanal and saving twenty-four thousand German soldiers trapped in the Stalingrad *Kessel* from the Soviet gulag. Despite tactical success, air transportation was no match for that of land or water. At Stalingrad, a German army of 250,000 accustomed to an adequate, if overstretched, supply line of trains, trucks, vehicles, and *Panje* carts, could not be supplied by air (see Figure C.4).

At Khe Sanh, the line of communication through the air could equal the capacity of land and water. Although sometimes food and water were scarce,

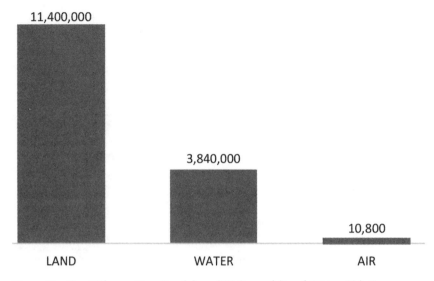

Figure C.4. Ton-Miles per Day, Guadalcanal/Stalingrad (Land, Water, Air). See appendix for source data. The following technologies represent the modes: railroad (land), liberty ship (water), C-47/Ju-52 (air).

American aircraft kept the base supplied. The United States may well have been able to supply the Marines at Khe Sanh for all time. So complete was the victory of American logistics that a postconflict debate between the US Marine Corps and the US Army ensued about whether Khe Sanh was ever under siege at all, and thus in need of Operation Pegasus. For the North Vietnamese, the venerable 2.5-ton truck delivered two divisions of combatants and over sixty days of supply down the Ho Chi Minh Trail. However, the capacity and the speed of the truck, and the threat of US airpower, forced the North Vietnamese to spend months building up their supplies at Khe Sanh. (See Figure C.5 for a comparison of how an NVA truck compared in speed and capacity to a US C-130 aircraft.) For the United States, the ability to move so much cargo by air provided great speed and capacity, but at great cost. In fact, the United States and perhaps the Soviet Union were the only two nations capable of such a feat of logistics in 1968.

Airpower still dominated logistics at Khe Sanh. With the computing power of the Muscle Shoals system, connected to the firepower and mobility of aircraft, the US pinned the North Vietnamese down. The Americans recorded every movement, offensive, or counterattack by the NVA and at-

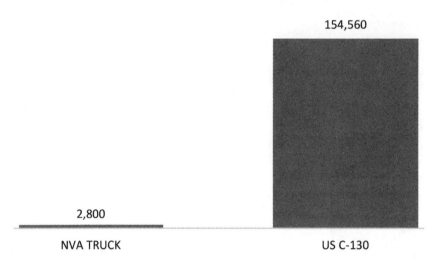

154,560

2,800

NVA TRUCK   US C-130

Figure C.5. Ton-Miles per Day, Khe Sanh (Truck and C-130). See appendix for source data.

tacked them relentlessly. While weather and darkness played a critical factor in limiting airpower in the Second World War, by the battle of Khe Sanh advanced technologies allowed the air campaign to become a near twenty-four-hour operation for the missions of firepower and logistics.

Though the United States won at the game of supply and inflicted heavy losses on the NVA at Khe Sanh, they still lost the war. The narrative of the small third-world country, besieging the Marines at Khe Sanh, and attacking US- and ARVN-controlled cities in South Vietnam, was enough to turn American public opinion against the war. In an obverse of Braddock's material largess rippling through the native allies of the French and calling them to fight after the defeat on the Monogahela, moving so many soldiers and supplies into South Vietnam despite their enemy's military might bolstered the view that North Vietnam was winning the war. The narrative triumphed over airpower and logistics. In postmodern war, ideological factors came to mean more than material ones.

CONTINUITIES

From Abercrombie's force losing its way on the north shore of Lake George, to the challenge of getting supplies from the helicopters to the hill outposts at Khe Sanh, the difficulty of transitioning between modes of transportation was a constant. This difficulty manifested itself in front-line logistics and rear-echelon logistics support.

For front-line logistics, moving from one mode of transportation to another required unloading or loading, the marrying of supplies and combatants, and movement forward. What seems like a simple process was tough to carry out in combat conditions. The initial landings of Marines at Red Beach are most representative of this difficulty. While the landings were a success, the cargo overflowing on the beach stalled the offensive to take the airfield. Water was in short supply and critical food floated away with the tide. The difficulties the Marines encountered to march three miles to Henderson Field resembled Abercrombie's failure to navigate the forest of the Adirondacks on the short path to Fort Carillon, his British and colonial soldiers jettisoning food all over the forest floor.

Proper planning for the transition between modes of transportation was necessary but not sufficient. Follow-through planning, beyond initial movements, was always important. In an example of failure to plan, the Japanese at Guadalcanal focused too much on concentration of troops and firepower, and waited too long for food. As a result, their ability to conduct offensives stalled for lack of sustenance. By contrast, Brigadier General Howe and Major General Vandegrift planned and prepared with much foresight before their offensives. Howe worked hard to build the navy to transport Abercrombie's army and practiced the complicated procedures to keep hundreds of boats in line as they rowed and sailed up Lake George. However, his lack of preparation for debarkation cost the army a critical delay of one day, allowing Montcalm to reinforce his fortifications, and contributed to the loss of Howe's own life in the melee of moving his men uphill. For Major General Vandegrift, the successful amphibious assault at Guadalcanal—theorized, tested, and practiced for decades in the Marine Corps—stalled in its efforts to reach the airfield and cost him precious supply because of the lack of logistics foresight.

While helicopter resupply missions to the hill outposts and cargo deliveries to the Khe Sanh runway were challenging, the Americans illustrated how to overcome the difficulty of transitioning between modes of transportation. For the helicopter deliveries, the Americans used the Super Gaggle—airpower as logistics support. For fixed-wing deliveries, the Marines adapted radar designed for aircraft approaches to guide USAF C-130s to airdrop cargo, along with other technological solutions such as LAPES. The efforts of the Luftwaffe to pull the German army forward with firepower and transportation in the summer of 1942 were another example of how to properly transition between modes. However, their failure to resupply the Stalingrad *Kessel* showed the opposite. Thus, at the tactical level, transporting supplies and combatants across modes required dedicated planning, proper coordination with combat power, and integrating applicable technologies for success. The transition required a network solution. From transport to tarmac and barge to bayou, intermodal planning proved critical to delivery of goods and people.

Rear-echelon logistics also struggled with the transition from one mode of transportation to another. Albany, the French ports in the Western Front in 1917, and Nouméa in 1942, all had backlogs. The speed of the transportation technologies of the time—the sloop, the ocean steamer, and the transport ship—overwhelmed the ports with cargo. At Albany, the British created a supply system at the docks, and developed a robust overland supply network with depots, to ensure the cargo survived the threat from Native American raids. Sir Eric Geddes's system with more cranes at the ports, more rail lines, and better information flow allowed the British to pursue their offensives of 1917. At Nouméa, Admiral Halsey simplified the system, rather than making it more robust, separating the army and navy cargo to speed up the deliveries to Guadalcanal. Thus, the solution for rear-echelon logistics required a network of disparate elements: information, technology, and dedicated logistics planning to solve the problem.

The technologies of the age also imposed a time-requirement to establish a successful network. The faster supplies and combatants moved to the front, the more quickly a supply network was needed. For example, the British took years to build their network from Albany to Lake George, which was sufficient in the era of wood, wind, and sail for the technology of the time, even if did not produce victory in 1755 as the Crown had hoped. On the Western Front in 1917, Sir Eric Geddes spent a year revamping British transportation in France. At Guadalcanal, the United States and Japan had months to get it right, where the United States succeeded in three months and the Japanese failed. At Stalingrad, the speed and capacity of the airplane required a network with the same attributes. The Germans lacked the network in place to handle such a cargo load. At Khe Sanh, the Americans possessed the network to handle the immediate surges of vast numbers of cargo aircraft. To make it work for the ensuring battle, the Americans had to establish the network of logistics in days versus the forty-eight months required of the British in 1755. In many ways, the successful creation of a network was as much about leadership and managerial acumen as it was about understanding how to adapt logistics to the battle at hand.[1] Captain Eyre at Lake George, Admiral Halsey at Guadalcanal, and General Chuikov all led their organizations to success through sometimes innovative and other times brutal means to keep their armies in the fight. Being able to manage a system of logistics, although much less glamourous than direct combat, meant the difference between victory and defeat.

The challenge of transitioning modes, and establishing the proper supply network to support that transition, illustrates how important joint operations were to logistics. Most notable in their lack of integration among the various services were the Germans at Stalingrad and the Japanese at Guadalcanal. For the Germans, the petty and sycophantic competition to curry favor with Hitler between the Luftwaffe and the *Ostheer* led to supply shortages at the front. For the Japanese, the inability of the army to understand how capable their enemy was and how hard it was to supply the island, coupled with the Imperial Japanese Navy's reluctance to interfere, led to the starvation of twenty-eight thousand troops. Thus, the joint force remains an enabler of the logistics in the same way that logistics enables the joint forces. This synergy appears continuous over the past three hundred years.

Despite the need for supply networks to match technological advances, the most striking continuity over the last three centuries was simpler: the impact of food and water on the outcome of battle. While this factor seems obvious in the eighteenth century, with wooden wagons, ships, and limited methods to preserve food in the field, food and water supplies for the belligerents at Khe Sanh were just as important as those at Lake George had been. Even with the modern firepower, computing power, and transportation possessed by the United States and the NVA, the key to the success of the Americans was access to water, and for the North Vietnamese to food.

Even on the Western Front in 1917, lack of food and water was at least partially responsible for the stalled British offensives at Ypres; and, more important, food supply at home shaped the operational planning for both sides. The British tried to strike at Ypres and toward Flanders, in part because of the threat the submarine posed to the food supplies of the British population. For the Germans, the pullback to the Hindenburg Line, the unleashing of the U-boats on shipping in the Atlantic, and their decision to stay on the defensive until the Russians capitulated in the East, was motivated by the lack of food for the civilian population.

Beyond the linking of food to tactical, operational, and strategic considerations for war, there was a temporal constant associated with food supplies—fifteen days. Whether Dieskau's troops who limped back to Fort Carillon starving, the Japanese at Guadalcanal, or the Germans in the *Kessel*, a fifteen-day food deficit represented the limit to effective operations. Any food deficit beyond a fortnight doomed the combatants. How quickly an army starves!

Even Carl Von Clausewitz, who understood the relationship between food and victory, believed food took second place to combat power when war reached its apex of intensity. Clausewitz theorized that supply was more important "on the other hand, where a state of equilibrium has set in, in which troops move back and forth for years in the same province, subsistence is likely to become the principal concern."[2] For Clausewitz the transition between the now and later of food importance seemed to take on a timeline of months—when, as this study has shown, it is days. Thus, the limit of the human body, much more than technological advance, determined the outcome of battle.

Given the limits of the human body, the feat of General Edward Braddock in getting his army to Fort Duquesne represented a logistic feat for the ages. To put Braddock's logistical prowess in historical context, the archetype general of the Preindustrial Era, Frederick the Great, "could march for a maximum of ten days before a pause became necessary."[3] Braddock, by contrast, had his army construct a road and move itself for a month, hungry but intact with a significant advantage in personnel and firepower over his enemies.[4] Braddock's overarching emphasis on food underpinned his success of logistics.[5] As we have seen in this study, not one army could keep itself internally supplied for a month and survive—save Braddock's. Yet for all of Braddock's success of logistics, it did not guarantee him victory, instead supplying his enemy with the heavy artillery the French needed to defend their empire from the British. Logistics was important, but it was not everything.

GEOPOLITICAL IMPACTS

Technological changes, by their impact on logistics, alter geopolitical balances. The railroad allowed land transportation to compete with water transportation, and coupled with the Late Industrial technology of the submarine allowed a land power in Germany to threaten to overturn centuries of British world dominance. The airplane, in turn, demanded control of the air to deliver logistics to the battlefield. Manufacturing bases, expenses, and the human capital needed to produce such an air force meant that only nations with vast air forces could compete on the stage as great powers, much as the requirement for a great navy determined world stature centuries before. The advancement of nuclear weapons and telecommunications in the Modern Era elevated the narrative of war over airpower. Despite profligate supply, and winning every battle, the United States lost the war. Thus, the Modern Era represents a clean break from the previous three centuries.

Since the eighteenth century, and battles like Fontenoy, the ability of either side to marshal its forces to battle and sustain them had underpinned victory. The "fustest with mostest" had held for three centuries. Although there were many exceptions at the tactical level, at the strategic level the nations that best moved and supplied their forces won—the British at Lake George, the allies on the Western Front in 1918 after the logistics of the Americans tilted the tie between sea and land power, the Soviets at Stalingrad, and the Americans at Guadalcanal. At Khe Sanh, the formula changed. Despite their ability to supply the Marines at will, a luxury all armies of the past three centuries would have envied, and the subsequent maiming of the NVA, the Americans and their South Vietnamese ally lost the war. We now live in this age. Ideas trump the material forces of war.

Appendix
Technologies of Transportation

The representative technologies of transportation of war are only a fraction of the various machines used throughout each era. The term ton-mile per day is measure of capacity and speed and used in modern logistics to compare capability across air, land, and water modes of transportation. Ton-mile is a *theoretical value* based on twenty-four hours of operation at a given speed and cargo load.[1] Although land and air technologies have difficulty meeting the twenty-four-hour limit because of fuel considerations or the limits of human and animal power, transportation by sea and water could often reach the number. In the conclusion, the total-ton miles for each era equals the sum of the maximum ton-miles per day of all three modes.[2]

Table A.1. Technologies of Transportation, Preindustrial Era

Technology	Power Source	Capacity (Tons)	Speed (mph)	Ton-Miles per Day
Wagon	Animal	2–8	1.5	72–288
Bateau	Current/Human/Wind	1/2–2	2–5*	24–240
River Sloop	Current/Animal/Wind	80	1–2.5	1,900–4,800
Sailing Ship	Wind/Current	100–260	2–20*	4800–124,800

Sources: Data adapted from Donald H. Berkebile, Conestoga Wagons in Braddock's Campaign, 1755 (Washington, DC: Smithsonian Institution, 1959); Joseph F. Meany Jr., "'Batteaux' and 'Battoe Men': An American Colonial Response to the Problem of Logistics in Mountain Warfare," unpublished (New York, 1998); J. Wheelwright, "J. Wheelwright's List of Supplies, Enclosed in Shirley to Johnson, June 9, 1755," in The Papers of Sir William Johnson (Albany: University of the State of New York, Division of Archives and History, 1921), 571; and Kellie Vanhorn, "Eighteenth Century American Colonial American Merchant Ship Construction" (Thesis, Texas A&M University, 2004), 160–164.
* Water dependent

Table A.2. Technologies of Transportation, Industrial Era

Technology	Power Source	Capacity (Tons)	Speed (mph)	Ton Miles per Day
Train[a]	Steam	500–1,500	7–30	84,000–1.08 Million
Trench Train[b]	Steam	10–15	5	1,200–1,800
Barge	Current/Animal/Steam	300	2.5	18,000
Ocean Steamer	Current/Wind/Steam	5,000	11*	1.3 Million

Sources: Data adapted from Alan Major Henniker, Transportation on the Western Front, 1914–1918 (London: H. M. Stationery Office, 1937), 110; William J. Wilgus, Transporting the A. E. F. In Western Europe, 1917–1919 (New York: Columbia University Press, 1931), 276; Christian Wolmar, Blood, Iron, & Gold: How the Railroads Transformed the World, 1st ed. (New York: Public Affairs, 2010), 263–264; Motor Rail & Tramcar Co. Ltd., "Old Kiln Light Railway: A Short History," http://www .oldkilnlightrailway.com/motorrail.php; Allied and Associated Powers (1914–1920), Military Board of Allied Supply, Report of the Military Board of Allied Supply, vol. 1 (Washington, DC: Government Publishing Office, 1924), 1041, 1043; Carl E. McDowell, Helen M. Gibbs, and E. L. Cochrane, Ocean Transportation (New York: Beard Books, 1999), 112; S. C. Tucker, World War I: The Definitive Encyclopedia and Document Collection (Santa Barbara, CA: ABC-CLIO, 2014), 1074; and Norman Friedman, Fighting the Great War at Sea: Strategy, Tactics and Technology (Annapolis, MD: Naval Institute Press, 2014), 283.
[a] Estimate for a train carrying fifty wagons. Speeds for trains varied based on type of cargo. During

Germany's mobilization in 1914, the rails were so full of trains meeting exact schedules that they moved as slow as a few miles per hour to stay on time.

[b] Estimate for a narrow-gauge train. Motor Rail & Tramcar (see source notes) wrote, "The War Office required 'Petrol Trench Tractors' of 600-mm gauge capable of drawing 10 to 15 Tons at 5 miles per hour."

*No wind

Table A.3. Technologies of Transportation (WW1), Late Industrial Era

Technology	Power Source	Capacity (Tons)	Speed (mph)	Ton-Miles per Day
Truck	Internal Combustion Engine	2–3	20	960–1,440
Airplane	Internal Combustion Engine	50–600 lbs	87–115	48–826

Sources: Data adapted from Allied and Associated Powers (1914–1920), Military Board of Allied Supply, *Report of the Military Board of Allied Supply,* vol. 1 (Washington, DC: Government Publishing Office, 1924), 659; Daniel R. Beaver, "Deuce and a Half": Selecting U.S. Army Trucks, 1920–1945," in John A. Lynn, ed., *Feeding Mars: Logistics in Western Warfare from the Middle Ages to the Present* (Boulder, CO: Westview Press, 1993), 253; Military Factory Staff Writer, "WW1 Aircraft Ranked by Speed," http://www.militaryfactory.com/aircraft/ww1-aircraft-ranked-by-speed.asp; and John Terraine, *White Heat: The New Warfare 1914–18* (London: Sidgwick & Jackson, 1982), 265.

Table A.4. Technologies of Transportation (Water), Late Industrial Era

Technology	Power Source	Capacity (Tons)	Speed (mph)	Ton-Miles per Day
Cargo Ship	Diesel to Steam Turbine	5,000–10,000	15	1,440,000–3,840,000
Troop Transport	Diesel to Steam Turbine	1,800–2,000	17	734,000–816,000

Sources: Data adapted from James L. Mooney, *Dictionary of American Naval Fighting Ships* (Washington, DC: Naval Historical Center, 1991); Second Demobilization Bureau, General Headquarters Far East Asia Command, "Japanese Monograph No. 98—Southeast Area Naval Operations—Part I, May 42–Feb 43" (1949); and S. C. Heal, *Ugly Ducklings: Japan's WWII Liberty Type Standard Ship* (Annapolis, MD: Naval Institute Press, 2003).

Note: These ranges are for both Japanese and American ships. Troop transport ships had armament and often carried landing craft as well. Transport ships could carry 1,000–1,500 troops and up to 1,700 tons of cargo. Some older Japanese cargo ships were paleotechnic—relying on coal and cruising as slow as nine knots (not represented).

Table A.5. Technologies of Transportation (Air), Late Industrial Era

Technology	Power Source	Capacity (Tons)	Speed (mph)	Ton-Miles per Day
Airplane	Internal Combustion Engine	2–3	150	8,000–10,800

Sources: Data for C-47/Ju-52 adapted from Boeing, "C-47 Skytrain Military Transport," accessed 7 January 2016, http://www.boeing.com/history/products/c-47-skytrain.page; Hans Detlef Herhudt Von Rhoden, "The Stalingrad Airlift: A Brief Summary of the Facts Involved," in *The Papers of Lt. Gen. William Tuner* (Maxwell Air Force Base, AL: Air Force Historical Research Agency, IRIS No. 10910955, 1949), 6; and Peter C. Smith and Martin Pegg, *Transporter, Volume Two: Luftwaffe Transport Units 1943–45* (London: Classic Publications, 2006), 133.

Table A.6. Technologies of Transportation (Land), Late Industrial Era

Technology	Power Source	Capacity (Tons)	Speed (mph)	Ton-Miles per Day
Train	Steam/Diesel	3,000–4,000	50–108	3.96–11.4 Million
Truck	Internal Combustion Engine	2	20–40	960–1,880

Sources: Data adapted from Avro L. Vecamer, "Deutsche Reichsbahn—The German State Railway in WWII," accessed 24 February 2016, http://www.feldgrau.com/dreichsbahn.htm; and "3-ton Opel Blitz," accessed 24 Febuary 2016, http://www.achtungpanzer.com/3-ton-opel-blitz-36-36-36-36s-4x2-4x4.htm.
Note: German trains were steam engines for their resources in coal. The Soviets converted some trains to diesel by the start of the war. The heaviest trains would have moved at 50 mph (or slower) over poor Soviet Rails.

Table A.7. Technologies of Transportation (Water), Modern Era

Technology	Power Source	Capacity (Tons)	Speed (mph)	Ton-Miles per Day
Cargo Ship	Diesel to Steam Turbine	20,000+	20	10,000,000

Source: Data adapted from "U.S. Merchant Marine, Military Sea Transportation Service, and Military Sealift Command in Vietnam," accessed 1 April 2016, http://www.usmm.org/vietnam.html.
Note: This is a conservative estimate of capacity for a container-carrying cargo ship. Oftentimes the ship will be full of volume (i.e., no space left), before the limit of its deadweight tonnage (maximum weight the ship can handle and still maneuver safely/stay afloat).

Table A.8. Technologies of Transportation (Land), Modern Era

Technology	Power Source	Capacity (Tons)	Speed (mph)	Ton-Miles per Day
Train	Steam/Diesel	3,000–4,000	50–108	3.96–11.4 million
Truck	Internal Combustion Engine	2	60	2,800

Sources: Data adapted from Avro L. Vecamer, "Deutsche Reichsbahn-The German State Railway in WWII," accessed 24 February 2016, http://www.feldgrau.com/dreichsbahn.htm; and 3-ton Opel Blitz," accessed 24 Febuary 2016, http://www.achtungpanzer.com/3-ton-opel-blitz-36-36-36-36s-4x2-4x4.htm.

Note: Higher truck speed and more dependable engine led to greater ton-miles per day than during the Late Industrial Era.

Table A.9. Technologies of Transportation (Air), Modern Era

Technology	Power Source	Capacity (Tons)	Speed (mph)	Ton-Miles per Day
Airplane	Internal Combustion Engine	20	270	154,560

Source: Data for C-130E adapted from Ray L. Bowers, *Tactical Airlift: The United States Air Force in Southeast Asia* (Washington, DC: Office of Air Force History, 1983), 34.

Note: Speed reduced from 370 mph to 308 mph for short sortie lengths to Khe Sanh versus a long-range airlift sortie.

NOTES

INTRODUCTION

1 Evan Charteris, *William Augustus, Duke of Cumberland, His Early Life and Times (1721–1748)* (London: E. Arnold, 1913), 211.

2 Charteris, *William Augustus*, 191.

3 Lewis Mumford, *Technics and Civilization* (New York: Harcourt, 1934), 93.

4 Mumford, *Technics and Civilization*, 109. Mumford used Eotechnic, Paleotechnic, and Neotechnic to define the technological eras. These titles correspond to the first three eras listed in Table I.1. For this analysis, the Modern Era encompasses the splitting of the atom as a source of power and a weapon. Although Mumford's eras described technology, they were as much about culture as artifacts and included crucial periods of social "preparation, when all the key inventions were either invented or foreshadowed" and the "existence of certain types of workers." Mumford also viewed each era in continuity with that before it; the transitions between epochs did not happen stochastically.

5 Although the Great War occurred a few years into the Industrial Era, weapons and logistics were dominated by industrial technologies perfected over the previous century—artillery, machine guns, trains, and steam ships.

6 Antoine Bousquet, *The Scientific Way of Warfare: Order and Chaos on the Battlefields of Modernity* (New York: Columbia University Press, 2010), 123–124.

7 Peter Dye, *The Bridge to Airpower: Logistics Support for Royal flying Corps Operations on the Western Front, 1914–18* (Annapolis, MD: Naval Institute Press, 2015), 1–19. Transportation and supply are two broad categories of logistics. Dye gives an outstanding account of the historiography and expanded definition of logistics encompassing everything from national manufacturing capacity to delivery supplies to troops in direct combat.

8 Winston S. Churchill, *The River War: An Account of the Reconquest of the Sudan* (Mineola, NY: Dover Publications, 2012), 162.

9. Theodore Ropp, *War in the Modern World* (Baltimore, MD: Johns Hopkins University Press, 2000), 184.

10 Francis Bacon, *The Essays of Lord Bacon* (London: Longmans, Green & Company, 1873), 130.

CHAPTER 1. CONESTOGA VERSUS CANOES: LAKE GEORGE, 1755–1759

1 Frederic Franklyn Van de Water, *Lake Champlain and Lake George* (New York: Bobbs-Merrill Company, 1946), 56.

2 The French called the lake Lac du Saint Sacrement. In 1755, Sir William Johnson, christened the waters Lake George when his colonial army arrived on the

south shore. In addition, the British named the French Fort of Saint-Frédéric, located just north of Lake George on Lake Champlain, Crown Point.

3   Eliot A. Cohen, *Conquered into Liberty: Two Centuries of Battles Along the Great Warpath That Made the American Way of War* (New York: Free Press, 2011), 2.

4   Plantations General, "Population of the British American Colonies," in *Documents Relative to the Colonial History of the State of New York Procured in Holland, England and France*, ed. John Romeyn Brodhead 15 vols., (Albany: Weed, Parsons, and Company, 1858), 6:993.

5   See Daniel Baugh, *The Global Seven Years' War, 1754–1763: Britian and France in a Great Power Contest*, 1st. ed. (Harlow, England: Pearson, 2011), 73; and Fred Anderson, *Crucible of War: The Seven Years' War and the Fate of Empire in British North America, 1754–1766* (Vintage, 2007), 32.

6   See Anderson, *Crucible of War*, 28. Anderson describes the proximate cause of the French and Indian War as a deal between British colonial merchants and the Iroquois League to establish Fort Cumberland as a British settlement. This agreement placed British interests in direct geographic and economic competition with French dominion over the internal river ways of the Old Northwest. See also Gail D. MacLeitch, *Imperial Entanglements: Iroquois Change and Persistence on the Frontiers of Empire*, Early American Studies (Philadelphia: University of Pennsylvania Press, 2011), 45–84.

7   Cohen, *Conquered into Liberty*, 6–9.

8   See Cohen, 27–28; MacLeitch, *Imperial Entanglements*, 24; and Anderson, *Crucible of War*, 11.

9   Baugh, *The Global Seven Years' War*, 63–64.

10   Baugh, 82–83.

11   Anderson, *Crucible of War*, 66–73.

12   Gilles Harvard, "'Protection' and 'Unequal Alliance': The French Conception of Sovereignty over Indians in New France," in *French and Indians in the Heart of North America, 1630–1815*, eds. Robert Englebert and Guillaume Teasdale (East Lansing: Michigan State University Press, 2013), 114. The French were often the communication vessel for one tribe to speak to another, and given the small size of the French population, French leaders were often at the mercy of tribal demands. Although the Native Americans often invoked patriarchal language to describe French leaders, the relationship "relied on considerations (*menagments*)—in other words, strategic accommodation."

13   See Francis Henry Bennett Skrine, *Fontenoy and Great Britain's Share in the War of the Austrian Succession, 1741–1748* (Edinburgh W. Blackwood and Sons, 1906), available online at http://catalog.hathitrust.org/Record/000556734. On the British side, the Duke of Cumberland commanded all British forces at Fontenoy; Braddock and St. Clair took part in the battle. On the French side, Dieskau saw action in the fight as a cavalry officer under de Saxe. Brigadier General Howe, General Amherst, and Lt. Col. Gage all fought at Fontenoy. French col-

onel Levis, Montcalm's second-in-command at Ticonderoga in 1758, was involved in other battles that summer in Flanders. Watching it all in horror was Louis XV. The two notable exceptions were Major General Abercrombie, who served as a British administrator at the time of the battle, and Montcalm, on the French side, who was involved in siege warfare in Italy.

14 Martin van Creveld, *Supplying War: Logistics from Wallenstein to Patton* (New York: Cambridge University Press, 1977), 39.

15 Frederick, *Frederick the Great on the Art of War*, ed. and trans. Jay Luvaas (New York: Free Press, 1966), 112–113.

16 See *Frederick the Great on the Art of War*, 109. Frederick the Great stated, "regimental wagons . . . carry an eight-day supply of bread." See also Maurice Saxe and William Fawcett, *Reveries, or, Memoirs Upon the Art of War* (London: Printed for J. Nourse, 1757), 9. Saxe recommended soldiers should have a seven- to nine-day supply of biscuits—"because it [a biscuit] is a composition which does not spoil with keeping."

17 Steven T. Ross, *From Flintlock to Rifle, Infantry Tactics, 1740–1866*, 2nd ed. (London: Frank Cass, 1996), 25.

18 See Van de Water, *Lake Champlain and Lake George*, 35; Samuel De Champlain et al., *The Works of Samuel de Champlain*, vol. 2 (Ontario, Canada: Champlain Society, 1922), 98–99; MacLeitch, *Imperial Entanglements*, 15; and Anderson, *Crucible of War*, 12. Champlain and three of his French companions fired into a massed formation of Iroquois warriors who had drawn their bows and spears to attack, and killed three of their chiefs. With this action, Champlain cemented animosity between the French and the Iroquois that remained until France no longer controlled Canada—framing the future alliances during the campaign for Lake George.

19 Armstrong Starkey, *European and Native American Warfare 1675–1815* (London: University College of London Press, 2002), 18.

20 Theodore Ropp, *War in the Modern World* (Baltimore: Johns Hopkins University Press, 2000), 12.

21 Anderson, *Crucible of War*, 87. Braddock gave "direction and energy to a war effort unlike any ever seen in North America."

22 Robert Orme, *The History of an Expedition Against Fort Du Quesne, in 1755 Under Major-General Edward Braddock* (Lippincott, Grambo, & Co., 1856), 286.

23 See Edward Braddock, "General Edward Braddock to Robert Napier Williamsburg, March 17, 1755," in *Military Affairs in North America, 1748–1765: Selected Documents from the Cumberland Papers in Windsor Castle*, ed. Stanley McCrory Pargellis (New York: D. Appleton-Century Company, 1936), 80; and "General Edward Braddock to Robert Napier, April 19, 1755," in Pargellis, *Military Affairs in North America, 1748–1765*, 82.

24 See Orme, *The History of an Expedition Against Fort Du Quesne*, 159; Charles R. Hildeburn and John St. Clair, "Sir John St. Clair, Baronet, Quarter-Master

General in America, 1755 to 1767," *Pennsylvania Magazine of History and Biography* 9, no. 1 (1885): 5–7. As quoted by the editor of Captain Orme's journal from the Shippen MSS papers.

25 Orme, *The History of an Expedition Against Fort Du Quesne,* 288.

26 See Edward Braddock, "A Return of His Majesty's Troops Encamped at Will's Creek—June the 8th 1755," in Pargellis, *Military Affairs in North America, 1748–1765,* 85; *The Writings of George Washington from the Original Manuscript Sources, 1745–1799,* ed. John Clement Fitzpatrick, vol. 1 of 39 (Washington, DC: Government Publishing Office, 1931), 116–139; Edward Braddock, *Major General Edward Braddock's Orderly Books From February 26 to June 17, 1755* (Cumberland, MD: W. H. Lowdermilk, 1878); and Orme, *The History of an Expedition Against Fort Du Quesne,* 288. The correspondence of Braddock, orderly logs for the campaign, and the correspondence of his aide-de-camps Lieutenant George Washington and Captain Orme, illustrate the urgency of Braddock's requests and the difficult progress in getting the wagons. George Washington mentioned the want of horses or wagons fourteen out of the twenty-seven of his correspondences from 11 May to 7 June 1755.

27 Benjamin Franklin, "Memorandum of Wagon Accounts, April 23, 1755," in *The Papers of Benjamin Franklin* (American Philosophical Society and Yale University).

28 "Advertisement for Wagons, April 26, 1755," in Franklin, *The Papers of Benjamin Franklin.*

29 Donald H. Berkebile, *Conestoga Wagons in Braddock's Campaign, 1755* (Washington, DC: Smithsonian Institution, 1959), http://BZ6FJ9FL8E.search.serials solutions.com/?V=1.0&L=BZ6FJ9FL8E&S=JCs&C=TC_007465407&T=marc .9.

30 William E. Burns, *Science and Technology in Colonial America* (Greenwood Publishing Group, 2005), 86.

31 Berkebile, *Conestoga Wagons in Braddock's Campaign, 1755,* Kindle version, 28.

32 Bryan Wright, "The Conestoga Wagon: The Colonial Workhorse," accessed 17 August 2015, http://colonialsense.com/Society-Lifestyle/Signs_of_the_Times /Conestoga_Wagon.php.

33 *Major General Edward Braddock's Orderly Books,* xxvii–xxix. Braddock issued orders on 28 and 29 April for several cavalry officers to act as a screening force for food to be pushed forward from several staging areas en route. Captain Horatio Gates, a future general in the American Revolution, was one of the cavalry officers directed to hasten the bring-up of supplies.

34 *Major General Edward Braddock's Orderly Books,* xxiii. Harsh punishment was common practice in the British Army of the nineteenth century.

35 Orme, *The History of an Expedition Against Fort Du Quesne,* 311. This quote illustrates Braddock's European understanding of logistics supplanted on the economic realities of North America. The general was accustomed to Euro-

pean practices of private sutlers and commissaries, who followed an army to sell food and alcohol and to run brothels. This type of arrangement allowed the army to pass the cost of moving food onto a private enterprise. There was no such system set up to support Braddock in colonial America.

36 Orme, *The History of an Expedition Against Fort Du Quesne*, 313.

37 *Major General Edward Braddock's Orderly Books*, xxxv.

38 Robert Dinwiddie, *The Official Records of Robert Dinwiddie: Lieutenant-Governor of the Colony of Virginia, 1751–1758*, 2 vols., ed. R. A. Brock (Richmond, VA: Virginia Historical Society, 1883), 2:48.

39 Orme, *The History of an Expedition Against Fort Du Quesne*, 317–322.

40 Orme, 322.

41 Orme, 323–324.

42 Orme, 331–332.

43 Berkebile, *Conestoga Wagons in Braddock's Campaign, 1755*, Kindle edition, 94.

44 Patrick Walsh, In discussion with the author, 1 Jun 2018. Walsh walked the ground of one steep section of hill near Fort Duquesne and noted, "The hill up the gap is little more than one-half mile long and rises about four hundred feet in elevation . . . the length and wagon, and team was around ten yards." The required each wagon to lurch up the hill in about forty-four movements, resting after each movement, to cover that short distance.

45 George Washington, "To John A. Washington, Winchester 25 May and 30 May 1755," in *The Writings of George Washington from the Original Manuscript Sources, 1745–1799*, ed. John Clement Fitzpatrick (Washington, DC: US Government Printing Office, 1931), 1:160–161. Officers often purchased their own horses for use during a campaign, with the expectation of reimbursement.

46 David L. Preston, *Braddock's Defeat: The Battle of the Monongahela and the Road to Revolution*, (New York, NY: Oxford University Press, 2015), 99. Albert Louise Zambone, *Daniel Morgan: A Revolutionary Life* (Yardley, PA: Westholme Publishing, 2018), 25.

47 Braddock, *Major General Edward Braddock's Orderly Books*, XLII.

48 See Berkebile, *Conestoga Wagons in Braddock's Campaign, 1755.* 9. The transportation wagons and carriages totaled two hundred vehicles—with approximately 143 wagons. See also Dinwiddie, *The Official Records of Robert Dinwiddie*, 55. On horses Dinwiddie states in his correspondence, "The Gen'l complains much for the want of Forage for the Horse . . . upwards of 1,500."

49 United States Department of Agriculture Forest Service, "Human Heritage of the Allegheny National Forest," accessed 11 September 2015, http://www.fs .usda.gov/main/allegheny/learning/history-culture.

50 See Sir John St. Clair, "Letter to Robert Napier (A.L.S.), Camp of the Van Guard of the Army at the Little Meadows, June 13th, 1755," in Pargellis, *Military Affairs in North America, 1748–1765*, 93–94; D. R. Cubbison, *On Campaign Against Fort Duquesne: The Braddock and Forbes Expeditions, 1755–1758, Through the Expe-*

riences of Quartermaster Sir John St. Clair (Jefferson, NC: McFarland, 2015), 72–98. Cubbison gives a detailed accounting of the work it took to cut the road.

51 Christopher Chantrill, "UK Public Spending: Public Spending Details for 1750," accessed 31 August 2015, http://www.ukpublicspending.co.uk/year_spen ding_1750UKbn_15bc1n_303433.

52 Orme, *The History of an Expedition Against Fort Du Quesne*, 348.

53 Preston, *Braddock's Defeat*, 191.

54 See "Extract of a Letter from Fort Cumberland, July 23, from The Public Advertiser October 31, 1755," *Pennsylvania Magazine of History and Biography* (1899), xxiii: 324. Christian Buchet, *The British Navy, Economy and Society in the Seven Years' War* (Woodbridge, UK: Boydell Press, 2013), 174.

55 *Major General Edward Braddock's Orderly Books*, lv.

56 Orme, *The History of an Expedition Against Fort Du Quesne*, 321.

57 Orme, 336.

58 Preston, *Braddock's Defeat*, 134. Three hundred men followed Beaujeu's larger forces in three separate and smaller convoys a week later.

59 Preston, 17–18.

60 Preston, 136.

61 Preston, 134–147. Although quick, Beaujeu's journey was fraught with dangerous river currents teeming with uncertain allies, and a brutal sixteen-mile portage near present-day Niagara, NY, that nearly exhausted his small force. Preston gives an outstanding account of his journey from newly discovered French sources.

62 Preston, 147.

63 Anderson, *Crucible of War*, 99 and Map 4 on xxxi.

64 Anderson, 99.

65 Stephen Brumwell, *White Devil: An Epic Story of Revenge from the Savage War That Inspired The Last of the Mohicans* (London: Phoenix Press, 2005), 60–61.

66 See Preston, *Braddock's Defeat*, 247; and Jack Babuscio and Richard Minta Dunn, *European Political Facts, 1648–1789* (New York, NY: Facts on File, 1984), 220.

67 Preston, *Braddock's Defeat*, 244.

68 Thomas Ord, "Return of Ordance by Thomas Ord and James Furnis (D.S) Little Bear Camp 18th July 1755," in Pargellis, *Military Affairs in North America, 1748–1765*, 96–97.

69 Ord, "Return of Ordance by Thomas Ord and James Furnis (D.S) Little Bear Camp 18th July 1755," in Pargellis, *Military Affairs in North America, 1748–1765*, 97.

70 Thomas Dunbar, "A return of the troops encamp'd at Wills's Creek, distinguishing the fit for duty, sick, and wounded July 25, 1755," in Pargellis, *Military Affairs in North America, 1748–1765*, 97.

71 Anonymous British Officer, "Anonymous Letter on British Campaign," in Pargellis, *Military Affairs in North America, 1748–1765*, 118.

72 Orme, *The History of an Expedition Against Fort Du Quesne*, 888. Capt. Orme said, "he [Braddock] departed this life, much lamented by the whole Army, and was decently, though privately, buried next morning."

73 Berkebile, *Conestoga Wagons in Braddock's Campaign, 1755.*, Kindle edition, 182.

74 Orme, *The History of an Expedition Against Fort Du Quesne*, 888.

75 Monsieur de Contrecoeur, "Extrait da La Lettre ecrite par Monsieur de Contrecoeur Commandant au fort Duquesne a Monsieur Le marquis De Vaudreuil Governeur General, date du dit fort le 14 Juillet 1755," in Pargellis, *Military Affairs in North America, 1748–1765*, 131.

76 See Marquis De Montcalm, "Account of Camp at Carillon, 26th September 1756," in Brodhead, *Documents Relative to the Colonial History of the State of New York*,10:490; Anonymous French Officer, "Abstract of Dispatches from Canada," in Brodhead, *Documents Relative to the Colonial History of the State of New York*,10:423; and Baugh, *The Global Seven Years' War, 1754–1763*, 132.

77 Edward Pierce Hamilton, "Colonial Warfare in North America," *Proceedings of the Massachusetts Historical Society* (1968), 80.

78 Marquis De Vaudreuil, "Journal of the Operations of the Army from 22d July to 30th September 1755," in Brodhead, *Documents Relative to the Colonial History of the State of New York*, 10:337.

79 John Rutherford "Extract from Letter to his Wife, Camp on Laurel Hill, 12 July 1755,"in *The Papers of Sir William Johnson*, 14 vols (Albany: The University of the State of New York, Division of Archives and History, 1921), 1:712.

80 See Preston, *Braddock's Defeat*, 297–298. Preston lists several incidents of the French using Braddock's artillery for future campaigns. He is the first author in the literature to directly connect Braddock's cannons to other campaigns. See also Vaudreuil, "Letter to Marquis De Massiac, 1 November 1758," 10: 863. Vaudreuil wrote, "Were it not for the ammunition furnished me successively by the Beautiful river [the Monongahela], Chouagouin and Fort George, I should not have had enough either for attack or defence."

81 Duke of Cumberland, "Sketch for Next Year's Campaign in North America. September 6, 1755," in Pargellis, *Military Affairs in North America, 1748–1765*.

82 Duke of Cumberland, "Sketch for Next Year's Campaign in North America. September 6, 1755," in Pargellis, *Military Affairs in North America, 1748–1765*, 134–135.

83 James De Lancey, "Letter from James De Lancey to William Johnson Esq, April 16, 1755," in *The Papers of Sir William Johnson*, 468–471. Johnson had an economic trading alliance and personal relationship with the Mohawk tribe of the Iroquois nation.

84 Anderson, *Crucible of War*, 81.

85 De Lancey, "Letter from James De Lancey to William Johnson Esq, April 16, 1755," 469.

86 De Lancey, 469.

87 De Lancey, 469.

88 Gipson, *The Great War for the Empire: The Years of Defeat 1754–1757,* 6:139–140.

89 William Johnson, "To Governor Shirley, 1 May 1755," in *The Papers of Sir William Johnson,* 1:483–484.

90 Johnson, "To Governor Shirley, 1 May 1755," in *The Papers of Sir William Johnson,* 1:484.

91 "To Edward Braddock (in handwriting of P. Wraxall) Mount Johnson 17th May 1755," in *The Papers of Sir William Johnson,* 514–515.

92 Goldsbrow Banyar, "Letter from Goldsbrow Banyar to William Johnson, New York, 6 June 1755," in *The Papers of Sir William Johnson,*1:563.

93 Howard Irving Chapelle, *American Small Sailing Craft: Their Design, Development, and Construction* (W.W. Norton & Company, 1951), 33.

94 See Joseph F. Meany Jr., "'Batteaux' and 'Battoe Men': An American Colonial Response to the Problem of Logistics in Mountain Warfare" (Albany: New York State Museum, 1998), 2; Chapelle, *American Small Sailing Craft,* 34–35.

95 Meany Jr., "'Batteaux' and 'Battoe Men,'" 6. With such ease of construction, the bateau fleets for future campaigns on Lake George by the French and British numbered in the thousands.

96 Stephen Webster, "Letter from Stephen Webster to William Johnson, Albany June 5th, 1755," in *The Papers of Sir William Johnson,* 1:563.

97 William Eyre, "Letter from William Eyre to William Johnson, Albany, 13th June 1755," in *The Papers of Sir William Johnson,* 1:585.

98 J. Wheelwright, "J. Wheelright's List of Supplies, Enclosed in Shirley to Johnson, June 9, 1755," in *The Papers of Sir William Johnson,* 1:571.

99 Wheelwright in *The Papers of Sir William Johnson,* 1: 571–574.

100 *The Papers of Sir William Johnson,* 673–810. These are the only actual bills listed as supplies from stores. There are also numerous other smaller charges and supply requests within Johnson's correspondence.

101 John Dies, "Bills of charges to province of New York for ordinance carriages and stores shipped to Albany, care of Messrs Schuyler and De Peyster, [New] York Juley, ye 17th: 1755," in *The Papers of Sir William Johnson,* 1:724–729. For example John Dies, a sutler, wrote a bill for "Charges of Smiths Work & Iron for 10 Carriages," labor for "making and materials to compleat [*sic*] 2 carriages," and costs for "running 560 weight of lead into Grape Shot."

102 See William Johnson, "Letter to Commanding Officer of Sir William Pepperrell's Regiment, Mount Johson 21 June 1755," in *The Papers of Sir William Johnson,* 1:642; "Indian Proceedings, Mount Johnson 15 May 1755-June 21, 1755," in *The Papers of Sir William Johnson* , 1:630. More important than weapons and food to the Mohawks was "some place of security built for our wives & children & we

hope you will now comply with it." Initially, Johnson housed the Mohawks at his homestead—humbly named Mount Johnson—about forty miles northwest of Albany, and then gathered them closer as he pushed north later in the summer.

103 "Letter from William Eyre to William Johnson, Albany, 21st. June 1755," in *The Papers of Sir William Johnson*, 1:623. Eyre wrote to Johnson that it would be better house the provincials away from Albany "where it will be impossible to keep them . . . from making beasts of themselves."

104 "Letter from William Eyre to William Johnson, Albany, 17th. June 1755," in *The Papers of Sir William Johnson*, 1:605. Eyre wrote Johnson to warn him that Shirley thought Eyre's "conduct irregular."

105 Anderson, *Crucible of War*, 114–116. In addition, Shirley and Johnson had a contentious relationship, as the two biggest leaders in the colonies for the early part of the undeclared war. Although Shirley was technically Johnson's superior during this time, Johnson actively campaigned against Shirley in dispatches back to England and colonial leadership.

106 See "Letter from Goldsbrow Banyar to William Johnson, New York, 19 July 1755, 1/2 past 7 PM.," in *The Papers of Sir William Johnson*, 1:746; and "Letter from Goldsbrow Banyar to William Johnson, New York, 19 July 1755, Satuday Evening, 10 oClock," in *The Papers of Sir William Johnson*, 1:747.

107 "Letter from Goldsbrow Banyar to William Johnson, New York, 26 July 1755, 9 oClock AM," in *The Papers of Sir William Johnson*, 1:767.

108 William Johnson, "Orders & Instructions for Col. Moses Titcom, Albany, 1 August 1755," in *The Papers of Sir William Johnson*, 1:816–818.

109 *The Parliamentary Register; or History of the Proceedings and Debates, of the House of Commons*, vol. 12 (London: Parliament of Great Britain, 1779), 174–176. This House of Commons proceeding discusses the difficulties of Burgoyne's British Army moving down the Hudson from Fort Edward (The Great Carrying Place) to Albany before the Battle of Saratoga in 1777. The journey would have been even more challenging in 1755.

110 Meany Jr., "'Batteaux' and 'Battoe Men,'" 5. The boats with their simple construction needed constant caulking before getting underway, and this task was the bane of a soldier's existence when using them.

111 William Johnson, "Orders & Instructions for Col. Moses Titcomb, Albany, 3 Aug 1755" in *The Papers of Sir William Johnson*,1:829–830.

112 See William Johnson, "Letter to James De Lancey, Albany 8 August 1755," in *The Papers of Sir William Johnson*, 1:842.; J. Wheelwright, "J. Wheelright's List of Supplies, Enclosed in Shirley to Johnson, June 9, 1755," in *The Papers of Sir William Johnson*, 1:571. Johnson had over 1500 lbs. of Oakum delivered in June and had used it all by early August.

113 William Johnson, "Letter to James De Lancey, Albany 8 August 1755," in *The Papers of Sir William Johnson*, 1:841–842. A militia regiment from New Hampshire was still on the march to upstate New York in early August.

114 William Johnson, "Letter to James De Lancey, Aug 24, 1755," in *The Papers of Sir William Johnson*, 1:879.

115 William Johnson, "Letter to the Commissaries at Albany, Camp at the Carrying Place, August 24, 1755," in *The Papers of Sir William Johnson*, 1:878.

116 William Johnson, "Letter to the Several Governors (P. Wraxall handwriting) Camp at the Great Carrying Place, Aug 24, 1755," in *The Papers of Sir William Johnson*, 1:880.

117 Johnson, "Letter to the Several Governors (P. Wraxall handwriting) Camp at the Great Carrying Place, Aug 24, 1755," in *The Papers of Sir William Johnson*, 1:881.

118 See Johnson, "Letter to the Several Governors," 1:881; and Wolter Groesbeck and Gysbert Oosterhoudt, "Letter to William Johnson, Camp at the Great Carrying Place, 22 August 1755," in *The Papers of Sir William Johnson*, 1:872–873. Lyman sent Johnson a list of waggoneers who deserted from Fort Edward on 22 August 1755 as well.

119 William Johnson, "Letter to Phineas Lyman (P. Wraxall Handwriting) Lake Sacrement 29 Aug 1755," in *The Papers of Sir William Johnson*,1:889.

120 Johnson, "Letter to Phineas Lyman (P. Wraxall Handwriting) Lake Sacrement 29 Aug 1755," in *The Papers of Sir William Johnson*, 1:889.

121 "Major-General Johnson to the Lords of Trade, September, 3 1755," in Brodhead, *Documents Relative to the Colonial History of the State of New York*, 6:997.

122 William Johnson, "Letter to William Shirley, Camp at Lake George 1 Sep 1755," in *The Papers of Sir William Johnson*, 1:892–893.

123 Anderson, *Crucible of War*, 115.

124 Anderson, 116–117.

125 Skrine, *Fontenoy and Great Britain's Share in the War of the Austrian Succession, 1741–1748*, 189–190.

126 Marquis De Montreuil, "Battle of Lake George, 8th September 1755," in Brodhead, *Documents Relative to the Colonial History of the State of New York*, 10:335.

127 See Anderson, *Crucible of War*, 118; and "Dialogue between Marshal Saxe and Baron de Dieskau in the Elysian Fields," in Brodhead, *Documents Relative to the Colonial History of the State of New York*, 10:341.

128 Wood Creek was ten miles east and ran directly parallel to Lake George. Since the creek was smaller than Lake George, it offered better concealment for the three hundred boats than the open water of the lake.

129 Gipson, *The Great War for the Empire*, 6:168.

130 Peter Wraxall, "Minutes of Council of War, Camp at Lake George, 7 Sep 1755," in *The Papers of Sir William Johnson*.2:15-16.

131 Montreuil, "Battle of Lake George, 8th September 1755," 339.

132 Anderson, *Crucible of War*, 118.

133 Gipson, *The Great War for the Empire*, 6:171.

134 See Montreuil, "Battle of Lake George, 8th September 1755," 339. Montreuil, a

French officer, recounted the French report and Dieskau's pronouncement to fix bayonets and "March, Let us force the place." See also "Letter from Petter Wraxall to Lake George, September 27th, 1755," in Pargellis, *Military Affairs in North America, 1748–1765,* 139. Wraxall gives the British account of the battle.

135 Gipson, *The Great War for the Empire,* 6:172–174.

136 Gipson, 6:174.

137 Gipson, 6:172–174.

138 Gipson, 6:172.

139 Montreuil, "Battle of Lake George, 8th September 1755," 340.

140 William Johnson, "Letter to the Mayor and Magistrates of Albany, Camp at Lake George, 15 Sept, 1755," in *The Papers of Sir William Johnson.* 2:42-43. In fairness to those supplying Johnson, he asked for the supplies to be brought up on 24 August, which necessitated a three-day journey home for the courier, followed by a ten-day trip back to the lake—an earliest possible arrival of 5 September.

141 Buchet, *The British Navy, Economy and Society in the Seven Years' War,* 144.

142 Berkebile, *Conestoga Wagons in Braddock's Campaign, 1755.* Kindle edition, 90–101. Although the capacity of wagons varied greatly, two thousand pounds per wagon is a good approximation of the maximum load over the rough roads of upstate New York. The famed prairie Conestoga of later decades had capacities in excess of twelve thousand pounds.

143 William Johnson, "Letter to the Mayor and Magistrates of Albany, Camp at Lake George, 15 Sept, 1755," in *The Papers of Sir William Johnson,* 2:42.

144 Fintan O'Toole, *White Savage: William Johnson and the Invention of America* (London: Farrar, Straus & Giroux 2015), 152.

145 William Johnson, "Letter to Spencer Phips, Camp at Lake George, 17 Sept 1755," in *The Papers of Sir William Johnson,* 2:48–54.

146 Peter Wraxall, "Minutes of Council of War, Camp at Lake George, 21 Sept. 1755 Sunday P.M.," in *The Papers of Sir William Johnson,* 2:70–71.

147 William Johnson, "Letter to the Mayor and Magistrates of Albany, Camp at Lake George, 15 Sept, 1755," in *The Papers of Sir William Johnson,* 2:42.

148 John Watts, "Extract of a Letter to William Cotterell, Nov 6, 1755," in *The Papers of Sir William Johnson,* 2:148.

149 David R. Starbuck, *Massacre at Fort William Henry* (Hanover, NH: University Press of New England, 2002), 8.

150 Anderson, *Crucible of War,* 336. Johnson emerged later in the war to lead the Iroquois to defend Fort Edward in 1757 and help with the capture of Fort Niagara in 1759.

151 Vaudreuil, "Letter to Marquis De Machault, 31 September 1755," in Brodhead, *Documents Relative to the Colonial History of the State of New York* 10:377.

152 "Letter from Marquis De Vaudreuil to Sieur De Lotbinere, Montreal, September 20, 1755; Translated from a manuscript in the collection of the Fort Ticonderoga Museum," in *Bulletin of the Fort Ticonderoga Museum* (1932), 2–3.

153 Marquis De Lobiniere, "Letter to Count d'Argenson, Camp at Carillon, 24 Sept 1755," in Brodhead, *Documents Relative to the Colonial History of the State of New York*,10:368–369.

154 Charles Hardy, "Extract of a Letter to Lord Halifax, Fort Geroge, November 27, 1755," in *The Papers of Sir William Johnson*2:339.

155 Gipson, *The Great War for the Empire*, 6:188. Major General Abercrombie was temporary commander of chief from March 1756 to August 1756, until Lord Loudoun arrived.

156 Baugh, *The Global Seven Years' War, 1754–1763*, 211. Loudoun's cutting of colonial profits coupled with his disdain for colonials, rod-iron fealty to the Crown, and constant demands for the quartering of British troops made him a hated figure in the colonies.

157 Gipson, *The Great War for the Empire*, 6:208.

158 Gipson, 6:208.

159 Jonathan R. Dull, *The French Navy and the Seven Years' War*, France Overseas (Lincoln: University of Nebraska Press, 2005), 56–55.

160 Baugh, *The Global Seven Years' War, 1754–1763*, 255.

161 "Examination of Francis Beaujour, Fort Edward, December ye 27th, 1755," in *The Papers of Sir William Johnson*, 2:398–399. Fort Edward's garrison interrogated a French deserter in December 1755 about the status of Fort Carillon. He reported one hundred men as the winter garrison force.

162 Peter Wraxall, "Minutes of a Meeting of Officers, Fort Edward, Fryday Morning the 28th November, 1755," in *The Papers of Sir William Johnson*, 2:353–354.

163 David V. Burley, "Proto-Historic Ecological Effects of the Fur Trade on Micmac Culture in Northeastern New Brunswick," *Ethnohistory* 28, no. 3 (1981): 206. The only exceptions were hunts for larger game in the winter.

164 Christian Ayne Crouch, *Nobility Lost: French and Canadian Martial Cultures, Indians, and the End of New France* (Ithaca, NY: Cornell University Press, 2014), 71.

165 See Saint Sauveur, "Conferences between M. de Vaudreuil and the Indians, 13 December 1756," in Brodhead, *Documents Relative to the Colonial History of the State of New York*, 10:503; and William Johnson, "Letter to the Mayor and Magistrates of Albany, Camp at Lake George, 15 Sept, 1755," in *The Papers of Sir William Johnson*, 1:880.

166 Ann M. Carlos and Frank D. Lewis, *Commerce by a Frozen Sea: Native Americans and the European Fur Trade* (Philadelphia: University of Pennsylvania Press, 2011), 172.

167 Robb Wolf, *The Paleo Solution* (Las Vegas: Victory Belt Publishing, 2017). Kindle edition, 284–292.

168 William Johnson, "To Colden and Kelly June 24th, 1755," in *The Papers of Sir William Johnson*, 1:653. Johnson wrote to Captains Colden and Kelly, whom he had sent on various supply runs to obtain equipment, "I have got up the guns

you sent me, which will not Answer for all, instead of being light Indians guns as I wrote for, I think they are old muskets vamped up anew. So large & wide a bore the Indians never use, neither would they carry them if they were paid never so much for it."

169 See Anderson, *Crucible of War*, 142.; Officer, "Journal of Occurrences in Canada from October 1755, to June, 1756," in Brodhead, *Documents Relative to the Colonial History of the State of New York*, 10: 401–402. French companies composed of colonial troops and native warriors departed from locations as far north as Montreal to attack the British posts on Lake George

170 Saint Sauveur, "Conferences between M. de Vaudreuil and the Indians, 13 December 1756," 10:499–518.

171 MacLeitch, *Imperial Entanglements*, 17.

172 MacLeitch, 22. The "Mourning War" of the Iroquois involved avenging death by the capture of enemies, whom the Iroquois forced to join their tribe in order to replace warriors killed in battle.

173 Officer, "Journal of Occurrences in Canada from October 1755, to June, 1756.," in Brodhead, *Documents Relative to the Colonial History of the State of New York* 10:405.

174 Nicholas Westbrook, "'Like Roaring Lions Breaking From Their Chains': The Highland Reigment at Ticonderoga Documents Compiled and Edited by Nicholas Westerbrook," *Bulletin of the Fort Ticonderoga Museum* (Vol. 16, no 1, 1998), 21–23.

175 Lemuel Wood "Extract from Diary, Amherst Campaign, 1759" *Bulletin of the Fort Ticonderoga Museum* (Vol 2, No 12, 1930), 252–253. Wood's description of Fort Carillon gives a solid accounting of how much timber was needed to construct colonial forts.

176 Michael Williams, *Americans and Their Forests: A Historical Geography* (Cambridge, England: Cambridge University Press, 1992), 94.

177 "Colonial America's Pre-Industrial Age of Wood and Water," Collections at Historic Bethlehem, PA, accessed 17 September 2015, http://www.engr.psu.edu/mtah/articles/colonial_wood_water.htm.

178 "The Naval Stores Act (14 March 1705)," in *English Historical Documents: American Colonial Documents to 1776*, ed. Merrill Jensen (New York: Oxford University Press, 1955), 417–418.

179 Stephen Brumwell, *White Devil*, 73. Rogers was eventually promoted to major and was the only colonial soldier to receive a full commission from the British Army at the end of the French and Indian War.

180 Brumwell, *White Devil*, 73.

181 "74th Ranger Regiment: Robert Rogers' Standing Orders," accessed 12 April 2016, http://www.goarmy.com/ranger/heritage/rodgers-orders.html.

182 William R. Nester, *The Epic Battles for Ticonderoga, 1758* (Albany: State University of New York Press, 2008), 10.

183 Montcalm, "Letter to Count d'Argenson, Montreal, 1 Nov 1756," in Brodhead, *Documents Relative to the Colonial History of the State of New York*, 10:491.

184 See Marquis De Vaudreuil, "Letter to Marquis de Machualt," 10:496–497.

185 Anderson, *Crucible of War*, 186.

186 Earl of Loudoun, "Loudoun to Webb, 20 June 1755," in Pargellis, *Military Affairs in North America, 1748–1765*, 371.

187 Anderson, *Crucible of War*, 186.

188 Babuscio and Dunn, *European Political Facts, 1648–1789*, 216.

189 Cadwallader Colden, *The Letters and Papers of Cadwallader Colden, 1711–1775*, vol. 6 of 9, 1755–1760 (New York: New York Historical Society, 1918), 163.

190 Brumwell, *White Devil*, 92.

191 Francis Parkman, *Montcalm and Wolfe* (New York: Collier Books, 1962). Kindle version, 218. Parkman translated and quoted Montcalm from *Circulaire du Marquis de Montcalm, 25 Juillet, 1757*.

192 Pierre-Joseph-Antoine Roubard, "Letter from Father * * * , Missionary to the Abnakis, October 21, 1757," in Reuben Gold Thwaites, ed., *The Jesuit Relations and Allied Documents, Travels and Explorations of the Jesuit Missionaries in New France*, vol. 70 of 73 (Cleveland, OH: Burrows Bros. Co., 1899), http://puffin .creighton.edu/jesuit/relations/relations_70.html. 125.

193 Cadwallader Colden, *The Letters and Papers of Cadwallader Colden, 1711–1775*, vol. 6 of 9, 1755–1760 (New York: New York Historical Society, 1918), 163.

194 Anderson, *Crucible of War*, 190.

195 See Anderson, 191; and Parkman, *Montcalm and Wolfe*, 219.

196 Parkman, *Montcalm and Wolfe*, 219.

197 Marquis De Bougainville, "Letter of M. de Bougainville to the Minister, with the Articles of Capitulation granted to Lieutenant-Colonel Munro, on the 19th of August, 1757," in Brodhead, *Documents Relative to the Colonial History of the State of New York*, 10:635.

198 Ian Kenneth Steele, *Betrayals: Fort William Henry and the Massacre* (New York: Oxford University Press, 1990). Steele gives the most balanced assessment of the incidents after the battle.

199 Pierre Pouchot and Catherine Broué, *Mémoires sur la dernière guerre de l'Amérique septentrionale entre la France et l'Angleterre*, vol. 1 of 2 (Yverdon, 1781), 107.

200 Steele, *Betrayals*, 130.

201 "Letter of M. de Bougainville to the Minister, with the Articles of Capitulation granted to Lieutenant-Colonel Munro, on the 19th of August, 1757," in Brodhead, *Documents Relative to the Colonial History of the State of New York*, 10:616.

202 Steele, *Betrayals*, 130. This speed contrasted with the five-day trip needed to make it to Albany from Fort William Henry overland.

203 Anderson, *Crucible of War*.

204 Montcalm, "Prices of Provisions, 1758," 711.

205 "Letter to Marquis de Moras, Quebec, 19th February 1758," in Brodhead, *Documents Relative to the Colonial History of the State of New York*, 10:686.

206 Pargellis, *Military Affairs in North America, 1748–1765*, 233–280. In several documents from Loudoun to Cumberland, the cost of operations was a constant concern.

207 William Pitt, "Letter to General Jeffrey Amherst," in *Papers of General Jeffrey Amherst* (London: Kew Archives, 1758). Public Record Office. War Office 34.

208 Julian Stafford Corbett, *England in the Seven Years' War* (Novato, CA: Presidio Press, 1992), 306.

209 See Nester, *The Epic Battles for Ticonderoga, 1758*, 119; and Alexander Moneypenny, "Extract from Capt Moneypenny's Orderly Book 30 June-7 July 1758," *Bulletin of the Fort Ticonderoga Museum* vol 2, no. 2 (1932): 56–67.

210 Westbrook, "'Like Roaring Lions Breaking From Their Chains,'" 24.

211 Westbrook, "'Like Roaring Lions Breaking From Their Chains,'" 30–31. Captain Hugh Arnot's Journal Entries as he moved from Fort Stillwater, Fort Edward, and Half-Way Brook show an orderly process of logistics. Whereas three years prior Johnson's forces just moved down the road, Arnot's regiment had specific directions and procedures for both movement and victualing.

212 Evelyn M Dinsdale, "Spatial Patterns of Technological Change: The Lumber Industry of Northern New York," *Economic Geography* (1965): 255. The sawmill at Lake George, based on the colonial sawmills of New York at the time, was likely a simple "single upright saw powered by an overshot water wheel, a direct application of water power" from a stream near the fort.

213 See Moneypenny, "Extract from Capt Moneypenny's Orderly Book 30 June–7 July 1758," 58.

214 See Moneypenny, "Extract from Capt Moneypenny's Orderly Book 30 June–7 July 1758," 64 and 66; Anderson, *Crucible of War*, 259.

215 Moneypenny, "Extract from Capt Moneypenny's Orderly Book 30 June–7 July 1758," 64–66.

216 Moneypenny, "Extract from Capt Moneypenny's Orderly Book 30 June–7 July 1758," 58.

217 Caleb Rea and F. M. Ray, *The Journal of Dr. Caleb Rea* (Salem, MA,1881), 122. Wagons crowded the roads from Albany to Fort William Henry. The Reverend Caleb Rea, who marched on 1 July 1758 from Fort Edward to Lake George, noted that there were between sixty and eighty wagons in front of his march, impeding his progress.

218 Moneypenny, "Extract from Capt Moneypenny's Orderly Book 30 June–7 July 1758," 62–67.

219 Monseuir Doriel, "Letter to Marshal de Belle Isle, Quebec, 16th June 1758," in Brodhead, *Documents Relative to the Colonial History of the State of New York*, 10:718.

220 Adjutant Malartic, "Narrative of Occurences on the Frontier of Lake St. Sacra-

ment, from the 30th June to the 10th July, inclusive," in Brodhead, *Documents Relative to the Colonial History of the State of New York*, 10:721.

221 Malartic, "Narrative of Occurences on the Frontier of Lake St. Sacrament, from the 30th June to the 10th July, inclusive," 10:723.

222 See Major General Abercrombie, "Letter to Mr. Secretary Pitt, Camp at Lake George, 12th July, 1758," in Brodhead, *Documents Relative to the Colonial History of the State of New York*, 10:725; and Hugh Arnot, "A Journal or Proceedings of the Army under the Command of Major Gen Abercrombie from June ye 17th untill July ye 9th Campaign 1758," *Bulletin of the Fort Ticonderoga Museum* 16, no. 1 (1998): 33–35. The width of the column was as wide as Lake George.

223 Robert Rogers and Franklin B. Hough, *Journals of Major Robert Rogers: Containing an Account of the Several Excursions He Made Under the Generals Who Commanded Upon the Continent of North America During the Late War* (Albany, NY: J. Munsell's Sons, 1883), 118.

224 Alexander Moneypenny, "Copy of Map from Major Moneypenny: Sent With Report of Lord Howe's death, Aug 1758 From Westport House, Ireland" (Fort Ticonderoga Museum Map Collection).

225 Rea and Ray, *The Journal of Dr. Caleb Rea*, 25.

226 See Rogers and Hough, *Journals of Major Robert Rogers*, 116; and Brumwell, *White Devil*, 121–123. From orderly journals to personal diaries, both superiors and his soldiers told of Howe's leadership. Howe was an enthusiastic supporter of changes to the British Army to help it perform better in the wilds of North America. Howe doffed his formal hat, cut his hair, ordered the leggings that retarded British soldiers discarded, and cut the coat length of British soldiers to give better movement during battle. He was a supporter of Major Robert Rogers and his Rangers—lobbying for Ranger regiments within the British Army. As part of this enthusiasm, he accompanied Rogers on patrol several times. Ultimately, Howe was killed before the main battle and was not responsible for Abercrombie's poor decisions after the landings.

227 United States Geological Survey and New York State Department of Environmental Conservation, "Topographic Map of the Adirondacks: Lake George Region" (Keene Valley, NY: Plinth, Quion & Cornice Associates, 1984). The highest elevation point from Monypenny's Map was 550 feet elevation, while Howe's landing point was 369 feet.

228 John Knox, *An Historical Journal of the Campaigns in North America, for the Years 1757, 1758, 1759 and 1760: Containing the Most Remarkable Occurrences of the Period; Particularly the Two Sieges of Quebec, &C. &C. The Orders of the Admirals and General Officers; Descriptions of the Countries Where the Author Has Served, with Their Forts and Garrisons; Their Climates, Soil, Produce; and a Regular Diary of the Weather. As Also Several Manifesto's a Mandate of the Late Bishop of Canada; the French Orders and Disposition for the Defence of the Colony, &C. &C. &C*, 2 vols. (London: Printed for the Author, 1769).

229 See Rea and Ray, *The Journal of Dr. Caleb Rea*, 27; and Salah Barnard, "Journal of Capt Barnard Salah, 1758 Campaign," in Fort Ticonderoga Research Collection, Fort Ticonderoga Museum.

230 Abercrombie, "Letter to Mr. Secretary Pitt, Camp at Lake George, 12th July, 1758," 10:727.

231 Major Ord was the artillery officer who abandoned the majority of British firepower to the French after the defeat at the Battle of the Monongahela.

232 Westbrook, "'Like Roaring Lions Breaking From Their Chains,'" 85.

233 William Eyre, "Letter from Capt William Eyre to Robert Napier, Description of the attack on Ticonderoga, Lake George, July 10, 1758," in Pargellis, *Military Affairs in North America, 1748–1765*, 420. Capt. Eyre was not involved in the Council of War in which Abercrombie decided to attack without the artillery, since he had been battlefield promoted to Field Grade officer and given command of an infantry regiment during the battle.

234 Westbrook, "'Like Roaring Lions Breaking From Their Chains,'" 56.

235 *Bulletin of the Fort Ticonderoga Museum*, vol. 7, no. 5: 18; as cited in Nester, *The Epic Battles for Ticonderoga, 1758*, 158.

236 Rea and Ray, *The Journal of Dr. Caleb Rea*, 30.

237 Rea and Ray, 30.

238 Van Schank, "Van Schank Orderly Book, 1758," in Fort Ticonderoga Research Collection, Fort Ticonderoga Museum (Fort Ticonderoga, NY).

239 James Abercrombie, "Abercrombie to Townsend Washington, 11 July 1758," in *Abercrombie Papers* (Huntingon Library, Huntington, CA).

240 Amos Richardson, "Amos Richardson Journal, 1758," in Fort Ticonderoga Research Collection, Fort Ticonderoga Museum (Fort Ticonderoga, NY), 10. Amos Richardson's colonial regiment arrived the morning that Abercrombie's force sailed and plundered the fort for any food left over from the army. The next day Richardson recorded his hunger, since he had not taken victualing provisions for eight days.

241 Amos Richardson, "Amos Richardson Journal, 1758," 16.

242 Rea and Ray, *The Journal of Dr. Caleb Rea*, 33.

243 William Green, "Letter to Abercrombie—Observations on the Plan for a Fort at the Oneida Carrying Place, 16 July 1758," in *Abercrombie Papers* (Huntington Library, Huntington, CA). Green expressed his reservations about building a fort at the Oneida Carrying Place due to the amount of labor, lumber, and time required, given that the campaign season was now into late summer. This note likely helped inform Abercrombie's decision not to stay put at the south end of Lake George over the winter.

244 New York State, Department of Environmental Conservation, "The Land Tortoise Underwater Perserve Site," accessed 29 Augist 2019, https://www.dec.ny.gov /outdoor/5076.html.

245 Anderson, *Crucible of War*, 250.

246 J. Clarence Webster, ed., *The Journal of Jeffrey Amherst: Recording the Military Career of General Amherst in America from 1758 to 1763* (Chicago: University of Chicago Press, 1931), 92.

247 See "Journal of Capt Barnard Salah, 1758 Campaign"; Meany Jr., "'Batteaux' and 'Battoe Men'"; and Department of Environmental Conservation, "The Land Tortoise."

248 Meany Jr., "'Batteaux' and 'Battoe Men,'" 6.

249 Skrine, *Fontenoy and Great Britain's Share in the War of the Austrian Succession, 1741–1748.*

250 Anderson, *Crucible of War,* 250.

251 Anderson, 250.

252 "Map: Project For the Attack of Ticonderoga Proposed to Be in Execution as Near as the Circumstances and Ground Will Admit of" (Fort Ticonderga Research Center Collection, 1759); Webster, *The Journal of Jeffrey Amherst,* 91-92. Amherst began the journey on 04 October 1758 and arrived 06 October 1758 to meet with Abercrombie.

253 *The Journal of Jeffrey Amherst,* 115–126.

254 *Journal of Jeffrey Amherst,* 126–127.

255 *Journal of Jeffrey Amherst,* 126–27.

256 Robert Webster, "Robert Webster's Journal: Fourth Connecticut Regiment, Amherst's Campaign, Apri 5th to November 23rd, 1759," *Bulletin of the Fort Ticonderoga Museum* 2, no. 4 (1931): 126.

257 Alexander Moneypenny, "Extract from Capt Moneypenny's Orderly Book, Fort William Henry to Crown Point, July 15th, 1759 to August 3rd, 1759, 55th Regiment of Foot (British Army)," *Bulletin of the Fort Ticonderoga Museum* 2, no. 12 (1932): 231–235.

258 Alexander Moneypenny, "Extract from Capt Moneypenny's Orderly Book, Fort William Henry to Crown Point, July 15th, 1759 to August 3rd, 1759, 55th Regiment of Foot (British Army)," *Bulletin of the Fort Ticonderoga Museum* 2, no. 12 (1932): 231–235.

259 See Moneypenny, "Extract from Capt Moneypenny's Orderly Book 30 June–7 July 1758."; and "Extract from Capt Moneypenny's Orderly Book, Fort William Henry to Crown Point, July 15th, 1759 to August 3rd, 1759, 55th Regiment of Foot (British Army)." The difference between the orderly books between 1758 and 1759 illustrates the superior strategy and logistics acumen of Amherst when compared to that of Abercrombie and Howe.

260 Robert Webster, "Robert Webster's Journal: Fourth Connecticut Regiment, Amherst's Campaign, Apri 5th to November 23rd, 1759," *Bulletin of the Fort Ticonderoga Museum* 2, no. 4 (1931), 131.

261 "Robert Webster's Journal," 133–134.

262 "Robert Webster's Journal," 133.

263 Daniel Marston, *The French-Indian War, 1754–1760*, Essential Histories (New York: Routledge, 2003), 53.

264 Thomas Ord, "Return of Ordance and Stores Taken at Ticonderoga and Crown Point, August 10, 1759," *Bulletin of the Fort Ticonderoga Museum* 2, no. 12 (1931): 251–252.

265 Ord, "Return of Ordnance": 251-252

266 "Robert Webster's Journal": 131.

267 See Anderson, *Crucible of War*, and Brumwell, *White Devil*. Anderson and Brumwell criticize Amherst's methodical nature and question his decision to build forts instead of moving to help Wolfe at Quebec.

268 "Robert Webster's Journal": 146–147. In early November, Webster reported on his hunger every day—at one point, the men had one biscuit every four days.

269 Doriel, "Letter to Marshal de Belle Isle, Quebec, 16th June 1758," 781.

270 Van Creveld, *Supplying War*, 36.

271 Benoit B. Mandelbrot, *The Fractal Geometry of Nature*, vol. 173 (New York: Macmillan, 1983), 342. Mandelbrot used the relationship between famous television comedians to describe the Lindy effect. He stated, "However long a person's past collected works, it will on the average continue for an equal additional amount. When it eventually stops, it breaks off at precisely half of its promise."

272 Ropp, *War in the Modern World*, 184.

273 James Kirby Martin and Mark Edward Lender, *A Respectable Army: The Military Origins of the Republic, 1763–1789*, 3rd ed. (Hoboken, NJ: John Wiley and Sons, 2015), 20.

274 S. L. Danver, *Revolts, Protests, Demonstrations, and Rebellions in American History: An Encyclopedia* (Santa Barbara, CA: ABC-CLIO, 2011), 183–188.

275 Danver, *Revolts, Protests, Demonstrations, and Rebellions in American History*, 183-188.

276 Ropp, *War in the Modern World*, 184.

CHAPTER 2. STEAM ON STEAM IN 1917: THE WESTERN FRONT

1 Norman Friedman, *Fighting the Great War at Sea: Strategy, Tactics and Technology*, (Annapolis, MD: Naval Institute Press, 2014), 283.

2 *Report of the Military Board of Allied Supply*, ed. Military Board of Allied Supply, Allied and Associated Powers (1914–1920), 2 vols. (Washington, DC: Government Printing Office, 1924), 1:352.

3 See appendix for a detailed comparison of weapons across the eras.

4 Ian F. W. Beckett, *The Great War: 1914–1918* (New York: Routledge, 2014), 223.

5 Lewis Mumford, *Technics and Civilization* (New York: Harcourt, 1934), 235–239.

6 Holger H. Herwig, *The Marne, 1914: The Opening of World War I and the Battle that Changed the World* (New York: Random House, 2011), xiii. The French used taxis during the Battle of the Marne to shepherd three thousand troops

to the front. This event had a bigger legend than actual wartime impact but proved that automobiles had utility during wartime.

7   Alan John Percivale Taylor, *War by Time-Table: How the First World War Began* (Ann Arbor, MI: Macdonald & Co, 1969), 44–45. At the start of the war, the Germans had 8.5 million men in the army and 39,439 miles of rail—as large as Russia, French, and Britain combined.

8   Rainer Fremdling, "Railroads and German Economic Growth: A Leading Sector Analysis with a Comparison to the United States and Great Britain," *Journal of Economic History* 37, no. 3 (1977): 601. Fremdling backs up Rostow's thesis that "The introduction of the railroad has been historically the most powerful single initiator of take-offs. It was decisive in the United States, Germany, and Russia. Perhaps most important for the take-off itself, the development of railways has led on to the development of modern coal, iron, and engineering industries."

9   Daniel Hughes, *Moltke on the Art of War: Selected Writings* (New York: Presidio Press, 2009), 102.

10 Larry H. Addington, *The Blitzkrieg Era and the German General Staff, 1865–1941* (New Brunswick, NJ: Rutgers University Press, 1971), 4.

11 Dennis E. Showalter, *Railroads and Rifles: Soldiers, Technology, and the Unification of Germany* (Hamden, CT: Archon Books, 1975), 44. Moltke and Bismarck spent great political capital integrating railway timetables and construction across Germany and neighboring states.

12 Addington, *The Blitzkrieg Era*, 10.

13 Addington, 10.

14 Martin van Creveld, *Supplying War: Logistics from Wallenstein to Patton* (New York: Cambridge University Press, 1977), 84, 100. For example, When the Prussians reached Paris in October 1870, the supply trains had only just broken through a backlog at the French Fortress of Metz, which was two hundred miles to the east.

15 Addington, *The Blitzkrieg Era*, 12.

16 Addington, 129

17 Edwin A. Pratt, *The Rise of Rail-power in War and Conquest, 1833–1914: With a Bibliography* (London, King, 1915), 286

18 Pratt, *The Rise of Rail-Power*, 152–153

19 Taylor, *War by Time-Table*, 44–45. France possessed the most submarines of any belligerent prior to the war, with seventy-three to Germany's twenty-three. The Germans had forty battleships to Great Britain's sixty-four.

20 Brown, *British Logistics on the Western Front*, 219.

21 Avner Offer, *The First World War: An Agrarian Interpretation* (Oxford: Clarendon Press, 1989), 1–4. Offer posits that the British used the possible blockade of populations as an early form of deterrence. In August 1914 this became a purposeful strategy of starvation of the German population

22 Jon Tetsuro Sumida, "Forging the Trident: British Naval Industrial Logistics,

1914–1918," in *Feeding Mars: Logistics in Western Warfare from the Middle Ages to the Present*, ed. John A. Lynn (Boulder, CO: Westview Press, 1993), 217.

23 Taylor, *War by Time-Table*, 44.

24 Taylor, *War by Time-Table*. This quote is from Taylor's title.

25 Herwig, *The Marne, 1914*, 48.

26 Van Creveld, *Supplying War*, 109–141. Van Creveld illustrates the limits of German railroads beyond their own borders during the invasion of France and Belgium in 1914.

27 Offer, *The First World War*, 406. Offer's magisterial work details the efforts of the British to starve the German population as a strategy, and the naval blockade as the key means to that end.

28 Michael Duffy, "The Battle of Verdun, 1916," firstworldwar.com, 22 August 2009, accessed 20 October 2015, http://www.firstworldwar.com/battles/verdun.htm; Michael Duffy, "The Second Battle of Ypres, 1915," firstworldwar.com, 22 August 2009, accessed 30 October 2015, https://www.firstworldwar.com/battles/ypres2.htm; Robert A. Doughty, *Pyrrhic Victory* (Cambridge, MA: Harvard University Press, 2005), 309.

29 Leon Wolff, *In Flanders Fields: The 1917 Campaign* (New York: Viking, 1958), 204.

30 Wolff, *In Flanders Fields*, 207.

31 The Arras and Aisne campaign was also called the Nivelle Offensive. The British refer to the Third Battle of Ypres as Passchendaele.

32 See Erich Von Falkenhayn, *The German General Staff and Its Decisions, 1914–1916* (Dodd, Mead, 1920), 48; and John Keegan, *The First World War* (London: Hutchinson, 1998), 136. The British also struggled with artillery shortages. Keegan records that British artillery units "were limited to firing six rounds per gun per day."

33 Eric Dorn Brose, *The Kaiser's Army: The Politics of Military Technology in Germany During the Machine Age, 1870–1918* (Oxford University Press, 2004), 227.

34 Brose, *The Kaiser's Army*, 228.

35 Erich Ludendorff, *Ludendorff's Own Story*, 2 vols., vol. 1 (New York: Harper & Brothers, 1919), 408.

36 Ludendorff, *Ludendorff's Own Story*, 407.

37 Eric Dorn Brose, *A History of the Great War: World War One and the International Crisis of the Early Twentieth Century* (Oxford University Press, 2010), 227.

38 Keegan, *The First World War*, 318.

39 Offer, *The First World War*, 63.

40 Brose, *A History of the Great War*, 277.

41 Alexander Watson, *Ring of Steel: Germany and Austria-Hungary in World War I* (New York: Basic Books, 2014), 415.

42 Watson, *Ring of Steel*, 414; Gerald Feldman, *Army, Industry and Labour in Germany, 1914–1918* (Princeton, NJ: Princeton University Press, 1966), 310–348.

Both Feldman and Watson offer extensive insight into how the Hindenburg Program and the Auxiliary Service Laws did little to help the war effort, and in fact ensured inefficiencies.

43 Holger H. Herwig, *The First World War: Germany and Austria-Hungary, 1914–1918*, Modern Wars (London: St. Martin's Press, 1997), 260.

44 Herwig, *The First World War*, 260.

45 Christopher M. Clark, *Iron Kingdom: The Rise and Downfall of Prussia, 1600–1947* (New York: Penguin Books, 2007), 609–611. The high demand of war supply, transportation, and manpower stretched the manufacturing and economic abilities of the German state and led Germany toward military dictatorship. While the German chancellor, Bethmann-Hollweg, attempted to reform the state along political lines to balance the interests of business, labor, and the manic wishes of Kaiser Wilhelm II, the demands of war strained the abilities of Germany's nascent democracy. By mid-1917, Hollweg had resigned, and the German government was in the hands of Hindenburg and Ludendorff as his quartermaster general.

46 David R. Woodward, *World War I Almanac*, Almanacs of American Wars (New York: Facts On File, 2009), 66.

47 Woodward, *World War I Almanac*, 74.

48 *Statistics of the Military Effort of the British Empire During the Great War: 1914–1920* (London: His Majesty's Stationery Office, 1922), 434. On 3 July 1914, the average for thirteen weeks was 1,198,898. On 27 January 1917, the average for four weeks was 5,349,505.

49 See Herwig, *The First World War*, 260; and Clark, *Iron Kingdom*, 609–611.

50 *History of the War*, ed. The Times of London (London: Printing House Square: 1918), 15:262–268.

51 Watson, *Ring of Steel*, 416–417.

52 Brown, *British Logistics on the Western Front*, 181.

53 Keith Grieves, *Sir Eric Geddes: Business and Government in War and Peace*, Business and Society (New York: Manchester University Press, 1989), 1–9.

54 *Ibid.*, Grieves, *Sir Eric Geddes*, 13.

55 Doughty, *Pyrrhic Victory*, 309.

56 Grieves, *Sir Eric Geddes*, 35.

57 Jobie Turner, "Technogeopologistics: Supply Networks and Military Power in the Industrial Age" (Thesis, Maxwell Air Force Base, AL: Air University, 2012), 71–73. The mine was the critical technology that kept the German Navy pinned inside the confined waters of the Baltic Sea, the English Channel, and the North Sea.

58 Brose, *A History of the Great War*, 113.

59 Keegan, *The First World War*, 265; Brose, *A History of the Great War*, 114. The sinking of the *Lusitania* and the outcry from the United States held the German

U-boats at bay for nearly two years in an effort by the Germans to keep the
United States out of the war.

60 Herwig, *The First World War*, 305.

61 Herwig, 315.

62 Herwig, 314, 318.

63 Woodward, *World War I Almanac*, 187.

64 Woodward, 216. British general Robertson wrote on 29 July 1917, "The Russians
broke, with the result that three Russian armies comprising some 60 to 70 divisions, well equipped with guns and ammunition, are now running away from
some 18 Austrian and German divisions."

65 Wolff, *In Flanders Fields*, 203.

66 Wolff, 323–324

67 David T. Zabecki, *Steel Wind: Colonel Georg Bruchmüller and the Birth of Modern Artillery* (Westport, CT: Praeger Publishers, 1994), 14. Ludendorff, *Ludendorff's Own Story*, 1, 323–325. At a conference in Cambrai in the fall of 1916, the
German army decided to readjust its tactics on the Western Front.

68 "Map Showing Narrow Gauge Railways in France and Flanders, ," in *Report of
the Military Board of Allied Supply*, Vol. 1, part 2, Chapter 16, Chart 9. Single-
line track could accept traffic from only one direction. Double line track could
accept traffic in both directions.

69 Ludendorff, *Ludendorff's Own Story*, 1, 318.

70 As quoted in J. E. Edmonds, *A Short History of World War I* (New York: Oxford
University Press, 1951), 215.

71 Lawrence Moyer, *Victory Must Be Ours* (Hippocrene Books: New York, 1995),
194. Famed historian Arnold Toynbee published a treatise entitled "German
Terror in France" in protest.

72 Y. Buffetaut and B. Lepretre, *The 1917 Spring Offensives: Arras, Vimy, Le Chemin
Des Dames* (New Line Books, 2006), 8–14.

73 See Herwig, *The First World War*, 247; "28.SW Trench Map 22 June 2016 Edition 6A," in *British First World War Trench Maps: 1915–1918* (National Library
of Scotland, 1916); and "28.SW Trench Map 01 April 1917, Edition 6A," in *British
First World War Trench Maps: 1915–1918* (National Library of Scotland, 1917).
The front around Arras shows the change in German lines before and after
their decision to retreat and build their elastic defense.

74 Herwig, *The First World War*, 250. Herwig also avers that the demands of the
Hindenburg Line brought all other rail traffic to a halt within Germany.

75 Alan Henniker, *Transportation on the Western Front, 1914–1918* (London: H. M.
Stationery Office, 1937), 179.

76 "Lines of Communcation—British Forces in France and Flanders," in *Report of
the Military Board of Allied Supply*,vol 1, part 2, Chapter 11, Chart 2.

77 Grieves, *Sir Eric Geddes*, 32.

78 "Area Calculator," Map Developers, accessed 6 October 2015, http://www.map developers.com/area_finder.php. The state of Connecticut is 5,100 square miles.

79 *Report of the Military Board of Allied Supply*, 2:304.

80 Brown, *British Logistics on the Western Front*, 103.

81 S. E. Fawcett, L. M. Ellram, and J. A. Ogden, *Supply Chain Management: From Vision to Implementation* (Upper Saddle River, NJ: Pearson Education, 2007), 10. Inadequate information shared between the destination of supplies and the origin can cause a "bullwhip effect" in which "demand variations are likely to be exaggerated as decisions are made up the [supply] chain."

82 *Report of the Military Board of Allied Supply*, 2:310. The Military Board of Allied Supply reported, "The general scheme was varied *sometimes in the following ways* [emphasis added]."

83 Frederick William Taylor, *The Principles of Scientific Management* (1911), http://www.gutenberg.org/cache/epub/6435/pg6435-images.html. E-book. Frederick Taylor first championed these methods at the turn of the century in the United States. Called "Taylorism," his business practices championed analytical methods to measure productivity and improve efficiency.

84 Grieves, *Sir Eric Geddes*, 18.

85 Henniker, *Transportation on the Western Front*, 190.

86 Henniker, 191.

87 *Statistics of the Military Effort of the British Empire During the Great War*, 593, 598. The British had extensive statistics on rail, barge, and truck movement beginning in October 1916. Before this time very little data exists other than the overall supply amounts which left Britain for the war. See part XVIII (p. 598) for railway statistics, part XVII (p. 593) for lorries, and part XVIII (p. 598) for inland barges.

88 *Statistics of the Military Effort of the British Empire During the Great War*, 593, 598. Underscoring this lack of two years of data the *Report of the Military Board of Allied Supply* begins with a sixteen-page summary listing all the supplies, personnel, and transportation available to the Allies on 31 October 1918, as a testament to the logistics system. It contains no reference or data to land transportation metrics until after Geddes initial reforms in late 1916.

89 Henniker, *Transportation on the Western Front*, 191.

90 Geddes and his team estimated this would take 6,096 full rail wagons per week.

91 Henniker, 185

92 Henniker, 236.

93 Henniker, 240.

94 Henniker, 236, 241. The British approved the channel ferry concept in January 1917, but it did not run until February 1918.

95 Henniker, 240–241. The more precise number was one thousand rail cars containing munitions every fourteen days.

96 Pratt, *The Rise of Rail-power in War and Conquest* 118–121. Pratt details German

railway troops, training, and practice of rail building. See also Grieves, *Sir Eric Geddes*, 33.

97 Grieves, *Sir Eric Geddes*, 33.

98 "Map Showing Narrow Gauge Railways in France and Flanders," in *Report of the Military Board of Allied Supply*, Vol. 1, part 2, Chapter 16, Chart 9; *Report of the Military Board of Allied Supply*, 1:364; and Pratt, *The Rise of Rail-power in War and Conquest*, 349. Writing from an allied perspective, Pratt made a case for light rail and its uses based on the German system he observed before the war.

99 Wolff, *In Flanders Fields*, 42. According to Wolff, the first international conference Lloyd George attended was a disaster because the prime minister attempted to move the entire Allied strategy to Italy without the proper support of his Allied generals or even his own British War Office.

100 Wolff, *In Flanders Fields*, 44; and Richard M. Watt, *Dare Call It Treason* (New York: Simon and Schuster, 1963), 155–156. Watt states, "It was anticipated that the British attack would open a few days before the French and thus draw the German reserves North to meet it, following which the French would erupt violently on the southern flank of the German salient and crush through it, opening a gap of approximately seventy miles in the German trench system through which the allies would flood and end the war."

101 Sir Douglas Haig as quoted in John Terraine, *The Road to Passchendaele: The Flanders Offensive of 1917, A Study in Inevitability* (London: Cooper, 1977), 31.

102 Grieves, *Sir Eric Geddes*, 35. The French highlighted their lack of capacity on their rail lines during the winter of 1916–1917. In one of his last acts as commander in chief of the French Army, Marshal Joffre argued for the British to ship three thousand to ten thousand wagons and 490 locomotives to France before 1917.

103 Robert Blake and Douglas Haig, *Private Papers of Douglas Haig, 1914–1919* (London: Eyre & Spottiswoode, 1952), 199.

104 Blake and Haig, *Private Papers of Douglas Haig*, 199.

105 Grieves, *Sir Eric Geddes*, 35. With the British economy moving toward total support for the war and American industry increasing its output and support as the country moved to Wilson's declaration of war on 4 April 1917, the British had confidence that their logistics transportation system could hold.

106 Buffetaut and Lepretre, *The 1917 Spring Offensives*, 12–14.

107 Blake and Haig, *Private Papers of Douglas Haig*, 210. Haig wrote of the change in plan and his discussion with Nivelle on 12 March 1917.

108 Blake and Haig, *Private Papers of Douglas Haig*, 216.

109 As quoted in Watt, *Dare Call It Treason*, 155; and Woodward, *World War I Almanac*, 188.

110 Blake and Haig, *Private Papers of Douglas Haig*, 216.

111 *Statistics of the Military Effort of the British Empire During the Great War*, 418–419.

112 Buffetaut and Lepretre, *The 1917 Spring Offensives,* 67.

113 Wolff, *In Flanders Fields,* 62.

114 As quoted in John Herbert Boraston, ed., *Sir Douglas Haig's Despatches: December 1915–April 1919* (London: Dent, 1919), 91.

115 Boraston, *Sir Douglas Haig's Despatches,* 93–95.

116 "51B.NW Trench Map, 4 March 1917" and "51B.NW Trench Map, 25 May 1917," *British First World War Trench Maps: 1915–1918,* National Library of Scotland (NLS), accessed 22 April 2019, https://maps.nls.uk/ww1/trenches/list.html. The NLS has outstanding color maps which show the elastic defense the Germans built after the retreat to the Hindenburg Line and how they fell back on their significant rail network to blunt the Nivelle Offensive.

117 Boraston, *Sir Douglas Haig's Despatches,* 77–78; and Blake and Haig, *Private Papers of Douglas Haig,* 216–217. For their efforts, Haig praised Sir Eric Geddes and the Canadian railway troops who had built the expanded narrow gauge system into Arras, both in his wartime diary and in his later postwar dispatches.

118 Wolff, *In Flanders Fields,* 64.

119 Wolff, 63.

120 Watt, *Dare Call It Treason,* 173 and; Ardant Du Picq, ed., *Battle Studies: Ancient and Modern Battle,* trans. John N. Greely and Robert C. Cotton, Roots of Strategy Book 2, 65. In the late nineteenth century Du Picq championed élan—the belief that human will could overcome any challenge put before it on the battlefield. Du Picq stated, "It often happens that those who discuss war, taking the weapon for the starting point . . . the human heart . . . is the starting point in all matters pertaining to war."

121 Watt, *Dare Call It Treason,* 218.

122 Paul Painlevé, "Address by the French Minister of War, July 7,1917," in *Source Records of the Great War,* ed. Charles F. Horne (Indianapolis, IN: American Legion, 1931), 166.

123 The French would participate in the Third Battle of Ypres and also undertake an offensive attack on Verdun in the fall of 1917, but not nearly with the same amount of forces as they had in previous operations prior to the Nivelle Offensive.

124 General Von Janson, "Account of the Spring Offensive in the West," in *Source Records of the Great War,* ed. Charles F. Horne, 7 vols, (Indianapolis, IN: American Legion, 1931), 5:165.

125 Von Janson, "Account of the Spring Offensive in the West," 5:166; and Erich Ludendorff, "Memorandum on the Western Front." Ludendorff was worried German heavy losses in the west, which caused troops to be diverted from elsewhere, both in the early spring and later at Passchendaele, would sap the German ability to go on the offensive in 1918.

126 Von Janson, "Account of the Spring Offensive in the West," 166; Erich Ludendorff, *The General Staff and Its Problems: The History of the Relations Between*

the High Command and the German Imperial Government as Revealed by Official Documents, 2 vols. (Boston: E.P Dutton and Company, 1920), 2:469–470. In July, Ludendorff reported in a war conference to Von Hindenburg and some members of the Reichstag, "The success that was anticipated for the U-boat operations has materialized. There is no doubt that our enemies have a smaller superiority."

127 As quoted in Ludendorff, The General Staff and Its Problems, 2:179.

128 Moyer, Victory Must Be Ours, 223. The voting of a peace proposal by the Reichstag in July 1917 was the proximate cause of Hollweg's removal and the final ascension of Hindenburg and Ludendorff.

129 Moyer, 224.

130 Wolff, In Flanders Fields, 125.

131 Blake and Haig, Private Papers of Douglas Haig, 210. Haig mentioned the ports twice in his five-point plan to Neville.

132 Wolff, In Flanders Fields, 108–109. This was a rehash of the same argument between Lloyd George and Haig—out in the open after the French plan failed.

133 Blake and Haig, Private Papers of Douglas Haig, 240–241.

134 Terraine, The Road to Passchendaele, 156–157.

135 As quoted in Wolff, In Flanders Fields, 113. See also Hubert Gough, Soldiering On: Being the Memoirs of General Sir Hubert Gough (London: A. Barker, 1954), 138. British general Hugh Gough, who commanded the British Fifth Army on the Western Front, wrote after the war, "Ever since he [Haig] assumed command of the British Army he had always wished to attack form the Ypres Salient and drive the Germans off the coast of Belgium. This plan was now also being urged by Admiral Jellicoe, who was becoming increasingly anxious about our losses at sea from German submarines."

136 All commonwealth soldiers would call it Passchendaele after the campaign's capture of the city just seven miles from Ypres in the last months of the campaign (October–November 1917).

137 Wolff, In Flanders Fields, 88. Wolff posits that this move by Haig was an attempt to draw the offensive to Flanders, Haig's focus for the entire war.

138 Wolff, 88. Wolff states, "there was hardly a point within the loop of ground held by his [Plummer's] Second Army which German guns could not enfilade or fire into from behind."

139 Wolff, 89

140 Keegan, The First World War, 356.

141 Wolff, In Flanders Fields, 101.

142 Paddy Griffith, Battle Tactics of the Western Front: The British Army's Art of Attack, 1916–18 (New Haven, CT: Yale University Press, 1994), 86.

143 Wolff, In Flanders Fields, 103.

144 Wolff, 104.

145 Peter Mead, The Eye in the Air: History of Air Observation and Reconnaissance for the Army, 1785–1945 (London: Her Majesty's Stationery Office, 1983), 87–88.

146 John Howard Morrow, *The Great War in the Air: Military Aviation from 1909 to 1921* (Washington, DC: Smithsonian Institution Press, 1993), 234–235. By the end of April, the British Royal Flying Corps had lost 238 pilots with another 105 wounded.

147 Mead, *The Eye in the Air,* 87.

148 Terraine, *The Road to Passchendaele,* 70. A British soldier remarked on 14 April 1917, "The weather, always the abominable weather, was the fiendish, relentless ally of the Germans." See also Watt, *Dare Call It Treason,* 79. On 15 April 1917, a cold rain turned to sleet over the French lines.

149 Herwig, *The First World War,* 250.

150 Herwig, 246–252.

151 Wolff, *In Flanders Fields,* 84.

152 *Statistics of the Military Effort of the British Empire During the Great War,* 601. To supplement the growing transportation effort, the support personnel to the railroads gained increasing strength. Total personnel working on railroads, road construction, transportation sources, and numerous other logistics efforts, jumped from 44,392 in May 1917 to 63,594 in October 1917. For direct support of light rail to the front, the number of personnel assigned workshop duties to repair the lines grew from zero to 1,560.

153 Herwig, *The First World War,* 332.

154 Feldman, *Army, Industry and Labour in Germany, 1914–1918,* 386. Feldman covers the debates, strikes, and political unrest caused by the demands of war on German society. He illustrates how close Germany came to internal revolution in the summer of 1917.

155 Ludendorff, *The General Staff and Its Problems,* 2:394.

156 Wolff, *In Flanders Fields,* 203.

157 Herwig, *The First World War,* 331.

158 *Statistics of the Military Effort of the British Empire During the Great War,* 416–418

159 *Statistics of the Military Effort of the British Empire During the Great War,* 601. The British would not eclipse this amount until of shells until the frantic last week of September 1918 as the Allies pounded the Germans in the final weeks of the war.

160 Herwig, *The First World War,* 332.

161 As quoted in Wolff, *In Flanders Fields,* 210.

162 Wolff, 210.

163 Herwig, *The First World War,* 331.

164 "The Wartime Memories Project: 118th Siege Battery, During the Great War," accessed 29 August 2019, https://www.wartimememoriesproject.com/greatwar/allied/rgartillery.php?pid=9509. Printed with permission from Chris Baker.

165 Wolff, *In Flanders Fields,* 210. Two of those tank officers present—J. F. C. Fuller and Liddell Hart—would make writing careers advocating for maneuver warfare after the disaster at Passchendaele.

166 Wolff, 238–240.

167 Brown, *British Logistics on the Western Front*, 239.

168 Winston S. Churchill, *The World Crisis Volume II: 1916–1918* (New York: Charles Scribner's Son, 1927), 63–90. Churchill gives a complete summary of the campaign.

169 Lee Kennett, *The First Air War* (New York: Free Press, 1991), 196–197.

170 Herwig, *The First World War*, 332.

171 Ludendorff, "Memorandum on the Western Front," 272–273.

172 "20 South East, Ypres Salient Trench Map 17 September 1917 Edition 4a," in *British First World War Trench Maps: 1915–1918*.

173 "20 South East, Ypres Salient Trench Map 17 September 1917 Edition 4a." A close up view of this location reveals the loading tracks and shunts, the Germans constructed on the sides of the road to support the loading of the trains.

174 "20 SE, Ypres Salient Trench Map 17 September 1917 Edition 4a," in *British First World War Trench Maps: 1915–1918*.

175 "20 SE, Ypres Salient Trench Map 17 December 1917 Edition 5A," in *British First World War Trench Maps: 1915–1918*. This is a conservative estimate of rail distance, since the original maps have rail routes that also run along standard roads, obscuring the marking of the new railways.

176 John Terraine, *White Heat: The New Warfare, 1914–18* (London: Sidgwick & Jackson, 1982), 240–242. Registering involved actual firing of artillery to range the weapon, which in turn warned the enemy of impending attack

177 See Terraine, *White Heat*, 217. At about the same time, German artillery under the command of Colonel Burchmuller was advancing surprise artillery tactics to take Riga. See also Zabecki, *Steel Wind*, 33–61. Zebecki details Bruchmuller's fire and move tactics.

178 Morrow, *The Great War in the Air*, 276. At Cambrai, the air effort had decidedly mixed results; some Royal Flying Corps units suffered as much as 30 percent losses in their low-flying missions to support the attack.

179 Terraine, *White Heat*, 242.

180 John Cotesworth Slessor, *Air Power and Armies* (Tuscaloosa: University of Alabama Press, 2009), 91.

181 Slessor, *Air Power and Armies*, 91. Interdiction is the operational term for striking targets beyond the front line, and in particular reinforcing forces and logistics.

182 Zabecki, *Steel Wind*, 17; Addington, *The Blitzkrieg Era*, 26.

183 *Statistics of the Military Effort of the British Empire During the Great War*, 561. The British averaged less than 7.1 million pounds per day in 1918.

184 Christian Wolmar, *Blood, Iron, & Gold: How the Railroads Transformed the World*, 1st ed. (New York: PublicAffairs, 2010), 280.

185 Keegan, *The First World War*, 1–6.

186 Turner, "Technogeopologistics: Supply Networks and Military Power in the Industrial Age," 55–56. This section was adapted in large part from this thesis.

187   Adam Tooze, *The Wages of Destruction: The Making and Breaking of the Nazi Economy* (New York: Penguin, 2006), 552–557.

CHAPTER 3. STAVING STARVATION: THE BATTLE FOR GUADALCANAL, 1942–1943

1   Jobie Turner, "Technogeopologistics: Supply Networks and Military Power in the Industrial Age" (Thesis, Air University, 2012), 121.

2   Jeremy Black, *World War Two: A Military History* (New York: Routledge, 2006), 31–32.

3   Richard B. Frank, *Guadalcanal* (New York: Random House, 1990), 12.

4   See appendix for detailed comparison. See Table A.4.

5   See appendix for detailed comparison. See Table A.5.

6   Williamson Murray and Allan Reed Millett, *Military Innovation in the Interwar Period* (Cambridge, England: Cambridge University Press, 1996), 53.

7   Edward S. Miller, *War Plan Orange: The U.S. Strategy to Defeat Japan, 1897–1945* (Annapolis, MD: Naval Institute Press, 1991), 350–351.

8   "Solomon Islands Campaign: I, Landings in the Solomons, 7–8 August 1942," in *Combat Narratives* (Washington, DC: United States Navy Office of Naval Intelligence,1943), 24.

9   "Solomon Islands Campaign," 24. Red Beach was six thousand yards to the east of Lunga Point.

10   The formal designations for the three types craft were LCP(L), LCV, and LCM(2) respectively. See "Solomon Islands Campaign," 34; and N. Friedman, *U.S. Amphibious Ships and Craft: An Illustrated Design History* (Annapolis, MD: Naval Institute Press, 2002), 92. This total was for the landings at Tulagi and Guadalcanal, with approximately eleven thousand of the nineteen thousand troops landing at Guadalcanal. Given this ratio, 266 of the 457 craft would have debarked their loads on Guadalcanal.

11   "Solomon Islands Campaign" 34.

12   Solomon Islands Campaign," 33.

13   Frank, *Guadalcanal*, 61–62.

14   This number is an estimate. According to Frank, 2571 Japanese engineers and conscripts arrived at Guadalcanal and Tulagi in the summer of 1942. The exact number located on Guadalcanal was uncertain, although the Japanese did operate Tulagi with a three-hundred-man garrison.

15   Stanley Coleman Jersey, *Hell's Islands: The Untold Story of Guadalcanal* (College Station: Texas A&M University Press, 2007), 115. Jersey quotes a Japanese seaman, "The fortunate ones were those who fled to the west where they found coconut groves and adequate water and so were able to survive."

16   "Solomon Islands Campaign" 38.

17   "Division Commanders Final Report on Guadalcanal Operations, Phase 2" (San Francisco: First Division United States Marine Corps, 1942), 15.

18 "Division Commanders Final Report on Guadalcanal Operations, Phase 2," 16. As if to underscore the lesson, Vandegrift stated, "Landings should not be attempted in the face of organized resistance if, by any combination of march or maneuver, it is possible to land unopposed . . . within striking distance of the objective."

19 Frank, *Guadalcanal,* 64–66.

20 "Japanese Monograph No. 98, Southeast Area Naval Operations Part I, May 42–Feb 43" (General Headquaters Far East Asia Command Second Demobilization Bureau, 1949), 10.

21 John B. Lundstrom, *The First Team and the Guadalcanal Campaign: Naval Fighter Combat from August to November 1942* (Annapolis, MD: Naval Institute Press, 1994), 44–45. Betty was the US identifier for the Mitsubishi G4M1 Type 1 land attack plane.

22 Lundstrom, *The First Team and the Guadalcanal Campaign,* 64. Val was the US identifier for the Aichi D3A1 Type 99 bomber.

23 Frank, *Guadalcanal,* 62.

24 "Division Commanders Final Report on Guadalcanal Operations, Phase 2," 17.

25 Frank, *Guadalcanal,* 62.

26 Thayer Soule, "Guadalcanal Invasion Part 2," YouTube video, accessed 9 December 2015, https://www.youtube.com/watch?v=bPAkAoT-8L8. USMC First Lieutenant Soule was in charge of the footage of the landing. His enlisted troops missed filming the landing due to the chaos of unloading on the beach. Footage of the later Bougainville campaign showed a dozen Marines forming a line to empty a landing craft, without a ramp, of its ammunition.

27 Jersey, *Hell's Islands,* 116.

28 See "Division Commanders Final Report on Guadalcanal Operations, Phase 2"; and Jersey, *Hell's Islands,* 118–119. Their maps were antiquated versions of *National Geographic* inserts cobbled together with information from a few British civilians who had worked on Guadalcanal's coconut plantations prior to the war.

29 "Division Commanders Final Report on Guadalcanal Operations, Phase 2." The poor communication on the ground with reconnaissance aircraft before and during the landings led to incomplete maps, which even ten days after landing still had areas labeled "Clouds" because aircraft had not seen the terrain enough to provide the information.

30 George Carroll Dyer, *The Amphibians Came to Conquer: The Story of Admiral Richmond Kelly Turner,* vol. 1 (Washington, DC: US Department of the Navy, 1972), Annex M(1) and 15–16. The after-action report focuses on the lack of salt in the water and salt tabs to overcome the heat, based on the medicine of the time. More than water with saline in it, the Marines needed water.

31 "Division Commanders Final Report on Guadalcanal Operations, Phase 2," 10.

32 Lundstrom, *The First Team and the Guadalcanal Campaign,* 62.

33 Lundstrom, 68.

34 See "Division Commanders Final Report on Guadalcanal Operations, Phase 2," 62. Despite this unsustainable loss rate, the US pilots and naval commanders were bolstered by the success in shooting down the vaunted Zeros. The hereto-fore-splendid performance of the Zero in battle made it seem like an immortal piece of technology. See also Lundstrum, *The First Team and the Guadalcanal Campaign*, 71.

35 "Division Commanders Final Report on Guadalcanal Operations, Phase 2," Annex N(5). This quote is located in the First Division's communication logs report.

36 "Division Commanders Final Report on Guadalcanal Operations, Phase 2," 15.

37 See "Division Commanders Final Report on Guadalcanal Operations, Phase 2," Annex N(6). The command post log notes, "Shore Party to CG—Unload-ing entirely out of hand X Supplies arriving much faster than we can handle X Imperative we stop ships unloading until we can clear beach 1000 tomorrow."; See also Dyer, *The Amphibians Came to Conquer*, 1:350.

38 Dyer, *The Amphibians Came to Conquer*, 1:1.

39 Dyer, 1:351.

40 Bruce Loxton and C. D. Coulthard-Clark, *The Shame of Savo: Anatomy of a Naval Disaster* (Annapolis, MD: Naval Institute Press, 1994), 240.

41 Lundstrom, *The First Team and the Guadalcanal Campaign*, 76–78.

42 See Samuel Eliot Morison, *History of United States Naval Operations in World War II: The Struggle for Guadalcanal, August 1942–February 1943* (Boston: Little, Brown and Co, 1949), 5:16; see also Lundstrom, *The First Team and the Guadal-canal Campaign*, 76–78.

43 Lundstrom, *The First Team and the Guadalcanal Campaign*, 78.

44 Thayer Soule, *Shooting the Pacific War: Marine Corps Combat Photography in WWII* (Lexington: University Press of Kentucky, 2000), 4.

45 "Division Commanders Final Report on Guadalcanal Operations, Phase 2," 17.

46 Frank, *Guadalcanal*, 93–95. The decision to withdraw the carriers is still a topic of disagreement within the United States Navy and the United States Marine Corps, with a significant literature. Every member of the USMC can recite the failure of the Navy chapter and verse seventy-four years later. Frank's discus-sion of the reasons behind the departure is the most concise and probing.

47 Frank, 58.

48 James D. Hornfischer, *Neptune's Inferno: The US Navy at Guadalcanal* (New York: Bantam, 2011), 65. The group consisted of one heavy, three standard, and three light cruisers.

49 Morison, *History of United States Naval Operations in World War II*, 5:24. Cloud cover masked Mikawa's force. B-17s from Gen. Macarthur's Southwest Pacific force missed the convoy since it skirted at the edge of his area of responsibil-ity while successive *Catalina* floatplanes could not cover the "slot" from down south due to the ranges involved.

50 Hornfischer, *Neptune's Inferno*, 63, 435.

51 The US Navy had seven cruisers and eight destroyers versus the seven cruisers and one destroyer of the IJN.

52 Frank, *Guadalcanal*, 118. The long-lance torpedo had a theoretical range of twenty NM.

53 United States Naval Institute, "Leading the Charge at Savo Island by Capt. Toshikazu Ohmae" accessed 10 August 2019, https://www.usni.org/magazines /naval-history-magazine/2017/august/leading-charge-savo-island.The postwar debate continued for decades. This famous analysis, completed at the US Naval War College with the help of Imperial Japanese Navy captain Ohmae states, "It is easy to say, now, that the enemy transports should have been attacked at all cost. There is now little doubt that it would have been worthwhile for *Chokai* to have turned back, even alone, ordering such of her scattered ships as could follow her in an attack on the enemy transports. And, if all had followed and all had been sacrificed in sinking the transports, it would have been well worth the price to effect the expulsion of the enemy from Guadalcanal."

54 Loxton and Coulthard-Clark, *The Shame of Savo*, 240. Loxton declares, "What a wonderful thing is hindsight and possession of almost unlimited resources!"

55 "Japanese Monograph No. 98" 11.

56 Iron Bottom Sound was the moniker for the waters between Tulagi, Savo Island, and Guadalcanal. In the sound, during the Battle of Guadalcanal, more than fifty vessels from PT boats and submarines to cruisers were sunk.

57 "Division Commanders Final Report on Guadalcanal Operations, Phase 2," 14.

58 Jersey, *Hell's Islands*, 205.

59 See Jersey, 195.; and Soule, "Guadalcanal Invasion Part 2." In a metaphor for future flying operations on the airfield, the PBY landed too far down the runway and had to be pulled out of a crater. As McCain stepped off the aircraft, a Japanese air raid caused the entire party to scatter to the shallow bunkers surrounding the airfield. There was little damage and the PBY-5 was refueled with small jerry cans. Lt. Soule recorded the plane landing, but not the crater incident, in his official movie for the campaign.

60 See "Division Commanders Final Report on Guadalcanal Operations, Phase 2," 14.; and Jersey, *Hell's Islands*, 191. This allowed the supplies to be stored in some former Japanese buildings and to be combined with the supplies from the Japanese, and to connect the supply line form the sea more directly to the airfield (See Map 2—Upper Left Map).

61 "Division Commanders Final Report on Guadalcanal Operations, Phase 3, 08 August–21 August 1942" (San Francisco: First Division United States Marine Corps, 1942), Annex C(4).

62 See A. A. Vandegrift and Robert B. Asprey, *Once a Marine: The Memoirs of General A.A. Vandegrift, United States Marine Corps* (New York: Norton, 1964), 133–135.; and "Division Commanders Final Report on Guadalcanal Operations, Phase 3, 08 August–21 August 1942, Annex C(4).

63 "Division Commanders Final Report on Guadalcanal Operations, Phase 3" Annex C(4).

64 Frank, *Guadalcanal*, 138.

65 Frank, 131.

66 Frank, 140.

67 Morison, *History of United States Naval Operations in World War II*, 5:74. Cactus was the US designation for Guadalcanal. Tulagi was called Ringbolt.

68 Vandegrift and Asprey, *Once a Marine*, 139.

69 Chester A. Nimitz, in *Command Summary and Running Estimate of Chester A. Nimitz: 1941–1945*, Microfilm Reel No. 1, 7 December 1941–31 December 1942 (Washington, DC: United States Navy), 829.

70 Richard M. Leighton and Robert W Coakley, *Global Logistics and Strategy: 1940–1943* (Washington, DC: Office of the Chief of Military History, Department of the Army, 1955), 399–404. Lighters were barges used to transfer cargo from ships to land.

71 Joseph Bykofsky and Harold Larson, *The Transportation Corps: Operations Overseas* (Washington, DC: Department of the Army, 1957), 490.

72 Leighton and Coakley, *Global Logistics and Strategy*, 399.

73 Leighton and Coakley, 399.

74 Leighton and Coakley, 404–406. Poor packing procedures were endemic to the South and Southwest Pacific theaters until late 1943.

75 Morison, *History of United States Naval Operations in World War II*, 5:81.

76 R. L. Ferguson, *Guadalcanal, The Island of Fire: Reflections of the 347th Fighter Group* (Blue Ride Summit, Pennsylvania: Aero Books, 1987), 60–61. Ferguson recounts loading a landing craft to meet the Formalhaut and running out of fuel during the three-mile trip to the ship.

77 "CINCPAC Daily Staff Summary 26 August 1942," in *Command Summary and Running Estimate of Chester A Nimitz: 1941–1945*, 835.

78 "CINCPAC Daily Staff Summary 26 August 1942," 835.

79 "CINCPAC Daily Staff Summary 26 August 1942," 835.

80 Frank, *Guadalcanal*, 143.

81 Frank, 143.

82 Frank, 143.

83 "Japanese Monograph No. 98," 11.

84 Morison, *History of United States Naval Operations in World War II*, 5:18.

85 Matome Ugaki et al., *Fading Victory: The Diary of Admiral Matome Ugaki, 1941–1945* (Pittsburgh, PA: University of Pittsburgh Press, 1991), 188.

86 Jonathan Parshall, "Oil and Japanese Strategy in the Solomons: A Postulate," accessed 16 December 2015, 29 August 2019/, http://www.combinedfleet.com /guadoil1.htm.

87 Parshall, "Oil and Japanese Strategy in the Solomons."

88 See Parshall; and "Logistics," The Pacific War Online Encyclopedia, accessed

23 December 2015, http://pwencycl.kgbudge.com/L/o/Logistics.htm#mozToc Id360123. See also Anthony Tully, "Sakito Maru Auxiliary Class Transport," accessed 6 January 2016, http://www.combinedfleet.com/Sakito_c.htm. Budge estimates the range of fuel consumption for a ship at .7 to .9 pounds per hour, per Shaft Horse Power (SHP). The larger Japanese cargo ships—Type A and C burned a range of 1.5 to 3.0 tons per hour at this rate (2000 to 2500 SHP). While this was respectable, the Japanese also had older ships which cruised t ten knots and burned coal—combining a slow speed with a power source that needed labor-intensive extraction when compared to oil. Transport ships for troops could move faster (seventeen knots) at the higher burn rate of oil at 5.8 to 8.5 tons of oil per hour (16,600 SHP), but could carry ten times the cargo.

89 *Standard Classes of Japanese Merchant Ships.* vol. oNI 208-J (Revised), Supplement 3 (Washington, DC: United States Government Printing Office, 1945). See also Parshall, "Oil and Japanese Strategy in the Solomons: A Postulate."

90 Frank, *Guadalcanal,* 22.

91 Frank, 145.

92 William H. Bartsch, *Victory Fever on Guadalcanal: Japan's First Land Defeat of World War II* (College Station: Texas A&M University Press, 2014), 77.

93 "Japanese Monograph No. 98," 13.

94 Bartsch, *Victory Fever on Guadalcanal,* 92–93.

95 Bartsch, 150–151.

96 Frank, *Guadalcanal,* 22.

97 Ugaki et al., *Fading Victory,* 185.

98 Paul S. Dull, *A Battle History of the Imperial Japanese Navy, 1941–1945* (Annapolis, MD: Naval Institute Press, 1978), 203.

99 "Japanese Monograph No. 98" 16.

100 Ugaki et al., *Fading Victory,* 193.

101 Ferguson, *Guadalcanal,* 72.

102 Hornfischer, *Neptune's Inferno,* 121.

103 Frank, *Guadalcanal,* 166. There were significant numbers of other surface craft and submarines involved, but in the confusing melee of carrier aircraft strikes and launches, most of the surface craft were lost in the confusion and did not see action.

104 Hornfischer, *Neptune's Inferno,* 119–120. With the *Enterprise* steaming back from repairs at Pearl Harbor, the *Hornet* was the only carrier in the South Pacific. In quick succession, Admiral's Fletcher and his replacement Admiral Noyes were relieved of command of the carrier task force.

105 See Lundstrom, *The First Team and the Guadalcanal Campaign,* 62, 147. These losses were mostly Val Bombers. Lundstrom disagrees with Frank's assessment in *Guadalcanal* that the Japanese lost more than seventy-five aircraft and disagrees with Fletcher's postbattle estimate of ninety. See also Ugaki et al., *Fading Victory,* 191. Both the Japanese and American leadership were disappointed

with the outcome and felt they missed opportunities to send the others carriers
to the bottom of the ocean.

106   See Hornfischer, *Neptune's Inferno*, 132–133.; and Lundstrom, *The First Team
and the Guadalcanal Campaign*, 227.

107   Lundstrom, *The First Team and the Guadalcanal Campaign*, 184. For the best
telling of the hodgepodge experience of airmen from three services flying during the campaign see Ferguson's Guadalcanal: The Island of Fire, which details
the experience of the Sixty Seventh Fighter Squadron of the United States Army
Air Forces.

108   Mark R. Peattie, *Sunburst: The Rise of the Japanese Naval Air Power, 1909–1941*
(Annapolis, MD: Naval Institute Press, 2001), 133. Japanese fighter ace Sakai
Saburo remarked, "During the 1930s, the Japanese Navy trained approximately
one hundred fliers a year. The rigid screening . . . reduced the many hundreds
of qualified students to the ridiculously low total of a hundred or fewer graduated pilots."

109   Lundstrom, *The First Team and the Guadalcanal Campaign*, 147.

110   "Japanese Monograph No. 98," 18.

111   Ugaki et al., *Fading Victory*, 197.

112   See Frank, *Guadalcanal*, 500.; and "Japanese Monograph No. 98" 19.

113   "Japanese Monograph No. 98," 20.

114   Dull, *A Battle History of the Imperial Japanese Navy, 1941–1945*, 209

115   See Morison, *History of United States Naval Operations in World War II*, 5:129;
and "Japanese Monograph No. 98," 28. See also Frank, *Guadalcanal*, 502. Frank
estimates 6,217 as the total number of Japanese soldiers delivered (after the
American invasion) by this time. With those left behind from the runway construction and the Ichiki deployment, 7,800 is a reasonable estimate. The Imperial Japanese Staff lamented, "Army unit launched a scheduled attack on the
evening of 12 September, but the main body was unable to advance rapidly
through the jungle, and launched an attack at 1200 hours on 13 September."
This statement understated the challenge of logistics.

116   Jersey, *Hell's Islands*, 232–233.

117   Frank, *Guadalcanal*, 246.

118   Frank, 279, 502. Oftentimes, destroyers carried troops as well and their food
supplies would dwindle to from ten to twenty tons. Most of the standard Tokyo
Express runs in October delivered between three hundred and four hundred
men and fifteen tons of supplies. See also Parshall, "Oil and Japanese Strategy
in the Solomons: A Postulate." As aforementioned, the destroyer could carry
forty tons of cargo total—supplies, food, and soldiers.

119   Parshall, "Oil and Japanese Strategy in the Solomons: A Postulate."

120   Edward Norman Peterson, *An Analytical History of World War II*, 2 vols. (New
York: Peter Lang, 1995), 1:422. Peterson estimated 9,000 soldiers, but based on

the record in Frank's *Guadalcanal*, 7,800 is likely more accurate. See "Summary of Supply," this chapter, for full estimate of food supplies during the campaign.

121 See Eric M. Bergerud, *Fire in the Sky: The Air War in the South Pacific* (Boulder, CO: Westview Press, 2000), 463; and Ferguson, *Guadalcanal*, 129. Radar was a boon to Cactus aviators because it allowed the ground station at Henderson to vector aircraft towards unseen Japanese attackers upwards of 150 miles away, overcoming line of sight and the obscuration of clouds. US Army Air Force Lt. Ferguson describes listening to "resurrection radio" to determine inbound Japanese aircraft.

122 Japanese Naval and Merchant Vessels Losses During World War II, All Causes" (Washington, DC: Joint Army-Navy Assesment Committee, 1947), 32. The submarines sunk more than fourteen thousand tons of shipping with these attacks.

123 "Division Commanders Final Report on Guadalcanal Operations, Phase 4, 20 Aug–18 Sep" (San Francisco: First Division United States Marine Corps, 1942), Annex(H) 3–4.

124 Morison, *History of United States Naval Operations in World War II*, 5:109, 111.

125 See "Division Commanders Final Report on Guadalcanal Operations, Phase 4," Annex C(4); and "Division Commanders Final Report on Guadalcanal Operations, Phase 4," Annex (H)3.

126 A. J. Baime, *The Arsenal of Democracy: FDR, Detroit, and an Epic Quest to Arm an America at War* (Boston: Houghton Mifflin Harcourt, 2014), 206. Baime postulates that FDR understood by the winter of 1942 that the "Arsenal of Democracy" he promised in 1940 was coming to fruition.

127 Lundstrom, *The First Team and the Guadalcanal Campaign*, 184, 200, 202, 210, 217, 219, 238, 249, 258, 264. The number of losses for both sides differed greatly—with both sides exaggerating the number of enemy planes shot down. Lundstrom peels the information from both sides to get a closer number to actual losses. Japanese lost twenty Aircraft between 21 August and 11 September, and thirty-five thereafter—in addition to sixteen on the first two days of the Marine landing. The Cactus Air Force lost sixty-five between 20 August (first day of operation) and 21 September 1942. They lost five more the in proceeding days. These losses do not count the carrier battle at the Eastern Solomons.

128 "Japanese Monograph No. 98," 39.

129 "Japanese Monograph No. 98," 39.

130 See Ugaki et al., *Fading Victory*, 227; and "Japanese Monograph No. 98," 29.

131 Frank, *Guadalcanal*, 252.

132 Ugaki et al., *Fading Victory*, 227.

133 "Japanese Monograph No. 98" 30.

134 Lundstrom, *The First Team and the Guadalcanal Campaign*, 241. Lundstrom records, "Rabaul received strong air reinforcements to the tune of forty-three

Type 1 land attack planes, thirty-eights Zero fighters (Long-Range Model 21s), and twelve Type 99 carrier bombers."

135 See "Japanese Monograph No. 98," 39.; and "Japanese Monograph No. 98," 33. Carving runways onto Pacific Islands, festooned with jungle and daily deluge of rain, was not easy. Due to delays in construction at Buin airfield, the Japanese had to postpone the planned landing by sea transport until October 15.

136 Nimitz, in *Command Summary and Running Estimate*, 829. August 27 dispatch from COMSOPAC to CINCPAC info COMINCH, CTF 61, 62, 63, CGSOPAC.

137 Millard F Harmon, "Headquarters USAFISPA to Chief Theater Group, Operations Division, War Department: 26 August 1942," in *Millard F. Harmon Papers* (United States Air Force Historical Agency, IRIS No. 260973, 1942).

138 "Division Commanders Final Report on Guadalcanal Operations, Phase 4," 16.

139 Peterson, *An Analytical History of World War II*, 1:422. This does not include the four thousand or so Marines still stationed across the sound at Tulagi.

140 Vandegrift and Asprey, *Once a Marine*, 165.

141 Frank, *Guadalcanal*, 284–285.

142 Millard F Harmon, "Headquarters USAFISPA to Chief Theater Group, Operations Division, War Department: 16 November 1942," in *Millard F. Harmon Papers* (United States Air Force Historical Agency, IRIS No. 260973, 1942). These numbers are from August until mid-November. Exact numbers for October would have been lower since the larger flow of US Army Air Forces into the theater began the first week of October.

143 *Japanese Naval and Merchant Vessels Sunk Losses During World War II*, , 33.

144 See Ugaki et al., *Fading Victory*, 220. On 29 September 1942 Admiral Ugaki recorded in his diary, "Twelve B-17s attacked destroyer *Akitsuki*." See also Millard F Harmon, "Headquarters USAFISPA to Commanding General Army Air Force, 28 August 1942," in *Millard F. Harmon Papers* (United States Air Force Historical Agency, IRIS No. 260973, 1942). Harmon lists five different B-17 attacks on Japanese surface forces, including the destroyer at Guadalcanal, by then end of August.

145 "The Slot" was the space between the New Georgian, San Isabel, and Guadalcanal island chains. All sea traffic proceeding to Guadalcanal had to proceed through the narrow passage of sea. See Figure 3.3.

146 Millard F Harmon, "Headquarters USAFISPA to COMSOPAC: 22 October 1942," in *Millard F. Harmon Papers*(United States Air Force Historical Agency, IRIS No. 260973, 1942). Harmon made the case to Admiral Ghormley that the B-17s needed to do less reconnaissance and more bombing.

147 See "Division Commanders Final Report on Guadalcanal Operations, Phase 4," Annex B(5).; and "Division Commanders Final Report on Guadalcanal Operations, Phase 5, 18 September–5 December 1942" (San Francisco: First Division United States Marine Corps, 1942), Annex T(8).

148 J. Britt McCarley, "General Nathan Farragut Twining: The Making of a Dis-

ciple of American Strategic Air Power, 1897–1953" (Disseration, Temple University, 1989), 60–61.

149 "Division Commanders Final Report on Guadalcanal Operations, Phase 4," 15. Vandegrift recorded, "The P-400s types were especially valuable in supporting ground activities although dive bombers were also employed on occasion. Both types were used with good effect in support of the Tasimboko raid [Marine raid of Japanese positions after Battle of Tenaru] in spite of poor air-ground communications"

150 Jersey, *Hell's Islands*, 249.

151 "Japanese Monograph No. 98" 39. On 17 September, the Japanese Imperial Naval staff recorded the shelling of supplies and the landing area at Tassafaronga point, which called off daytime operations.

152 "Division Commanders Final Report on Guadalcanal Operations, Phase 4," Annex C(4).

153 Bergerud, *Fire in the Sky*, 140–141.

154 Ugaki et al., *Fading Victory*, 200–201.

155 "Japanese Monograph No. 98" 33.

156 Bergerud, *Fire in the Sky*, 115–116.

157 Lundstrom, *The First Team and the Guadalcanal Campaign*, 289.

158 "Japanese Monograph No. 98" 32.

159 See Morison, *History of United States Naval Operations in World War II*, 5:149; and "Division Commanders Final Report on Guadalcanal Operations, Phase 5," Annex C(2). The only thing that interrupted these runs was the domination of Japanese destroyers by the Cactus Air Force on the morning of 8 October 1942 and again on the 9th, damaging one cruiser and one destroyer.

160 List of equipment and supplies from Boeicho Boei Kenshujo, Senshishitsu, and Asagumo Shin bun Sha, "War History Series, Southeast Area Navy Operations, Part 2, Up to Withdrawal from Guadalcanal, Vol. 83" (Japan: Defense Research Institute Defense Agency, Office of War History, 1975), as quoted in Frank, *Guadalcanal*, 330. The artillery pieces were 70 and 75 mm versions.

161 Morison, *History of United States Naval Operations in World War II*, 5:149.

162 Their rapid increase of soldiers from nine thousand in mid-September to more than twenty thousand via the Tokyo Express stretched their food supplies thin. On 1 September 1942, the Japanese had a food reserve of five days; with the extra troops and the limited capacity of the Tokyo Express, that reserve was consumed by the end of the month and was a deficit beyond ten days by early September. (See "Summary of Supply," this chapter, for a full discussion).

163 Robert Ghormley, "COMSOPAC to CINPAC Info COMAIRSOPAC, HARMON," in *Command Summary and Running Estimate of Chester A. Nimitz: 1941–1945*, 892. On 12 October 1942 Ghormley dispatched a note to Admiral Nimitz and Maj. Gen. Harmon discussing plans for bigger runways and bringing bombers onto the island—not for defensive purposes, but rather to use

Guadalcanal as the staging base for offensive movement further into the Solomons.

164   Hornfischer, *Neptune's Inferno*, 165.

165   Hornfischer, 168.

166   Hornfischer, 165.

167   Frank, *Guadalcanal*, 293.

168   Frank, 314.

169   Dull, *A Battle History of the Imperial Japanese Navy, 1941–1945*, 224. Naval Seabees worked furiously to repair the holes throughout the day on 13 October.

170   Hornfischer, *Neptune's Inferno*, 195.

171   "Division Commanders Final Report on Guadalcanal Operations, Phase 5," Annex Q(3). Before the bombing, the Cactus Air had thirty-nine SBDs, forty-one F4Fs, four P-400s, and six P-39s.

172   "Division Commanders Final Report on Guadalcanal Operations, Phase 5," Annex Z(8).

173   Morison, *History of United States Naval Operations in World War II*, 5:176.

174   "Division Commanders Final Report on Guadalcanal Operations, Phase 5," Annex Q(3).

175   Morison, *History of United States Naval Operations in World War II*, 5:179.

176   Morison, *History of United States Naval Operations in World War II*, 5:179–180.

177   "Division Commanders Final Report on Guadalcanal Operations, Phase 5," Annex Q(3).

178   See Frank, *Guadalcanal*, 324;"Japanese Monograph No. 98", 36; and Ugaki et al., *Fading Victory*, 232–233. The exact amount delivered is unknown. Frank estimates about two-thirds; Admiral Ugaki and the Japanese staff estimate put the delivered cargo at 80 percent. The transports also had many heavy artillery pieces and ammunitions. In another attempted delivery in November the Japanese used eleven transports (versus six) to deliver a thirty-day supply of food for thirty-thousand soldiers, about five thousand tons. Given this number, a reasonable estimate was two thousand tons of food for this delivery. See "Summary of Supply," this chapter, for full discussion.

179   Morison, *History of United States Naval Operations in World War II*, 5:177.

180   Frank, *Guadalcanal*, 328.

181   Millard F Harmon, "Headquarters USAFISPA to AGWAR WASH DC, 17 October 1942," in *Millard F. Harmon Papers* (United States Air Force Historical Agency, IRIS No. 260973, 1942).

182   As quoted in Frank, *Guadalcanal*, 405.

183   Nimitz, "CINCPAC to COMINCH, 16 October 1942," in *Command Summary and Running Estimate of Chester A Nimitz: 1941–1945*, 895.

184   "CINCPAC to COMINCH Info COMSOPAC, 27 October 1942," in *Command Summary and Running Estimate of Chester A. Nimitz: 1941–1945*, 898. Eight days after taking command, Halsey asked Nimitz for "1 or more carriers" of the British

Eastern Fleet. Given the paucity of British resources to hold Burma and cover the ocean between New Guinea and Australia, this speaks to Halsey's aggressiveness.

185 Leighton and Coakley, *Global Logistics and Strategy: 1940–1943*, 402.

186 "Division Commanders Final Report on Guadalcanal Operations, Phase 5," Annex Z(9).

187 See Washburne, *The Thirsty 13th*, 153. A C-47 navigator recorded in an interview with the author, "Typically four to five planes from each of the three squadrons [1 AAF and 2 USMC] went over per day, so twelve to fifteen planes, so we would see other planes, but not until we got close." See also Morison, *History of United States Naval Operations in World War II*, 5:179. The Americans also tried to up deliveries of aviation fuel by using whatever naval transportation vehicles they had. In just one example, the submarine *Amerijack* delivered almost ten thousand gallons of fuel and bombs to Lunga Point after the barrage.

188 See Frank, *Guadalcanal*, 365–366; and Washburne, *The Thirsty 13th*, 147.

189 Frank, *Guadalcanal*, 365–366. This was about 50 percent of their estimated strength.

190 Ferguson, *Guadalcanal*, 156–157.

191 "Division Commanders Final Report on Guadalcanal Operations, Phase 5," Annex I(6).

192 See Morison, *History of United States Naval Operations in World War II*, 5:204–206; and Hornfischer, *Neptune's Inferno*, 226.

193 Hornfischer

194 Lundstrom, *The First Team and the Guadalcanal Campaign*, 467. Thirteen of the aircraft were inoperable.

195 Frank, *Guadalcanal*, 426.

196 Frank, 434–435.

197 See Lundstrom, *The First Team and the Guadalcanal Campaign*, 447; and Hornfischer, *Neptune's Inferno*, 256–257. The new cruisers had the most advanced radar-guided antiaircraft guns of any navy of the time.

198 Lundstrom, *The First Team and the Guadalcanal Campaign*, 447.

199 See Lundstrom, 475.; and K. C. Carter and R. Mueller, *The Army Air Forces in World War II: Combat Chronology, 1941–1945* (Washington, DC: US Government Printing Office, 1975), 58.

200 Hornfischer, *Neptune's Inferno*, 256–257.

201 Hornfischer, 436.

202 Hornfischer, 325.

203 Frank, *Guadalcanal*, 464.

204 Frank, 465.

205 Frank, 465.

206 "Japanese Monograph No. 98," 48.

207 Frank, *Guadalcanal*, 486. Lee stated, "It should not be forgotten now, that our entire superiority was due almost entirely to our possession of radar."

208 Hornfischer, *Neptune's Inferno*, 436.
209 Frank, *Guadalcanal*, 487. Admiral Mikawa, the Eighth Fleet Commander, objected because this would make the landings more difficult.
210 *Japanese Naval and Merchant Vessels Losses During World War II*, 34. The exact units which "killed" the ships was indeterminate on 14 November (Cactus Air Force, *Enterprise*, or USAAF aircrew); on 15 November the destruction was entirely due to the aircraft from Henderson Field.
211 "Japanese Monograph No. 98," 490.
212 Frank, *Guadalcanal*, 502.
213 Frank, 502.
214 "Japanese Monograph No. 98," 56.
215 Hornfischer, *Neptune's Inferno*, 395.
216 Frank, *Guadalcanal*, 500–502.
217 "Japanese Monograph No. 98" 56.
218 As quoted in Frank, *Guadalcanal*, 527.
219 Hornfischer, *Neptune's Inferno*, 396.
220 Hornfischer, 396.
221 Frank, *Guadalcanal*, 552; Jersey, *Hell's Islands*, 382. First Lt. Marvin Ayers recorded in his diary on 5 February 1943, "Took supplies by mule to Company K."
222 Carter and Mueller, *The Army Air Forces in World War II*, 81–82. For example, on 14 and 15 January 1943, P39s dropped improvised bombs, with gasoline as incendiary, to assist the taking of Mount Austen.
223 Frank, *Guadalcanal*, 554–555.
224 Frank, 565.
225 Hornfischer, *Neptune's Inferno*, 404.
226 Hornfischer, 405–406.
227 Frank, *Guadalcanal*, 588.
228 Frank, 596. Numerous PT boats were also involved in the action, but the weather and haze disrupted them on one night and the Japanese caught them by surprise on the first night of deployment.
229 Frank, 597. The exact number of Japanese that were evacuated and casualties is approximate (some the Japanese were evacuated during Tokyo Express runs)
230 Vandegrift and Asprey, *Once a Marine*, 217–218.
231 Frank, *Guadalcanal*, 588.
232 "Japanese Monograph No. 98" 68.
233 See Dull, *A Battle History of the Imperial Japanese Navy, 1941–1945*, 216.; and Peterson, *An Analytical History of World War II*, 1:422.
234 See Hornfischer, *Neptune's Inferno*, 238–239; and Parshall, "Oil and Japanese Strategy in the Solomons: A Postulate."
235 Hornfischer, *Neptune's Inferno*, 408.
236 Frank, *Guadalcanal*. 329.
237 Frank, 329. Nimitz and King hoped the submarines would net a carrier or bat-

tleship by cruising in the waters off Truk and Rabaul. However, these were also the greatest areas of concentration for sea mines and antisubmarine warfare efforts of the Japanese.

238 S. P. Rosen, *Winning the Next War: Innovation and the Modern Military* (Ithaca, NY: Cornell University Press, 1991), 144–146.

239 *Japanese Naval and Merchant Vessels Losses During World War II*, vi. The thousands of ships added up to 4 million tons of shipping destroyed.

CHAPTER 4. SUMMER AND WINTER ON SOVIET STEPPES: STALINGRAD, 1942–1943

1 James S. Corum, *The Luftwaffe: Creating the Operational Air War, 1918–1940* (Lawrence: University Press of Kansas, 1997), 200.

2 Jobie Turner, "Technogeopologistics: Supply Networks and Military Power in the Industrial Age" (Thesis, Air University, 2012), 148–149.

3 Richard J. Overy, "Transportation and Rearmament in the Third Reich," *Historical Journal* 16, no. 2 (1973): 398.

4 See Turner, "Technogeopologistics," 150.; and Avro L. Vecamer, "Deutsche Reichsbahn—The German State Railway in WWII," German Armed Forces Research 1918–1945, accessed 20 January 2016, http://www.feldgrau.com/dreichs bahn.htm. In addition, the number of trains traveling to the east swelled from 84 per day after the invasion of Poland, to 220 trains by the beginning of Barbarossa.

5 Overy, "Transportation and Rearmament in the Third Reich," 406.

6 Keith Earle Bonn, ed., *Slaughterhouse: The Handbook of the Eastern Front* (Bedford, PA: Aberjona Press, 2005), 18.

7 See Appendix for comparison of technologies across all eras.

8 Martin van Creveld, *Supplying War: Logistics from Wallenstein to Patton* (New York: Cambridge University Press, 1977), 167.

9 Richard R. Muller, *The German Air War in Russia* (Baltimore: Nautical & Aviation Publishing Company of America, 1992), 41.

10 Bonn, *Slaughterhouse*, 18.

11 Van Creveld, *Supplying War*, 155, 160. Van Creveld remarks that this was "a procedure probably unique in the annuals of modern war."

12 See "Google Maps: Driving Directions from Brest to Moscow," accessed 20 January 2016, https://www.google.com/maps/dir/Moscow,+Russia/Brest,+Belarus /@53.1074896,21.8239257,7z/data=!4m13!4m12!1m5!1m1!1s0x46b54afc73d4b0c9:0 x3d44d6cc5757cf4c!2m2!1d37.6173!2d55.755826!1m5!1m1!1s0x47210c0223630975: 0x4d319ea41f64ae99!2m2!1d23.7340503!2d52.0976214; and Van Creveld, *Supplying War*, 155. Distances from the German forces in the south approached nine hundred miles.

13 Bonn, *Slaughterhouse*, 17.

14 See James S. Corum, *Wolfram Von Richthofen: Master of the German Air War*

(Lawrence: University Press of Kansas, 2008), 261. Corum avers, "The Soviet air force in 1941 was strong on paper—but only on paper." Stalin's purge of the officer corps of the military department in the late 1930s plagued all the services at the start of the war—the Red air force most acutely. See also Muller, *The German Air War in Russia*, 38. The Germans had 3,904 aircraft on the Eastern Front at the start of the invasion; of those, 3,032 were available for operations by June 1942. See also Larry H. Addington, *The Blitzkrieg Era and the German General Staff, 1865–1941* (New Brunswick, NJ: Rutgers University Press, 1971), 4–5.

15 Generalmajor a.D. Fritz Morzik, "German Air Force Airlift Operations," Research Studies Instititute, USAF Historical Division (Maxwell Air Force Base, AL: Air University, 1961), 137.

16 Morzik, "German Air Force Airlift Operations," 137

17 Morzik, "German Air Force Airlift Operations," 168. Supply by parachute drops is also called airdrop.

18 Morzik, "German Air Force Airlift Operations," 137.

19 Morzik, "German Air Force Airlift Operations," 137. There were still battles all over the front; in fact, Demyansk was not completely free of Soviet encirclement until May 1942, but the major campaigns ended as the muddy season began in late winter.

20 Antony Beevor, *Stalingrad: The Fateful Siege 1942–1943* (London: Viking, 1998), 32–33. Hitler did not supply his army with winter gear and in fact avoided the logistics of the campaign in part due to "a superstitious avoidance of Napoleon's footsteps" and also because "he ignored practical problems," such as the fundamentals of logistics.

21 See David M. Glantz and Jonathan M. House, *To The Gates of Stalingrad: Soviet-German Combat Operations, April–August 1942* (Lawrence: University Press of Kansas, 2009), 5; and Bonn, *Slaughterhouse*, 205.

22 Glantz and House, *To The Gates of Stalingrad*, 46.

23 Beevor, *Stalingrad*, 82.

24 "Wehrkraft der Wehrmacht im Frühjahr 1942, F.H. Qu., den 6 Juni 1942," in *1939–1945: Der Zweite Weltkrieg in Chronik und Dokumenten*, ed. Hans-Adolf Jacobsen (Darmstadt, Germany: Wehr und Wissen, 1961), 319–320.

25 Stephen G. Fritz, *Ostkrieg: Hitler's War of Extermination in the East* (Lexington: The University Press of Kentucky, 2011), 223. Fritz's magisterial work gives a full accounting of the Third Reich's plans to conquer, exploit, and exterminate all those living in the East to create *lebensraum* for German peoples. The slave labor camps were inefficient and too ideologically bound to *Arbeit Macht Frei* to produce meaningful results.

26 As quoted in Beevor, *Stalingrad*, 62.

27 Joseph Goebbels, "Aus den Goebbels-Tagebuchen: 20 Marz 1942 (Frietag)," in *1939–1945: Der Zweite Weltkrieg in Chronik und Dokumenten*, 296.

28 Goebbels, "Aus den Goebbels-Tagebuchen: 20 Marz 1942 (Frietag)," 296.

29 Adolf Hitler, "Weisung 41, F.H. Qu, Der Fuhrer under Oberste Befehlshaber der Werhmact an Geheime Kommandosache / Chef-Sache / Nur Durch Offizier, den 5.4.1952," in *1939–1945: Der Zweite Weltkrieg in Chronik und Dokumenten*, 297.

30 I. C. B. Dear and M. R. D. Foot, *The Oxford Companion to World War II* (New York: Oxford University Press, 1995), 1059. The Germans lost two hundred thousand in the final encirclement of the Soviet Union at Stalingrad and six hundred thousand in the battles preceding the isolation of the Sixth Army.

31 Erhard Rauss et al., *Fighting in Hell: The German Ordeal on the Eastern Front* (London: Greenhill Books, 1995), 176–177.

32 Max Bork, "Comments on Russian Railroads and Highways," All World Wars, accessed 2 February 2016, http://www.allworldwars.com/Comments-on-Russian-Roads-and-Higways-by-Max-Bork.html.

33 Bork, "Comments on Russian Railroads and Highways."

34 Rauss et al., *Fighting in Hell*, 176–177. The Germans attempted to compensate for the smaller numbers of vehicles available by scrounging from conquered territories and captured Soviet machines; however, Barbarossa and the winter environment had claimed too many for a full replacement

35 Omer Bartov, *Hitler's Army: Soldiers, Nazis, and War in the Third Reich* (New York: Oxford University Press, 1991), 12–28.

36 *Military Improvisations During the Russian Campaign*, vol. CMH Pub 104–1 (Washington, DC: Center of Military History, US Army, 1986), 51–52.

37 Vecamer, "Deutsche Reichsbahn—The German State Railway in WWII."

38 See Corum, *Wolfram Von Richthofen*, 281; Glantz and House, *To The Gates of Stalingrad*, 8; and Muller, *The German Air War in Russia*, 39. Two thousand is an approximation. Corum lists the number as 1,700, Glantz at 2,635; both are secondary sources. Muller lists 3,082 operational in 1941 from the German staff reports of the time.

39 Glantz and House, *To The Gates of Stalingrad*, 5.

40 Glantz and House, *To the Gates of Stalingrad*, 7.

41 Adam Tooze, *The Wages of Destruction: The Making and Breaking of the Nazi Economy* (New York: Penguin, 2006), 326–327.

42 Fritz, *Ostkrieg*, 223.

43 Tooze, *The Wages of Destruction*, 277.

44 In the infamous "Stab in the Back" mythology, a critical component of Nazi justification for war, it was the collapse of the home-front economy, not the loss on the battlefield, that caused Germany's defeat in the Great War.

45 Fritz, *Ostkrieg*, 223.

46 David M. Glantz, *Colossus Reborn: The Red Army at War, 1941–1943* (Lawrence: University Press of Kansas, 2005), 17.

47 Walter S. Dunn, *The Soviet Economy and the Red Army, 1930–1945* (Santa Barbara, CA: Greenwood Publishing Group, 1995), 43.

48 Sanford R. Lieberman, "The Evacuation of Industry in the Soviet Union During World War II," *Soviet Studies* 35, no. 1 (1983): 90–91.
49 Lieberman, "The Evacuation of Industry," 91.
50 Dunn, *The Soviet Economy and the Red Army, 1930–1945,* 75.
51 Gerhard L. Weinberg, *A World at Arms: A Global History of World War II* (New York: Cambridge University Press, 1994), 308.
52 See Dunn, *The Soviet Economy and the Red Army, 1930–1945,* 699–705; and D. A. Bertke, G. Smith, and D. Kindell, *World War II Sea War, Vol 6: The Allies Halt the Axis Advance* (Dayton, OH: Bertke Publications, 2014), 171.
53 Dunn, *The Soviet Economy and the Red Army, 1930–1945,* 70. Dunn states, "In only a few days the Germans sank as many tanks as the combined Russian and British land forces were able to destroy in two months."
54 David M. Glantz, *Kharkov, 1942: Anatomy of a Military Disaster* (Rockville Center, NY: Sarpedon, U.S., 1998), 20.
55 Joseph Stalin, "Order of the Day No. 130, May 1, 1942," in *On the Great Patriotic War of the Soviet Union* (Moscow: Foreign Languages Publishing House, 1946), 55.
56 Glantz and House, *To The Gates of Stalingrad,* 85; and Glantz and House, *To the Gates of Stalingrad,* 77. Before moving to attack Sevastopol, the German army needed to clear the Kerch peninsula to isolate the Soviet army in the Fortress of Sevastopol.
57 Glantz and House, *To the Gates of Stalingrad,* 75.
58 "Opisanie operatsii voisk iugo-zapadnom fronta na khar'kovskom napravlenii v mae 1942 goda (Account of Operations by Southwestern Front Forces on the Kharkov Axis in May 1942)," in *Collection of Military-Historical Materials of the Great Patriotic War,* Issue 5 (Moscow: Classified Secret 1951, Declassified 1964), as translated in Glantz, *Kharkov, 1942,* 45–48.
59 See "Opisanie operatsii voisk iugo-zapadnom fronta na khar'kovskom napravlenii v mae 1942 goda (Account of Operations by Southwestern Front Forces on the Kharkov Axis in May 1942)," as translated in Glantz, *Kharkov, 1942,* 260. These pages list armies and the equipment. See also G. F. Krivosheev, *Grif sekretnosti sniat: poteri Voruzhennykh Sil SSSR v voinakh, boevykh deistviiakh i voennykh konfliktakh: statisticheskoe issledovanie* (Moscow: Voenizdat, 1993), as translated in David M. Glantz and Jonathan M. House, *When Titans Clashed: How the Red Army Stopped Hitler* (Lawrence: University Press of Kansas, 1995), 295. This page lists personnel sizes. See also Von Hardesty, *Red Phoenix: The Rise of Soviet Air Power, 1941–1945,* 1st ed. (Washington, DC: Smithsonian Institution Press, 1982), 288.
60 "Opisanie operatsii voisk iugo-zapadnom fronta na khar'kovskom napravlenii v mae 1942 goda (Account of Operations by Southwestern Front Forces on the Kharkov Axis in May 1942)," as translated in Glantz, *Kharkov, 1942,* 58.
61 Glantz and House, *To The Gates of Stalingrad,* 79.

62 Glantz and House, *To the Gates of Stalingrad*, 79.

63 "Opisanie operatsii voisk iugo-zapadnom fronta na khar'kovskom napravlenii v mae 1942 goda (Account of Operations by Southwestern Front Forces on the Kharkov Axis in May 1942)," as translated in Glantz, *Kharkov, 1942*, 122.

64 As quoted in Glantz, *Kharkov, 1942*, 123.

65 Glantz and House, *To The Gates of Stalingrad*, 79–81.

66 "Opisanie operatsii voisk iugo-zapadnom fronta na khar'kovskom napravlenii v mae 1942 goda (Account of Operations by Southwestern Front Forces on the Kharkov Axis in May 1942)," as translated in Glantz, *Kharkov, 1942*, 235.

67 As quoted in Glantz, *Kharkov, 1942*, 123.

68 Andrew J. Brookes, *Air War Over Russia* (Shepperton, United Kingdom: Ian Allan Publishing, 2003), 78.

69 "Opisanie operatsii voisk iugo-zapadnom fronta na khar'kovskom napravlenii v mae 1942 goda (Account of Operations by Southwestern Front Forces on the Kharkov Axis in May 1942)," as translated in Glantz, *Kharkov, 1942*, 235.

70 "Opisanie operatsii voisk iugo-zapadnom fronta na khar'kovskom napravlenii v mae 1942 goda (Account of Operations by Southwestern Front Forces on the Kharkov Axis in May 1942)," as translated in Glantz, *Kharkov, 1942*, 235–236.

71 Glantz and House, *To The Gates of Stalingrad*, 79.

72 Glantz and House, *To the Gates of Stalingrad*, 80.

73 Krivosheev, *Grif sekretnosti sniat: poteri Voruzhennykh Sil SSSR v voinakh, boevykh deistviiakh i voennykh konfliktakh: statisticheskoe issledovanie*, as translated in Glantz and House, *When Titans Clashed*, 295.

74 Fritz, *Ostkrieg*, 262–263.

75 Richard J. Overy, *The Air War, 1939–1945* (Washington, DC: Potomac Books, 2005), 55.

76 Erich von Manstein and Anthony G. Powell, *Lost Victories* (Novato, CA: Presido Press, 1994), 268. Added to this, the head of the Luftwaffe, Hermann Göring, began to promise Luftwaffe ground units, made up of highly skilled maintenance troops, to help bolster the *Wehrmacht* after its losses in the first year of war in the east. In his memoirs, General Von Manstein noted the grandiose promise was not based on reality: "To form these excellent troops into divisions within the framework of the Luftwaffe was sheer lunacy. . . . Where were they to get the battle experience so vital in the east? And where was the Luftwaffe to find divisional, regimental and battalion commanders?"

77 Hermann Plocher, "The Russian Campaign 1941–1945, Volume 4: Employment of the Luftwaffe in the Eastern Theater, 1942," in *Personal Papers of Lt. Gen. William H. Tunner* (USAF Historical Research Center, IRIS No. 468075), 1. Plocher was the chief of staff for the *Lufwaffen-Kommando Ost* and commander of the *1.Flieger Division* in 1942.

78 "Luftversorgung der Festung Demjansk während ihrer Einschließ ung vom

15.11 bei zum 19.V.1942," in Karlsruhe Collection (Maxwell Air Force Base, AL: Air Force Historical Research Agency, IRIS Number 468333, 1956), 52.

79 Glantz and House, *To The Gates of Stalingrad*, 121.

80 Glantz and House, *To The Gates of Stalingrad*, 124.

81 Joel S. A. Hayward, *Stopped at Stalingrad: The Luftwaffe and Hitler's Defeat in the East, 1942–1943* (Lawrence: University Press of Kansas, 1998), 135.

82 Hayward, *Stopped at Stalingrad*, 137.

83 As quoted in Glantz and House, *To The Gates of Stalingrad*, 133. General Vasilevsky, chief of the Red Army General Staff, replaced Golikov due to his lack of ability to "control his forces effectively" in the face of the German offensive.

84 Glantz and House, *To The Gates of Stalingrad*, 149.

85 Glantz and House, *To The Gates of Stalingrad*, 152–153. According to Glantz, the Luftwaffe broke off attacks against Soviet tanks if they were too close to German units.

86 Glantz and House, *To The Gates of Stalingrad*, 149.

87 Glantz and House, *To The Gates of Stalingrad*, 165. Glantz avers, "Although the Soviets enjoyed a better than twofold superiority in armor along both axes during Blau I, in the end the Soviets' lamentably poor logistical support system—particularly with regard to vital fuel and ammunition—and the inability of its tank force commanders to lead their armies . . . largely negated this advantage."

88 Glantz and House, *To The Gates of Stalingrad*, 165; and Beevor, *Stalingrad*, 75–76. The "10-Kilometer" quote is from Beevor.

89 Beevor, *Stalingrad*, 77.

90 Beevor, 78.

91 Glantz and House, *To The Gates of Stalingrad*, 191.

92 Glantz and House, *To The Gates of Stalingrad*, 191. Hitler fired Bock for his disagreement and replaced him with General Von Wiechs. The debate on how complicit the German General Staff and the *Wehrmacht* Army were in the decision to split the forces is important in the historiography of Stalingrad. Glantz has an even approach—Hitler taking much of the blame, but German officers also suffered from overoptimistic thinking in the wake of the victories that piled up in the summer of 1942.

93 Glantz and House, *When Titans Clashed*, 295. The exact total of Soviet casualties and material losses on 9 July 1942 are unknown. This total includes those Soviet losses as the 4th Panzer Army drove to encircle the Soviets around Rostov as well.

94 Hitler, "Weisung Nr. 45 für die Fortsetzung der Operation 'Braunschweig,'" 338–340.

95 Glantz and House, *To The Gates of Stalingrad*, 207–208.

96 Glantz and House, *To The Gates of Stalingrad*, 319.

97 Glantz and House, *To The Gates of Stalingrad*, 319.

98 As quoted in Beevor, *Stalingrad*, 101, 107.

99 Glantz and House, *To The Gates of Stalingrad,* 319.

100 "Conversations with a Stuka Pilot: Paul-Werner Hozzel" (Washington, DC: National War College, Air Force Historical Research Agency, IRIS No. 1095079, 1978), 219–220.

101 Christer Bergstrom and Martin Pegg, *The War in Russia: January–October 1943,* Vol. 4, Section 3, *Jagdwaffe* (Sheppterton, United Kingdom: Classic Publications, 2004). The internal instrumentation of German fighters was such that flying in the clouds was more of an emergency procedure than an everyday operation. By late fall, the Luftwaffe would begin to improve its abilities with navigation beacons and receiver sets placed on transportation aircraft to help guide through the clouds, but in the summer of 1942, with good weather, this was not a concern.

102 See chapter 3 for similar examples during Guadalcanal.

103 "Tagesaoschulessmelding, 7.17.42, Generalkommando, VIII Fliegerkorps," in Karlsruhe Collection (Maxwell Air Force Base, AL: Air Force Historical Research Agency, IBIS No. 468332, 1942), Slide 0090. This specific end-of-day record states that seven hundred railcars were stationary at the Krasnodar train station, the major rail intersection south of Rostov and adjacent to the Kersch Peninsula. The reports from July 11, 12, and 16 also mention Soviet rail positions.

104 Hayward, *Stopped at Stalingrad,* 142.

105 See Muller, *The German Air War in Russia,* 92. Muller was the first scholar to note that "the employment of the Luftwaffe in an emergency air transport role was not an unusual practice on the eastern front by late 1942." See also Hans Detlef Herhudt Von Rhoden, "The Stalingrad Airlift: A Brief Summary of the Facts Involved," in *The Papers of Lt. Gen. William Tunner* (Maxwell Air Force Base, AL: Air Force Historical Research Agency, IRIS No. 10910955, 1949), 6; and Peter C. Smith and Martin Pegg, *Transporter:* Luftwaffe *Transport Units 1943–45: V. 2* (Shepperton, United Kingdom: Classic Publications, 2006), 133. The capacity of a Ju-52 was 1.5–2 tons. It could carry seventeen fully loaded troops or cargo. The C-47 of the United States military had a larger capacity of 3 tons.

106 Glantz and House, *To The Gates of Stalingrad,* 267. See Table 16.

107 See "Tiger I information center—the Maybach engine," accessed 4 February 2016, http://www.alanhamby.com/maybach.shtml; and Carnegie Library of Pittsburgh. Science Technology Department, *Science and Technology Desk Reference: 1,500 Answers to Frequently-Asked or Difficult-to-Answer Questions* (Farmington Hills, MI: Gale Research, 1993), 539. Tiger 1 tanks had 150-gallon tanks. Gasoline for vehicles weighed 6.3 pounds per gallon. The Germans did not have diesel variants in their engines. The tons here are metric tons or 2,200 lbs.

108 Dear and Foot, *The Oxford Companion to World War II,* 695; "Divisional Struc-

ture (Germany, UK, France USA)," accessed 4 February 2016, http://www
.mnstarfire.com/ww2/history/land/division.html.This website lists the German
fuel usage as three hundred tons per day per division. By the summer of 1942,
there were fewer vehicles than the full complement of three thousand due to
attrition from the war.

109   Glantz and House, *To The Gates of Stalingrad*, 267. At the time, the Sixth Army
was composed of the Sixth and Twenty-Fourth Panzer Divisions and the Third
and Sixtieth Motorized Divisions based on the numbers of tanks associated
with each division—the Sixth Army was a little larger than two divisions in
mechanized strength.

110   Von Rhoden, "The Stalingrad Airlift," 6.

111   See "BMW 132," Wikimedia Foundation, accessed 5 February 2016, https://
en.wikipedia.org/wiki/BMW_132. At cruise, the BMW 132 engine burned 0.53
pounds of gasoline per horsepower per hour and produced 779 hp. Each engine burned 412 pounds per hour or roughly 1,240 pounds per hour for the
three engines on the Ju-52. See also "Opel Blitz: Multi-Purpose Medium
Truck," accessed 29 August 2019. https://www.militaryfactory.com/armor/de
tail.asp?armor_id=519. The range of an Opel truck in rugged conditions was
130 miles with a 21.5-gallon tank—6 miles per gallon. At a speed of 20 miles
an hour, the fuel burn rate for an Opel equated to 21 pounds of fuel per hour.
See also Robert Forczyk, *Tank Warfare on the Eastern Front 1941–1942: Schwerpunkt* (South Yorkshire, England: Pen & Sword Books Limited, 2014), 29.
Forcyzk states, "Each *Panzer* Division required one V.S. (Verbrauchssatz) of
fuel, equivalent to . . . 92.3 tons. . . . Each *Panzer* division started with three organic fuel companies with 30 trucks that could carry 75cbm of fuel or 0.6 V.S."
Each Opel 36S truck carried 1.846 tons. One aircraft could move between 1.5–2
tons of cargo, the same as the Opel 36S German fuel truck with a potential to
deliver the cargo over a farther distance faster.

112   Horst Boog, "Luftwaffe and Logistics in the Second World War," *Aerospace
Historian* 35, no. 2 (1988), 103–104. Boog details the complex, stove-piped, and
bureaucratic system of Logistics that supported the Luftwaffe.

113   Beevor, *Stalingrad*, 267. In one example of many, "Hitler's chief adjutant . . .
was preoccupied with 'alterations to the uniforms of officers and Wehrmacht
officials.'"

114   Von Rhoden, "The Stalingrad Airlift," 6.

115   Beevor, *Stalingrad*, 77. Beevor recounts numerous instances of the vast looting
that took place in all of the Soviet villages: "There is an unsettling disparity in
many accounts, with no connections made between horrifying scenes and their
involvement, 'A really small boy stood in our way,' wrote a twenty year-old the-
ology student in a letter. 'He no longer begged, he just muttered: "*Pan*, bread."
It was eerie how much sorrow suffering and apathy could exist in a child's
face.'"

116 See Fritz, *Ostkrieg*, 217–218. Fritz sums up the strategic thinking with Hitler and leaders of the Third Reich about how to best deal with those conquered populations. See also Center for Military, *Military Improvisations During the Russian Campaign*, CMH Pub 104-1, 40–42. The actions of the Germans against those conquered peoples most naturally aligned to become future allies did not make much difference in the successful headlong pushes to the Caucuses and Stalingrad in the summer of 1942. During their long retreat over the next three years, their previous hostility gained the Wehrmacht significant numbers of partisan enemies who attacked their rail and supply lines from the Fatherland.

117 As quoted in Beevor, *Stalingrad,* 88.

118 Beevor, 92.

119 Beevor, 91.

120 "Opisanie operatsii voisk iugo-zapadnom fronta na khar'kovskom napravlenii v mae 1942 goda (Account of Operations by Southwestern Front Forces on the Kharkov Axis in May 1942)" as translated in Glantz, *Kharkov, 1942,* 128.

121 Glantz and House, *To The Gates of Stalingrad,* 308. The Stalingrad Front facing the Germans had anywhere between 0.28 and1.9 days of ammunitions and 1.4–3.2 days of fuel during the late summer fighting.

122 General Staff of the Red Army, "Death to the German Invaders: Collection of Materials on the Study of War Experince No. 2, September–October 1942, Position Concerning the Organization and Operation of the Army Rear," in *Soviet Documents on the Use of War Experience,* ed. and trans. Harold S. Orenstein (Portland, OR: Frank Cass, 1991), 231.

123 General Staff of the Red Army, "Death to the German Invaders," 231.

124 General Staff of the Red Army, "Death to the German Invaders," 232.

125 General Staff of the Red Army, "Death to the German Invaders," 232.

126 General Staff of the Red Army, "Death to the German Invaders," 218–219.

127 General Staff of the Red Army, "Death to the German Invaders," 222.

128 General Staff of the Red Army, "Death to the German Invaders," 222.

129 See General Staff of the Red Army, "Death to the German Invaders," 227, 230. See also People's Commissar of Defense, "Death to the German Invaders: Collection of Materials on the Study of War Experince No. 2, September–October 1942, Order of the People's Commissar of Defense No. 325, 16 Ocober 1942," in *Soviet Documents on the Use of War Experience,* ed. and trans. Harold S. Orenstein (Portland, OR: Frank Cass, 1991), 239. The *Stavka* recommended the same command-and-control arrangement for direct combat support and reinforcement: "After uninterrupted combat actions action 5–6 days, it is necessary for the corps to have 2–3 days to renew material and replenish reserves. . . . It is necessary to cover reliably from the air and reinforce combat actions . . . with air defense artillery means and aviation.

130 For the Soviets, centralized control of logistics fit neatly within the ideological bounds of communism and was thus political safe to recommend.

131 Joseph Stalin, "NKO Order No. 227 (28 July 1942)," in *Companion to Colossus Reborn: Key Documents and Statistics* ed. David M. Glantz (Lawrence: University Press of Kansas, 2005), 18.

132 Glantz and House, *To The Gates of Stalingrad*, 484.

133 Glantz and House, *To The Gates of Stalingrad*, 480.

134 Glantz and House, *To The Gates of Stalingrad*, 480.

135 Glantz and House, *To The Gates of Stalingrad*, 483.

136 Williamson Murray, *Strategy for Defeat, the* Luftwaffe, *1933–1945* (Maxwell Air Force Base, AL: Air University Press, 1983), 114.

137 Murray, *Strategy for Defeat*, 124.

138 Adolf Hitler, "Weisung 41, F.H. Qu, Der Fuhrer under Oberste Befehlshaber der Werhmact an Geheime Kommandosache / Chef-Sache / Nur Durch Offizier, den 5.4.1952," 299–300. Stalingrad was a subgoal and to be isolated versus taken in the original plan for Operation Blau.

139 See Muller, *The German Air War in Russia*, 90; and "Die Staerke der Deutschen Luftwaffe an der Ostfront," in Karlsruhe Collection, IRIS No. 468332, Slides 0608–0611 (Maxwell Air Force Base, AL: Air Force Historical Research Agency), 2–6.

140 As quoted in Beevor, *Stalingrad*, 103. "Die Staerke der Deutschen Luftwaffe an der Ostfront," 2–6. Luftflotte 4 had 642 operational aircraft on 20 August 1942, not including eight seaplanes.

141 Beevor, *Stalingrad*, 148.

142 See David M. Glantz, *Armageddon in Stalingrad: September–November 1942* (Lawrence: University Press of Kansas, 2009), 198; Hayward, *Stopped at Stalingrad*, 201. German casualties are from Hayward.

143 David M. Glantz, *Companion to Colossus Reborn: Key Documents and Statistics* (Lawrence: University Press of Kansas, 2005), 82–88. In Appendix 2 Glantz translated Soviet General Staff meeting notes, which recorded the beginnings of Operation Uranus starting on 27 September 1942.

144 Hayward, *Stopped at Stalingrad*, 210.

145 As quoted in Muller, *The German Air War in Russia*, 91.

146 Beevor, *Stalingrad*, 89.

147 Glantz, *Armageddon in Stalingrad: September–November 1942*, 107.

148 V. I. Chuĭkov, *The Battle for Stalingrad* (New York: Holt, 1964), 113.

149 Chuĭkov, *The Battle for Stalingrad*, 115.

150 Chuĭkov, *The Battle for Stalingrad*, 115.

151 Chuĭkov, *The Battle for Stalingrad*, 117.

152 Hayward, *Stopped at Stalingrad*, 199.

153 Beevor, *Stalingrad*, 213.

154 Beevor, 200.

155 Beevor, 155.

156 Chuĭkov, *The Battle for Stalingrad*, 207.

157 Beevor, *Stalingrad*, 431.

158 Chuĭkov, *The Battle for Stalingrad*, 207.

159 As quoted in Glantz, *Armageddon in Stalingrad*, 699.

160 Glantz, *Armageddon in Stalingrad*, 293.

161 Glantz, *Armageddon in Stalingrad*, 107.

162 Glantz, *Armageddon in Stalingrad*, 293. The attack on the Worker's Village was supported by "as many as 7,000 bombs on defenders.

163 Glantz, *Armageddon in Stalingrad*, 293.

164 Vasily Grossman, Antony Beevor, and Luba Vinogradova, *A Writer at War: Vasily Grossman with the Red Army, 1941–1945* (New York: Pantheon Books, 2006), 167.

165 Grossman et al., *A Writer at War* 167–170. As at Guadalcanal, the Volga Flotilla cursed moonlight nights, which made crossing the water, in view of German artillery spotters, very dangerous.

166 "Conversations with a Stuka Pilot: Paul-Werner Hozzel," 125.

167 Murray, *Strategy for Defeat*, 114.

168 As quoted in Hayward, *Stopped at Stalingrad*, 209.

169 Hayward, 225.

170 Hayward, 208. Hayward states, "[On October 10,] even in the absence of most German fighter groups, which flew south to escort bombers and dive-bombers attacking Tuapse and enemy troops opposing German armies, the VVS seemed unable to exploit the situation and press home their attacks with greater safety and consequent success.

171 Hayward, , 265.

172 Hayward, , 300–301.

173 Morzik, "German Air Force Airlift Operations," 165.

174 Hayward, *Stopped at Stalingrad*, 219.

175 Hayward, 252–253.

176 Hayward, 226–227.

177 Frank Ellis, *The Stalingrad Cauldron: Inside the Encirclement and Destruction of the 6th Army*, Modern War Studies (Lawrence: University Press of Kansas, 2013), 12.

178 Beevor, *Stalingrad*, 211.

179 Glantz, *Armageddon in Stalingrad*, 373.

180 As quoted in Glantz, *Armageddon in Stalingrad*, 462.

181 As quoted in Glantz, *Armageddon in Stalingrad*, 463see also 715–717. Glantz gives the two numbers as an estimate and lays out in detail the sources and contradictions in both. While the losses of the Axis armies of Germany, Hungary, Italy, and Romanian did not approximate the Soviet numbers of 1.2 million, by the middle of November two hundred thousand Axis soldiers were casualties.

182 Beevor, *Stalingrad*, 211.

183 Beevor, 211. Beevor has no reference for this information; however, the data

from Glantz, *Companion to Endgame at Stalingrad*, 251, reflects similar information from primary sources of the Sixth Army.

184   Beevor, 211.

185   David M. Glantz, *Companion to Endgame at Stalingrad* (Lawrence: University Press of Kansas, 2014), 251. Glantz uses two separate primary source references from Oberkommando 6 staff reports—one from 16 November the other from 15 December—to piece together the capability of the Sixth Army to move before and after the Soviet counterattack.

186   Glantz, *Companion to Endgame at Stalingrad*, 251.

187   Grossman et al., *A Writer at War*, 170.

188   See Grossman et al., 170–171; and Glantz, *Armageddon in Stalingrad*, 315.

189   "Conversations with a Stuka Pilot: Paul-Werner Hozzel," 127–128.

190   See "Conversations with a Stuka Pilot: Paul-Werner Hozzel," 127–128. See also Hayward, *Stopped at Stalingrad*, 194. In 1978, German Luftwaffe pilot, Major Hozell, recalled a maximum of 800 per day. Richthofen however in his official correspondence noted an average of 938 sorties per day, across the whole front, to include the Caucasus.

191   Glantz, *Armageddon in Stalingrad*, 716.

192   Chuĭkov, *The Battle for Stalingrad*, 209.

193   Hayward, *Stopped at Stalingrad*, 220–221.

194   "Appendix 2—Soviet Strategic Planning and Genesis of Plan Uranus, " in Glantz, *Companion to Endgame at Stalingrad*, 82. In this appendix, Glantz translated and collated numerous primary sources from the Soviet archives to trace the planning for Operation Uranus. See Appendix 2, 97, 101, 103, and 104 for Soviet archival source data.

195   "Appendix 4: Table 10—The Russian View on the Correlation of Opposing Forces in Operation Uranus," in Glantz, *Companion to Endgame at Stalingrad*, 136. Glantz considers these numbers the most accurate. He states, "The fifth and probably most accurate assessment was compiled by Aleksei Isaev in his 2008 book *Stalingrad: There Is No Land for us Beyond the Volga River.*" Glantz presents an exhaustive look at the historiography of Soviet sources and the numbers of troops engaged in Operation Uranus, which correlate to official Soviet propaganda and ideology at the time of research.

196   See Commander of the 5th Tank Army, "Combat Order no. 01/op, Headquarters, 5th TA [Tank Army], Izbushenskii, 11 November 1942," in Glantz, *Companion to Endgame at Stalingrad*, 113.

197   See "Combat Directive of the Commander of the Forces of the Stalingrad Front to the Commander of the 5th Tank Army, 8 November 1942," in Glantz, *Companion to Endgame at Stalingrad*, 109.

198   Hans Ulrich Rudel, *Stuka Pilot*, trans. Lynton Hudson (Dublin, Ireland: Euphorion Books, 1952), 63.

199   Glantz, *Colossus Reborn*, 103–104, 125.

200 Hayward, *Stopped at Stalingrad,* 219–220.

201 Hayward, 224.

202 Glantz, *Armageddon in Stalingrad,* 682.

203 As quoted Beevor, *Stalingrad,* 213–214. According to Antony Beevor, "His speech ranked among the greatest examples of hubris in history.

204 See "Die Staerke der Deutschen Luftwaffe an der Ostfront, 20.10.1942," in Karlsruhe Collection, IRIS No. 468332 (Maxwell Air Force Base, AL: Air Force Historical Research Agency), Slides 0612–15; and "Die Staerke der Deutschen Luftwaffe an der Ostfront, 20.11.1942," in Karlsruhe Collection, IRIS No. 468332 (Maxwell Air Force Base, AL: Air Force Historical Research Agency), Slides 0620–23. Fliegerkorps IV also had five seaplanes. Even though the majority of these aircraft supported Stalingrad, there were still many aircraft stationed down south, attempting to help the stalled offensive of Army Group A.

205 Fritz, *Ostkrieg,* 311.

206 Glantz, *Companion to Endgame at Stalingrad,* 251.

207 Fritz, *Ostkrieg,* 310.

208 Rudel, *Stuka Pilot,* 65.

209 Hayward, *Stopped at Stalingrad,* 228–230.

210 Friedrich Paulus, "Funksrpuch geh. K.dos., Chefsache! An OKH, 2345 Uhr, 23.11.42," in Glantz, *Companion to Endgame at Stalingrad,* 188. This is Glantz's translation; he titles the document "Message from General Paulus to Higler, 2345 hours on 23 November 1942 versus Paulus's urgent and somewhat informal (Chefsache! [translated loosely as a "Matter for the boss!"])

211 Fritz, *Ostkrieg,* 310.

212 Beevor, *Stalingrad,* 277–278. This is not to say that Soviet logistics were perfect—they also suffered in the cold weather, which slowed the offensive. In addition, the sheer size of the army led to inevitable supply shortages for certain units.

213 See David M. Glantz and Jonathan M. House, *Endgame at Stalingrad* (Lawrence: University Press of Kansas, 2014), 14. Glantz references the Luftwaffe staff's estimate that 750 tons a day was the required number, with 500 tons a day the "get by" amount and 300 tons a day the minimum. See also Hayward, *Stopped at Stalingrad,* 243–246.; and Muller, *The German Air War in Russia,* 92–101. Hayward and Muller have full discussions on the tonnage and the decision to airlift.

214 Hayward, *Stopped at Stalingrad,* 246.

215 The German word for cauldron or kettle was *Kessel.*

216 Hayward, *Stopped at Stalingrad,* 248.

217 Muller, *The German Air War in Russia,* 93.

218 Hayward, *Stopped at Stalingrad,* 248.

219 See Mike Thyssen, "A Deseprate Struggle to Save a Condemned Army—A Critical Review of the Stalingrad Army" (Thesis, Air University 1997), 9; and Hay-

ward, *Stopped at Stalingrad*, 235. Hayward avers that 750 tons was a theoretical limit—"an almost impossible tonnage to deliver.

220 Hayward, 249; Muller, *The German Air War in Russia*, 93. Muller also lists Svervo and Novocherkassk as other fields used during the airlift.

221 Muller, *The German Air War in Russia*, 95. Muller avers that in the pocket, "Gumrak, Karpovka, and Stalingradskii were marginal at best.

222 Muller, 94.

223 Muller, 95–96. Muller collated the information from General Milch's *Kriegstagebuch*.

224 See Beevor, *Stalingrad*, 297, 302; and Alan Clark, *Barbarossa: The Russian-German Conflict, 1941–45* (New York: W. Morrow, 1965), 250–252. After the surrounding of the Sixth Army generals Manstein and Guderian were "selected as the architects of recovery." Manstein was dispatched from Army Group Center and was Hoth's boss during the attempt to break the Sixth Army out of the *Kessel*.

225 Beevor, *Stalingrad*, 302.

226 Hayward, *Stopped at Stalingrad*, 296–302.

227 Hayward, 272.

228 Hayward, 272.

229 Hayward, 284.

230 Hayward, 307.

231 Hayward, 305.

232 As quoted in Hayward, 305. Major Freudenfeld was the signals officer.

233 Beevor, *Stalingrad*, 306.

234 Beevor, 298.

235 See Hayward, *Stopped at Stalingrad*, 255;.and Muller, *The German Air War in Russia*, 96–98. Hayward and Muller are the most thorough and surpass Glantz on the primary source data for the airlift.

236 Morzik, "German Air Force Airlift Operations," 193. Metric tons (2,200 lbs.) listed.

237 See Morzik, 193; andMuller, *The German Air War in Russia*, 99.

238 See Martin Fiebig, "Extracts from General Fiebig's Diary," in Karlsruhe Collection (Maxwell Air Force Base, AL: Air Force Historical Research Agency, IRIS No. 1038188, 1942–1943), 1; and HansDetlef Herhudt MajorGeneral Von Rhoden, "The Most Significant German Air Force Air Supply Operatons: 1939–1945," in *The Papers of Lt. Gen. William Tunner* (Maxwell Air Force Base, AL: Air Force Historical Research Agency, IRIS No. 1038188), 5. Von Rhoden also describes the difficulty of communicating with the *Kessel* and Soviet attempts to disrupt the communications.

239 See Paulus, "Funkspruch an Heeresgruppe B, Armee-Oberkommando 6, Abt.—la. A. H. Qu. 22.11.1942, 1900 Uhr," 6. This is Glantz's translation of the

primary source document. See also Fiebig, "Extracts from General Fiebig's Diary," 1.

240 "Excerpt from Teletype Message from General Schulz, the Chief of Staff of Army Group Don, to General Schmidt, the Chief of Staff of Sixth Amry, at 1650 hours on 28 December 1942," in Glantz, *Companion to Endgame at Stalingrad,* 479.

241 See Major General Schulz, "Supply Problems of the "Luftwaffe" in the Ukraine," in Karlsruhe Collection (Maxwell Air Force Base, AL: Air Force Historical Research Agency, IRIS No. 1038188), 1–5.; and Boog, "Luftwaffe and Logistics in the Second World War." Boog describes the convoluted system of logistics support within the Luftwaffe and between the Luftwaffe and industry.

242 "Report of Major Thiel, Commanding Officer III Combat Wing 27 and Captain Meyer, SQDR.CPT.9./C. Wing 27, 20 Jan 1943," in Karlsruhe Collection (Maxwell Air Force Base, AL: Air Force Historical Research Agency, IRIS No. 1038188), 1.

243 "Report of Major General Pickert, Commander of the 9th Flak Division of Stalingrad, January 18, 1943 13.20 Hours," in Karlsruhe Collection (Maxwell Air Force Base, AL: Air Force Historical Research Agency, IRIS No. 1038188, 1943), 1–2.

244 See "Report of Major General Pickert," 1–2; and Hayward, *Stopped at Stalingrad,* 258.

245 "Air Force Instruction 32–1002: Snow and Ice Control" (Washington, DC: United States Air Force, 2015), 4.

246 Thyssen, "A Deseprate Struggle to Save a Condemned Army—A Critical Review of the Stalingrad Army," 17. The lack of runway preparation at Gumrak was the most pronounced.

247 "Report of Major Thiel," 1.

248 Morzik, "German Air Force Airlift Operations," 197.

249 Morzik, 197.

250 Glantz and House, *Endgame at Stalingrad,* 13. Based on map provided by Glantz.

251 As quoted in Ellis, *The Stalingrad Cauldron,* 196.

252 Ellis, 332, 335. Ellis does a masterful job illustrating the German delineation between Soviet soldiers who joined the Germans with intention (*Hiwis*) and those prisoners of war captured by the army. Ellis quotes German Author Jochen Loser who stated, "*Hiwis* formed the backbone of the supply chain.

253 Beevor, *Stalingrad,* 257.

254 Walter Görlitz, "Paulus and Stalingrad: A Life of Field-Marshal Friedrich Paulus, with Notes, Correspondence, and Documents from His Papers," in Glantz, *Companion to Endgame at Stalingrad,* 429. This amount was calculated by the Sixth Army in late December 1942.

255 See "The Comparative Mobility of German Sixth Army's Divisions on 16 No-

vember and 15 December 1942," in Glantz, *Companion to Endgame at Stalingrad*, 336–338. See also Glantz, *Companion to Endgame at Stalingrad*, 339.

256 See Beevor, *Stalingrad*, 305; and Loren Cordain et al., "Plant-Animal Subsistence Ratios and Macronutrient Energy Estimations in Worldwide Hunter-Gatherer Diets," *American Journal of Clinical Nutrition* 71, no. 3 (2000): 688–690. A diet without enough fat will cause the liver to fail.

257 "Diary of General Pickert, c.g. 9th Flak Division: Air Supply of the Sixth-Army from 25 November 1942–1 November 1943," in *The Papers of Lt. Gen. William Tunner* (Maxwell Air Force Base, AL: Air Force Historical Research Center, IRIS No. 1038188), Slide 119.

258 Görlitz, "Paulus and Stalingrad," 429.

259 See "A Conversation between Generals Schmidt and Schulz, the Respective Chiefs of Staff of Sixth Army and Army Group Don, 1800–1900 hours on 20 December 1942" (2014), 422–424.;"A Conversation between Generals Schmidt and Schulz, the Respective Chiefs of Staff of Sixth Army and Army Group Don, 1710–1745 hours on 22 December 1942," in Glantz, *Companion to Endgame at Stalingrad*, 425–426. This is Glantz's translation of these primary sources taken from *Die Anlagenbander zu den Kriegstagebuchen der 6. Armee Band II*, 296–298 and 321–322.

260 Bartov, *Hitler's Army*, 12.

261 Alvin R. Sunseri, "Patrick J. Hurley at the Battle of Stalingrad: An Oral History Interview," *Military Affairs* 50, no. 2 (1986): 92.

262 "Diary of General Pickert, c.g. 9th Flak Division: Air Supply of the Sixth-Army from 25 November 1942–1 November 1943," Slide 119. This diary, along with numerous other papers in IRIS No. 1038188, were put together for Lt. Gen. Tunner as attempted to place the Berlin Airlift within historical context.

263 As quoted in "A Transcript of the Proceedings" (paper presented at the From the Don to the Dnepr: Soviet Offensive Operations-—December 1942 to August 1943, US Army War College, 1984), 419. General Friedrich von Mellenthin made this observation about Soviet logistics after the war.

264 Clark, *Barbarossa*, 288–290. Clark details several conversations with Hitler and his staff officers after Stalingrad, which illustrates the bizarre machinations of decision making within the Third Reich. Decisions were based less on reality on more on Hitler's perceptions about the loyalty of his officers, which he often conflated with battlefield success.

265 Fritz, *Ostkrieg*, 354.

266 Fritz, 418.

CHAPTER 5. KHE SANH, 1967–1968: THE TRIUMPH OF THE NARRATIVE

1 Lewis Mumford, *Technics and Civilization* (New York: Harcourt, 1934), 368.

2 Thomas C. Schelling, *Arms and Influence* (New Haven, CT: Yale University Press, 2008), 23.

NOTES TO PAGES 208–212 [337]

3 Paul N. Edwards, *The Closed World: Computers and the Politics of Discourse in Cold War America*, Inside Technology (Cambridge, MA: MIT Press, 1996), 15.

4 Krzysztof Lewandowski, "Long Way of Standardization Containers in Europe" (paper presented at the Carpathian Logistics Congress, Kracow, Poland, 2013), 4–5.

5 "All About Shipping Containers," accessed 20 August 2019, http://www.isbu -association.org/history-of-shipping-containers.htm.

6 Sam Howe Verhovek, *Jet Age: The Comet, the 707, and the Race to Shrink the World* (New York: Avery, 2010), 198–200.

7 William H. Tunner, *The Berlin Airlift* (Ramstein Air Base, Germany: Office of History, United States Air Forces in Europe, 1998), 222.

8 "OECD Data: United States," accessed 28 March 2016, https://data.oecd.org /united-states.htm.

9 Stewart O'Nan, ed. *The Vietnam Reader: The Definitive Collection of American Fiction and Nonfiction on the War* (New York: Knopf Doubleday Publishing Group, 2000), 7.

10 Frederik Logevall, *Embers of War: The Fall of an Empire and the Making of America's Vietnam* (New York: Random House, 2012), Kindle version, Prologue Section III.

11 Logevall, *Embers of War*, Prologue Section III.

12 Martin Windrow, *The Last Valley: Dien Bien Phu and the French Defeat in Vietnam* (Cambridge, MA: Da Capo Press, 2006),550–552.

13 Windrow, *The Last Valley*, 649–650.

14 Windrow, 651.

15 George Donelson D. Moss and Paul Conway, *A Vietnam Reader: Sources and Essays* (London, England: Pearson Education, 1990), 4.

16 "The President's New Conference of April 7, 1954," in David C. Eberhart, ed., *Public Papers of the Presidents of the United States: Dwight D. Eisenhower, Containing the Public Messages, Speeches, and Statements of the President: January 1 to December 31, 1954* (Washington, DC: Office of the Federal Register, 1954), 72–73.

17 Moss and Conway, *A Vietnam Reader: Sources and Essays*, 4.

18 Windrow, *The Last Valley*, 651.

19 Campbell Craig, *Destroying the Village: Eisenhower and Thermonuclear War* (New York: Columbia University Press, 1998), 55.

20 Craig, *Destroying the Village*, 55. Hence, the best deterrent was to *guarantee* nuclear war to dissuade war between the superpowers. Craig argues that Eisenhower was the first leader in the Cold War era to understand the logic of mutually assured destruction.

21 Moss and Conway, *A Vietnam Reader*, 7–8.

22 See Moss and Conway, 8.; John F. Kennedy, "Inaugural Address, January 20, 1961," accessed 4 March 2016, http://www.jfklibrary.org/Research/Research -Aids/Ready-Reference/JFK-Quotations/Inaugural-Address.aspx.

23 Maxwell D. Taylor, *The Uncertain Trumpet*, 2nd ed. (New York: Harper, 1960), 160. Roll-on and Roll-Off Shipping allows wheeled vehicles to be driven off the ship onto land. This reduces the time to bring cargo over the hold via crane or lighterage.

24 Taylor, *The Uncertain Trumpet*, 142, 144.

25 See appendix for comparison of technologies across all eras.

26 See appendix for comparison of technologies across all eras.

27 As quoted in Mark Clodfelter, *The Limits of Air Power: The American Bombing of North Vietnam* (Lincoln: University of Nebraska Press, 2006), 45.

28 Clodfelter, *The Limits of Air Power*, 67.

29 "All About Shipping Containers," 118–124.

30 Robert Anthony Pape, *Bombing to Win: Air Power and Coercion in War* (Ithaca, NY: Cornell University Press, 1996), 175. This is not to say that if the "politicians had gotten out of the way" that the bombing campaign would have succeeded— a time-honored lament from military generals to their civilian masters.

31 Clodfelter, *The Limits of Air Power*, 142.

32 Cloldfelter, 134.

33 Cloldfelter, 134.

34 Cloldfelter, 131.

35 As quoted in Robert S. McNamara and Brian VanDeMark, *In Retrospect: The Tragedy and Lessons of Vietnam*, 1st ed. (New York: Times Books, 1995), 289.

36 Clodfelter, *The Limits of Air Power*, 134.

37 William Thomas Allison, *The Tet Offensive: A Brief History with Documents* (New York: Routledge, 2008), 7.

38 Jacob Van Staaveren, "The Air Force in Vietnam: The Search for Military Alternatives, 1967" (Washington, DC: Office of Air Force History, 1969), vi.

39 Allison, *The Tet Offensive*, 13.

40 Allison, 15.

41 Lien-Hang T. Nguyen, *Hanoi's War: An International History of the War for Peace in Vietnam* (Chapel Hill: University of North Carolina Press, 2012), 77.

42 Nguyen, *Hanoi's War*, 77.

43 P. B. Davidson, *Vietnam at War: The History, 1946–1975* (Oxford University Press, 1991), 20. The North Vietnamese were wary of the Chinese due to long-standing animosity and attempted Chinese dominance of their land. Therefore, the North Vietnamese, including Giap, tended to align their ideology with Soviet (versus Sino) origins. However, the link to Mao is clear in how Ho Chi Minh and his leaders approached the Vietnam War.

44 United States Marine Corps, "FMFRP 12–18: Mao Tse-Tung on Guerrilla Warfare" (Washington, DC: United States Department of the Navy, 1989), 21.

45 *Ibid.*, United States Marine Corps, "FMFRP 12–18," 22.

46 Davidson, *Vietnam at War*, 20.

47 Francis Fitzgerald, Fredrik Logevall, and Lien-Hang T. Nguyen, "Fifty Years

After the Tet Offensive: Lessons From the Vietnam War," Council on Foreign Relations, https://www.cfr.org/event/fifty-years-after-tet-offensive-lessons-vietnam-war.

48 Lien-Hang T. Nguyen, *Hanoi's War: An International History of the War for Peace in Vietnam* (Chapel Hill: The University of North Carolina Press, 2012), 81. Nguyen was the first scholar with access to previously locked North Vietnamese records.

49 Nguyen, *Hanoi's War*, 81–82.

50 WP Central Committee, "Resolution of the 14th Plenum (January 1968)," in *The Vietnam War: A Documentary Reader,* ed. Edward Miller (Malden, MA: Wiley, 2016), 148–152.

51 "Notes of a Meeting at the White House (July 21, 1965)," in Miller, *The Vietnam War,* 110.

52 Fitzgerald et. al. "Fifty Years After the Tet Offensive." Lien-Hang T. Nguyen noted about the increase of troops and blunting of the North's effort before 1968, "in a sense, they stole Hanoi's victory from the jaws of defeat, or stole that for Saigon.

53 "Minutes of the Irregular Conference at Chau Thanh District Supply Council, 7 January 1967," in *Vietnam Documents and Research Notes Series Microform: Translation and Analysis of Significant Viet Cong/North Vietnamese Documents* (Carlisle Barracks, PA: Library of the US Army Military History Institute, 1967), Slide 168, 4.

54 "Minutes of the Irregular Conference at Chau Thanh District Supply Council, 7 January 1967," 4.

55 Allison, *The Tet Offensive,* 22.

56 As summarized in Allison, *The Tet Offensive,* 22.

57 See Allison, *The Tet Offensive,* 25, 38. Allison details the differing viewpoints on the importance of Khe Sanh on pages 37–39. See also Fitzgerald et al. "Fifty Years After the Tet Offensive.

58 E. E. Moïse, *The Myths of Tet: The Most Misunderstood Event of the Vietnam War* (Lawrence: University Press of Kansas, 2017), Kindle eBook, Introduction, Paragraph 5.

59 "A Study: Prospects for the Vietcong," in *Vietnam Documents and Research Notes Series microform : Translation and Analysis of Significant Viet Cong/North Vietnamese Documents,* ed. Robert Lester (Carlisle Barracks, PA: Library of the US Army Military History Institute, 1966), 13, Slide 0076. Document is now declassified.

60 Le Duan, "The Path of the October Revolution and the World Situation, 4 Nov 1967," in Robert Lester (Ed.) *Vietnam Documents and Research Notes Series Microform: Translation and Analysis of Significant Viet Cong/North Vietnamese Documents* (Carlisle Barracks, PA: Library of the US Army Military History Institute, 1966), 6, 9, 11,13. Document is now declassified.

61 Lien-Hang T. Nguyen, *Hanoi's War: An International History of the War for Peace in Vietnam* (Chapel Hill: University of North Carolina Press, 2012), 81–82.

62 This quote was translated by Dang Hoa Ho for Bowden from Dang Kinh's, *The Famous Guerrilla General* (Hanoi: Le Dong Publishing House, 2013). Bowden's research has an extensive list of new primary sources from North Vietnamese/ Viet Cong sources.

63 Bowden, *Huế 1968*, 58.

64 VWP Central Committee, "Resolution of the 14th Plenum (January 1968)," in *The Vietnam War: A Documentary Reader*, ed. Edward Miller (Malden, MA: Wiley, 2016), 148.

65 VWP Central Committee, "Resolution of the 14th Plenum (January 1968)," 150.

66 VWP Central Committee, "Resolution of the 14th Plenum (January 1968)," 151.

67 Nguyen, *Hanoi's War*, 102.

68 Edwards, *The Closed World: Computers and the Politics of Discourse in Cold War America* (Cambridge, MA: MIT Press, 1997), 3–5. The strong-point obstacle system was a fence with guards and a massive integrated system of electronic sensors and computers to detect movement.

69 William C. Westmoreland, *A Soldier Reports*, 1st ed. (Garden City, NY: Doubleday, 1976), 336.

70 Westmoreland, *A Soldier Reports*, 336.

71 Jack Shulimson, *U.S. Marines In Vietnam: The Defining Year, 1968* (Washington, DC: History and Museums Division, Headquarters, US Marine Corps, 1997), 59–60.

72. Shulimson, *U.S. Marines in Vietnam*, 61.

73 John Prados and Ray W. Stubbe, *Valley of Decision: The Siege of Khe Sanh* (Boston: Houghton Mifflin, 1991), 102–103.

74 Shulimson, *U.S. Marines in Vietnam*, 60–61.

75 Shulimson, 61.

76 Shulimson, 61.

77 See Shulimson, 61; and Prados and Stubbe, *Valley of Decision*, 153.

78 See ; and Prados and Stubbe, *Valley of Decision*, 153.

79 "Telegram from General Westmoreland, COMUSMACV, to General Wheeler, CJCS December 10, 1967," in *The Tet Offensive: A Brief History with Documents*, ed. William Thomas Allison (New York: Routledge, 1967), 113–114.

80 "Telegram from General Westmoreland, COMUSMACV, to General Wheeler, CJCS December 10, 1967," 114.

81 Westmoreland, *A Soldier Reports*, 337.

82 Westmoreland, 336.

83 "Telegram from General Westmoreland, COMUSMACV, to General Wheeler, CJCS December 10, 1967," 113.

84 Harold G. Moore and Joseph L. Galloway, *We Were Soldiers Once . . . and Young: Ia Drang—The Battle That Changed the War in Vietnam* (New York:

Random House, 1991), 9–10. This book sums up the mobile helicopter tactics that became a blueprint for US operations, and NVA countertactics, throughout the Vietnam War.

85 Shulimson, *U.S. Marines in Vietnam*, 61.

86 As quoted in Shulimson, 64.

87 Lance Burton, "North Vietnam's Logistics System: Its Contribution to the War, 1961–1969" (Fort Leavenworth, KS: US Army Command and General Staff College, 1977), 28. Document is now declassified.

88 Edward Valentiny, "Project Contemporary Historical Examination of Current Operations (CHECO) Report: USAF Operations from Thailand 1 January 1967 to 1 July 1968" (Directorate Tactical Evaluation HQ Pacific Air Forces, 1968), 19. Document is now declassified.

89 As transcribed in Valentiny, "Project Contemporary Historical Examination of Current Operations (CHECO) Report," 40.

90 Valentiny, 40.

91 Valentiny, 40.

92 Clodfelter, *The Limits of Air Power*, 133.

93 Clodfelter, 133.

94 Valentiny, "Project Contemporary Historical Examination of Current Operations (CHECO) Report," 41.

95 Valentiny, 41–42.

96 Valentiny, 41.

97 See Valentiny, 39; and "Muscle Shoals Six Month Summary Evaluation Report, 31 May 1968" (Maxwell Air Force Base, AL: United States Military Assistance Command Vietnam, Air Force Historical Research Agency, IRIS No. 1000577, 1968), 34. Document is now declassified.

98 Valentiny, "Project Contemporary Historical Examination of Current Operations (CHECO) Report," 19.

99 Valentiny, 48, 51.

100 Yuen Foong Khong, *Analogies at War : Korea, Munich, Dien Bien Phu, and the Vietnam Decisions of 1965* (Princeton, NJ: Princeton University Press, 1992), 129. Khong illustrates the administration's worry about nuclear war from 1965 onward as the US increased its men and material.

101 Valentiny, "Project Contemporary Historical Examination of Current Operations (CHECO) Report," 45–46.

102 Valentiny, 40. Later during the build-up to Khe Sanh, the NVA positioned their long-range artillery pieces in Laos for the same reasons.

103 Valentiny, 41.

104 Valentiny, 43.

105 Valentiny, 67.

106 Valentiny, 67, Figure 6.

107 Valentiny, 67, Figure 7.

108 Shulimson, *U.S. Marines in Vietnam*, 36.

109 John Prados, "Khe Sanh: The Other Side of the Hill," accessed 10 August 2019, http://archive.vva.org/archive/TheVeteran/0807/khesanh.html.

110 Prados, "Khe Sanh." Although Prados cites the statistics of what they moved, he explains that "this amounted to a substantial force, enough to mount a threat, but not a Dien Bien Phu given the combat capability and logistics support of the Marines at Khe Sanh." Prados misses the difficulty the NVA faced moving such a large force down the Ho Chi Minh Trail under threat of US airpower.

111 Windrow, *The Last Valley*, 715–716. The exact numbers of Viet Minh weapons at Dien Bien Phu is an estimate. Windrow lists sixty howitzers (75 mm and 105 mm), fifty mortars (82 or 120 mm), and more than seventy-five heavy weapons including "Japanese Type 94 mountain guns" and "60 x 75 mm recoilless rifles.

112 Prados and Stubbe, *Valley of Decision*, 318.

113 Prados and Stubbe, 319–320.

114 Prados and Stubbe, 320.

115 See "Strategic/Tactical Study Prepared by Assistant Chief of Staff, J-5, March 1968" (Vietnam Headquarters Military Assistance Command, Saigon), E-4. Document is now declassified.

116 See "Strategic/Tactical Study Prepared by Assistant Chief of Staff, J-5, March 1968," (Vietnam Headquarters Military Assistance Command, Saigon), B-5–1; and Prados and Stubbe, *Valley of Decision*, 102–103, 429–430. After the siege ended, the Marines recovered 13,500 tons of food. At full rations, this was twenty-one-day supply of food based on US estimates of 700 short tons per day to support both NVA divisions surrounding Khe Sanh.

117 Prados, "Khe Sanh.

118 Prados and Stubbe, *Valley of Decision*, 320.

119 Bui Tin, "The Ho Chi Minh Trail," in *The Vietnam Wars: Documents in Contemporary History*, ed. Kevin Ruane (New York: Manchester University Press, 2000), 106.

120 Bowden, *Huế 1968*, 80–82. Bowden's interviews with Le Huu Tong and other NVA soldiers paint a harrowing picture of the difficulties of traveling down the Ho Chi Minh Trail.

121 Nguyen Trong Nghi, "Our Future Selves," in *Vietnam: A Portrait of its People at War*, ed. David Chanoff and Van Toai Doan (London; New York: I. B. Tauris), 68.

122 "Strategic/Tactical Study Prepared by Assistant Chief of Staff, J-5, March 1968," B-2–1.

123 Prados, "Khe Sanh." In this article Prados uses more recent NVA archives to give more exact numbers for the NVA men and material surrounding Khe Sanh.

124 "Working Paper No. 14–66, Real Time Air Interdiction System, 17 May 1966," in *Project Corona Harvest* (Maxwell Air Force Base, AL: USAF Scientific Re-

search Advisory Group, United States Air Force Historical Agency, IRIS No. 0581360, 1966). Document is now declassified.

125 "Muscle Shoals Six Month Summary Evaluation Report, 31 May 1968," 5. Muscle Shoals was renamed Igloo White in June 1968 after its first operational tests at Khe Sanh yielded tactics, techniques, and procedures for broader use across South Vietnam and the Ho Chi Minh Trail.

126 "Muscle Shoals Six Month Summary Evaluation Report, 31 May 1968," 29–30.

127 "Memorandum from the President's Assistant (Jones) to President Johnson, 2 November 1967," in Allison, The Tet Offensive, 106–108.

128 "Muscle Shoals Six Month Summary Evaluation Report, 31 May 1968," 33.

129 Shawn P. Callahan, Close Air Support and the Battle for Khe Sanh (Quantico, VA: History Division, United States Marine Corps, 2009), 33.

130 Erol Morris, dir., The Fog of War (Sony Pictures Classics, 2003). McNamara was the archetype for the rationality of the Cold War as one of the "Whiz-Kids" of the Kennedy administration. He was an analyst during World War II for the United States. His job was to determine the effectiveness of the bombing of Japanese cities. In the postwar world, McNamara led Ford Motor Corporation and championed the use of statistics to make decisions—resulting in the successful manufacturing and marketing of seat belts to increase driver safety.

131 Edwards, The Closed World, 310. Muscle Shoals evolved into the Igloo White program.

132 Prados and Stubbe, Valley of Decision, 187–188.

133 "Muscle Shoals Six Month Summary Evaluation Report, 31 May 1968," 6.

134 Prados and Stubbe, Valley of Decision, 331.

135 Callahan, Close Air Support and the Battle for Khe Sanh, 62–64. Niagara I began on 5 January 1968 with reconnaissance of the area and Niagara II on 15 January 1968. B-52s had been prohibited from missions along or near Ho Chi Minh Trail during Rolling Thunder

136 "7th Air Force, Significant Events (TACO): Niagra II Sortie Recap, 21 to 31 Jan 1968," (Maxwell Air Force Base, AL: Air Force Historical Research Agency, IRIS No. 525200, 1968), 1. Document is now declassified.

137 "Muscle Shoals Six Month Summary Evaluation Report, 31 May 1968," 9.

138 Callahan, Close Air Support and the Battle for Khe Sanh, 65.

139 Callahan, 65.

140 Bruce M. Geiger, (1Lt Geiger , 1/44 Artillery, Khe Sanh 1967–1968), interview with the author, 17 March 2016; Ray W. Stubbe, "Transcript of an Oral History Interview with Rev. Ray W. Stubbe, Navy Chaplain, Vietnam War," ed. Jim Kurtz (Madison: Wisconsin Veterans Museum Research Center, 2005), 55.

141 "Strategic/Tactical Study Prepared by Assistant Chief of Staff, J-5, March 1968," E-1. Document is now declassified. Seventh Air Force listed 5,567 sorties in the two-week period from 23 January to 8 February. The sortie counts stabilized and were at or above this rate for the rest of the siege.

142 See "Strategic/Tactical Study Prepared by Assistant Chief of Staff, J-5, March 1968," E-3; and "7th Air Force, Significant Events (TACO): Niagra II Sortie Recap, 21 to 31 Jan 1968," 1–43. According to General Momyer's staff, the force of B-52s could fly a maximum of forty-eight sorties per day.

143 "Strategic/Tactical Study Prepared by Assistant Chief of Staff, J-5, March 1968," E-3. This tonnage was for the range of twenty-four to forty-eight sorties. A few days of bad weather limited Operation Niagara sorties to as low as nine.

144 Case A. Cunningham, "William W. Momyer: A Biography of an Airpower Mind" (PhD diss., Maxwell Air Force Base, AL: Air University, 2013), 330–331. As at Guadalcanal, the separation of the Marines from their aircraft was a significant emotional event. In a controversial decision, Westmoreland sided with the United States Air Force and placed all Khe Sanh air missions, including the aircraft of the US Marines, under the command and control of Seventh Air Force and General Momyer in April 1968.

145 Callahan, *Close Air Support and the Battle for Khe Sanh*, 62.

146 See Prados and Stubbe, *Valley of Decision*, 360, photo page 4; and Dwight Jon Zimmerman, "The Guns at Khe Sahn," Argunners Magazine, April 10, 2018, http://argunners.com/the-guns-at-khe-sanh-1968/.

147 Callahan, *Close Air Support and the Battle for Khe Sanh*, 72–73. Colonel Lownds was critiqued before, during, and after the siege for the lack of trenching of the Marine positions at the air base and the hill outposts.

148 Shulimson, *U.S. Marines in Vietnam*, 59.

149 Prados and Stubbe, *Valley of Decision*, 274.

150 Houng Van Ba, "Regroupee: Back Down the Trail," in Chanoff and Doan, *Vietnam: A Portrait of its People at War*, 154.

151 Moyers S. Shore, *The Battle for Khe Sanh* (Washington, DC: Historical Branch, G-3 Division, Headquarters, US Marine Corps, 1969, repr. 1977), 102.

152 Shore, *The Battle for Khe Sanh*, 114.

153 "Muscle Shoals Six Month Summary Evaluation Report, 31 May 1968," 35.

154 "Muscle Shoals Six Month Summary Evaluation Report, 31 May 1968," 32–35.

155 "Muscle Shoals Six Month Summary Evaluation Report, 31 May 1968," 36.

156 "Muscle Shoals Six Month Summary Evaluation Report, 31 May 1968," 66.

157 "Muscle Shoals Six Month Summary Evaluation Report, 31 May 1968," 37.

158 "Muscle Shoals Six Month Summary Evaluation Report, 31 May 1968," 37.

159 "Muscle Shoals Six Month Summary Evaluation Report, 31 May 1968," 37. The official report does not give the exact date, but it appears to be sometime in mid-March, when 881 South received its most concentrated assaults from NVA troops.

160 "Muscle Shoals Six Month Summary Evaluation Report, 31 May 1968," 37.

161 As quoted Prados and Stubbe, *Valley of Decision*, 302.

162 Shore, *The Battle for Khe Sanh*, 103.

163 Shore, 104.

164 "Muscle Shoals Six Month Summary Evaluation Report, 31 May 1968," 66.

165 See Prados, "Khe Sanh"; and Shore, *The Battle for Khe Sanh*, 66.

166 Prados and Stubbe, *Valley of Decision*, 327.

167 Callahan, *Close Air Support and the Battle for Khe Sanh*, 82.

168 See Geiger, interview with the author; and Prados and Stubbe, *Valley of Decision*, 110.

169 Ray L. Bowers, *Tactical Airlift: The United States Air Force in Southeast Asia* (Washington, DC: Office of Air Force History, 1983), 34. C-7s had a three-ton payload. C-123s had a five-ton payload. C-130s had a sixteen- to twenty-two-ton payload.

170 Bowers, *Tactical Airlift*, 299.

171 Prados and Stubbe, *Valley of Decision*, 112.

172 John J. Lane, *Command and Control and Communications Structures in Southeast Asia*, The Air War in Indochina (Maxwell Air Force Base, AL: Air University, 1981), 19–22.

173 Burl W. McLaughin, "Khe Sanh: Keeping an Outpost Alive," *Air University Review* 20, no. 1 (November–December 1968), 61–62.

174 McLaughlin, "Khe Sanh: Keeping an Outpost Alive," 161.

175 See McLaughlin, "Khe Sanh: Keeping an Outpost Alive"; 66-67, and Geiger, interview with the author.

176 Bowers, *Tactical Airlift*, 300.

177 McLaughlin, "Khe Sanh: Keeping an Outpost Alive," 59–61. Khe Sanh did have a Tactical Air Navigation (TACAN) beacon, but approaches to the field in the weather were much less accurate with this signal than the radar-guided GCA system.

178 Bowers, *Tactical Airlift*, 301–302.

179 Prados and Stubbe, *Valley of Decision*, 377.

180 McLaughlin, "Khe Sanh: Keeping an Outpost Alive," 61. Due to the risk of LAPES, the Marines also developed the Ground Proximity Extraction System (GPES). The GPES was a hook system, similar to the trap on an aircraft carrier. The pilot would land on the ground and catch a cable with a hook connected to the cargo pallet. The cable would pull the cargo out of the plane and the aircraft would continue down the runway for a takeoff.

181 Prados and Stubbe, *Valley of Decision*, 378. Errant cargo from the LAPES system killed two Marines and there were several instances of injury.

182 Prados and Stubbe, 379.

183 Bowers, *Tactical Airlift*, 303.

184 See Bowers, *Tactical Airlift*, 303.; and United States Air Force, "Air Force Instruction 13–217: Drop Zone and Landing Zone Operations" (Washington, DC: HQ USAF/A3OS, 2007), 9–11. C-130s airdrop at 130 knots—two nautical miles per minute or seventy-five yards per second.

185 Peter Brush, "Lifeline to Khe Sanh: The 109th Quatermaster Company (Air

Delivery)," accessed 3 March 2016, https://msuweb.montclair.edu/~furrg/Viet nam/pb109.html. These crews worked twenty-four hours on and six hours off for the length of the siege.

186 Bowers, *Tactical Airlift*, 379. There were 601 airdrops and 352 landings between C-130s and C-123s. C-130 lifted more than 90 percent of the cargo (counting both methods of delivery).

187 Callahan, *Close Air Support and the Battle for Khe Sanh*, 76–77. Based on the sortie counts, Callahan estimates, Marine C-130 delivers at 1,178 tons, with helicopters delivering 1,822 tons.

188 Callahan, 74.

189 See Callahan, 76; and Prados, "Khe Sanh: The Other Side of the Hill." This number, like many statistics of the US military from Vietnam, is likely inflated. John Prados avers that the total number of AAA pieces, not just 37 mm, brought down the Ho Chi Minh Trail was 184.

190 Shore, *The Battle for Khe Sanh*, 76.

191 Shore, 86.

192 As quoted in Shore, 89.

193 Carlton B. Crenshaw, "Letters Home, Another Perspective " accessed 31 March 2016, http://www.hmm-364.org/warriors-web-site/crenshaw-ltrs.html.

194 John T. Esslinger, "The Hill 881S Ice Cream Delivery," accessed 15 March 2016, http://www.hmm-364.org/warriors-web-site/esslinger-tj-icecream.html.

195 Shore, *The Battle for Khe Sanh*, 131.

196 Sedgwick D. Tourison, *B5-T8 in 48 QXD—The Secret Official Hisotry of the North Vietnamese Army at the Siege of Khe Sanh, Vietnam, Spring, 1968* (Wauwatosa, WI: Khe Sanh Veterans, 2006), cited in Callahan, *Close Air Support and the Battle for Khe Sanh*, 83.

197 As quoted in Prados and Stubbe, *Valley of Decision*, 412.

198 As quoted in Prados and Stubbe, 167.

199 Prados and Stubbe, 429–430.

200 Jon M. Van Dyke, *North Vietnam's Strategy for Survival* (Palo Alto, CA: Pacific Books, 1972), 122. This report was from North Vietnam, where food was more prevalent than in combat areas in the South, such as Khe Sanh.

201 As quoted in Ronald J. Drez and Douglas Brinkley, *Voices of Courage: The Battle for Khe Sanh, Vietnam*, 1st ed. (New York: Bulfinch Press, 2005), 156.

202 Eric M. Hammel, *Khe Sanh: Siege in the Clouds, An Oral History* (Pacifica, CA: Pacifica Press, 2000), 346–347.

203 As quoted in Hammel, *Khe Sanh*, 216.

204 Michael Ewing, *Khe Sanh: Illustrated History of the Vietnam War* (New York: Bantam Books, 1987), 138.

205 *Victory in Vietnam: The Official History of the People's Army of Vietnam, 1954–1975*, The Military History Institute of Vietnam, trans. Merle L. Pribbenow (Lawrence: University Press of Kansas, 2002), 230.

206 As quoted in Hammel, *Khe Sanh*, 37.
207 Shulimson, *U.S. Marines in Vietnam*, 289.
208 Geiger, interview with the author.
209 Stubbe, "Transcript of an Oral History Interview," 61.
210 Geiger, Geiger, interview with the author.
211 See Geiger, interview with the author. and Shulimson, *U.S. Marines in Vietnam*, 289. It was not standard practice to bring in water by helicopter, but the US successfully moved water buffaloes in several times during the siege.
212 "Sgt. Prentice: Oral History Interview," http://www.hmm-364.org/warriors-web-site/oral-histories/oral-history-prentice.html.
213 Stubbe, "Transcript of an Oral History Interview," 61.
214 Geiger, "Interview with Bruce Geiger.
215 Shulimson, *U.S. Marines in Vietnam*, 289. Shulimson sums up USMC Lieutenant General Krulak's view that the NVA did not cut the water because they "had no intention of undertaking an all-out assault on the base.
216 There were other sources of water, such as bamboo plants and natural springs, but this was not enough water for two divisions to maintain an offensive.
217 Callahan, *Close Air Support and the Battle for Khe Sanh*, 83.
218 Shulimson, *U.S. Marines in Vietnam*, 283.
219 Prados and Stubbe, *Valley of Decision*, 418.
220 Prados and Stubbe, 419.
221 Callahan, *Close Air Support and the Battle for Khe Sanh*, 86–87; Shulimson, *U.S. Marines in Vietnam*, 287.
222 Callahan, 289.
223 As quoted in Callahan,, 284.
224 Callahan, 289.
225 Callahan, , 81.
226 Callahan, 78.
227 Stubbe, "Transcript of an Oral History Interview" ," 55.
228 Tourison, *B5-T8 in 48 QXD*, 3–4, cited in Callahan, *Close Air Support and the Battle for Khe Sanh*, 83.
229 Shulimson, *U.S. Marines in Vietnam*, 326.
230 Allison, *The Tet Offensive*, 57.
231 Allison, 57.
232 Callahan, *Close Air Support and the Battle for Khe Sanh*.
233 "Strategic/Tactical Study Prepared by Assistant Chief of Staff, J-5, March 1968." The study is 200 pages in length.
234 Bowden, *Huế*, 226–237. Lt. Col. Dick Sweet's Second of the Twelfth Cavalry battalion was nearly wiped out by a National Liberation Front unit, which surrounded the battalion on the outskirts of Hu . His continual requests for support and to retreat were ignored at MACV.
235 Bowden, *Huế*, 519.

236 Prados and Stubbe, *Valley of Decision*, 429–430.

237 Bowden, *Hué*, 80–82.

238 Moïse, *Myths of Tet*, Kindle e-book, Introduction, Paragraph 5.

239 Allison, *The Tet Offensive*, 62.

240 Westmoreland, *A Soldier Reports*, 355.

241 General Tran Van Tra, "Tet: The 1968 General Offensive and General Uprising," in *The Vietnam War: Vietnamese and American perspectives*, eds. Mark
Bradley, Jayne S. Werner, and Luu Doan Huynh (Armonk, NY: M. E. Sharpe,
1993), 57.

242 Westmoreland, *A Soldier Reports*, 358, 361.

243 Lyndon B. Johnson, "Address to the Nation 31 March 1968," in *The Vietnam
Wars: Documents in Contemporary History*, ed. Kevin Ruane (New York: Manchester University Press, 2000), 126.

244 Muller, *The German Air War in Russia* (Baltimore: Nautical & Aviation Publishing Company of America, 1992), 96–98.

245 Taylor, *The Uncertain Trumpet*, 142, 144.

246 Callahan, *Close Air Support and the Battle for Khe Sanh*, 78–79. Callahan chron-
icles the debates and the sources of contention.

247 The C-130 variants used at Khe Sanh burned four thousand pounds of fuel per
hour. Each mission to Khe Sahn was roughly two hours in length.

248 Herman I. Gilster, *The Air War in Southeast Asia: Case Studies of Selected Campaigns* (Maxwell Air Force Base, AL: Air University Press, 1993), 49.

249 Ray L. Bowers, *Tactical Airlift* (Washington, DC: Office of Air Force History,
1983), 34. A C-130 Transport aircraft could carry twenty tons, a standard truck
about two to four tons.

250 William M. Momyer, "Memorandum for General Ellis, Subject: USAF Airlift
Activities in Support of Operations in Southeast Asia 1 Janary 1965–31 March
1968," in *CORONA HARVEST* (Air Force Historical Research Agency, IRIS No.
1028237, 1974), 8. Document is now declassified. The USAF commissioned several studies to revamp the air transportation efforts. In this lengthy document,
General Momyer lists in detail the many failures and improvements needed for
air mobility operations to compete with the Soviets.

CONCLUSION

1 Walter Millis, *Arms and Men: A Study in American Military History* (New
Brunswick, NJ: Rutgers University Press 1981), 208. Millis's classic details the
managerial revolution, especially in the American military context in the third
chapter.

2 Carl Von Clausewitz, *On War*, ed. Michael Howard and Peter Paret (Princeton,
NJ: Princeton University Press, 1984), 338–339.

3 William Hardy McNeill, *The Pursuit of Power: Technology, Armed Force, and
Society Since A.D. 1000* (Chicago: University of Chicago Press, 1982), 159.

4 See Fred Anderson, *Crucible of War: The Seven Years' War and the Fate of Empire in British North America, 1754–1766* (Vintage, 2007), 99; Robert Orme, *The History of an Expedition Against Fort Du Quesne, in 1755 Under Major-General Edward Braddock* (Lippincott, Grambo, & Co., 1856), 336; and Edward Braddock, *Major General Edward Braddock's Orderly Books From February 26 to June 17, 1755,* (Cumberland, MD: W. H. Lowdermilk, 1878), XLII. Braddock reached the battle with thirteen hundred men and dozens of artillery pieces, against nine hundred French and Indians, with no localized artillery. The French had artillery at Fort Duquesne, but it was a mile to the west of the Battle of the Monongahela. The British also had one hundred rounds per man extra musket shot in addition to the twenty-four rounds each man carried on with him.

5 Even in defeat and near death, Braddock concerned himself greatly with the routed army making it back to their food supplies to the west.

APPENDIX: TECHNOLOGIES OF TRANSPORTATION

1 R. T. Brigantic and J. M. Mahan, *Defense Transportation: Algorithms, Models, and Applications for the 21st Century* (Amsterdam, Netherlands: Elsevier, 2004). See this book for a full accounting of ton-miles for air, land, and sea modes of transportation.

2 For Khe Sanh this includes the railroad for a comparison across the ages. The railroad had similar capacity in 1968 as those of the Second World War.

BOOKS, ARTICLES, AND PUBLISHED SECONDARY SOURCES

Addintong, Larry H. *The Blitzkrieg Era and the German General Staff, 1865–1941*. New Brunswick, NJ: Rutgers University Press, 1971.

"Air Force Instruction 13-217: Drop Zone and Landing Zone Operations." Edited by United States Air Force. Washington, DC: HQ USAF/A30S, 2007.

"Air Force Instruction 32-1002: Snow and Ice Control." Edited by United States Air Force . Washington, DC, HQ USAF/A4CX, 2015.

Allison, William Thomas. *The Tet Offensive: A Brief History with Documents*. New York: Routledge, 2008.

American Military History. Vol. 1. Center of Military History, US Army, 1989.

Anderson, Fred. *Crucible of War: The Seven Years' War and the Fate of Empire in British North America, 1754–1766*. New York: Vintage, 2007.

Babuscio, Jack, and Richard Minta Dunn. *European Political Facts, 1648–1789*. New York: Facts on File, 1984.

Bacon, Francis. *The Essays of Lord Bacon*. Longmans, Green & Company, 1873.

Baime, A. J. *The Arsenal of Democracy: FDR, Detroit, and an Epic Quest to Arm an America at War*. Boston: Houghton Mifflin Harcourt, 2014.

Bartov, Omer. *Hitler's Army: Soldiers, Nazis, and War in the Third Reich*. New York: Oxford University Press, 1991.

Bartsch, William H. *Victory Fever on Guadalcanal: Japan's First Land Defeat of World War II*. College Station: Texas A&M University Press, 2014.

Baugh, Daniel. *The Global Seven Years' War, 1754–1763: Britian and France in a Great Power Contest*. 1st. ed. Harlow, England: Pearson, 2011.

Beaver, Daniel R. "'Deuce and a Half': Selecting U.S. Army Trucks, 1920–1945." In *Feeding Mars: Logistics in Western Warfare from the Middle Ages to the Present*, edited by John A. Lynn (Boulder, CO: Westview Press, 1993).

Beckett, Ian FW. *The Great War: 1914–1918*. New York: Routledge, 2014.

Beevor, Antony. *Stalingrad: The Fateful Siege: 1942–1943*. London: Viking, 1998.

Bergerud, Eric M. *Fire in the Sky: The Air War in the South Pacific*. Boulder, CO: Westview Press, 2000.

Bergstrom, Christer, and Martin Pegg. *The War in Russia: January–October 1943*. Vol. 4, Section 3, *Jagdwaffe*. Sheppterton, United Kingdom: Classic Publications, 2004.

Berkebile, Donald H. *Conestoga Wagons in Braddock's Campaign, 1755*. Washington, DC: Smithsonian Institution, 1959. http://BZ6FJ9FL8E.search.serialssolutions.com/?V=1.0&L=BZ6FJ9FL8E&S=JCs&C=TC_007465407&T=marc.

Bertke, D. A., G. Smith, and D. Kindell. *World War II Sea War*. Vol. 6, *The Allies Halt the Axis Advance*. Dayton, OH: Bertke Publications, 2014.

Black, Jeremy. *World War Two: A Military History*. New York: Routledge, 2006.

Bonn, Keith Earle, ed. *Slaughterhouse: The Handbook of the Eastern Front*. Bedford, PA: Aberjona Press, 2005.

Boog, Horst. "Luftwaffe and Logistics in the Second World War." *Aerospace Historian* 35, no. 2 (1988): 103–110.

Bousquet, Antoine. *The Scientific Way of Warfare: Order and Chaos on the Battlefields of Modernity*. New York: Columbia University Press, 2010.

Bowden, Mark. *Huế 1968: A Turning Point of the American War in Vietnam*. New York: Atlantic Monthly Press, 2017.

Bowers, Ray L. *Tactical Airlift: The United States Air Force in Southeast Asia*. Washington, DC: Office of Air Force History, 1983.

Brigantic, R. T., and J. M. Mahan. *Defense Transportation: Algorithms, Models, and Applications for the 21st Century*. San Diego: Elsevier, 2004.

Brookes, Andrew J. *Air War Over Russia*. Shepperton, United Kingdom: Ian Allan Publishing, 2003.

Brose, Eric Dorn. *A History of the Great War: World War One and the International Crisis of the Early Twentieth Century*. Oxford, England: Oxford University Press, 2010.

———. *The Kaiser's Army: The Politics of Military Technology in Germany During the Machine Age, 1870–1918*. Oxford, England: Oxford University Press, 2004

Brown, Ian "Logistics." In *The Cambridge History of the First World War*. Vol. 2, *The State*, edited by Jay Winter, 218–239. Cambridge, England: Cambridge University Press, 2014.

Brown, Ian Malcolm. *British Logistics on the Western Front: 1914–1919*. Westport, Connecticut: Praeger, 1998.

Brumwell, Stephen. *White Devil: An Epic Story of Revenge from the Savage War that Inspired The Last of the Mohicans*. London: Phoenix Press, 2005.

Buchet, Christian. *The British Navy, Economy and Society in the Seven Years' War* [Originally published in French as *Marine, économie et société: Un exemple d'interaction: l'avitaillement de la Royal Navy durant la guerre de sept ans*. Paris: Champion, 1999.]. Woodbridge, United Kingdom: Boydell Press, 2013.

Buffetaut, Y. *The 1917 Spring Offensives: Arras, Vimy, Le Chemin Des Dames*. Paris: Casemate Press, 1997.

Burley, David V. "Proto-Historic Ecological Effects of the Fur Trade on Micmac Culture in Northeastern New Brunswick." *Ethnohistory* 28, no. 3 (1981): 203–216.

Burns, William E. *Science and Technology in Colonial America*. Westport, CT: Greenwood Publishing Group, 2005.

Burton, Lance. "North Vietnam's Logistics System: Its Contribution to the War, 1961–1969." Fort Leavenworth, KS: US Army Command and General Staff College, 1977.

Bykofsky, Joseph, and Harold Larson. *The Transportation Corps: Operations Overseas*. Washington, DC: Department of the Army, 1957.

Callahan, Shawn P. *Close Air Support and the Battle for Khe Sanh*. Quantico, VA: History Division, United States Marine Corps, 2009.

Campbell, John. *Naval Weapons of World War Two*. Annapolis, MD: Naval Institute Press, 1985.

Carlos, Ann M, and Frank D. Lewis. *Commerce by a Frozen Sea: Native Americans and the European Fur Trade*. Philadelphia: University of Pennsylvania Press, 2011.

Carnegie Library of Pittsburgh. Department of Science and Technology. *Science and Technology Desk Reference: 1,500 Answers to Frequently-Asked or Difficult-to-Answer Questions*. Ann Arbor, MI: Gale Research, 1993.

Carter, K. C., and R. Mueller. *The Army Air Forces in World War II: Combat Chronology, 1941–1945*. Washington, DC: Government Publishing Office, 1975.

Chapelle, Howard Irving. *American Small Sailing Craft: Their Design, Development, and Construction*. New York: W. W. Norton, 1951.

Charteris, Evan. *William Augustus, Duke of Cumberland, His Early Life and Times (1721–1748)*. London: E. Arnold, 1913.

Chartrand, René. *Ticonderoga 1758: Montcalm's Victory Against All Odds*. Westport, CT: Praeger, 2004.

Cipolla, Carlo M. *Guns, Sails and Empires: Technological Innovation and the Early Phases of European Expansion, 1400–1700*. New York: Thomas Y. Crowell, 1965.

Clark, Alan. *Barbarossa: The Russian-German Conflict, 1941–45*. New York: W. Morrow, 1965.

Clark, Christopher M. *Iron Kingdom: The Rise and Downfall of Prussia, 1600–1947*. New York: Penguin Books, 2007.

Clausewitz, Carl Von. *On War*. Edited by Michael Howard and Peter Paret. Princeton, NJ: Princeton University Press, 1984.

Clodfelter, Mark. *The Limits of Air Power: The American Bombing of North Vietnam*. Lincoln: University of Nebraska Press, 2006.

Cohen, Eliot A. *Conquered into Liberty: Two Centuries of Battles Along the Great Warpath That Made the American Way of War*. New York: Free Press, 2011. Kindle.

Corbett, Julian Stafford. *England in the Seven Years' War*. Novato, CA: Presidio Press, 1992.

Cordain, Loren, Janette Brand Miller, S. Boyd Eaton, Neil Mann, Susanne H. A. Holt, and John D. Speth. "Plant-Animal Subsistence Ratios and Macronutrient Energy Estimations in Worldwide Hunter-Gatherer Diets." *American Journal of Clinical Nutrition* 71, no. 3 (2000): 682–692.

Corum, James S. *The Luftwaffe: Creating the Operational Air War, 1918–1940*. Lawrence: University Press of Kansas, 1997.

———. *Wolfram Von Richthofen: Master of the German Air War*. Lawrence: University Press of Kansas, 2008.

Craig, Campbell. *Destroying the Village: Eisenhower and Thermonuclear War*. New York: Columbia University Press, 1998.

Crouch, Christian Ayne. *Nobility Lost: French and Canadian Martial Cultures, Indians, and the End of New France.* Ithaca, New York: Cornell University Press, 2014.

Cubbison, D. R. *On Campaign Against Fort Duquesne: The Braddock and Forbes Expeditions, 1755–1758, Through the Experiences of Quartermaster Sir John St. Clair.* Jefferson, NC: McFarland, 2015.

Danver, S. L. *Revolts, Protests, Demonstrations, and Rebellions in American History: An Encyclopedia.* Santa Barbara, CA: ABC-CLIO, 2011.

Davidson, P. B. *Vietnam at War: The History, 1946–1975.* Oxford University Press, 1991.

Dear, I. C. B., and M. R. D. Foot. *The Oxford Companion to World War II.* New York: Oxford University Press, 1995.

Dinsdale, Evelyn M. "Spatial Patterns of Technological Change: The Lumber Industry of Northern New York." *Economic Geography* (1965): 252–274.

Doughty, Robert A. *Pyrrhic Victory.* Cambridge, MA: Harvard University Press, 2005.

Drez, Ronald J., and Douglas Brinkley. *Voices of Courage: The Battle for Khe Sanh, Vietnam.* 1st ed. New York: Bulfinch Press, 2005.

Dull, Jonathan R. *The French Navy and the Seven Years' War.* Lincoln: University of Nebraska Press, 2005.

Dull, Paul S. *A Battle History of the Imperial Japanese Navy, 1941–1945.* Annapolis, MD: Naval Institute Press, 1978.

Dunn, Walter S. *The Soviet Economy and the Red Army, 1930–1945.* Westport, CT: Greenwood Publishing Group, 1995.

Du Picq, Ardant. *Battle Studies: Ancient and Modern Battle.* Translated by John N. Greely and Robert C. Cotton, 9-300. Harrisburg, PA: Stackpole Books, 1987.

Dye, Peter. *The Bridge to Airpower: Logistics Support for Royal Flying Corps Operations on the Western Front, 1914–18.* Annapolis, MD: Naval Insitute Press, 2015.

Dyer, George Carroll. *The Amphibians Came to Conquer: The Story of Admiral Richmond Kelly Turner.* Vol. 1. Washington, DC: US Department of the Navy, 1972.

Edmonds, J. E. *A Short History of World War I.* New York: Oxford University Press, 1951.

Edwards, Paul N. *The Closed World: Computers and the Politics of Discourse in Cold War America.* Cambridge, MA: MIT Press, 1996.

Ellis, Frank. *The Stalingrad Cauldron: Inside the Encirclement and Destruction of 6th Army.* Lawrence: University Press of Kansas, 2013.

Ewing, Michael. *Khe Sanh: Illustrated History of the Vietnam War.* New York: Bantam Books, 1987.

Fawcett, S. E., L. M. Ellram, and J. A. Ogden. *Supply Chain Management: From Vision to Implementation.* Upper Saddle River, NJ: Pearson Education, 2007.

Feldman, Gerald. *Army, Industry and Labour in Germany, 1914–1918.* Princeton, NJ: Princeton University Press, 1966.

Ferguson, R. L. *Guadalcanal, The Island of Fire: Reflections of the 347th Fighter Group.* Blue Ride Summit, PA: Aero Books, 1987.

"FMFRP 12-18: Mao Tse-Tung on Guerrilla Warfare." Edited by United States Marine Corps. Washington, DC: United States Department of the Navy, 1989.

Forczyk, Robert. *Tank Warfare on the Eastern Front 1941–1942: Schwerpunkt.* South Yorkshire, England: Pen & Sword Books Limited, 2014.

Frank, Richard B. *Guadalcanal.* New York: Random House, 1990.

Frederick, and Jay Luvaas. *Frederick the Great on the Art of War.* New York: Free Press, 1966.

Fremdling, Rainer. "Railroads and German Economic Growth: A Leading Sector Analysis with a Comparison to the United States and Great Britain." *Journal of Economic History* 37, no. 03 (1977): 583–604.

Friedman, N. *U.S. Amphibious Ships and Craft: An Illustrated Design History.* Annapolis, MD: Naval Institute Press, 2002.

Friedman, Norman. *Fighting the Great War at Sea: Strategy, Tactics and Technology.* Annapolis, MD: Naval Institute Press, 2014.

Fritz, Stephen G. *Ostkrieg: Hitler's War of Extermination in the East.* Lexington: University Press of Kentucky, 2011.

Gilster, Herman L. *The Air War in Southeast Asia: Case Studies of Selected Campaigns.* Maxwell Air Force Base, AL: Air University Press, 1993.

Gipson, Lawrence Henry. *The Great War for the Empire: The Years of Defeat, 1754–1757.* New York: Albert A. Knopf, 1946.

Glantz, David M. *Armageddon in Stalingrad: September–November 1942.* Lawrence: University Press of Kansas, 2009.

———. *Colossus Reborn: The Red Army at War, 1941–1943.* Lawrence: University Press of Kansas, 2005.

———. *Kharkov, 1942: Anatomy of a Military Disaster.* Rockville Center, NY: Sarpedon, US., 1998.

Glantz, David M., and Jonathan M. House. *Endgame at Stalingrad.* Lawrence: University Press of Kansas, 2014.

———. *To The Gates of Stalingrad: Soviet-German Combat Operations, April–August 1942.* Lawrence: University Press of Kansas, 2009.

———. *When Titans Clashed: How the Red Army Stopped Hitler.* Lawrence: University Press of Kansas, 1995.

Görlitz, Walter. "Paulus and Stalingrad: A Life of Field-Marshal Friedrich Paulus, with Notes, Correspondence, and Documents from His Papers." In *Companion to Endgame at Stalingrad,* edited by David M. Glantz, 429–430. Lawrence: University Press of Kansas, 1964.

Gough, Hubert. *Soldiering On: Being the Memoirs of General Sir Hubert Gough.* London: A. Barker, 1954.

Grieves, Keith. *Sir Eric Geddes: Business and Government in War and Peace.* New York: Manchester University Press, 1989.

Griffith, Paddy. *Battle Tactics of the Western Front.* New Haven, CT: Yale University Press, 1994.

Grossman, Vasily, Antony Beevor, and Luba Vinogradova. *A Writer at War: Vasily Grossman with the Red Army, 1941–1945*. New York: Pantheon Books, 2006.

Hamilton, Edward Pierce. "Colonial Warfare in North America." *Proceedings of the Massachusetts Historical Society* 80 (1968): 3–15.

Hammel, Eric M. *Khe Sanh: Siege in the Clouds, An Oral History*. Pacifica, CA: Pacifica Press, 2000.

Hardesty, Von. *Red Phoenix: The Rise of Soviet Air Power, 1941–1945*. 1st ed. Washington, DC: Smithsonian Institution Press, 1982.

Harvard, Gilles. "'Protection' and 'Unequal Alliance': The French Conception of Sovereignty over Indians in New France." In *French and Indians in the Heart of North America, 1630–1815*, edited by Robert Englebert and Guillaume Teasdale, 113–138. East Lansing: Michigan State University Press, 2013.

Hayward, Joel S. A. *Stopped at Stalingrad: The Luftwaffe and Hitler's Defeat in the East, 1942–1943*. Lawrence: University Press of Kansas, 1998.

Heal, S. C. *Ugly Ducklings: Japan's WWII Liberty Type Standard Ship*. Annapolis, MD: Naval Institute Press, 2003.

Henniker, Alan. *Transportation on the Western Front, 1914–1918*. London: H. M. Stationery Office, 1937.

Herwig, Holger H. *The First World War: Germany and Austria-Hungary, 1914–1918*. London: St. Martin's Press, 1997.

———. *The Marne, 1914: The Opening of World War I and the Battle that Changed the World*. New York: Random House, 2011.

Hildeburn, Charles R., and John St. Clair. "Sir John St. Clair, Baronet, Quarter-Master General in America, 1755 to 1767." *Pennsylvania Magazine of History and Biography* 9, no. 1 (1885): 1–14.

Hind, Henry Youle, Thomas C. Keefer, John George Hodgins, Charles Robb, Moses Henry Perley, and William Murray. *Eighty Years' Progress of British North America*. Ithaca, NY: L. Stebbins, 1864.

History of the War. Vol. 15. Edited by *The Times of London*, 1918.

Hornfischer, James D. *Neptune's Inferno: The US Navy at Guadalcanal*. New York: Bantam, 2011.

Hughes, Daniel. *Moltke on the Art of War: Selected Writings*. New York: Presidio Press, 2009.

Hughes, Thomas Alexander. *Admiral Bill Halsey: A Naval Life*. Cambridge, MA: Harvard University Press, 2016.

Jersey, Stanley Coleman. *Hell's Islands: The Untold Story of Guadalcanal*. College Station: Texas A&M University Press, 2007.

Joint Army-Navy Assesment Committee. *Japanese Naval and Merchant Vessels Losses During World War II, All Causes* (Washington, DC: Joint Army-Navy Assesment Committee, 1947).

Jones, H. A. *The War in the Air: Being the Story of the Part Played in the Great War by the Royal Air Force*. Oxford, England: Clarendon Press, 1934.

Keegan, John. *The First World War.* London: Hutchinson, 1998.

Kennett, Lee. *The First Air War.* New York: The Free Press, 1991.

Khong, Yuen Foong. *Analogies at War: Korea, Munich, Dien Bien Phu, and the Vietnam Decisions of 1965.* Princeton, NJ: Princeton University Press, 1992.

Lane, John J. *Command and Control and Communications Structures in Southeast Asia.* Maxwell Air Force Base, AL: Air University, 1981.

Leighton, Richard M., and Robert W. Coakley. *Global Logistics and Strategy: 1940–1943.* Washington, DC: Office of the Chief of Military History, Department of the Army, 1955.

Lewandowski, Krzysztof. "Long Way of Standardization Containers in Europe." Paper presented at the Carpathian Logistics Congress, Kracow, Poland, 2013.

Lieberman, Sanford R. "The Evacuation of Industry in the Soviet Union During World War II." *Soviet Studies* 35, no. 1 (1983): 90–102.

Logevall, Frederick. *Embers of War: The Fall of an Empire and the Making of America's Vietnam.* New York: Random House, 2012.

Loxton, Bruce, and C. D. Coulthard-Clark. *The Shame of Savo: Anatomy of a Naval Disaster.* Annapolis, MD: Naval Institute Press, 1994.

Lundstrom, John B. *The First Team and the Guadalcanal Campaign: Naval Fighter Combat from August to November 1942.* Annapolis, MD: Naval Institute Press, 1994.

MacLeitch, Gail D. *Imperial Entanglements: Iroquois Change and Persistence on the Frontiers of Empire.* Philadelphia: University of Pennsylvania Press, 2011.

Mandelbrot, Benoit B. *The Fractal Geometry of Nature.* Vol. 173. New York: Macmillan, 1983.

Marston, Daniel. *The French-Indian War, 1754–1760.* New York: Routledge, 2003.

Martin, James Kirby, and Mark Edward Lender. *A Respectable Army: The Military Origins of the Republic, 1763–1789.* 3rd ed. Hoboken, NJ: John Wiley and Sons, 2015.

McCarley, J. Britt. "General Nathan Farragut Twining: The Making of a Disciple of American Strategic Air Power, 1897–1953." PhD diss., Temple University, 1989.

McDowell, Carl E., Helen M. Gibbs, and E. L. Cochrane. *Ocean Transportation.* Washington, DC: Beard Books, 1999.

McLaughlin, Burl W. "Khe Sanh: Keeping an Outpost Alive." *Air University Review* 20, no. 1 (November–December 1968).

McNeill, William Hardy. *The Pursuit of Power: Technology, Armed Force, and Society Since A.D. 1000.* Chicago: University of Chicago Press, 1982.

Mead, Peter. *The Eye in the Air: History of Air Observation and Reconnaissance for the Army, 1785–1945.* London: Her Majesty's Stationery Office, 1983.

Meany Jr., Joseph F. "'Batteaux' and 'Battoe Men': An American Colonial Response to the Problem of Logistics in Mountain Warfare." New York State Military Museum, 1998.

Merriam, Ray, ed. *US Warplanes of World War II.* Hoosick Falls, NY: Merriam Press, 2000.

Military Improvisations During the Russian Campaign. Edited by Center of Military History, Vol. CMH Pub 104-1. Washington, DC: US Army, 1986.

Miller, Edward, ed. *The Vietnam War: A Documentary Reader.* Malden, MA: Wiley, 2016.

Miller, Edward S. *War Plan Orange: The U.S. Strategy to Defeat Japan, 1897–1945.* Annapolis, MD: Naval Institute Press, 1991.

Moïse, E. E. *The Myths of Tet: The Most Misunderstood Event of the Vietnam War.* Lawrence: University Press of Kansas, 2017. Kindle.

Mooney, James L. *Dictionary of American Naval Fighting Ships.* Vol. 4, edited by Naval Historical Center (US). Washington, DC: Naval Historical Center, 1991.

Moore, Harold G., and Joseph L. Galloway. *We Were Soldiers Once . . . and Young: Ia Drang: The Battle That Changed the War in Vietnam.* New York: Random House, 1991.

Morison, Samuel Eliot. *The Struggle for Guadalcanal, August 1942-February 1943.* Vol. 5 of *History of United States Naval Operations in World War II.* Boston: Little, Brown, 1949.

Morrow, John Howard. *The Great War in the Air: Military Aviation from 1909 to 1921.* Washington, DC: Smithsonian Institution Press, 1993.

Moyer, Lawrence. *Victory Must Be Ours.* New York: Hippocrene Books, 1995.

Muller, Richard R. *The German Air War in Russia.* Baltimore· Nautical & Aviation Publishing Company of America, 1992.

Mumford, Lewis. *Technics and Civilization.* New York: Harcourt, 1934.

Murray, Williamson. *Strategy for Defeat: The Luftwaffe, 1933–1945.* Maxwell Air Force Base, AL: Air University Press, 1983.

Murray, Williamson, and Allan Reed Millett. *Military Innovation in the Interwar Period.* New York: Cambridge University Press, 1996.

Nester, William R. *The Epic Battles for Ticonderoga, 1758.* Albany: State University of New York Press, 2008.

Nguyen, Lien-Hang T. *Hanoi's War: An International History of the War for Peace in Vietnam.* Chapel Hill: The University of North Carolina Press, 2012.

Offer, Avner. *The First World War: An Agrarian Interpretation.* Oxford, England: Clarendon Press, 1989.

O'Toole, Fintan. *White Savage: William Johnson and the Invention of America.* London: Farrar, Straus & Giroux 2015.

Overy, Richard J. *The Air War, 1939–1945.* Washington, DC: Potomac Books, 2005.

———. "Transportation and Rearmament in the Third Reich." *Historical Journal* 16, no. 2 (1973): 389–409.

"Pamphlet, No. 20–290: Terrain Factors in the Russian Campaign." Washington, DC: Department of the Army, 1951.

Pape, Robert Anthony. *Bombing to Win: Air Power and Coercion in War.* Ithaca, NY: Cornell University Press, 1996.

Parkman, Francis. *Montcalm and Wolfe.* New York: Collier Books, 1962. Kindle.

Peattie, Mark R. *Sunburst: The Rise of the Japanese Naval Air Power, 1909–1941*. Annapolis, MD: Naval Institute Press, 2001.

Peterson, Edward Norman. *An Analytical History of World War II*. Vol. 1. New York: Peter Lang, 1995.

Prados, John, and Ray W. Stubbe. *Valley of Decision: The Siege of Khe Sanh*. Boston: Houghton Mifflin, 1991.

Pratt, Edwin A. *The Rise of Rail-Power in War and Conquest, 1833–1914*. London: King, 1915.

Preston, David L. *Braddock's Defeat: The Battle of the Monongahela and the Road to Revolution*. New York: Oxford University Press, 2015. Kindle.

Rauss, Erhard, Hans von Greiffenberg, Waldemar Erfurth, and Peter G. Tsouras. *Fighting in Hell: The German Ordeal on the Eastern Front*. London: Greenhill Books, 1995.

Rentz, John M. *Marines in the Central Solomons*. Arlington, VA: Headquarters, US Marine Corps, 1952. https://www.ibiblio.org/hyperwar/USMC/USMC-M-CSol /index.html#contents.

Ropp, Theodore. *War in the Modern World*. Baltimore, MD: Johns Hopkins University Press, 2000.

Rosen, S. P. *Winning the Next War: Innovation and the Modern Military*. Ithaca, NY: Cornell University Press, 1991.

Ross, Steven T. *From Flintlock to Rifle: Infantry Tactics, 1740–1866*. 2nd ed. London: Frank Cass, 1996.

Schelling, Thomas C. *Arms and Influence*. New Haven, CT: Yale University Press, 2008.

Schulz, Major General. "Supply Problems of the "Luftwaffe" in the Ukraine." In Karlsruhe Collection. Maxwell Air Force Base, AL: Air Force Historical Research Agency, IRIS No. 1038188.

Shaw, Henry I. *The Marine Campaign For Guadalcanal*. Washington, DC: Marine Corps Historical Center, 1992.

Shore, Moyers S. *The Battle for Khe Sanh*. Washington, DC: Historical Branch, G-3 Division, Headquarters, US Marine Corps, 1969, repr. 1977.

Showalter, Dennis E. *Railroads and Rifles: Soldiers, Technology, and the Unification of Germany*. Hamden, CT: Archon Books, 1975.

Shulimson, Jack. *U.S. Marines in Vietnam: The Defining Year, 1968*. Washington, DC: History and Museums Division, Headquarters, US Marine Corps, 1997.

Skrine, Francis Henry Bennett. *Fontenoy and Great Britain's Share in the War of the Austrian Succession, 1741–1748*. Edinburgh, England: W. Blackwood and Sons, 1906. http://catalog.hathitrust.org/Record/000556734.

Slessor, John Cotesworth. *Air Power and Armies*. Tuscaloosa: University of Alabama Press, 2009.

Smith, Peter C., and Martin Pegg. *Transporter, Volume Two: Luftwaffe Transport Units 1943–45*. Sheppterton, UK: Classic Publications, 2006.

"Solomon Islands Campaign: I, Landings in the Solomons, 7–8 August 1942." In *Combat Narratives*.Washington, DC: United States Navy Office of Naval Intelligence 1943.

Sondhaus, L. *Shooting the Pacific War: Marine Corps Combat Photography in WWII.* Lexington: University Press of Kentucky, 2000.

———. *World War One: The Global Revolution.* Cambridge University Press, 2011.

Standard Classes of Japanese Merchant Ships. Edited by Division of Naval Intelligence. Vol. oNI 208-J (revised), Supplement 3. Washington, DC: Government Publishing Office, 1945.

Starbuck, David R. *Massacre at Fort William Henry.* Hanover, NH: University Press of New England, 2002.

Starkey, Armstrong. *European and Native American Warfare 1675–1815.* New York: Routledge, 2002.

Steele, Ian Kenneth. *Betrayals: Fort William Henry and the Massacre.* New York: Oxford University Press, 1990.

Sumida, Jon Tetsuro. "Forging the Trident: British Naval Industrial Logistics, 1914–1918." In *Feeding Mars: Logistics in Western Warfare from the Middle Ages to the Present,* edited by John A. Lynn (Boulder, CO: Westview Press,1993), 223–231, 1993.

Sunseri, Alvin R. "Patrick J. Hurley at the Battle of Stalingrad: An Oral History Interview." *Military Affairs* 30, no. 2 (1986). 88–92.

Taylor, Alan John Percivale. *War by Time-Table: How the First World War Began.* Ann Arbor, MI: Macdonald & Co, 1969.

Taylor, Frederick William. *The Principles of Scientific Management.* 1911. E-book. http://www.gutenberg.org/cache/epub/6435/pg6435-images.html.

Taylor, Maxwell D. *The Uncertain Trumpet.* 2nd ed. New York: Harper, 1960.

Terraine, John. *The Road to Passchendaele: The Flanders Offensive of 1917, A Study in Inevitability.* London: Cooper, 1977.

———. *White Heat: The New Warfare 1914–18.* London: Sidgwick & Jackson, 1982.

Tooze, Adam. *The Wages of Destruction: The Making and Breaking of the Nazi Economy.* New York: Penguin, 2006.

Tourison, Sedgwick D. *B5-T8 in 48 QXD: The Secret Official Hisotry of the North Vietnamese Army at the Siege of Khe Sanh, Vietnam, Spring, 1968.* Wauwatosa, WI: Khe Sanh Veterans, 2006.

Townsend, Joan B. "Firearms against Native Arms: A Study in Comparative Efficiencies with an Alaskan Example." *Arctic Anthropology* 20, no. 2 (1983): 1–33.

"A Transcript of the Proceedings." Paper presented at the From the Don to the Dnepr: Soviet Offensive Operations—December 1942 to August 1943, US Army War College, Carlisle, PA, 1984.

Tregaskis, Richard. *Guadalcanal Diary.* New York: Random House, 1955.

Tucker, S. C. *World War I: The Definitive Encyclopedia and Document Collection.* Santa Barbara, CA: ABC-CLIO, 2014.

Tunner, William H. *The Berlin Airlift.* Ramstein Air Base, Germany: Office of History, United States Air Forces in Europe, 1998.

Van Creveld, Martin. *Supplying War: Logistics from Wallenstein to Patton.* New York: Cambridge University Press, 1977.

Van de Water, Frederic Franklyn. *Lake Champlain and Lake George.* New York: Bobbs-Merrill, 1946.

Van Dyke, Jon M. *North Vietnam's Strategy for Survival.* Palo Alto, CA: Pacific Books, 1972.

Van Staaveren, Jacob. "The Air Force in Vietnam: The Search for Military Alternatives, 1967." Washington, DC: Office of Air Force History, 1969.

Verhovek, Sam Howe. *Jet Age: The Comet, the 707, and the Race to Shrink the World.* New York: Avery, 2010.

Victory in Vietnam: The Official History of the People's Army of Vietnam, 1954–1975. Edited by the Military History Institute of Vietnam. Lawrence: University Press of Kansas, 2002.

Von Falkenhayn, Erich. *The German General Staff and Its Decisions, 1914–1916.* New York: Dodd, Mead, 1920.

Washburne, Seth P. *The Thirsty 13th: The US Army Air Forces 13th Troop Carrier Squadron, 1940–1945.* Chelsea, MI: Thirsty 13th LLC, 2011.

Watson, Alexander. *Ring of Steel: Germany and Austria-Hungary in World War I.* New York: Basic Books, 2014.

Watt, Richard M. *Dare Call It Treason.* New York: Simon & Schuster, 1963.

Weinberg, Gerhard L. *A World at Arms: A Global History of World War II.* New York: Cambridge University Press, 1994.

Wilgus, William J. *Transporting the A. E. F. in Western Europe, 1917–1919.* New York: Columbia University Press, 1931.

Willbanks, J. H. *Machine Guns: An Illustrated History of Their Impact.* Santa Barbara, CA: ABC-CLIO, 2004.

Williams, Michael. *Americans and Their Forests: A Historical Geography.* Cambridge, England: Cambridge University Press, 1992.

Windrow, Martin. *The Last Valley: Dien Bien Phu and the French Defeat in Vietnam.* Cambridge, MA: Da Capo Press, 2006.

Wolf, Robb. *The Paleo Solution.* Las Vegas, NV: Victory Belt Publishing, 2010.

Wolff, Leon. *In Flanders Fields: The 1917 Campaign.* New York: Viking Books, 1958.

Wolmar, Christian. *Blood, Iron, & Gold: How the Railroads Transformed the World.* 1st ed. New York: PublicAffairs, 2010.

Woodward, David R. *World War I Almanac.* New York: Facts On File, 2009.

Zabecki, David T. *Steel Wind: Colonel Georg Bruchmüller and the Birth of Modern Artillery.* Westport, CT: Praeger Publishers, 1994.

Zambone, Albert Louis. *Daniel Morgan: A Revolutionary Life.* Yardley, PA: Westholme Publishing, 2018.

Ziemke, Earl Frederick, and Magna E. Bauer. *Moscow to Stalingrad: Decision in the*

East. Washington, DC: Center of Military History, Government Publishing Office, 1987.

PRIMARY SOURCES, PRIMARY SOURCE COLLECTIONS,
AND PUBLISHED PAPERS

"1/26 After Action Report, 11 May 1968." Edited by United States Marine Corps, 1968.

"7th Air Force, Significant Events (TACO): Niagara II Sortie Recap, 21 to 31 Jan 1968." Maxwell Air Force Base, AL: Air Force Historical Research Agency, IRIS No. 525200, 1968.

Abercrombie Papers. Huntington, CA: Huntingon Library.

Allied and Associated Powers. *Report of the Military Board of Allied Supply (1914–1920),* 2 Vols. Washington, DC: Government Publishing Office, 1924.

Allison, William Thomas, ed. *The Tet Offensive: A Brief History with Documents,* New York: Routledge, 1967.

Arnot, Hugh. "A Journal or Proceedings of the Army under the Command of Major Gen. Abercrombie from June ye 17th untill July ye 9th Campaign 1758." *Bulletin of the Fort Ticonderoga Museum* 16, no. 1 (1998).

Barnard, Salah. "Journal of Capt. Barnard Salah, 1758 Campaign." In Fort Ticonderoga Research Collection. Fort Ticonderoga, New York.

Blake, Robert, and Douglas Haig. *Private Papers of Douglas Haig, 1914–1919.* London: Eyre & Spottiswoode, 1952.

Boraston, John Herbert, ed. *Major General Edward Braddock's Orderly Books From February 26 to June 17, 1755.* Cumberland, MD: W. H. Lowdermilk, 1878.

———. *Sir Douglas Haig's Despatches: December 1915–April 1919.* London: Dent, 1919.

Brodhead, John Romeyn, ed. *Documents Relative to the Colonial History of the State of New York Procured in Holland, England and France,* Vol 6, Vol 7, Vol 10. Albany: Weed, Parsons, and Company, 1858.

Chester A. Nimitz Command Summary and Running Estimate: 1941–1945: 7 Dec 1941–31 Dec 1942 (Microfilm Reel No. 1) Washington, DC: United States Navy.

Chuikov, V. I. *The Battle for Stalingrad.* New York: Holt, 1964.

Churchill, Winston S. *The River War: An Account of the Reconquest of the Sudan.* Mineola, NY: Dover Publications, 2012.

———. *The World Crisis, Volume II: 1916–1918.* New York: Charles Scribner's Sons, 1927.

"CINCPAC Daily Staff Summary 26 August 1942." In *Command Summary and Running Estimate of Chester A Nimitz: 1941–1945* (Microfilm Reel No. 1, 7 Dec. 1941–31 Dec. 1942). Washington, DC: United States Navy.

Companion to Endgame at Stalingrad, edited by David M. Glantz, Lawrence: University Press of Kansas, 2014.

"Conversations with a Stuka Pilot: Paul-Werner Hozzel." Maxwell Air Force Base, AL: Air Force Historical Research Agency, IRIS No. 1095079, 1978.

De Champlain, Samuel, Henry Percival Biggar, Hugh Hornby Langton, William Francis Ganong, John Home Cameron, John Squair, and William Dawson LeSueur. *The Works of Samuel de Champlain.* Vol. 2. Toronto, Canada: Champlain Society, 1922.

Defense, People's Commissar of. "Death to the German Invaders: Collection of Materials on the Study of War Experince No. 2, September–October 1942, Order of the People's Commissar of Defense No. 325, 16 Ocober 1942." In *Soviet Documents on the Use of War Experience,* Vol. 2, edited and translated by Harold S. Orenstein, 232. Portland, OR: Frank Cass, 1991.

Dinwiddie, Robert. *The Official Records of Robert Dinwiddie: Lieutenant-Governor of the Colony of Virginia, 1751–1758.* 2 vols., edited by R. A. Brock. Richmond, VA: Virginia Historical Society, 1883.

"Division Commanders Final Report on Guadalcanal Operations" Phases 2-5, San Francisco: First Division United States Marine Corps, 1942.

Duan, Le. "The Path of the October Revolution and the World Situation, 4 Nov 1967." In *Vietnam Documents and Research Notes Series Microform : Translation and Analysis of Significant Viet Cong/North Vietnamese Documents.* Carlisle Barracks, PA: Library of the US Army Military History Institute, 1967.

"Extract of a Letter from Fort Cumberland, July 23, from The Public Advertiser Ocober 31, 1755." *The Pennsylvania Magazine of History and Biography* xxiii (1899).

Geiger, Bruce M. (1Lt, 1/44 Artillery, Khe Sanh 1967–1968) "Interview with Bruce Geiger: Reference Khe Sanh Water Supplies." By the author (17 Mar 2016).

Glantz, David M. *Companion to Colossus Reborn: Key Documents and Statistics.* Lawrence: University Press of Kansas, 2005.

Jacobsen, Hans-Adolf, ed. *1939–1945: Der Zweite Weltkrieg in Chronik und Dokumenten.* Darmstadt, Germany: Wehr und Wissen, 1961.

Janson, General Von. "Account of the Spring Offensive in the West." In *Source Records of the Great War,* Vol. 5, edited by Charles F. Horne, 166–167. Indianapolis, IN: The American Legion, 1931.

"Japanese Merchant Vessels Sunk During World War II." Washington, DC: The Joint Army-Navy Assesment Committee, 1947.

"Japanese Monograph No. 98, Southeast Area Naval Operations Part I, May 42–Feb 43." Edited by General Headquarters Far East Asia Command Second Demobilization Bureau, 1949.

Johnson, Lyndon B. "Address to the Nation 31 March 1968." In *The Vietnam Wars: Documents in Contemporary History,* edited by Kevin Ruane. New York: Manchester University Press, 2000.

Karlsruhe Collection, IRIS No. 468332, 468335, 1038188 Maxwell Air Force Base, AL: Air Force Historical Research Agency.

Kenshujo, Boeicho Boei, Senshishitsu, and Asagumo Shin bun Sha. "War History Series, Southeast Area Navy Operations, Part 2, Up to Withdrawal from Guadalcanal, Vol. 83." Japan: Defense Research Institute Defense Agency, Office of War History, 1975.

Krivosheev, G. F. *Grif sekretnosti sniat: poteri Voruzhennykh Sil SSSR v voinakh, bo-evykh deistviiakh i voennykh konfliktakh: statisticheskoe issledovanie.* Moscow: Voenizdat, 1993. Translated by David Glantz in *When Titans Clashed: How the Red Army Stopped Hitler.* Lawrence: University Press of Kansas, 1995.

"Lao Dong Party [North Vietnam Communist Party] Document on Tet, March 1968." In *Vietnam Documents: American and Vietnamese Views of the War,* edited by George Katsiaficas. Armonk, NY: M. E. Sharpe, 1992.

The Letters and Papers of Cadwallader Colden, 1711–1775. New York,: New York Historical Society, 1918.

Ludendorff, Erich. *The General Staff and Its Problems: The History of the Relations Between the High Command and the German Imperial Government as Revealed by Official Documents.* Vol. 2. Boston: E. P Dutton, 1920.

———. *Ludendorff's Own Story.* Vol. 1. New York: Harper & Brothers, 1919.

"Luftversorgung Stalingrad." In Karlsruhe Collection. Maxwell Air Force Base, AL: Air Force Historical Research Agency: IRIS No. 468335 Slide 1458, 1942.

Malartic, Adjutant. "Narrative of Occurences on the Frontier of Lake St. Sacrament, from the 30th June to the 10th July, inclusive." Translated by Edmund B. O'Callaghan. In *Documents Relative to the Colonial History of the State of New York Procured in Holland, England and France,* Vol. 10, edited by John Romeyn Brodhead. Albany: Weed, Parsons, and Company, 1858.

Manstein, Erich von, and Anthony G. Powell. *Lost Victories.* Novato, CA: Presido Press, 1994.

McNamara, Robert S., and Brian VanDeMark. *In Retrospect: The Tragedy and Lessons of Vietnam.* 1st ed. New York: Times Books, 1995.

Millard F. Harmon Papers. United States Air Force Historical Agency, IRIS No. 260973, 1942.

Momyer, William M. "Memorandum for General Ellis, Subject: USAF Airlift Activities in Support of Operations in Southeast Asia 1 Janary 1965–31 March 1968." In *CORONA HARVEST.* Maxwell Air Force Base, AL: Air Force Historical Research Agency, IRIS No. 1028237, 1974.

Moneypenny, Alexander. "Copy of Map from Major Moneypenny: Sent With Report of Lord Howe's Death, Aug 1758 From Westport House, Ireland." Fort Ticonderoga, NY: Fort Ticonderoga Museum Map Collection.

———. "Extract from Capt Moneypenny's Orderly Book 30 June–7 July 1758." *Bulletin of the Fort Ticonderoga Museum* 2, no. 2 (1932): 57–67.

———. "Extract from Capt Moneypenny's Orderly Book, Fort William Henry to Crown Point, July 15th, 1759 to August 3rd, 1759, 55th Regiment of Foot (British Army)." *Bulletin of the Fort Ticonderoga Museum* 2, no. 12 (1932): 219–251.

Morzik, Generalmajor a.D. Fritz. "German Air Force Airlift Operations." Edited by Research Studies Instititute, USAF Historical Division. Maxwell Air Force Base, AL: Air University, 1961.

Moss, George Donelson D., and Paul Conway. *A Vietnam Reader: Sources and Essays.* Upper Saddle River, NJ:: Pearson Education, 1990.

"Muscle Shoals Six Month Summary Evaluation Report, 31 May 1968." Edited by United States Military Assistance Command Vietnam. Maxwell Air Force Base, AL: Air Force Historical Research Agency, IRIS No. 1000577, 1968.

"The Naval Stores Act (14 March 1705)." In *English Historical Documents: American Colonial Documents to 1776,* Vol. 9, edited by Merrill Jensen. New York: Oxford University Press, 1955.

Nghi, Nguyen Trong. "Our Future Selves." In *Vietnam: A Portrait of its People at War,* edited by David Chanoff and Van Toai Doan. New York: I. B. Tauris.

Ohmae, Toshikazu. "The Battle of Savo Island." *USNI Proceedings* 83, no. 12 (1957).

O'Nan, Stewart, ed. *The Vietnam Reader: The Definitive Collection of American Fiction and Nonfiction on the War.* New York: Knopf Doubleday Publishing Group, 2000.

"Opisanie operatsii voisk iugo-zapadnom fronta na khar'kovskom napravlenii v mae 1942 goda [Account of Operations by Southwestern Front Forces on the Kharkov Axis in May 1942]." In *Collection of Military-Historical Materials of the Great Patriotic War, Issue 5.* Moscow, Classified Secret 1951, Declassified 1964.

Ord, Major Thomas. "Return of Ordance and Stores Taken at Ticonderoga and Crown Point, August 10, 1759." *Bulletin of the Fort Ticonderoga Museum* 2, no. 12 (1931): 251–252.

Orme, Robert. *The History of an Expedition Against Fort Du Quesne, in 1755 Under Major-General Edward Braddock.* Lippincott, Grambo, & Co., 1856.

Painlevé, Paul, and Ferdinand Foch. *Comment j'ai nommé Foch et Pétain.* Paris: Alcan, 1923.

Papers of Benjamin Franklin. American Philosophical Society and Yale University.

Papers of General Jeffrey Amherst. Kew Archives, London.

Papers of Lt. Gen. William Tunner. Maxwell Air Force Base, AL: Air Force Historical Research Agency, IRIS No. 10910955, 1949.

Paragellis, Stanley McCrory, ed. *Military Affairs in North America, 1748–1765: Selected Documents from the Cumberland Papers in Windsor Castle.* New York: D. Appleton-Century Company, 1936.

"The Parliamentary Register; or History of the Proceedings and debates, of the House of Commons." London: Parliament of Great Britain, 1779.

Pouchot, Pierre, and Catherine Broué. *Mémoires sur la dernière guerre de l'Amérique septentrionale entre la France et l'Angleterre.* Vol. 1. Yverdon, Switzerland: 1781.

"The President's New Conference of April 7, 1954." In *Public Papers of the Presidents of the United States: Dwight D. Eisenhower, Containing the Public Messags, Speeches, and Statements of the President: January 1 to December 31, 1954,* edited by David C. Eberhart. Washington, DC: Office of the Federal Register, 1954.

"Range Tables for His Majesty's Fleet, 1910." ADM 186/81:541+33. The National Archives, Kew, England, 1911.

Rea, Caleb, and F. M. Ray. *The Journal of Dr. Caleb Rea.* Salem, MA: 1881.

Richardson, Amos. "Amos Richardson Journal, 1758." In Fort Ticonderoga Research Collection, Fort Ticonderoga Museum, Fort Ticonderoga, NY.

Rogers, Robert, and Franklin B. Hough. *Journals of Major Robert Rogers: Containing an Account of the Several Excursions He Made Under the Generals Who Commanded Upon the Continent of North America During the Late War.* Albany, NY: J. Munsell's Sons, 1883.

Roubard, Pierre-Joseph-Antoine. "Letter from Father * * * , Missionary to the Abnakis, October 21, 1757." In *The Jesuit Relations and Allied Documents: Travels and Explorations of the Jesuit Missionaries in New France,* edited by Reuben Gold Thwaites. Cleveland, OH: Burrows Bros. Co., 1899. http://puffin.creighton.edu /jesuit/relations/relations_70.html.

Rudel, Hans Ulrich. *Stuka Pilot.* Translated by Lynton Hudson. Dublin, Ireland: Euphorion Books, 1952.

Saxe, Maurice, and William Fawcett. *Reveries, or, Memoirs Upon the Art of War.* London: Printed for J. Nourse, 1757.

Schank, Van. "Van Schank Orderly Book, 1758." In Fort Ticonderoga Research Collection, Fort Ticonderoga Museum, Fort Ticonderoga, NY.

Source Records of the Great War, Vol. 5, edited by Charles F. Horne, Indianapolis, IN: The American Legion, 1931.

Soviet Documents on the Use of War Experience, Vol. 1 and Vol. 2, edited and translated by Harold S. Orenstein, 232. Portland, OR: Frank Cass, 1991.

Stalin, Joseph. "NKO Order No. 227 (28 July 1942)." In *Companion to Colossus Reborn: Key Documents and Statistics,* edited by David M. Glantz. Lawrence: University Press of Kansas, 2005.

———. "Order of the Day No. 130, May 1, 1942." In *On the Great Patriotic War of the Soviet Union,* 51–66. Moscow: Foreign Languages Publishing House, 1946.

"Strategic/Tactical Study Prepared by Assistant Chief of Staff, J-5, March 1968." Edited by Vietnam Headquarters Military Assistance Command. Saigon.

Stubbe, Ray W. "Transcript of an Oral History Interview with Rev. Ray W. Stubbe, Navy Chaplain, Vietnam War." By Jim Kurtz (2005).

Sullivan, James, ed. *The Papers of Sir William Johnson,* Vol 1 and Vol 2. Albany: The University of the State of New York, Division of Archives and History, 1921.

The Tet Offensive: A Brief History with Documents, edited by William Thomas Allison, New York: Routledge, 2008.

Tin, Bui. "The Ho Chi Minh Trail." In *The Vietnam Wars: Documents in Contemporary History,* edited by Kevin Ruane, 105–107. New York: Manchester University Press, 2000.

Tunner, Lt Gen. William H. *The Papers of Lt. Gen. William H. Tunner.* Maxwell Air Force Base, AL: Air Force Historical Research Center, IRIS No. 1038188.468075.

Ugaki, Matome, Gordon William Prange, Donald M. Goldstein, and Katherine V.

Dillon. *Fading Victory: The Diary of Admiral Matome Ugaki, 1941–1945.* Pittsburgh, PA: University of Pittsburgh Press, 1991.

Valentiny, Edward. "Project Contemporary Historical Examination of Current Operations (CHECO) Report: USAF Operations from Thailand 1 January 1967 to 1 July 1968." Edited by Directorate Tactical Evaulation HQ Pacific Air Forces. 1968.

Van Ba, Houng. "Regroupee: Back Down the Trail." In *Vietnam: A Portrait of its People at War,* edited by David Chanoff and Van Toai Doan, 152–158. New York: I. B. Tauris, 1996.

Vandegrift, A. A., and Robert B. Asprey. *Once a Marine: The Memoirs of General A. A. Vandegrift, United States Marine Corps.* New York: Norton, 1964.

Van Tra, Tran. "Letter from Marquis De Vaudreuil to Sieur De Lotbinere, Montreal, September 20, 1755; Translated from a manuscript in the collection of the Fort Ticonderoga Museum." In *Bulletin of the Fort Ticonderoga Museum* 1, no. 3, 1932.

———. "Tet: The 1968 General Offensive and General Uprising." In *The Vietnam War: Vietnamese and American Perspectives,* edited by Mark Bradley, Jayne S. Werner and Luu Doan Huynh. Armonk, NY: M.E. Sharpe, 1993.

Vietnam Documents and Research Notes Series Microform: Translation and Analysis of Significant Viet Cong/North Vietnamese Documents. Carlisle Barracks, Pennsylvania: Library of the US Army Military History Institute, 1966.

Vietnam Documents and Research Notes Series Microform: Translation and Analysis of Significant Viet Cong/North Vietnamese Documents. Carlisle Barracks, PA: Library of the US Army Military History Institute, 1967.

Voltaire. "The Henriade with the Battle of Fontenoy." In *Select Works of Voltaire,* Vol. 2, edited by O. W. Wight. New York: Derby & Jackson, 1859.

Walsh, Patrick. "Interview with Patrick Walsh: Reference Movement of Conestoga Wagons in the Seven Years' War." By the author (01 Jun 2016).

War Office, ed. *Statistics of the Military Effort of the British Empire During the Great War: 1914–1920.* London: His Majesty's Stationery Office, 1922.

The Writings of George Washington from the Original Manuscript Sources, 1745–1799, Vol. 1, edited by John Clement Fitzpatrick, George Washington Bicentennial Commission (US), and David Maydole Matteson. Washington, DC: Government Publishing Office, 1931.

Webster, J. Clarence, ed. *The Journal of Jeffrey Amherst: Recording the Military Career of General Amherst in America from 1758 to 1763.* Chicago: University of Chicago Press, 1931.

Webster, Robert. "Robert Webster's Journal: Fourth Connecticut Regiment, Amherst's Campaign, Apri 5th to November 23rd, 1759." *Bulletin of the Fort Ticonderoga Museum* 2, no. 4 (1931): 120–153.

Webster, Stephen. "Letter from Stephen Webster to William Johnson, Albany June 5d, 1755." In *The Papers of Sir William Johnson,* Vol. 1. Albany, NY: University of the State of New York, Division of Archives and History, 1921.

Westbrook, Nicholas. "'Like Roaring Lions Breaking From Their Chains': The Highland Reigment at Ticonderoga Documents Compiled and Edited by Nicholas Westerbrook." *Bulletin of the Fort Ticonderoga Museum*, 1998, 16–91.

Westmoreland, William C. *A Soldier Reports.* 1st ed. Garden City, NY: Doubleday, 1976.

"Working Paper No. 14–66, Real Time Air Interdiction System, 17 May 1966." In *Project Corona Harvest.* Edited by USAF Scientific Research Advisory Group. Maxwell Air Force Base, Air Force Historical Agency, IRIS No. 0581360, 1966.

ELECTRONIC SOURCES

"74th Ranger Regiment: Robert Rogers' Standing Orders." Accessed 12 April 2016, http://www.goarmy.com/ranger/heritage/rodgers-orders.html.

Acred, Matthew Laird. "Battles of the Russian Offensive." Accessed 31 January 2016, https://www.asisbiz.com/Battles/Russian-Offensive.html.

"All About Shipping Containers." Accessed 20 August 2019, http://www.isbu-association.org/history-of-shipping-containers.htm.

"Area Calculator." Accessed 6 October 2015, http://www.mapdevelopers.com/area_finder.php.

"BAAM-CI: BAAM Printed Projects." Accessed 2 May 2016, http://www.e-ci.com/baam-3d-printed-projects/.

"BMW 132." Wikimedia Foundation. Accessed 5 February 2016, https://en.wikipedia.org/wiki/BMW_132.

Bork, Max. "Comments on Russian Railroads and Highways." Accessed 2 February 2016, http://www.allworldwars.com/Comments-on-Russian-Roads-and-Highways-by-Max-Bork.html.

Brush, Peter. "Lifeline to Khe Sanh: The 109th Quartermaster Company (Air Delivery)." Accessed 3 Mar 2016, https://msuweb.montclair.edu/~furrg/Vietnam/pb109.html.

Budge, Kent J. "Destroyers (DD)." Pacific Online Encyclopedia. Accessed 29 December 2015, http://pwencycl.kgbudge.com/D/e/Destroyers.htm.

———. "Logistics." Pacific Online Encyclopedia. Accessed 23 December 2015, http://pwencycl.kgbudge.com/L/o/Logistics.htm#mozTocId360123.

"C-47 Skytrain Military Transport." Boeing Corporation. Accessed 7 January 2016, http://www.boeing.com/history/products/c-47-skytrain.page.

Chantrill, Christopher. "UK Public Spending: Public Spending Details for 1750." http://www.ukpublicspending.co.uk/year_spending_1750UKbn_15bc1n_303433 (accessed 31 August 2015).

Clement, L. W. "Interview by Gary Hayes in Vietnam Archive: Oral History Project, Texas Tech University." Accessed 29 August 19. https://www.vietnam.ttu.edu/reports/images.php?img=/OH/OH0021/OH0021.pdf&from=website.

"Colonial America's Pre-Industrial Age of Wood and Water." Collections at Historic Bethlehem, PA. Accessed 17 September 2015, http://www.engr.psu.edu/mtah/articles/colonial_wood_water.htm.

Crenshaw, Carlton B. "Letters Home, Another Perspective." Accessed 31 Mar 2016, http://www.hmm-364.org/warriors-web-site/crenshaw-ltrs.html.

Department of Environmental Conservation, New York State. "The Land Tortoise Underwater Perserve Site." Accessed 29 August 2019. https://www.dec.ny.gov /outdoor/5076.html.

"Divisional Structure." Accessed 4 February 2016, http://www.mnstarfire.com/ww2 /history/land/division.html.

Duffy, Michael. "The Battle of Verdun—1916." Firstworldwar.com. Accessed 30 October 2015, http://www.firstworldwar.com/battles/verdun.htm.

———. "The Second Battle of Ypres—1915." Accessed 30 October 2015, https://www .firstworldwar.com/battles/ypres2.htm.

Esslinger, John T. "The Hill 881S Ice Cream Delivery." Accessed 15 March 2016, http://www.hmm-364.org/warriors-web-site/esslinger-tj-icecream.html).

Fitzgerald, Francie, Fredrik Logevall, and Lien-Hang T. Nguyen, "Fifty Years After the Tet Offensive: Lessons From the Vietnam War." February 8, 2018, https:// www.cfr.org/event/fifty-years-after-tet-offensive-lessons-vietnam-war.

"The German Retreat to the Hindenburg Line." Accessed 10 August 2019, https:// www.longlongtrail.co.uk/battles/battles-of-the-western-front-in-france-and -flanders/pursuit-of-the-german-retreat-to-the-hindenburg-line/.

"The Gunners at Khe Sahn." Argunners Magazine. Accessed 30 Mar 1968, http:// argunners.com/the-guns-at-khe-sanh-1968/.

Kafka, Peter. "Google Wants Out of the Creepy Military Robot Business." 17 March 2016, http://recode.net/2016/03/17/google-wants-out-of-the-creepy-military-robot-business/.

Kennedy, John F. "Inaugural Address, January 20, 1961." Accessed 4 March 2016, http://www.jfklibrary.org/Research/Research-Aids/Ready-Reference/JFK-Quota tions/Inaugural-Address.aspx.

"McDonnell Douglas F-4 Phantom II." Aviation History Online Museum. Accessed 1 May 2016, http://www.aviation-history.com/mcdonnell/f4.html.

McLaughin, Burl W. "Khe Sanh: Keeping an Outpost Alive." Air University. Accessed 4 April 2016, http://www.airpower.maxwell.af.mil/airchronicles/aureview /1968/nov-dec/mclaughlin.html.

"OECD Data: United States." Accessed 28 March 2016, https://data.oecd.org/united -states.htm.

"Opel Blitz: Multi-Purpose Medium Truck." Accessed 29 August 2019, https://www .militaryfactory.com/armor/detail.asp?armor_id=519.

Parshall, Jonathan. "Oil and Japanese Strategy in the Solomons: A Postulate." Accessed 29 August 2019/, http://www.combinedfleet.com/guadoil1.htm.

Prados, John. "Khe Sanh: The Other Side of the Hill." Accessed 10 August 2019, http://archive.vva.org/archive/TheVeteran/0807/khesanh.html.

Randolph, Eric. "3D Printing Could Revolutionize Modern Warfare." 5 January 2015, http://www.businessinsider.com/afp-how-3d-printing-could-revolutionise-war -and-foreign-policy-2015-1.

"Sgt. Prentice: Oral History Interview." http://www.hmm-364.org/warriors-web -site/oral-histories/oral-history-prentice.html.

Soule, Thayer. "Guadalcanal Invasion Part 2." YouTube video. Accessed 9 December 2015, https://www.youtube.com/watch?v=bPAkAoT-8L8.

"Sunrise and Sunset Times, Volgograd, August 1997." Accessed 11 February 2016, http://www.timeanddate.com/sun/russia/volgograd?month=8&year=1997.

"Tiger I information center—the Maybach engine." Accessed 4 February 2016, http:// www.alanhamby.com/maybach.shtml.

Tully, Anthony. "Sakito Maru Auxiliary Class Transport." Accessed 6 January 2016, http://www.combinedfleet.com/Sakito_c.htm.

United States Department of Agriculture, Forest Service. "Human Heritage of the Allegheny National Forest." Accessed 11 September 2015, http://www.fs.usda.gov /main/allegheny/learning/history-culture.

"US Merchant Marine, Military Sea Transportation Service, and Military Sealift Command in Vietnam." Accessed 1 Apr 2016, http://www.usmm.org/vietnam .html.

Vecamer, Avro L. "Deutsche Reichsbahn—The German State Railway in WWII." Feldgrau.com. Accessed 20 January 2016, http://www.feldgrau.com/dreichsbahn .htm.

"The Wartime Memories Project: 118th Siege Battery, During the Great War," Accessed 29 August 2019, https://www.wartimememoriesproject.com/greatwar/al lied/rgartillery.php?pid=9509.

Wright, Bryan. "The Conestoga Wagon: The Colonial Workhorse." Colonial Sense. Accessed 17 August 2015, http://colonialsense.com/Society-Lifestyle/Signs_of_the _Times/Conestoga_Wagon.php.

MAPS

"20 SE, Ypres Salient Trench Map 17 December 1917 Edition 5A." In *British First World War Trench Maps: 1915–1918*. National Library of Scotland, 1917.

"20 SE, Ypres Salient Trench Map 17 September 1917 Edition 4A." In *British First World War Trench Maps: 1915–1918*. National Library of Scotland, 1917.

"28.SW Trench Map 01 April 1917, Edition 6A." In *British First World War Trench Maps: 1915–1918*. National Library of Scotland, 1917.

"28.SW Trench Map 22 June 2016 Edition 6A." In *British First World War Trench Maps: 1915–1918*. National Library of Scotland, 1916.

"51B.NW Trench Map, 4 March 1917." In *British First World War Trench Maps: 1915– 1918*. National Library of Scotland, 1917.

"51B.NW Trench Map, 25 May 1917." In *British First World War Trench Maps: 1915– 1918*. National Library of Scotland, 1917.

"Google Maps: Driving directions from Brest to Moscow." Accessed 20 January 2016, https://www.google.com/maps/dir/Moscow,+Russia/Brest,+Belarus/@53.107489 6,21.8239257,7z/data=!4m13!4m12!1m5!1m1!1s0x46b54afc73d4b0c9:0x3d44d6cc575

7cf4c!2m2!1d37.6173!2d55.755826!1m5!1m1!1s0x47210c0223630975:0x4d319ea41f64a e99!2m2!1d23.7340503!2d52.0976214.

Hoodinski. "Map of French and Indian War." Wikimedia Commons.

Lacock, John Kennedy "Map of Braddock's Military Road." Wikimedia Commons, 1912.

"Map of the Pacific Theatre." Accessed 10 December 2015, http://www_nzhistory_net _nz/media/photo/japanse-expansion-in-WW2.

"Map: Project For the Attack of Ticonderoga Proposed to Be in Execution as Near as the Circumstances and Ground Will Admit of." Fort Ticondergo Research Center Collection, 1759.

"Map Showing Narrow Gauge Railways in France and Flanders, Chart 9, Chapter 16." In *Report of the Military Board of Allied Supply,* Vol. 1, part 2, edited by Allied and Associated Powers (1914–1920). Washington, DC: Government Publishing Office, 1924.

Martini, Frank. "Battle of Cambrai, 20 November–5 December 1917." West Point, New York: Department of History, United States Military Academy.

———. "Battle of Messines—21 May–7 June 1917." West Point, New York: Department of History, United States Military Academy.

———. "The Guadalcanal Campaign, August–October 1942." West Point, New York: Department of History, United States Military Academy.

———. "Southwest Russia, 1942." West Point, New York: Department of History, United States Military Academy.

———. "Third Battle of Ypres." West Point, New York: Department of History, United States Military Academy.

NYSDEC, USGS and. "Topographic Map of the Adirondacks: Lake George Region." Keene Valley, New York: Plinth, Quion & Cornice, 1984.

"Rivers of New York." Edited by Mapsof.net, 2012.

Wikipedia, Gdr at English.

———. "Eastern Front: 7 May-18 November 1942." https://commons.wikimedia. org/wiki/World_War_II_maps_(Europe)#/media/File:Eastern_Front_1942-05 _to_1942-11.png.

———. "Eastern Front: 22 June 1941–5 December 1941."https://commons.wikimedia. org/wiki/World_War_II_maps_(Europe)#/media/File:Eastern_Front_1941-06 _to_1941-09.png.

OTHER MEDIA

Davies, Thomas. "Painting of the View of the Lines at Lake George." Fort Ticonderoga, NY: Fort Ticonderoga Thompson/Pell Research Center, 1759.

Morris, Erol, dir. *The Fog of War.* Sony Pictures Classics, 2003.

UNPUBLISHED WORKS

Cunningham, Case A. "William W. Momyer: A Biography of an Airpower Mind." PhD diss., Air University, 2013.

Thyssen, Mike. "A Desperate Struggle to Save a Condemned Army—A Critical Review of the Stalingrad Army." Thesis, Air University, 1997.

Turner, Jobie. "Technogeopologistics: Supply Networks and Military Power in the Industrial Age." Thesis, Air University, 2012.

Vanhorn, Kellie. "Eighteenth Century American Colonial American Merchant Ship Construction." Thesis, Texas A&M University, 2004.

INDEX